A PERFECT MORAL STORM

ENVIRONMENTAL ETHICS AND SCIENCE
POLICY SERIES

General Editor: Kristin Shrader-Frechette

Democracy, Risk, and Community
Technological Hazards and the Evolution of Liberalism
Richard P. Hiskes

Environmental Justice
Creating Equality, Reclaiming Democracy
Kristin Shrader-Frechette

Across the Boundaries
Extrapolation in Biology and Social Science
Daniel Steel

Is a Little Pollution Good For You?
Incorporating Societal Values in Environmental Research
Kevin C. Elliott

A Perfect Moral Storm
The Ethical Tragedy of Climate Change
Stephen M. Gardiner

A PERFECT MORAL STORM

The Ethical Tragedy
of Climate Change

STEPHEN M. GARDINER

OXFORD
UNIVERSITY PRESS

OXFORD
UNIVERSITY PRESS

Oxford University Press, Inc., publishes works that further
Oxford University's objective of excellence
in research, scholarship, and education.

Oxford   New York
Auckland   Cape Town   Dar es Salaam   Hong Kong   Karachi
Kuala Lumpur   Madrid   Melbourne   Mexico City   Nairobi
New Delhi   Shanghai   Taipei   Toronto

With offices in
Argentina   Austria   Brazil   Chile   Czech Republic   France   Greece
Guatemala   Hungary   Italy   Japan   Poland   Portugal   Singapore
South Korea   Switzerland   Thailand   Turkey   Ukraine   Vietnam

Copyright © 2011 by Oxford University Press, Inc.

Published by Oxford University Press, Inc.
198 Madison Avenue, New York, New York 10016

www.oup.com

Oxford is a registered trademark of Oxford University Press

Gardiner, Stephen Mark.
A perfect moral storm : the ethical tragedy of climate
change / Stephen M. Gardiner.
p. cm. — (Environmental ethics and science policy series)
ISBN 978-0-19-537944-0 (alk. paper)
1. Environmental ethics.   2. Global warming—Moral and ethical aspects.
3. Climatic changes—Moral and ethical aspects.   4. Environmental responsibility.   I. Title.
GE42.G37 2011
179′.1—dc22
2010030958

3 5 7 9 8 6 4

Printed in the United States of America
on acid-free paper

For
Lynn, Ben and Matthew,
Safe Harbor in a Storm

Contents

Preface

Those of us working on global ethics and political philosophy tend to think about grand theories of justice and rights, trying to figure out which are the best, how they apply to the world that we live in, and how they might guide us in making it better. However, this is not that kind of book. Instead, my aim is to characterize our predicament—humanity's and especially that of richer nations and peoples. This seems to me where the action is right now. We need to understand what the problem is that we are trying to solve, and why it is so persistent. Until we do, attempts at solutions are likely to be shallow.

In the hope of piquing your interest, let me gesture at the main claims of the book by announcing eight propositions.

PROPOSITION 1: RUNAWAY EMISSIONS

We are currently accelerating hard into the most serious global environmental problem that humanity has ever faced. If the scientists are to be believed, the planet is at serious risk of a shift in global climate comparable in magnitude to an ice age (albeit in the other direction), but occurring over decades rather than millennia. Yet, despite more than twenty years of awareness, we are neither slowing down nor stabilizing, let alone actually reducing, our collective input to the problem. Instead, we continue to add more fuel to the fire, faster and faster, producing an almost exponential rise in anthropogenic emissions of carbon. This, arguably, is the most striking fact of our time.

PROPOSITION 2: A DUBIOUS FRAMING

In public discussion, we do not understand the striking fact in the most relevant terms, and so conceive of the problem in the wrong way. The dominant discourses about the nature of the climate threat are scientific and economic. But the deepest challenge is ethical. What matters most is what we do to protect those vulnerable to our actions and unable to hold us accountable, especially the global poor, future generations, and nonhuman nature.

PROPOSITION 3: A PROFOUND CHALLENGE

Our problem is profoundly global, intergenerational, and theoretical. When these factors come together they pose a "perfect moral storm" for ethical action. This casts doubt on the adequacy of our existing institutions, and our moral and political theories.

PROPOSITION 4: A PROBLEMATIC PARADIGM

In the environmental discourse, the presence of the perfect moral storm is obscured by the dominance and pervasiveness of an alternative, narrower analysis. According to this account, climate change is a paradigmatically global problem best understood as a prisoner's dilemma or tragedy of the commons played out between nation states who adequately represent the interests of their citizens in perpetuity. However, such models assume away many of the main issues, and especially the intergenerational aspect of the climate problem. Hence, they are inadequate in this case, and perhaps many others. This point has theoretical as well as practical implications.

PROPOSITION 5: A THREATENED DISCOURSE

In the perfect moral storm, our position is not that of idealized neutral observers, but rather judges in our own case, with no one to properly hold us accountable. This makes it all too easy to slip into weak and self-serving ways of thinking, supported by a convenient apathy or ideological fervor. Moreover, the devices of such corruption are sophisticated, and often function indirectly, by infiltrating the terms of ethical and epistemic argument.

PROPOSITION 6: SHADOW SOLUTIONS

Given this, we are susceptible to proposals for action that do not respond to the real problem. This provides a good explanation of what has gone wrong in the last two decades of climate policy, from Rio to Kyoto to Copenhagen. However, the form of such "shadow solutions" is likely to evolve as the situation deteriorates. Some recent arguments for pursuing geoengineering may represent such an evolution.

PROPOSITION 7: A DEFENSIVE STRATEGY

The perfect storm constitutes a nonneutral evaluative setting, and this poses special challenges for ethical action. Because we are judges in our own case, there is a role for "defensive" moral and political philosophy, especially in the public sphere. In particular, we should work as hard at identifying bad arguments, policies, and theories as on developing the good; and we must pay attention to the ways important values are articulated, since the likelihood of their perversion is high.

PROPOSITION 8: EARLY GUIDANCE

Although the theoretical component of the perfect moral storm is serious, it does not follow that nothing useful can be said about confronting the ethical challenge. Instead, there are serious constraints on moral and political reasoning involving many of the main aspects of the climate problem, such as scientific uncertainty, intergenerational ethics, and intragenerational justice. Paying attention to these suggests that the current public debate about climate should be reoriented.

These eight propositions seem to me difficult to dispute. If they are correct, the issues before us are serious and deep-rooted. I hope that we will
rise to the occasion.

Stephen Gardiner
Seattle

June 2010

Acknowledgments

My interest in the intergenerational aspect of climate change, and specifically what I now call "the perfect moral storm," began in the late 1980s, as an undergraduate in Oxford, when climate change was first becoming a topic of mainstream scientific and political concern. In the nineties, I moved to the United States for graduate school, first to Colorado, and then to Cornell, and was lucky enough to study with three pioneers in the field: Dale Jamieson, Henry Shue, and (for a summer in the early 1990s at *Resources for the Future*) Mike Toman. I learned a huge amount from each, and would like to thank them publicly for that here.

Despite my fortunate education, for a long time I resisted making climate change and global environmental problems my focus. One reason was because I wanted to pursue other philosophical interests, in contemporary moral and political theory in general, and Aristotelian virtue ethics in particular. For this, my other inspiring philosophical teachers—especially Roger Crisp, Terry Irwin, Mike Otsuka, and Nick Sturgeon—were largely responsible. Their influence is present in almost everything that I have done since, only one narrow aspect of which is represented in this book. So, I'd also like to acknowledge my debt to them.

A second reason for my delay in writing this book was that for a long time I hoped that humanity would quickly rise to the ethical challenge it uncovers, and so render its central message less urgent. However, by the late 1990s, this stance had become untenable. So, having finished a dissertation on Aristotle and fallen into a wonderful faculty job in New Zealand, I decided to take a break from my regular research to write a conference paper on the intergenerational problem. I thank Derek Browne, Philip Catton, Graham Macdonald, and David Novitz for their encouragement back then, even though I've been struggling to take a break in the other direction ever since.

Many others have contributed to the evolution of my thinking in the last decade. Earlier versions of some chapters were read at meetings of the

American Philosophical Association, the Australasian Association of Philosophy, and the International Society for Environmental Ethics, and at workshops organized by the National Academy of Sciences, and the European Science Foundation. Some were also presented at the following universities and colleges: Arizona State, Auckland, Bern, Bremen, Canterbury, California (at San Diego), Colorado (at Boulder), Delaware, Delft, Fordham, Iowa State, Leeds, Lewis and Clark, Melbourne, Ohio, Oregon, Oslo, Oxford, Penn State, Princeton, Reading, San Diego State, Simon Fraser, Stanford, Utah, and Washington. I thank those audiences for their many valuable suggestions, and in particular Neil Adger, Chrisoula Andreou, Richard Arneson, Ken Arrow, Sandy Askland, Peter Atterton, Paul Baer, David Battisti, Tim Bayne, Jeremy Bendik-Keymer, Cecilia Bitz, David Brink, Simon Blackburn, Andrew Brennan, Simon Caney, Paula Casal, Deen Chatterjee, Ralph Cicerone, Tony Coady, Richard Daggar, Justin D 'Arms, Paul Ehrlich, Nir Eyal, James Fleming, Dave Frame, Leslie Francis, Espen Gamlund, Michael Gillespie, Olivier Godard, Bob Goodin, Axel Gosseries, Nicole Hassoun, Kristen Hessler, Margaret Holmgren, Mathew Humphrey, Rosalind Hursthouse, Aaron James, Monte Johnson, Karen Jones, Willett Kempton, Berit Kristoffersen, Neil Levy, Stephen Macedo, Graham Macdonald, Catriona MacKinnon, Andrew McGonigal, Don Maier, Richard Miller, Lije Millgram, Darrel Moellendorf, John Meyer, Lukas Meyer, Adam Moore, Julie Nelson, James Nickel, Cara Nine, David Nobes, Karen O 'Brien, Jay Odenbaugh, Michael Oppenheimer, Philip Pettit, Christopher Preston, Alan Robock, William Rodgers, Debra Satz, David Schmidtz, Kristin Shrader-Frechette, Peter Singer, Angela Smith, Richard Somerville, Asuncion St Clair, Behnam Taebi, Ted Toadvine, Allen Thompson, Steve Vanderheiden, Mike Wallace, Michael White, Harlan Wilson, and Clark Wolf. I am especially indebted to Michael Blake, Lauren Hartzell, and Bill Talbott for reading a draft of the entire manuscript, prompting several important changes, and to Peter Ohlin for shepherding the project through its many stages. I also gratefully acknowledge research support from the Center for Human Values at Princeton University (in the form of a Laurance S. Rockefeller Fellowship), the University of Canterbury, the Centre for Applied Philosophy and Public Ethics at the University of Melbourne, and the University of Washington.

Earlier versions of some chapters previously appeared as:

2006. "A Perfect Moral Storm: Climate Change, Intergenerational Ethics and the Problem of Moral Corruption," *Environmental Values* 15, 397–413. (Chapter 1)

2003. "The Pure Intergenerational Problem," *The Monist*, Vol. 86, No. 3, 481–500. Special Issue on Moral Distance, edited by Deen Chatterjee. (Chapter 5)

2009. "Saved By Disaster? Abrupt Climate Change, Political Inertia and the Possibility of an Intergenerational Arms Race," *Journal of Social Philosophy* Vol. 20, No. 4, 140–162. Special Issue on Global Environmental Issues, edited by Carol Gould and Tim Hayward. (Chapter 6)

2010. "Climate Change as a Global Test for Contemporary Political Institutions and Theories." In Karen O'Brien, Asuncion Lera St. Clair, and Berit Kristoffersen, eds., *Climate Change, Ethics and Human Security*, Cambridge University Press. (Chapter 7)

2010. "Is 'Arming the Future' with Geoengineering Really the Lesser Evil? Some Doubts About the Ethics of Intentionally Manipulating the Climate System." In Stephen Gardiner, Simon Caney, Dale Jamieson, and Henry Shue, eds. *Climate Ethics: Essential Readings.* Oxford University Press. (Chapter 10)

I have also made use of parts of several other pieces at various points during the book. These include:

2011. "Climate Justice." In John Dryzek, David Schlosberg and Richard Norgaard, eds. *Oxford Handbook of Climate Change and Society.* Oxford University Press.

2011. "Is No One Responsible for Global Environmental Tragedy? Climate Change as a Challenge to Our Ethical Concepts." In Denis Arnold, ed., *Ethics and Climate Change.* Cambridge University Press.

2010. "Ethics and Climate Change: An Introduction." *Wiley Interdisciplinary Reviews: Climate Change* 1.1, 54–66.

2006. "Protecting Future Generations." In Jörg Tremmel, ed., *Handbook of Intergenerational Justice.* Cheltenham: Edgar Elgar Publishing, 148–169.

2004. "Ethics and Global Climate Change," *Ethics* 114, 555–600.

2004. "The Global Warming Tragedy and the Dangerous Illusion of the Kyoto Protocol," *Ethics and International Affairs* 18. 1, 23–39.

2001. "The Real Tragedy of the Commons," *Philosophy and Public Affairs* 30.4, 387–416.

I am grateful to the original publishers for allowing me to draw on this work here.

My most important debt is to my family. My parents, Anne and Peter Gardiner, and my sister, Kate, supported me lovingly and unflinchingly throughout my early education, and have continued to do so ever since. In recent years, Lynn, Ben, and Matthew patiently endured "Daddy's book" for longer than anyone could reasonably expect, and still managed to smile about it at the end. I thank them for this, and all else.

A PERFECT MORAL STORM

Introduction:
The Global Environmental Tragedy

Sometimes the best way to make progress in solving a problem is to clarify what the problem is. That is the aim of this book. Its subject is the coming global environmental crisis. Still, this is not a work of natural science. It does not seek to explain humanity's effects on the earth's physical, biological, and ecological systems. These facts are, I take it, reasonably well known.[1] My concern is with why, given that the relevant facts are known, effective action is so difficult, and indeed has so far eluded us. This is the real global environmental tragedy, and it is what needs to be explained.

I. MY APPROACH

In my view, the global environmental tragedy is most centrally an ethical failure, and one that implicates our institutions, our moral and political theories, and ultimately ourselves, considered as moral agents. In a moment, I will introduce my explanation of how the tragedy comes about through the metaphor of the perfect moral storm. But first let me say something about the kind of project I am engaged in, some of the assumptions I am making, and the audience for which this book is intended.

Much work in moral and political philosophy, and especially in its more applied or practical areas, takes the form of announcing, developing, and defending a set of principles (or norms) for guiding institution-building or policy decisions in a particular area. This is a worthy endeavor;

1. See, for example, IPCC 2007a; UNEP 2007. I do not mean to imply that everything about the natural science is known with certainty. Indeed, part of the problem of global environmental change is precisely that it involves uncertainty. My point is rather that those facts essential to action are known, where this includes the fact that there are some deep uncertainties. See also chapter 11 and Appendix 2.

however, it is not my aim in this book. Instead, my goal is to get clearer about the nature of the problem itself, as a preliminary to generating and assessing potential solutions.[2]

Such a project has precedents in at least two traditions of moral and political theorizing. The first is perhaps best exemplified by the social contract tradition in political philosophy in general, and the work of Thomas Hobbes in particular.[3] Hobbes sets out to say what the basic problem of political organization really is. (Infamously, he claims that it is to avoid the scenario of continual war in a state of nature where life is "nasty, brutish and short.") He then treats this account as the background against which potential solutions should be formulated and judged. As it happens, Hobbes's statement of the problem has turned out to be of more enduring interest than his own attempt at a solution. Still, his contribution is not regarded as any less important because of that. Sometimes clearly identifying the problem is a crucial step.[4]

The second tradition is most clearly evident in what might broadly be called virtue theory, although it is also present in other approaches to normative ethics, as well as in some areas of professional ethics, and in literature. This tradition seeks to identify the characteristic "temptations" present in certain situations, positions, or ways of life, where these are understood as vulnerabilities to behaving badly to which many are likely to be susceptible. Such work is helpful not only for thinking about how to resist acting badly, but also in coming to understand ourselves as moral agents.[5] "Who we are," morally speaking, is a significant ethical issue, and one which (as we shall see in chapter 10) has considerable bearing on the global environmental tragedy.

2. For solution-oriented material, see chapter 11, Gardiner et al. 2010, Garvey 2008, Page 2006, and Vanderheiden 2008a, 2008b.

3. Locke 1988, Rousseau 1997, Rawls 1999, Dworkin 2000, and Nozick 1974 also fit into the more general tradition, even though not all are contract theorists.

4. A similar point might be made in epistemology about Descartes's method of doubt. This is set up as the criterion against which solutions to the problem of knowledge should be judged. Again, Descartes's own solution has not been influential; but his effort to set out the problem provides the backdrop for centuries of further work.

5. Consider, for example, Plato's discussion of conflicts between the three parts of the soul, Aristotle's account of the excess and deficiency related to each virtue, and Hume's analysis of the "monkish" and other virtues. Some recent writings on "moral psychology" also fit this mold.

Let us turn now to assumptions. In setting out my account of the global environmental tragedy I will be taking for granted a number of claims that I shall not attempt to justify within the confines of this book. These include that we have strong reason to believe that climate change poses a real and potentially catastrophic threat to human and other life on this planet,[6] that scientific concern about the threat is robust and not driven by some kind of left-wing or green conspiracy, and that people in all nations have a shared responsibility to act together to address the threat.[7] I shall also assume that ethical concerns matter in deciding exactly why and how we must act; and that it is not only inaction that might be morally wrong (in ways to be discussed), but also inappropriate action (such as a retreat of the affluent into their own "fortress world," or predatory geoengineering). Nevertheless, in keeping with the goal of clearly identifying the problem, I will try to couch the ethical risks of our current predicament in the broadest possible terms. My hope is to specify the global environmental tragedy in language that almost all morally serious people can accept, and so I will try not to beg any contentious theoretical questions. Presumably, potential solutions to the tragedy will have to go further, and make claims that are more controversial. Still, in my view, it is better not to build in such assumptions at the beginning. As we shall see, one of my main claims is that we are already vulnerable to distraction from the imperative to act, and act well. So, one of my aims in this book is to keep such distractions to a minimum.

Who should read the book? My hope is that it will be useful to a wide audience, both inside and outside the academy. Though I am a philosopher by training, this work is aimed at the problem—the global environmental tragedy—rather than at a particular discipline or institution, and so reflects the fact that the challenge transcends traditional boundaries. In my view, the issue is one that concerns all of us, simply as moral agents. The future of our own societies, of humanity, and of many of the earth's species is at stake, and with them our own moral legacy. Hence, I have tried to make my discussion accessible to as many people as possible, avoiding as much tangential complexity as I can. This is not a time for purely parochial concerns, or local academic niceties.

6. IPCC 2007a; Oreskes 2005.
7. See chapter 11.

That being said, some parts of the book are clearly more technical than others, and some may be of special interest to particular audiences. I try to indicate this (and especially which sections might be safely skipped) in the outline offered below, and in the main text itself. However, I also believe that most chapters can be safely read in isolation, especially if one already has the first two in hand. Hence, the more confident reader should feel free to skip around. For those looking for a "fast and dirty" grasp of the book, I suggest reading chapters 1, 2, 5, 7, and 9 first.

One final point about my approach is perhaps worth emphasizing. This book tries to identify our moral situation, including the temptations to which we are subject, and the ways in which they make us vulnerable to a certain kind of corruption. Some may take a peculiar kind of pleasure in this, and rejoice in pointing fingers at those they see as most liable to moral criticism. But I want to stress right from the start that my objective is not to vilify any particular individuals, groups, classes, or nations. Indeed, the point is not really to apportion blame at all, but rather to help us understand our own predicament (see chapter 7). This is a tragedy in which most of the world's more affluent people play a part. Hence, almost all those able to read this book are ethically vulnerable to at least some extent, in many parts of our lives, and through membership in a wide range of social and political communities. If the moral quality of our lives is not to be compromised (see chapter 10), we must seek to address it together.

II. INTRODUCING THE PERFECT STORM METAPHOR

The global environmental tragedy has many causes and aspects. But in this book I will highlight three central contributions through invoking the metaphor of "a perfect moral storm." I borrow the phrase "a perfect storm" from Sebastian Junger's book of that name, and the subsequent Hollywood film.[8] Junger recounts the true story of the *Andrea Gail*, a fishing vessel caught at sea during the rare convergence of three particularly bad storms, and ultimately destroyed as a result. Given this, I take a perfect

8. Junger 1999.

storm to involve the unusual intersection of a number of serious, and mutually reinforcing, problems, which creates an unusual and perhaps unprecedented challenge. In my metaphor of the perfect moral storm, the three problems (or "storms") are all obstacles to our ability to behave ethically. Like the *Andrea Gail*, we are beset by forces that are likely at least to throw us off course, and may even sink us into the bargain.

Each of the first two storms involves a serious asymmetry of power, where the possibility of some taking undue advantage[9] of others is pronounced. The first storm is global. Its key feature is that the world's most affluent nations, and especially the rich within those nations, have considerable power to shape what is done, and to do so in ways which favor their own concerns, especially over those of the world's poorer nations, and poor people within those nations.

The second storm is intergenerational. Its key feature is that the current generation has similar, but more pronounced, asymmetric power over the prospects of future generations: roughly speaking, earlier generations can affect the prospects of future generations, but not vice versa. In my view, the intergenerational storm is the most prominent of the three. Here the possibilities for taking advantage are deep.

The third storm is theoretical. In dealing with the first two storms, it would be nice if we had robust general theories to guide us. Unfortunately, this is not the case. In particular, existing theories are extremely underdeveloped in many of the relevant areas, including intergenerational ethics, international justice, scientific uncertainty, and the human relationship to animals and the rest of nature. This not only complicates the task of behaving well, but also renders us more vulnerable to the first two storms.

Each of the three storms hampers the cause of ethical action, and threatens to blow it seriously off course. But taken together they are mutually reinforcing, and the challenge becomes profound. Moreover, this interaction also brings on new problems. Most prominently, the

---

9. In keeping with my aim of begging as few theoretical questions as possible, I shall use the phrase "taking undue advantage" (or just "taking advantage") as a placeholder, to be filled in by a more nuanced philosophical account of the moral wrong at stake. (I take it that this is often the function of that phrase.) For example, one might try to flesh it out with notions such as "exploitation" (Bertram 2009) or "domination" (Nolt 2011), or by appeal to violations of the principles of a particular moral or political theory, such as Rawls's (cf. Gardiner 2011a).

perfect storm puts pressure on the very terms in which we discuss the environmental crisis, tempting us to distort our moral sensibilities in order to facilitate the exploitation of our global and intergenerational position. I call this "the problem of moral corruption."

III. CLIMATE CHANGE

In this book, I explore the perfect moral storm through a discussion of one central example, that of global climate change. I do so both because this is the leading environmental problem of our age, and because it is an especially good example of the storm.

First, the sources and impacts of climate change are spread across space, time, and species. The temporal aspect is particularly striking. Once emitted, molecules of the main greenhouse gas, carbon dioxide, typically persist in the atmosphere and contribute to warming for centuries. Moreover, a significant percentage of these emissions remains for thousands, and even tens of thousands, of years. Given this, the full impacts of our current activities are realized over a very long period, making the problem they pose profoundly intergenerational.

Second, climate change seems to provide a compelling case study of how the storm can undermine effective policy. On the matter of substance, there is a serious problem of political inertia (see chapters 3 and 4). Leaders and their countries have been promising to act for nearly two decades now. But this has been a sad history of delay, obstruction, and broken promises.

In the early 1990s, the nations of the world announced the objective of avoiding dangerous climate change for the sake of protecting current and future generations against its impacts, and with the understanding that ecosystems should not be pushed beyond their capacities to adapt. In line with this, many industrialized countries (including the United States, Canada, Japan, New Zealand, and Norway) said that they would voluntarily stabilize their emissions at 1990 levels by 2000. As it turned out, almost no one did so, and most had risen by around 10% by that time.[10]

---

10. Marland 2008. Germany and the United Kingdom did post reductions, although these were for unrelated economic reasons.

Moreover, subsequent negotiations around the Kyoto Protocol have at best had only limited effect. Despite a few notable efforts, emissions in most countries continued to grow through the next decade, even as the science suggested that reductions were becoming much more urgent. The United States, for example, saw growth of just over 20% in the period 1990–2005, while global emissions increased by almost 30%.

More recently, in the period 2007–09, much energy was invested in the idea that a United Nations meeting in Copenhagen in December 2009 would produce a new, more ambitious, and binding global treaty to replace Kyoto. However, as things turned out, that gathering delivered only a vague and weak political accord, accompanied by widespread dismay and angry recriminations.

It is difficult to see this experience as anything other than a geopolitical disaster. As Connie Hedegaard, the Danish Minister for Climate and Energy (and subsequently EU commissioner on climate action), put it two months before Copenhagen: "If the whole world comes to Copenhagen and leaves without making the needed political agreement, then I think it's a failure that is not just about climate. Then it's the whole global democratic system not being able to deliver results in one of the defining challenges of our century. And that . . . should not be a possibility."[11]

As a matter of public discourse, the geopolitical disaster has been facilitated by the fact that the current generation in the developed countries has spent much of the last two decades conveniently distracted and confused about the problem. On the one hand, governments have persistently had "other priorities," and citizens have failed to see climate change even as a serious environmental problem, let alone one of humanity's largest problems per se.[12] On the other hand, we have seen much hand wringing about the soundness of the science (albeit almost all by nonscientists, or scientists who don't work on climate), active campaigns of misinformation, and a tendency to reduce the issue to tangential matters such as recycling. In short, few seem interested in really dealing with the problem despite its catastrophic potential. All of this seems difficult to explain away in any normal way. Unfortunately, in a perfect moral storm, it makes perfect sense. The temptation to pass the buck on to the future, the poor, and nature is very strong. So, the incentive to disengage is high.

11. Von Bulow 2009.
12. Leiserowitz 2005, 2009; Pew 2005; see also Jamieson 2006.

In my view, then, the perfect moral storm poses a very serious and deep ethical challenge, and one that is manifest in the climate policy of the last two decades. Still, mine is not a council of despair. First, even given the theoretical storm, the broad outlines of what must be done are relatively clear and well-known, especially in the short- to medium-term (see chapter 11). Even lacking robust theory, intermediate guidance is possible using indirect methods, such as identifying intuitively clear cases of failure, trying to articulate ethical constraints based on those cases, searching for levels of overlapping consensus across existing theories, and defending such benchmarks against the forces of moral corruption. Such strategies suggest two things. To begin with, global emissions must be put onto a sensible pathway that takes seriously the needs and aspirations of both present and future people. Given the extreme risk facing future generations, this mandates that they must peak sometime in the next few decades and then decline significantly for the foreseeable future. In addition, the developed nations are morally required to take the lead, and the heaviest burdens, at least in the short- to medium-term.

Second, though achieving this will be a serious challenge, the more central problem seems to be with engaging and then making operative the motivations that will bring it about. This is within our control. If climate change is a perfect moral storm, it is concerns about what we are doing to the poor, future generations, and nature that justify most of what needs to be done. I am optimistic that most of us have such concerns, and take them seriously. (Others are less so, but that is another story.) Still, what seems clear is that we lack the appropriate institutions to make these concerns effective in the world of policy. Markets and democratic elections may be good at registering short-term and local interests, but they look more dubious in the face of the perfect storm. We must find new ways to engage such institutions, and probably also develop additional institutions to help.

Here it is useful to recognize that the biggest obstacles to effective action may be our own attitudes of complacency and procrastination. Much of what passes for even the most progressive discussion of climate change these days is devoted to persuading us that dealing with the problem will not be costly in terms of our current lifestyles, and so is compatible with ways of living that many take to be in their best interests. This is comforting talk, and I am hopeful that it may turn out to be substantially true. Still, it seems to me that this is the wrong discussion to be having. Our reasons for acting on climate change are not (or at least not primarily) that doing so will be good (or at least not bad) *for us*; they are deeper and more morally serious than that. In my view, seeing this should make it easier for us to act. To dither when one might prevent moderate harms to oneself by taking modest precautionary action is folly to be sure, but its moral import is limited. By contrast, to engage in willful self-deception and moral corruption when the lives of future generations, the world's poor, and even the basic fabric of life on the planet is at stake is a much more serious business. We should wake up to that fact, and demand more of our institutions, our leaders, and ourselves.

IV. THE WIDER RELEVANCE OF THE MODEL

The focus of this book is on climate change. This is a vitally important topic. Still, I want to emphasize that the perfect moral storm analysis does not stand or fall with this case alone. In my view, the analysis is relevant to environmental affairs more generally, and indeed beyond them to other areas of human life. Importantly, I suspect that other instances of the storm are both possible, and indeed likely, to emerge over the coming decades and centuries. As humanity's activities become ever more extensive, it seems probable that the potential for the global and intergenerational problems to manifest themselves also increases. Some suggestion of this potential may come from the fact that climate change is already the second genuinely global environmental problem to come along in just a few decades (after ozone depletion), and another (ocean acidification) comes fast on its heels.[13] Another indication comes

---

13. Ozone depletion does not seem to fit the perfect moral storm model, partly because it has substantial intragenerational effects that seem sufficient to motivate action. But ocean acidification may share some of the crucial characteristics.

from the thought that we may have already seen degenerate forms[14] of the storm in other areas—such as nuclear proliferation, and financial deregulation prior to the Great Depression and current recession.

One way to see the wider relevance of the perfect storm is by contrasting it with the traditional "tragedy of the commons" analysis originally made popular by Garrett Hardin. This model is ubiquitous in discussions of environmental (and many other) problems. But, for reasons which should become clear, I believe that the perfect moral storm is sometimes more fundamental, and the intergenerational storm often so. This has practical consequences. Hardin's model, though useful in many contexts and respects, would underestimate the seriousness of some problems, and misdirect our energies in searching for solutions.[15] Given this, it should sometimes give way.

Another reason that the perfect storm analysis has more general relevance is that ultimately we are in need of a political philosophy and an ethic to address it, and especially its intergenerational aspect. This is especially so if, as I suggest elsewhere, the challenge of the storm is in some ways more fundamental than the one much conventional theory tries to address.[16] Surely philosophy would be remiss if it did not try to rise to the challenge and provide an "ideal theory" to resolve this deep problem.[17]

In the case of climate change, of course, the problem is too urgent to wait, so we must muddle through without strong theory, and within existing institutions. Hence, as well as ideal theory, we must also seek an

14. I say more about the idea of degenerate forms in chapter 5. But one example would be if we see the convergence of the intergenerational and theoretical storms at a national or regional level. At first glance, this would not be a perfect moral storm in my sense, since it is not global in scope. Still, it might retain many of the same characteristics, so that much of what we say about the perfect storm remains apt. More deeply, from the theoretical point of view I would argue that the crucial features of what I have been calling the "global" storm are not essentially tied to a single planet considered as such (let alone this planet), but rather to certain kinds of systems that are largely self-contained. I call the storm "global" since, at this stage in human history, the earth is such a system for humanity, and because many of our prominent political and theoretical problems are at this level (see chapter 7).

15. On Hardin's application of the commons metaphor to world population, see Appendix 1.

16. Gardiner 2009a, 2011a.

17. Rawls 1999.

"ethics for the transition." As already mentioned, here we are fortunate that the basic parameters of what needs to be done morally-speaking are fairly clear, at least in the short- to medium-term. Nevertheless, there remains work to be done in fleshing out the details, and in defending this ethical consensus against the forces of moral corruption. Moreover, how to get existing political institutions to act, or how to create and fashion new (even transitional) ones, is not obvious. Hence, in addition to pointing in the general direction we should be heading, it would be useful for the ethics of the transition to offer some guidance in how to get there, and what to do while we figure out both of these things.

In this book, I comment only briefly on these tasks, deferring deeper engagement for another occasion. Here my aim is to clearly identify the problem, trusting that in the current context this is itself a contribution to progress. If we persistently see global environmental problems in general, and climate change in particular, through other lenses (e.g., the scientific, economic, or short-term geopolitical), this may prevent us from reaching a solution. As Henry Shue likes to say, "sometimes sunlight is the best antiseptic."[18] I hope that in this case it is.

V. OUTLINE OF THE BOOK

The basic structure of the book is as follows. Part A offers an overview of the perfect moral storm analysis. Chapter 1 presents the basic metaphor, distinguishes its main elements, and explains why these are especially problematic in the case of climate change. Chapter 2 addresses two initial objections. One suggests that the analysis relies on too selfish and unethical an account of human agency; and the other that it neglects the potential for a "green energy revolution." I argue that the perfect storm can accommodate both concerns.

Part B discusses the global storm. Chapters 3 and 4 consider two competing diagnoses of the structure of the current international problem. (These chapters involve some modestly technical sections that may be safely skipped by general readers.) According to the optimistic analysis, addressing climate change does not really require truly global cooperation, but only that of a substantial, "critical mass" of countries.

18. Shue 1980, 341.

According to a more pessimistic analysis, truly global cooperation is necessary. I argue that the facts of climate change make the optimistic analysis largely untenable for the global storm considered as such, and in ways that support the more pessimistic case. However, I go on to claim that the more pessimistic analysis is itself not bleak enough, since it neglects the background presence of the intergenerational storm. Given this, we might expect nations to indulge in a modest "wait and see" policy that focuses on only short- to medium-term concerns. Unfortunately, we see evidence for such "shadow solutions" in the history of global climate policy, and especially in the Kyoto framework. Interestingly, their existence may help to explain the initial appeal of the optimistic analysis.

Part C considers the intergenerational storm more directly, and constitutes the theoretical heart of the book. Chapter 5 sets out the basic structure of the intergenerational problem, suggesting that it operates at various social levels. Chapter 6 assesses whether its application to climate change is undermined by the possibility that severe impacts may be imminent: if catastrophe is coming soon, the thought goes, doesn't the intergenerational problem disappear? I argue that it does not, and moreover that (counterintuitively) the temporal proximity of major negative impacts may make matters worse, even perhaps to the extent of setting off the equivalent of an intergenerational arms race.

Part D discusses the theoretical dimension of the perfect moral storm. Chapter 7 introduces a global test for political institutions and moral and political theories, and argues that we have strong grounds for thinking that current versions of both are failing this test. It also suggests that theories can be opaque, complacent, and evasive in the face of serious problems, and that this is a live worry in the case of climate change. Chapter 8 offers as an example of these problems attempts to apply economic cost-benefit analysis, the leading public policy tool of the day, to climate change. Such analysis is often criticized by philosophers and environmentalists; but in the present case, it also comes under pressure from many of its usual supporters.

Part E discusses the problem of moral corruption. Chapter 9 explains the basic problem and then illustrates its relevance through a comparison of some of the current debate about climate change with a classic piece of corrupt reasoning discussed by Jane Austen. In light of such worries, chapter 10 explores recent arguments for the pursuit of geoengineering, and considers how the perfect storm analysis might illuminate them. In addition, it assesses what might be at stake when we do wrong, even when that wrong might be in some sense justified as a "lesser evil,". Through this, it suggests that there is a value at stake in global environmental tragedy that casts further light on the ethical challenge of the perfect storm.

Part F brings the book to a close. Chapter 11 briefly makes steps towards an ethics of the transition through commenting on some basic concerns about scientific uncertainty, precautionary action, responsibility for past emissions, the allocation of future emissions, and the shape of individual responsibility. The conclusion summarizes the main claims of the book, and says something about the prospects for the immediate future. Appendix 1 considers and rejects Garrett Hardin's identification of the global environmental tragedy with world population growth. Appendix 2 illustrates how we may be vulnerable to epistemic as well as moral corruption though a discussion of three of Michael Crichton's claims in the author's message accompanying his novel *State of Fear*.

PART A

Overview

CHAPTER 1

A Perfect Moral Storm

We are heading substantially—and rapidly—in the wrong direction.

—Dieter Helm (Helm 2008, 214)

I. WHY ETHICS?

In 2001, the most authoritative scientific report on climate change, from the United Nations Intergovernmental Panel on Climate Change (IPCC),[1] began by saying:

> Natural, technical, and social sciences can provide essential information and evidence needed for decisions on what constitutes "dangerous anthropogenic interference with the climate system." At the same time, *such decisions are value judgments.*[2]

There are good grounds for this statement. Climate change is complex problem raising issues across and between a large number of disciplines, including the physical and life sciences, political science, economics, and psychology, to name just a few. But without wishing for a moment to

1. The IPCC is charged with providing member governments with state of the art assessments of "the science, the impacts, and the economics of—and the options for mitigating and/or adapting to—climate change" (IPCC 2001c, p. vii). In 2007, it shared the Nobel Peace Prize with Al Gore.

2. IPCC 2001a, 2; emphasis added. See also IPCC 2007c, 19. The passage continues "to be determined through sociopolitical processes taking into account considerations such as development, equity, and sustainability, as well as uncertainties and risk." Hence, the IPCC takes a position on the way in which decisions will be made, and on some of the relevant criteria. These are themselves value judgments (albeit not highly controversial ones). But see also chapter 8.

marginalize the contributions of these disciplines, ethics does seem to play a fundamental role.

Why so? At the most general level, the reason is that we cannot get very far in discussing why climate change is a problem without invoking ethical considerations. If we do not think that our own actions are open to moral assessment, or that various interests—our own; those of our kith, kin, and country; those of distant people, future people, animals, and nature—matter, then it is hard to see why climate change (or much else) poses a problem. But once we see this, then we appear to need some account of moral responsibility, morally important interests, and what to do about both. This puts us squarely in the domain of ethics.

At a more practical level, ethical questions are fundamental to the main policy decisions that must be made, such as where to set a global ceiling for greenhouse gas emissions, and how to distribute the emissions permitted by such a ceiling. Consider first where the global ceiling is set at a particular time. In large part, this depends on how the interests of the present are weighed against those of the future. As the IPCC said in its 2007 report: "Choices about the scale and timing of [greenhouse gas] mitigation involve balancing the economic costs of more rapid emission reductions now against the corresponding medium-term and long-term climate risks of delay."[3]

One way of making this point vivid is to imagine an extreme case. Suppose that the president of the United States went on television tonight and said that he and other world leaders were declaring a global state of emergency and ordering an immediate radical cut in emissions (e.g., complete cessation, or an 80% cut). Such a cut would dramatically reduce the risks to future generations of catastrophic impacts from climate change. Still, the proposal is surely unreasonable and unethical. Since the global economic system—on which most people's way of life depends—is substantially driven by fossil fuels, an immediate radical cut in emissions would cause a social and economic catastrophe for current people. Since there is no way that the system could cope with an overnight change of this magnitude, such a policy would probably lead to mass starvation, rampant disease, and war. Civil society would collapse. Even if this did "solve" the climate problem for future generations, the moral objections to such an approach would be overwhelming.

3. IPCC 2007c, 23.

The instant radical cut strategy is thus not discussed, and for good reason. Nevertheless, the prospect raises important questions. Suppose, for the sake of argument, that such a cut would be what is best for future people.[4] For example, suppose that it would be awful for those living through it, but that at some point later generations would be better off than under any alternative climate policy, and at least as well off as we are now. If such an option were available, the question would become: how far are current people entitled to inflict risks on the future in order to protect themselves? If the threat to the present were imminent and widespread social collapse, it seems that they are so entitled. But what if it were not? What if, instead, the cost facing the current generation were merely a slightly lower standard of living than they are currently used to? Moreover, what if this were necessary to save the future from a genuine catastrophe? The crucial thought here is that presumably at some point the interests of future people become so important, and those of current people relatively less so, that the balance tips to the future. This is relevant because a decision on where to set a global cap at a particular time implicitly answers the question of where we think this tipping point is. Of course, even without an explicit cap, our actual behavior— the emissions we allow at a particular time—also implicitly answers the question. At the time of writing, this answer is very strongly in our favor. Indeed, it suggests the view that our interests have absolute priority over the interests of the future: any interest of ours (however trivial) is sufficient to outweigh any interest of theirs (however serious).

Consider now the second main policy issue: once a global cap for a particular time is set, how do we decide how emissions are to be distributed under it? This is a very important question. Given that fossil fuel consumption is currently fundamental to our economic systems and likely to remain important for decades, even as we transition towards alternatives, how we answer the question of who is allowed to emit how much will have major social, economic, and geopolitical consequences. But many of the issues underlying any answer are ethical. Any allocation must (explicitly or implicitly) take a position on the importance of factors such as historical responsibility for the problem, the current needs and future aspirations of particular societies, and the appropriate

---

4. I consider an objection to this assumption in the next chapter.

role of energy consumption in people's lives. Consider the following. Does it matter that the developed nations are responsible for the overwhelming majority of emissions historically?[5] Is it important that their populations are, on average, much richer than those of the less developed nations, and likely to remain so during the transition?[6] What are we to say about the fact that some people's emissions are largely "spent" on luxury items (such as maintaining large houses at a constant temperature of 72 degrees F, or driving large and relatively energy-inefficient vehicles, or taking exotic vacations far from home) whereas others are the basis of bare subsistence?[7]

The relevance of ethics to substantive climate policy thus seems clear, and the topic deserves serious independent treatment. This is a project to which I have contributed elsewhere.[8] Still, it is not my focus in this book. Instead, I address a further—and to some extent more basic—way in which ethical reflection sheds light on our present predicament. This has nothing much to do with the substance of a defensible climate regime; instead, it concerns the making of climate policy.

My thesis is this. The peculiar features of the climate change problem pose substantial obstacles to our ability to make the hard choices necessary to address it. Climate change is a perfect moral storm. One consequence of this is that, even if the difficult ethical questions could be answered, we might still find it difficult to act. For the storm makes us extremely vulnerable to moral corruption.[9]

Let us say that a perfect storm is an event constituted by an unusual convergence of independently harmful factors where this convergence is likely to result in substantial, and possibly catastrophic, negative

---

5. World Resources Institute 2007.

6. Baer et al. 2007.

7. Shue 1993.

8. For introductions to the relevant literature, see Gardiner 2004b and 2010a. Gardiner et al. 2010 collects some central papers.

9. One might wonder why, despite the widespread agreement that climate change involves important ethical questions, there is relatively little public discussion of them. The answer to this question is no doubt complex. But my thesis may constitute part of that answer.

outcomes. The term "the perfect storm" seems to have become prominent in popular culture from Sebastian Junger's book of that name, and the associated film.[10] Junger's tale is based on the true story of the *Andrea Gail*, a fishing vessel caught at sea during a convergence of three particularly bad storms. The sense of the analogy is that climate change appears to be a perfect moral storm because it involves the convergence of a number of factors that threaten our ability to behave ethically.[11]

As climate change is a complex phenomenon, I cannot hope to identify all of the ways in which its features cause problems for ethical behavior.[12] Instead, I will identify three especially salient problems – analogous to the three storms that hit the *Andrea Gail* – that converge in the climate change case. These three "storms" arise in the global, intergenerational, and theoretical dimensions, and I will argue that their interaction helps to exacerbate and obscure a lurking problem of moral corruption that may be of greater practical importance than any one of them.

10. Junger 1999.

11. The term '"perfect storm"' is in wide usage. However, it is difficult to find definitions. An online dictionary of slang offers the following: "When three events, usually beyond one's control, converge and create a large inconvenience for an individual. Each event represents one of the storms that collided on the *Andrea Gail* in the book/movie titled *The Perfect Storm*" (Urbandictionary.com, 3/25/05). More recently, Wikipedia states: "The phrase *perfect storm* refers to the simultaneous occurrence of events which, taken individually, would be far less powerful than the result of their chance combination. Such occurrences are rare by their very nature, so that even a slight change in any one event contributing to the perfect storm would lessen its overall impact" (Wikipedia, accessed 6/29/2007).

12. For example, Chrisoula Andreou draws our attention to the relevance of the psychological and philosophical literature on procrastination for understanding environmental decision making (Andreou 2006, 2007). She does not apply this analysis to climate change specifically; but I suspect that it is relevant, and worth pursuing. Nevertheless, the procrastination model is unlikely to be dominant in this case. It focuses on the challenges to decision making faced by a single, unified agent; hence, it does not reveal, and is unlikely to account for, the practical and moral import of the fragmentations of agency I am emphasizing.

II. THE GLOBAL STORM

The climate challenge is usually understood in spatial, and especially geopolitical, terms. We can make sense of this by pointing out three important characteristics of the problem: dispersion of causes and effects, fragmentation of agency, and institutional inadequacy.

1. The Basic Storm

Let us begin with the *dispersion of causes and effects*. Climate change is a truly global phenomenon. Emissions of greenhouse gases from any geographical location on the earth's surface enter the atmosphere and then play a role in affecting climate globally. Hence, the impact of any particular emission of greenhouse gases is not realized solely at its source, either individual or geographical; instead, impacts are dispersed to other actors and regions of the earth. Such spatial dispersion has been widely discussed.

The second characteristic is *fragmentation of agency*. Climate change is not caused by a single agent, but by a vast number of individuals and institutions (including economic, social, and political institutions) not unified by a comprehensive structure of agency. This is important because it poses a challenge to humanity's ability to respond.

In the spatial dimension, this feature is usually understood as arising out of the shape of the current international system, as constituted by states. Then the problem is that, given that there is not only no world government but also no less centralized system of global governance (or at least no effective one), it is very difficult to coordinate an effective response to global climate change.

This general argument is typically given more bite through the invocation of a certain familiar theoretical model.[13] For the international situation is usually understood in game theoretic terms as a prisoner's dilemma, or what Garrett Hardin calls a tragedy of the commons. Let us

---

13. The appropriateness of this model even to the spatial dimension requires some further specific, but usually undefended, background assumptions about the precise nature of the dispersion of effects and fragmentation of agency. But I pass over that issue here.

consider each of these models in turn (see also chapters 3 and 4). (*The details of the next few paragraphs can be safely overlooked by those uninterested in more technical matters.).*)

A prisoner's dilemma is a situation with a certain structure.[14] In the standard example, two prisoners are about to stand trial for a crime that they are accused of committing together.[15] Each faces the following proposition. He can either confess or not confess. If both confess, then each gets five years. If neither confesses, then each gets one year on a lesser charge. But if one confesses and the other does not, then the confessor goes free, and the nonconfessor gets ten years. Neither knows for sure what the other will do; but each knows that the other faces the same choice situation.

Given this scenario, each person has the following preference ranking:

1st Preference: I confess, the other criminal doesn't. (Go free)
2nd Preference: Neither of us confess. (1 year)
3rd Preference: Both of us confess. (5 years)
4th Preference: I don't confess, but the other criminal does. (10 years.)

This situation is usually expressed with a diagram of the following sort:

	B don't confess	B confess
A don't confess	1, 1 (2nd, 2nd)	10, 0 (4th, 1st)
A confess	0, 10 (1st, 4th)	5, 5 (3rd, 3rd)

The reason why the situation is called a dilemma is as follows. Suppose I am one of the prisoners. I cannot guarantee what the other prisoner will do, and I lack any effective means to make it that I can do so. So I need to consider each possibility. Suppose he confesses. Then it is better for me to confess also (since 5 years in jail is better than 10). Suppose he does not confess. Then it is better for me to confess (since going free is better than 1 year in jail). So, whatever he does, I should confess.

---

14. The next few paragraphs are drawn from Gardiner 2001a.

15. The title and illustration are attributed to Albert Tucker, who used them to popularize ideas developed by Merrill Flood and Melvin Dresher in investigating global nuclear strategy (Kuhn 2001).

Unfortunately, the situation is exactly the same for him. So, reasoning in the same way I do, he will also confess. This means that the outcome will be that both of us confess (getting 5 years each). But this is suboptimal: each of us prefers the outcome that comes from us both not confessing (1 year each) over the outcome that comes from us both confessing (5 years each).[16]

For current purposes, the central difficulty can be (roughly) characterized as follows:

> (PD1) It is *collectively rational* to cooperate: each agent prefers the outcome produced by everyone cooperating over the outcome produced by no one cooperating.
> (PD2) It is *individually rational* not to cooperate: when each individual has the power to decide whether or not she will cooperate, each person (rationally) prefers not to cooperate, whatever the others do.

PD1 and PD2 generate the paradox as follows. In prisoner's dilemma situations, each individual has the power to decide whether or not she will cooperate. Hence, given PD2, if each person is individually rational, no one cooperates. But this means that each person ends up with an outcome that they disprefer over an outcome that is available. For, according to PD1, each prefers the cooperative over the noncooperative outcome. Obviously, this is unsatisfactory, by each agent's own lights.

The tragedy of the commons model is perhaps more familiar in environmental contexts than the prisoner's dilemma, but seems to have the same underlying logic. In essentials, the tragedy of the commons appears to be a prisoner's dilemma involving a single common resource. (I offer a more complex account of the relationship between the two models in chapter 4.) In his classic example, Hardin imagines a group of herdsmen grazing their cattle on common land. Each herdsman is considering whether or not he should add to his herd. Hardin assumes that the relevant factors to consider are: on the positive side, the benefit of an extra cow, which is roughly the price it will fetch in the market place; and, on

16. But neither of us can get there as things stand. Suppose one of us thinks, "It's a prisoner's dilemma, so we should not confess." Then, the other person knows that we know this. But if they think we are not going to confess, the rational thing for them to do is to confess, since this gives them a better outcome. Remember that the previous reasoning showed that a prisoner should confess, *no matter what the other prisoner does*.

the negative side, the effects of this cow's grazing on what is left for other animals. But, he observes, these benefits and costs are distributed differently: whereas the benefit accrues only to the individual herdsman, the costs are spread across all the cattle in the pasture, and so are shared by all herdsmen.[17] Suppose then that each herdsman has as his goal the maximization of his own profit. Given the distribution of costs and benefits, each will find himself with a strong incentive to add extra cattle; and so all will. But if they do, this will result in the systematic overgrazing of the commons, which is disastrous for everyone.

The force of Hardin's example is as follows. The situation facing the herdsmen is paradoxical. On the one hand, each prefers the outcome of everyone restricting their own herd (i.e., the commons remaining intact) over the outcome produced by no one doing so (i.e., the collapse of the commons). But, on the other hand, when each is deciding what to do in his own case, each prefers to add more cattle to his own herd. Unfortunately, it is this latter preference that drives the outcome. Since each herdsman makes his decision in isolation, all add cattle. This destroys the commons, to their mutual ruin.

Hardin's description of this kind of situation as a tragedy is apt. For what happens is more than simply a bad thing. The initial situation drives people by an inexorable process towards an outcome that is worse by their own lights, and away from one that is better. Indeed, it is the very same values that make cooperation preferable that drive each agent away from it. In Hardin's example, each herdsman wants the maximum profit, which is why all prefer collective constraint; still, when they act as individuals, it is their desire for profit that drives them to pursue more (and more) cattle, and so leads to the collapse of the commons.[18]

The basic features of the herdsmen example can be generalized to fit other cases in the same way as those of the prisoner's dilemma. Roughly speaking, the tragedy of the commons holds when: (TC1) each agent prefers the outcome produced by everyone restricting their consumption over the outcome produced by no one doing so; but (TC2) each agent has the power to decide whether or not she will restrict her consumption, each (rationally) prefers not to do so, whatever the others do. Again, this

17. Hardin 1968, 1244; Hardin 1993, 217–18.

18. Note that, though the values Hardin talks about in this example are self-interested ones, the generalized tragedy of the commons model does not mandate this. See chapter 2.

is paradoxical: according to the first claim, each agent accepts that it is *collectively rational* to cooperate; but, according to the second, each agent believes that it is *individually rational* not to cooperate. Moreover, if the second claim dominates—if the parties all act on individual rationality—the situation generates tragedy. All are lead to a situation that they agree is worse than another that is potentially available.

The tragedy of the commons has become the standard analytical model for understanding regional and global environmental problems in general, and climate change is no exception. Typically, the reasoning goes as follows. Think of climate change as an international problem, and conceive of the relevant parties as individual countries, who represent the interests of their countries in perpetuity. Then, the above claims about collective and individual rationality appear to hold. On the one hand, no country wants catastrophic climate change. Hence, each prefers the outcome produced by everyone restricting their own emissions over the outcome produced by no one doing so, and so it is collectively rational to cooperate and restrict global emissions. But, on the other hand, each country prefers to free-ride on the actions of others. Hence, when each country has the power to decide whether or not she will restrict her emissions, each prefers not to do so, whatever the others do.[19;]

If climate change is a normal tragedy of the commons, this is a matter of concern. Still, there is a sense in which this turns out to be encouraging news. In the real world, commons problems are often resolvable under certain circumstances, and at first glance climate change seems to satisfy these conditions.[20] In particular, it is widely said that parties facing a commons problem can solve it if they benefit from a wider context of interaction—that is, if they have reasons to cooperate with one another over other matters of mutual concern. This appears to be the case with climate change, since countries interact with each other on a number of broader issues, such as trade and security.

This brings us to the third characteristic of the climate change problem, *institutional inadequacy*. There is wide agreement that the

19. For a deeper analysis, see chapter 4.

20. A genuine prisoner's dilemma is literally irresolvable under standard assumptions about its nature. As Ken Binmore puts it in his introduction to game theory: "rational players don't cooperate in the Prisoner's Dilemma because the conditions for rational cooperation are absent" (Binmore 2007, 19). For relevant discussion, see Shepski 2006, Ostrom 1990, and chapter 4.

appropriate means for resolving commons problems under the favorable conditions just mentioned is for the parties to agree to change the existing incentive structure through the introduction of a system of enforceable sanctions. (Hardin calls this "mutual coercion, mutually agreed upon."[21]) This transforms the decision situation by foreclosing the option of free-riding, so that the collectively rational action also becomes individually rational. Theoretically, then, matters seem simple; but in practice things are different. The need for enforceable sanctions poses a challenge at the global level because of the limits of our current (largely national) institutions, and the lack of an effective system of global governance. In essence, addressing climate change appears to require global regulation of greenhouse gas emissions, where this includes establishing a reliable enforcement mechanism; but the current global system—or lack of it—makes this difficult, if not impossible.

The implication of the familiar (spatial) analysis, then, is that the main thing needed to solve the climate problem is an effective system of global governance (at least for this issue). There is a sense in which this is still good news. In principle at least, it should be possible to motivate countries to establish such a regime, since they ought to recognize that it is in their long-term interests to eliminate the possibility of free riding and so make genuine cooperation the rational strategy at the individual as well as collective level.

2. Exacerbating Factors

Unfortunately, however, this is not the end of the story. There are other features of the climate change case that make the necessary global agreement more difficult, and so exacerbate the basic global storm.[22] Prominent amongst these is scientific uncertainty about the precise

---

21. Hardin 1968, 1247.

22. There is one fortunate convergence. Several writers (e.g., Shue 1999, Singer 2002) have emphasized that the major ethical arguments all point in the same direction: that the developed countries should bear most of the costs of the transition—including those accruing to developing countries—at least in the early stages of mitigation and adaptation. See, also chapter 11.

magnitude and distribution of effects, particularly at the national level.[23] One reason for this is that the lack of trustworthy data about the costs and benefits of climate change at the national level casts doubt on the collective rationality claim—that no one wants serious climate change. Perhaps, some nations wonder, we might be better off with at least a moderate amount of climate change than without it. More importantly, some might ask whether, faced with a given serious change, they will at least be *relatively* better off than other countries, and so might get away with paying less to avoid the associated costs.[24] Such factors complicate the game theoretic situation, and so make agreement more difficult.

In other contexts, the problem of scientific uncertainty might not be so serious. But a second characteristic of the climate problem exacerbates matters in this setting. The source of climate change is located deep in the infrastructure of current civilizations; hence, attempts to combat it may have substantial ramifications for social life. Climate change is caused by human production of greenhouse gases, primarily carbon dioxide. Such emissions are brought about by the burning of fossil fuels for energy. But it is this energy that supports existing economies. Hence, if halting climate change requires deep cuts in projected global emissions over time, we can expect that such action will have profound effects on the basic economic organization of the developed countries and on the aspirations of the developing countries.

The "deep roots" problem has several salient implications. First, it suggests that those with vested interests in the continuation of the current system—for example, many of those who have substantial political and economic power, or who expect to gain such power, through selling emissions-intensive resources—will resist such action. Second, unless ready substitutes are found, real mitigation can be expected to have

23. Rado Dimitrov argues that we must distinguish between different kinds of uncertainty when we investigate the effects of scientific uncertainty on international regime building, and that it is uncertainties about national impacts that undermines regime formation (Dimitrov 2003).

24. This consideration appears to have played a role in U.S. deliberation about climate change, where it is often asserted that the U.S. faces lower marginal costs from climate change than other countries. See, for example, Mendelsohn 2001, Nitze 1994, Posner and Sunstein 2008.

profound impacts on how humans live and how human societies evolve. Hence, action on climate change is likely to raise serious, and perhaps uncomfortable, questions about who we are and what we want to be. Third, this suggests a status quo bias in the face of uncertainty. Contemplating change is often uncomfortable; contemplating basic change may be unnerving, even distressing. Since the social ramifications of action appear to be large, perspicuous, and concrete, but those of inaction appear uncertain, elusive, and indeterminate, it is easy to see why uncertainty might exacerbate social inertia.[25]

A third and very important feature of the climate change problem that exacerbates the basic global storm is that of skewed vulnerabilities. The climate challenge interacts in some unfortunate ways with the present global power structure. For one thing, the responsibility for historical and current emissions lies predominantly with the richer, more powerful nations, and the poor nations are badly situated to hold them accountable. For another, the limited evidence on regional impacts suggests that it is the poorer nations that are most vulnerable to the worst impacts of climate change, at least in the short- to medium-term.[26] Finally, action on climate change creates a moral risk for the developed nations. Implicitly, it embodies a recognition that there are international norms of ethics and responsibility, and reinforces the idea that international cooperation on issues involving such norms is both possible and necessary. Hence, it may encourage attention to other moral defects of the current global system, such as global poverty and inequality, human rights violations, and so on. If the developed nations are not ready to engage on such topics, this creates a further reason to avoid action on climate change. Indeed, the unwillingness to engage puts pressure on the claim that there is a broader context of interaction within which the climate problem can be solved. If some nations do not wish to engage with

25. Much more might be said here. I discuss some psychological aspects of political inertia and the role these play independently of scientific uncertainty in chapter 6.

26. This is because they tend to be located in warmer lower latitudes, because a greater proportion of their economies are in climate-sensitive sectors such as agriculture, and because—being poor—they are worse placed to deal with those impacts. See Stern 2007, 139, citing Tol et al. 2004.

issues of global ethics, and they believe that creating a climate regime leads down this path, then this lessens the incentive to cooperate.[27]

III. THE INTERGENERATIONAL STORM

The global storm emerges from a spatial reading of the characteristics just mentioned (i.e., dispersion of causes and effects, fragmentation of agency, and institutional inadequacy). However, these characteristics are also highly relevant in the temporal dimension, and this gives rise to a more serious, but relatively neglected, challenge. I call this "the intergenerational storm."

1. The Basic Storm

Consider first the dispersion of causes and effects. Human-induced climate change is a severely lagged phenomenon. This is partly because some of the basic mechanisms set in motion by the greenhouse effect, such as sea level rise, take a very long time to be fully realized. But it is also because by far the most important greenhouse gas produced by human activities is carbon dioxide, and once emitted molecules of carbon dioxide can spend a surprisingly long time in the atmosphere.[28]

27. Of course, it has not helped that over much of the last decade climate discussion has occurred in an unfortunate geopolitical setting. International negotiations have taken place against a backdrop of distraction, mistrust, and severe inequalities of power. For many years, the dominant global actor and lone superpower, the United States, refused to address climate change, and was distracted by the threat of global terrorism. Moreover, the international community, including many of America's historical allies, distrusted its motives, its actions, and especially its uses of moral rhetoric; so there was global discord. This unfortunate state of affairs was especially problematic in relation to the developing nations, whose cooperation must be secured if the climate change problem is to be addressed. One issue was the credibility of the developed nations' commitment to solving the climate change problem. (See the next section.) Another was the North's focus on mitigation to the exclusion of adaptation. A third concern was the South's fear of an "abate and switch" strategy on the part of the North. (Note that considered in isolation, these factors do not seem sufficient to explain political inertia. After all, the climate change problem originally became prominent during the 1990s, a decade with a much more promising geopolitical environment.)

28. For more on both claims, see IPCC 2001a, 16–17.

Let us dwell for a moment on this second factor. In the past, the IPCC has said that the average time spent by a molecule of carbon dioxide in the atmosphere is in the region of 5–200 years. This estimate is long enough to create a serious lagging effect; nevertheless, it obscures the fact that a significant percentage of carbon dioxide molecules remain in the atmosphere for much longer periods of time, of the order of thousands and tens of thousands of years. For instance, the climatologist David Archer says:

> The carbon cycle of the biosphere will take a long time to completely neutralize and sequester anthropogenic CO_2. We show a wide range of model forecasts of this effect. For the best-guess cases . . . we expect that 17–33% of the fossil fuel carbon will still reside in the atmosphere 1kyr from now, decreasing to 10–15% at 10kyr, and 7% at 100 kyr. The mean lifetime of fossil fuel CO2 is about 30–35 kyr.[29]

This is a fact, he states, which has not yet "reached general public awareness."[30] Hence, he suggests that "a better shorthand for public discussion [than the IPCC estimate] might be that CO2 sticks around for hundreds of years, plus 25% that sticks around forever."[31]

The fact that carbon dioxide is a long-lived greenhouse gas has at least three important implications. The first is that climate change is a *resilient* phenomenon. Given that currently it does not seem practical to remove large quantities of carbon dioxide from the atmosphere, or to moderate its climatic effects, the upward trend in atmospheric concentration is not easily reversible. Hence, a goal of stabilizing and then reducing carbon dioxide concentrations requires advance planning. Second, climate change impacts are *seriously backloaded*. The climate change that the earth is currently experiencing is primarily the result of emissions from some time in the past, rather than current emissions. As an illustration, it is widely accepted that by 2000 we had already committed ourselves to a rise of at least 0.5 and perhaps more than 1 degree Celsius over the then-observed

29. Archer 2006, 5. "Kyr" means "thousand years." See also Archer 2009; Archer et al. 2009.

30. Archer 2005.

31. Archer 2005; a similar remark occurs in Archer 2006, 5. The discrepancy between the IPCC's range and Archer's is apparently caused by a terminological confusion rather than any scientific dispute. See Archer et al. 2009.

rise of 0.6C.[32] Third, climate change is a *substantially deferred* phenomenon. Backloading implies that the full, cumulative effects of our current emissions will not be realized for some time in the future.

Temporal dispersion creates a number of problems. First, as is widely noted, the resilience of climate change implies that sustained action across many decades is required, and that this needs to anticipate (and so avoid or moderate) negative impacts that are some way off. Given this, periods of procrastination and vacillation have serious repercussions for our ability to manage the problem. Second, backloading implies that climate change poses serious epistemic difficulties, especially for normal political actors. Backloading makes it hard to grasp the connection between causes and effects, and this may undermine the motivation to act[33]; it also implies that by the time we realize that things are bad, we will already be committed to much more change, undermining the ability to respond. Third, the deferral effect calls into question the ability of standard institutions to deal with the problem. Democratic political institutions have relatively short time horizons—the next election cycle, a politician's political career—and it is doubtful whether such institutions have the wherewithal to deal with substantially deferred impacts. Even more seriously, substantial deferral is likely to undermine the will to act. This is because there is an incentive problem: the bad effects of current emissions are likely to fall, or fall disproportionately, on future generations, whereas the benefits of emissions accrue largely to the present.[34]

These three points already raise the specter of institutional inadequacy. But to appreciate this problem fully, we must first say something about the temporal fragmentation of agency. To begin with, there is some reason to think that this might be worse than spatial fragmentation even considered in isolation. In principle, spatially fragmented agents may actually become unified and so able to act as a single agent; but temporally fragmented agents cannot actually become unified, and so may at best only act *as if* they were a single agent. Hence, there is a sense in which

<hr />

32. Wigley 2005; Meehl et al. 2005; Wetherald et al., 2001.

33. This is exacerbated by the fact that the climate is an inherently chaotic system in any case, and that there is no control against which its performance might be compared.

34. The possibility of nonlinear effects, such as in abrupt climate change, complicates this point, but I do not think it undermines it. See chapter 6.

temporal fragmentation may be more intractable than spatial fragmentation. At a minimum, theoretical accounts of how we might act so as to overcome temporal fragmentation seem even more pressing than in the spatial case.

More substantively, the kind of temporal dispersion that characterizes climate change seems clearly much more problematic than the associated spatial fragmentation. Indeed, the presence of backloading and deferral together brings on a new kind of collective action problem that not only adds to the global storm, but is also more difficult to resolve. This problem might aptly be described as one of "intergenerational buck-passing."

We can illustrate the buck-passing problem in the case of climate change if we relax the assumption that countries can be relied upon adequately to represent the interests of both their present and future citizens. Suppose that this is not true. Assume instead that existing national institutions are biased towards the concerns of the current generation: they behave in ways that give excessive weight to those concerns relative to the concerns of future generations. Then, if the benefits of carbon dioxide emission are felt primarily by the present generation[35] (in the form of cheap energy), whereas the costs are substantially deferred to future generations (in the form of the risk of severe and perhaps catastrophic climate change), climate change may provide an instance of a severe intergenerational collective action problem. For one thing, the current generation may "live large" and pass the bill on to the future. For another, the problem may be iterated. As each new generation gains the power to decide whether or not to act, it faces the same incentive structure, and so if it is motivated primarily by generation-relative concerns, it will continue the overconsumption. Thus, the impacts on those generations further into the future are compounded, and more likely to be catastrophic. If in the long-term there are positive feedback mechanisms, or dangerous nonlinearities in the system (as some scientists suspect), this worry increases.

---

35. Some may object to this assumption on the grounds that such benefits drive economic growth that does benefit future generations. This issue does complicate matters. Still, the assumptions (a) that economic growth will continue even in the face of catastrophic climate change, and (b) that it compensates for climate risks need to be scrutinized. See chapters 6 and 8.

Chapter 5 argues that we gain some insight into the shape of this intergenerational problem if we consider a pure version, where the generations do not overlap.[36] I call this "the central problem of intergenerational buck-passing" (CPIBP or "the central problem"), and think of it as the core concern of distinctively intergenerational ethics ("the pure intergenerational problem," or PIP). The main idea is that future generations are extremely vulnerable to their successors. They are subject to what we might call an ongoing "tyranny of the contemporary" that is parallel in some ways to the problem of the "tyranny of the majority" that exercises a great deal of traditional political theory.

It is useful to compare the pure intergenerational problem to the more traditional prisoner's dilemma or tragedy of the commons. The two have strong similarities. Suppose we envision a paradigm form of intergenerational buck-passing, a case where earlier generations inflict serious and unjustifiable pollution on later generations. On an optimistic understanding of things, this situation might involve the following claims about collective and individual rationality:[37]

> (PIP1) Almost every generation prefers the outcome produced by everyone restricting its pollution over the outcome produced by everyone overpolluting.
> (PIP2) When each generation has the power to decide whether or not it will overpollute, each generation (rationally) prefers to do so, whatever the others do.

We might notice that PIP2, the claim about individual rationality, is structurally identical to PD2 in the prisoner's dilemma, and that PIP2, the claim about collective rationality, is also very similar to PD1. Still, even given this similarity, there are important differences. On the one hand, PIP1 is worse than PD1 because in intergenerational buck-passing not all of the actors prefer the cooperative outcome; instead, the first generation is left out, because it prefers noncooperation. (The cooperation of its successors does not benefit it; and since the costs of its overpollution are passed on to the future, holding back does not benefit it either, but requires a pure sacrifice.) Worse, because of this, there is a new problem

36. Generational overlap complicates the picture in some ways, but I do not think that it resolves the basic problem. See Gardiner 2009a and chapter 5.

37. For the reasons for focusing on this form, see chapter 5.

of defection. Since subsequent generations have no reason to comply if their predecessors do not, noncompliance by the first generation reverberates so as to undermine the collective project. If the first generation does not cooperate, then the second generation does not gain from cooperation, and so is put in the same position as the first. Hence, it does not cooperate, and so puts the third generation in the same position as the first; so, it does not cooperate, and so on. In short, the defection of the first generation is enough to unravel the entire scheme of cooperation.

On the other hand, the claim about individual rationality is worse in intergenerational buck-passing because the reason for it is deeper. Both claims about individual rationality hold because the parties lack access to mechanisms (such as enforceable sanctions) that would make defection unattractive. But whereas in normal tragedy of the commons cases this obstacle is largely practical, and can be resolved by the affected parties creating appropriate institutions together, in the pure intergenerational problem the parties do not coexist, and so the afflicted are in principle unable to directly influence the behavior of their predecessors.

This problem of interaction produces the second respect in which the pure intergenerational problem is worse than the tragedy of the commons. This is that it is more difficult to resolve, because the standard solutions to the tragedy of the commons are unavailable. One cannot appeal to a wider context of mutually beneficial interaction, nor to the usual notions of reciprocity. First, the appeal to broad self-interest relies on there being repeated interactions between the parties where mutually beneficial behavior is possible. But between present and future generations there is neither repeated interaction (by definition, there is no interaction at all), nor mutual benefit (there is no way for future generations to benefit present generations).[38] Second, in this context, an appeal to reciprocal fairness initially seems more promising. In particular, if one generation unilaterally restricts its pollution, then subsequent generations can owe the obligation to their forefathers to restrict theirs for the sake of future generations. (Subsequent generations get a benefit from not inheriting an overpolluted planet, but then must, out of fairness, pass this on, so that there is a kind of indirect reciprocity.) However, one problem with this is

---

38. Thus, the situation violates Axelrod's two conditions for resolution: there can be no reciprocity, and the future does not cast the relevant shadow over the parties.

that we need to assume that the initial generation makes a pure sacrifice, with no compensation. So, their action cannot be justified by an appeal to (even indirect) reciprocity.[39]

These problems reflect the difference in structure of the cases already mentioned. In the prisoner's dilemma case, most of the proposed solutions rely on rearranging the situation so as to provide some kind of guarantee of the behavior of others when one cooperates. But in the PIP, the situation cannot be rearranged in this way.[40] If the parties cannot interact, future generations are in no position to benefit or to engage in reciprocal acts with their forbears.

The upshot of all this is that the intergenerational analysis will be less optimistic about solutions than the prisoner's dilemma analysis. When applied to climate change, the intergenerational analysis suggests that current populations may not be motivated to establish a fully adequate global regime. Given the temporal dispersion of effects—and especially the substantial deferral and backloading of impacts—such a regime is probably neither in their interests nor responsive to their concerns (see chapter 2).[41] This is a significant moral problem. Moreover, since in my view the intergenerational storm dominates the global in climate change, the problem may become acute.

39. For more on these issues, see Gardiner 2009a; Gosseries 2009.

40. The point can be made clearer by looking at the preference structures which underlie the tragic situation. We might imagine that the intergenerational problem begins with a prisoner's dilemma structure:

1st preference: I pollute, previous generation don't.
2nd preference: Neither I nor previous generation pollutes.
3rd preference: I pollute, previous generation pollutes.
4th preference: I don't pollute, previous generation pollutes.

But for the first generation capable of serious overpollution, this becomes simply:

1st preference: I pollute
2nd preference: I don't pollute.

So, this fixes the third option for the next generation, and so on for subsequent generations.

41. This may be because they see themselves as the first generation, or the second generation given that the first failed to cooperate, or (as the Fairy Story in chapter 5 suggests) as a mid-sequence generation that does not care about intergenerational cooperation, and is happy simply to take advantage of its temporal position.

2. Exacerbating Factors

Intergenerational buck-passing is bad enough considered in isolation. But in the context of climate change it is also subject to morally relevant multiplier effects. First, climate change is not a static phenomenon. In failing to act appropriately, the current generation does not simply pass an existing problem along to future people. Instead, it adds to it, making the problem substantially worse. For one thing, it increases the costs of coping with climate change. Failing to act now increases the magnitude of future climate change and so its effects. For another, in failing to act now the current generation makes mitigation more difficult because it allows additional investment in fossil fuel-based infrastructure in developed and especially less developed countries. Hence, inaction raises transition costs, making future change harder than change now. Finally, and perhaps most importantly, the current generation does not add to the problem in a linear way. Rather, it rapidly accelerates the problem, since global emissions are increasing at a substantial rate. For example, total carbon dioxide emissions have increased more than four-fold in the last fifty years:

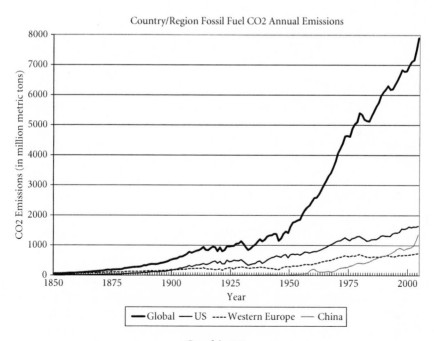

Graphic 1.1

Both global emissions and the emissions of most major countries have been increasing steadily during this period. For example, from 1990–2005, global emissions rose by almost 30% (from 6164 to 7985 million metric tons of carbon), and U.S. emissions by just over 20%.[42] In addition, global emissions have been growing even more rapidly in the recent past, from an average of 1.5–2% per annum in the late 1990s to nearly 3% in 2007. Though 2% may not seem like much, the effects of compounding make it significant, even in the near term: "continued growth of CO2 emissions at 2% per year would yield a 22% increase of emission rate in 10 years and a 35% increase in 15 years."[43] Moreover, the magnitude of the most recent growth is shocking. As the *Washington Post* put it late in 2008, "The rise in global carbon dioxide emissions last year outpaced international researchers' *most dire projections*."[44]

The second multiplier effect is that insufficient action may make some generations suffer unnecessarily. Suppose that, at this point in time, climate change seriously affects the prospects of generations A, B, and C. Suppose, then, that if generation A refuses to act, the effect will continue for longer, harming generations D and E. This may make generation A's inaction worse in a significant respect. In addition to failing to aid generations B and C (and probably also increasing the magnitude of harm inflicted on them), generation A now harms generations D and E, who otherwise would be spared. On some views, this might count as especially egregious, since it might be said that it violates a fundamental moral principle of 'do no harm'.[45]

The third multiplier effect is that generation A's inaction may create situations where *tragic choices* must be made. One way in which a generation may act badly is if it puts in place a set of future circumstances that make it morally required for its successors (and perhaps even itself) to make other generations suffer either unnecessarily, or at least more than would otherwise be the case. For example, suppose that

42. Marland et al., 2008.

43. Hansen 2006, 9.

44. Eilperin 2008, emphasis added. Numbers for 2009 are likely to be substantially lower because of the global economic crisis. But, by itself, this gives no reason to think that underlying trends will change.

45. I owe this suggestion to Henry Shue. (I leave aside here the non-identity problem. For more on this, see chapter 5.)

generation A could and should act now in order to limit climate change, and if it did so that generation D would be kept below some crucial climate threshold, but delay would mean that they would pass that threshold.[46] If passing the threshold imposes severe costs on generation D, then their situation may be so dire that they are forced to take action that will harm generation F (such as emitting even more greenhouse gases) than they would otherwise not need to consider. One possibility is this. Under some circumstances actions that harm innocent others may be morally permissible on grounds of self-defense, and such circumstances may arise in the climate change case.[47] In short, if there is a self-defense exception to the prohibition on harming innocent others, one way in which generation A might behave badly is by creating a situation such that generation D is forced to call on this exception, and so inflict extra suffering on generation F.[48] Worse, this problem can become iterated: perhaps generation D's actions force generation F to call on the self-defense exception too, with the result that it inflicts harm on generation H, and so on. (This is one instance of a more general scenario I refer to as the "intergenerational arms race" in chapter 6. See also chapters 10 and 11.)

IV. THE THEORETICAL STORM

The final storm I want to highlight is constituted by our current theoretical ineptitude. We are extremely ill-equipped to deal with many problems characteristic of the long-term future. Even our best moral and political theories face fundamental and often severe difficulties addressing basic issues such as intergenerational equity, international justice, scientific uncertainty, contingent persons, and the human relationship to animals and nature more generally. But climate change involves all of these matters and more. Given this, our theories are poorly placed to respond. Theoretically, we are currently "inept," in the (nonpejorative) sense of lacking the skills and basic competence for the task.

46. O'Neill and Oppenheimer 2002; Lenton et al. 2008.
47. Traxler 2002, 107.
48. For a related case, see Shue 2005, 275–6.

One sign of our theoretical problems comes from the leading economic approach, cost-benefit analysis (CBA). Much work has been done trying to analyze climate change in these terms. But it tends to point in radically different directions. There is an explanation for this. Here is what John Broome, White's Professor of Moral Philosophy at Oxford, and formerly a Professor of Economics at the University of Bristol, has to say about the method when applied to climate change:

> Cost-benefit analysis, when faced with uncertainties as big as these, *would simply be self-deception*. And in any case, it *could not be a successful exercise*, because the issue of our responsibility to future generations is too poorly understood, and too little accommodated in the current economic theory.[49]

Unlike many concerned with environmental issues, Broome is a defender of CBA in normal contexts.[50] Nevertheless, he thinks that there are special problems in this setting that undermine its application (see chapter 8). Given such worries, we should be surprised at the continued predominance of economic analysis in policy discourse. Why indulge in "self-deception"? Unfortunately, other components of the perfect moral storm provide an answer. (See below.)

A second sign of our theoretical problems comes from the relative silence of most of the prominent political philosophies of the day on global environmental problems.[51] Of course, there is a feeling that such theories *ought* to have something to say about climate change. After all, such change is likely to be severely detrimental to concerns that they hold dear, such as happiness, individual rights, and the integrity of national cultures. Still, in practice, these approaches seem peculiarly reticent in the face of the threat. This raises the worry that they may facilitate the perfect moral storm. Chapter 7 explores this worry by asking whether contemporary political theory and the institutions it tends to support are guilty of failing an important global test. If a set of institutions and theories leave humanity open to, or even encourage, self-inflicted disaster, should they not be criticized, or even rejected, because of this?

49. Broome 1992, 19; emphasis added.
50. Broome 1992, 18–19.
51. In the last few years, the situation has shifted from one of complete silence. But a much fuller engagement is needed.

A third sign of possible theoretical trouble comes from the fact that the global test is stated in purely anthropocentric terms, and instrumental ones at that. But surely a more general worry about the human exploitation of nature also lurks in the background.

To be sure, to a significant extent, the problem posed by the perfect moral storm is that nature becomes a vehicle through which injustice is visited on other people. It facilitates the exploitation of the poor by the rich in the global storm, and of the future by the present in the intergenerational storm.[52] Such injustice is made vivid even in narrowly instrumental terms. Environmental injustice impacts the wealth, health, and so on of vulnerable human beings.

Nevertheless, there may be more to consider if one thinks that nature may have noninstrumental value. To see this, consider an example. Many years ago, I came across a magazine article by an economist that argued that climate change is not a problem because future generations of humanity could always live in massive domes on the earth's surface if they needed to.[53] (Call this scenario *dome world*.) This claim is troubling for many reasons. But one that is especially striking is that it suggests that the disappearance of nonhuman animals and the rest of nature would not be a serious loss (or, at best, that it would be a compensable one). I take this to be a profound claim with which many people would disagree. On the one hand, many will object because they believe that a good relationship with the natural world is, or should be, constitutive of a flourishing human life. In that case, dome world involves another important manifestation of the global and intergenerational storms. On the other hand, some will insist that the dome world scenario is also morally horrifying because the loss of other living beings and systems on the planet would be a tragedy in itself, independently of its effects on human interests. This suggests a further, "ecological storm."

It is plausible to think that the structure of the distinctively ecological storm bears some similarity to the tragedy of the commons or intergenerational buck-passing models. Consider the following simple metaphor,

52. Such worries are at the heart of much green political theory and environmental ethics. See, for example, Shrader-Frechette 2002, Schlosberg 2007.

53. Unfortunately, I no longer have either the article or the reference. (If others do, I would be glad to know.) Still, I hope that this does not undermine the example: the point would hold even if I were talking about a merely hypothetical economist.

which I shall call *kick the dog*. In the old story, the farmer kicks his wife, his wife kicks the child, and the child kicks the dog. In the perfect moral storm, the parallel is likely to be that the current rich "kick" the current poor, and both "kick" future generations. But the "kicking" is unlikely to stop there. Chances are that many of the costs of our problematic ways of life will be passed on to other species through the ecological systems on which they depend. Some of this will be done directly by the rich, but some will also be done by the initial victims, the current poor and future generations. In other words, the initial bad behavior may set off a chain reaction towards the end of which stands not just the most vulnerable humans, but also many animals, plants, and places. Moreover, if and when the natural world kicks back, it may just induce a further cycle of further buck-passing. (This might parallel the "intergenerational arms race" discussed in chapter 6.)

The kick the dog scenario has strong initial plausibility. The signs are that such ecological buck-passing is already rife in the global environmental tragedy more generally. Humanity as such is kicking the atmosphere, the rainforests, the Arctic, and so on, and thorough them the polar bear, the big cats, and many other species. Much of this buck-passing is disguised by the complicated causal routes through which it occurs. But the fact that it is disguised does not mean that it is not happening.

What should we say about the status of the ecological storm? It is tempting to include it as one of the main constituents of the perfect moral storm proper, instead of subsuming it under the theoretical storm. I have not done so both for the sake of simplicity and because its existence as a distinct "storm" is itself a matter of theoretical controversy. This does not imply that it is not important or central. (I have not counted the problem of skewed vulnerabilities separately for similar reasons. Yet it is of profound importance.) Instead, it reflects my attempt, signaled in the Introduction, to beg as few theoretical questions as possible in the sketching of the basic moral problem. This does not in any way preclude those with strong ethical commitments to animals and the rest of nature from conceiving of the ecological storm as a distinct problem that should be addressed by any positive account that deserves our respect. (A similar point can be made about the problem of skewed vulnerabilities.) These are simply matters to be taken up elsewhere.[54]

54. For suggestions that climate change poses problems for conventional environmental ethics, see Palmer 2011.

V. THE PROBLEM OF MORAL CORRUPTION

This brings us to the last problem I wish to identify. When the global, intergenerational and theoretical storms meet, they encourage a distinct problem for ethical action on climate change, the problem of moral corruption. This can be illustrated if we focus for a moment on the intergenerational storm. Acknowledging that one is engaging in intergenerational buck-passing is morally uncomfortable, especially when the consequences of such buck-passing may be severe, or even catastrophic, for the victims. Presumably, this is discomfort that we would like to avoid. Given this, if the current generation engages in buck-passing, it will welcome ways to obscure what it is doing. This is important because it suggests that climate policy is not made or discussed in a neutral evaluative context. The perfect moral storm clouds the debate.

One way to facilitate buck-passing is by avoiding real engagement with the issue. This might be achieved in a wide variety of ways, many of which are familiar from other contexts. Consider, for example:

- Distraction
- Complacency
- Selective attention
- Unreasonable doubt
- Delusion
- Pandering
- Hypocrisy

Now, I suspect that close observers of two decades of political debate about climate change will recognize many of these mechanisms as being in play. In their most obvious forms, they facilitate a relatively quick evasion of the whole topic. But such strategies are also relevant to more substantive discussions.

Of special concern from an ethical and philosophical point of view is the fact that, if the current generation favors buck-passing, but does not want to face up to what it is doing, it is likely to welcome any rationale that appears to justify its behavior. Hence, it may be attracted to weak or deceptive arguments that appear to license buck-passing, and so give them less scrutiny than it ought. A particularly deep way of doing this is thorough the corruption of the very terms of the debate, moral and otherwise. In other words, the perfect moral storm may work to subvert our understanding of what is at stake.

The idea that agents may subvert moral language and arguments for their own purposes is hardly unfamiliar in normal political life. Moreover, it is highly plausible to think that the self-serving approach to morality has been alive and well in much of what has passed for social and political discourse about climate change in the last twenty years or so. Still, the presence and prevalence of the intergenerational storm reveals a new and powerful potential for such trouble. In many normal contexts, the tendency towards the corruption of discourse faces a strong challenge from the likely victims of immoral behavior. But this is not the case in the intergenerational setting. Since the victims are not yet around to defend the discourse, the potential for moral corruption is especially high.[55] This problem is exacerbated by the iteration of buck-passing, which implies that when they are around, future people may themselves become vulnerable to moral corruption.

In chapter 9, I try to illustrate the problem more clearly by drawing a comparison between a classic instance of moral corruption in Jane Austen's *Sense and Sensibility* and the recent climate debate. For now, let me focus on just way in which moral corruption may be facilitated, by selective attention. Since climate change involves a complex convergence of problems, it is easy to engage in *manipulative or self-deceptive* behavior by applying one's attention to only some of the considerations that make the situation difficult. This may happen in a variety of ways.

At the level of practical politics, such strategies are all too familiar. For example, many political actors emphasize considerations that appear to make inaction excusable, or even desirable (such as uncertainty, or simple economic calculations with high discount rates) and action more difficult and contentious (such as the need for lifestyle change) at the expense of those that seem to impose a clearer and more immediate burden (such as scientific consensus and intergenerational buck-passing).

However, selective attention strategies may also manifest themselves more generally. This prompts an unpleasant thought. Perhaps there is a

---

55. The same issue arises in the kick the dog scenario. The potential for moral corruption is also high in the global storm when the victims are contemporaries but spatially distant and relatively close to powerless.

problem of corruption in the standard way in which we frame the issue itself. Most prominently, *perhaps the prevalence of the global storm model is not independent of the existence of the intergenerational storm, but instead is encouraged by it.*

In particular, perhaps it simply suits our buck-passing purposes to continue discussing climate change primarily in geopolitical terms, assuming that states represent the interests of their citizens in perpetuity. After all, the current generation may find such a framing highly advantageous. On the one hand, a focus on the global storm tends to draw attention towards various issues of global politics and scientific uncertainty (mentioned above) that seem to problematize action, and away from issues of intergenerational ethics, which tend to demand it. Thus, an emphasis on the global storm at the expense of the other problems may *facilitate* a strategy of procrastination and delay. On the other hand, since it usually stipulates that the relevant actors are nation-states who represent the interests of their citizens in perpetuity, the global storm analysis has the effect of *assuming away* the intergenerational aspect of the climate change problem. For one thing, it presumes that there is no motivation problem. It is just taken for granted that current governments and populations automatically take the interests of their successors into account, and to the appropriate extent. For another, it suggests that failure to act will result in a collectively self-inflicted harm (by those states to themselves), rather than in a potentially severe injustice to innocent and vulnerable others.

As the intergenerational analysis makes clear, these last claims are too quick. First, the current generation contributes significantly to climate change, but the effects will predominantly fall in the future, to other people (and species). Hence, the issue of how to understand and motivate appropriate moral concern, and especially intergenerational concern, is right at the heart of the climate problem. Second, these are not predominantly "self-inflicted" harms, but something significantly morally worse. This fact should also have motivational consequences. Given these points, an undue emphasis on the global storm obscures much of what is at stake in making climate policy, and in a way that benefits present people.

In conclusion, the threat of moral corruption reveals another sense in which climate change may be a "perfect" moral storm. Its complexity may turn out to be *perfectly convenient* for us, the current generation, and indeed for each successor generation as it comes to occupy our position. For one thing, it provides each generation with the cover under which it can seem to be taking the issue seriously – by negotiating weak and largely substanceless global accords, for example, and then heralding them as great achievements (see chapters 3–4)—when really it is simply exploiting its temporal position. For another, all of this can occur without the exploiting generation actually having to acknowledge that this is what it is doing. If it can avoid the appearance of overtly selfish (or self-absorbed) behavior, an earlier generation can take advantage of the future without the unpleasantness of admitting it—either to others, or, perhaps more importantly, to itself.

CHAPTER 2

The Consumption Tragedy

Chapter 1 set out an outline of the main thesis of this book. Before fleshing out that thesis in the following chapters, it is worth pausing to confront two serious objections. The first is that the perfect moral storm analysis relies on flawed, egoistic assumptions which make it both unrealistic and unsuitable as a basis for talking about the ethics of climate change. The second objection is that the perfect storm fails to appreciate the extent to which considerations of self-interest can drive a solution. In particular, the thought goes, the analysis overplays the possibility of international and intergenerational conflict by neglecting the win-win potential of a technology-driven "green energy revolution," and the fact that current social and economic systems are not clearly in the interests of much of the world's population, including perhaps even many of those who on the surface seem to profit from them.

This chapter aims to blunt such worries. It argues that the perfect moral storm analysis can (and in the case of climate change largely does) rely on weaker assumptions than the objections suggest, and so is able to accommodate many of the criticisms. In addition, I claim that taking such criticisms seriously reveals ways in which the perfect storm may actually be morally worse than is initially apparent. Perhaps our behavior is absurd or shallow, rather than nakedly self-interested.

The chapter proceeds as follows. Section I articulates the first objection in terms of three distinct concerns about the role of game theory in ethical analysis. Section II argues that such analysis is compatible with nonegoistic assumptions about motivation, and puts forward my own favored assumptions. Section III addresses the "green energy revolution" objection. Section IV briefly considers the relevance of game theoretic models to thinking about the relation between consumption and happiness.

I. WHAT'S THE POINT OF GAME THEORY?

The models introduced in chapter 1—the prisoner's dilemma, the tragedy of the commons, and intergenerational buck-passing—all owe something to game theoretic analysis.[1] Against this approach, some will complain that game theory is misguided in general, and in any case irrelevant to the *ethics* of international affairs. In particular, they will object that it relies on an outdated and dangerous model of human motivation, that embodied in an account of self-interest seen in narrow, purely economic, terms.

This worry raises issues far beyond the scope of this book, and I cannot attempt a full account of the role of game theory in ethical analysis here. Still, a few remarks might help to disarm the criticism and motivate my approach. To begin with, it is worth identifying three distinct concerns lurking behind the basic objection.

1. The Kind of Analysis

The first is that game theory provides the wrong *kind* of analysis. According to one version of this complaint, game theory is primarily a descriptive, not a normative, enterprise. It tells us how things are or will be, not what ought to be. Hence, the objection goes, a game theoretic analysis of climate change can tell us nothing about the ethics of climate change, because it does not tell us what, morally, we should do. By contrast, according to a second version of the complaint, game theory is not purely descriptive, but also normative. But it is normative in the wrong sense. It tells us what we ought to do if we are concerned only with our own interests.[2] But, the objection continues, this egoistic point of view contrasts with morality—indeed it is the principal obstacle to ethical behavior—and hence, this kind of game theory focuses on exactly the wrong considerations for ethical discussion.

---

1. It is not clear whether my own intergenerational problem should, *strictly speaking*, be conceived of as game theoretic. Future generations do not literally participate in any game with earlier generations, and there is no reciprocity. Still, it is clearly informed by game theory.

2. Of course, some argue that (enlightened) self-interest is the basis of morality. I ignore that complication here. For one thing, future generations' cases constitute one of the standard objections to that approach.

2. The Content of Game Theory

The second concern with game theory involves its *content*. If game theoretic models typically assume that individuals (and countries) are exclusively self-interested, some critics will object that this assumption is descriptively either false, or (at least) seriously misleading. There are two main complaints here. The first is that, if the claim is that agents are only interested in getting benefits for themselves, people do not seem to be *self*-interested in this sense. Specifically, they are not so self-absorbed: they care for their spouses, their children, their friends, their communities, their nations, and perhaps also for humanity as such, and other species too.

Against this, it is often said that these concerns are still *theirs*, so that agents do benefit when they are satisfied, because their preferences are satisfied. Still, to many, this reply appears to beg a crucial question, since it is far from clear that the satisfaction of an agent's preference always confers a benefit on them. Sometimes agents want to see art and literature flourish, the Arctic Wildlife Refuge and other wildernesses protected, the memory of those killed in foreign wars honored, and so on. But it is not easy to see how—by itself—the achievement of such things makes the agent *better off* in any meaningful (or nonquestion-begging) sense. Hence, the complaint continues, the claim that there is anything crucially self-directed going on here is unmotivated.[3]

The second main complaint about content is that even within the domain of self-interest, game theory has the wrong view. It tends to focus on short-term economic interests narrowly construed, and especially those captured by consumption behavior in a market system. But—the critics charge—at best, such behavior registers only a modest part of an agent's true interests, and, at worst, much consumption actually inhibits, rather than promotes, overall well-being.

3. The Effects of Game Theory

The third distinct concern with game theory concerns the *effects* of game theoretic analysis on people's behavior. Critics maintain that game

3. Gardiner 2001c.

theory tends to be morally undermining: it obstructs ethical solutions to policy problems. This is so for a number of reasons. One is that it casts a veil of legitimacy over behavior that could not otherwise be justified.[4] The mere presence of a game theoretic rationale for a certain kind of behavior tends to validate it in the eyes of some people, even when the behavior would conventionally be regarded as illegitimate (e.g., as selfish, extortionate, and so on). A second reason is that—partly because of the veil of legitimacy—the study of game theory, like the study of economics in general, tends to make people more selfish, and so less liable to act in an ethical manner, and to cooperate in ethical ventures.[5]

How might one respond to these criticisms? One approach would be simply to reject them. After all, many who study international affairs profess "Realism," or Neo-Hobbesianism. They would either reject certain elements of the criticisms, or refuse to count them as criticisms—claiming either that game theory is right to ignore ethical considerations, or that its focus on self-interest gives the only sense to ethics that can be given. If one took this view, the perfect moral storm analysis would still apply. Still, this is not my position. As it happens, I have a great deal of sympathy for the critics. (I mention the first response only to make it clear that the Realists and Neo-Hobbesians also have a reason to read on.) Nevertheless, I do not believe that the standard criticisms undermine the use of game theory in this instance.

II. MOTIVATING THE MODELS

To see why, let us begin with the concern about the kind of analysis present in game theory. Suppose that the role of game theory is descriptive. Then, how can an account of "how things are" be relevant to what *ought* to be done? Stated in this bald way, this objection is almost self-refuting. As I stated in the Introduction, I believe that often the best way to make progress in solving a given ethical problem is to get clear on what the problem actually is. This is one reason why

---

4. Hausman and McPherson 1996; Blackburn 1998, chapters 5–6.
5. Frank et al. 1993.

genuinely *practical*[6] ethics is so important: details of how real world problems are actually constituted are often of profound moral significance. In my view, descriptive game theoretic analyses are sometimes helpful here. Some evidence for this comes from their continued popularity in the literature on environmental issues in general, and climate change in particular.[7] Knowing how agents would behave *if* narrowly self-interested or economic motivations are operative can be useful. It can reveal where problems may arise, and illuminate the roles that other motivations—such as moral motivations—might play in preventing or addressing them.

1. On Guidance

What of the normative role of game theory? Does the fact that self-interested agents would act in a certain way provide us with any guidance? This is complex. First, some critics might simply refuse to offer self-interest any normative role, claiming that game theory is useful only in describing people's behavior as it is, and in order to criticize it. Hence, they might claim that self-interest never has normative priority over morality, or perhaps never has normative force at all.

Still, this position seems extreme. Hence, second, more moderate critics of game theory will want to acknowledge that self-interested motivations are normative in at least some cases. This seems plausible. For one thing, the fact that a course of action would be bad for me is usually some kind of reason not to do it; so we have reason to take game theoretic analysis seriously. For another, in a collective action problem like the prisoner's dilemma, the fact that the outcome of a set of actions would be bad for all those agents who participate in them is relevant to both describing and solving the problem. If we do not regard self-interest as at all normative, it is hard to see what the problem is. In addition, the normativity of self-interest (even narrowly economic self-interest) supports a solution to the problem at hand: each agent has a reason to

6. The term 'applied ethics' is now more widely used to describe work in areas such as medical and environmental ethics. However, it tends to suggest a model whereby theory is made independently of practice and then simply imposed on cases. This picture seems to me seriously mistaken, and potentially dangerous. Hence, I prefer the less common term.

7. For the enormous and lingering popularity of Garrett Hardin's account of the tragedy of the commons, see Burger and Gochfield 1998.

reject the tragic scenario and embrace the cooperative solution if it can be secured.

Third, accepting the normative relevance of self-interest in some cases falls far short of claiming that it reigns supreme in all. (This would remain true even if one went further and claimed that self-interest sometimes overrides reasons of morality.) Moreover, acknowledging that self-interest is normative to some extent does not require conceding that game theory as conventionally understood rests on a reasonable account of self-interest, or provides any kind of guide to how we should live more generally. In short, there is plenty of conceptual space in which the game theoretic models can remain relevant to ethics without overwhelming it.

2. On Content

Let us turn now to concerns about content, and the assumption of self-interest. Despite the above, my central defense of the perfect moral storm analysis does not appeal to anything like the claim that actual human individuals or states are (or ought to be) exclusively self-interested, or the claim that their interests are exclusively economic. (Indeed, I would reject such claims.) Instead, I shall argue that the relevant assumptions can be much more limited. Let me begin with some general remarks about game theory, and then turn to my own thoughts about the motivations that drive the perfect moral storm.

The first point is that, despite popular misconceptions, models such as the prisoner's dilemma, the tragedy of the commons, and the problem of intergenerational buck-passing do not stand or fall with claims about self-interested motivation. Consider, for example, the prisoner's dilemma. It is true that in the standard story, one central assumption is that each of the prisoners has self-interested preferences regarding jail time: each prefers less for himself. Still, this assumption is not crucial to the basic dynamic of the situation. Instead, what matters is the overall structure of preferences; and this may be produced by preferences with very different content. (*Those uninterested in the technicalities may skip the next three paragraphs.*)

This becomes clear when one considers the basic matrix of preferences characteristic of the prisoner's dilemma:

TABLE 2.1

	Agent B: Coordinate	Agent B: Don't Coordinate
Agent A: Coordinate	2nd preference (for agent A) 2nd preference (for agent B)	4th preference (for agent A) 1st preference (for agent B)
Agent A: Don't Coordinate	1st preference (for agent A) 4th preference (for agent B)	3rd preference (for agent A) 3rd preference (for agent B)

In this matrix, the content of the relevant preference is left completely unspecified; all that is said is that the preferences have this ordering. Given this, there is no need to call on self-interest to generate the matrix: the same structure may arise even when mixed, or even completely altruistic, motivations are in play.

To illustrate this, consider the following example.[8] Suppose that rather than two prisoners, we imagine two humanitarian aid workers. Each is offered a meeting with a major donor. Each wants to win assistance for a particular project, one in the Sudan and the other in Cambodia; each is motivated purely by the aim of benefiting the poor in the region for which he advocates. Both know the following. The donor has ten million dollars that she is considering donating. If either aid worker tries a really hard sell, but the other does not, then this aggressive approach will secure the whole ten million for his favored project. However, if both do so, then this will alienate the donor (who hates conflict), and she will only give one million to each. Finally, if both adopt a more measured tone, the donor will split the money between the projects, giving five million to each. Given this scenario, each aid worker's preferences are:

1st Preference: My project wins all ($10 m), the other gets nothing.
2nd Preference: Each project wins half of the grant ($5 m).
3rd Preference: Each project wins one tenth of the grant ($1 m).
4th Preference: My project loses, and the other wins all ($10 m).

8. A similar case can be generated by altering the prisoner's dilemma story so that it is not the prisoners that must decide whether or not to confess, but each of their lawyers who must decide what advice to give their clients. (Suppose also that the lawyers cannot interact.) The lawyers face the same structural problem; and this is so even if they are not at all *self*-interested, but care only for the interests of their own clients. (If one has trouble with the concept of altruistic lawyers, try mothers or best friends.)

This corresponding matrix is thus:

TABLE 2.2

	Cambodia: Soft Sell	Cambodia: Hard Sell
Sudan: Soft Sell	$5 m, $5m (2nd, 2nd)	0, $10 (4th, 1st)
Sudan: Hard Sell	$10 m, 0 (1st, 4th)	$1 m, $1 m (3rd, 3rd)

This is structurally identical to the prisoner's dilemma matrix, with the same results. Each aid worker would prefer the cooperative over the noncooperative outcome: that is, the money secured by both advocates soft selling ($5 m each) over that produced by their both trying the hard sell ($1 m each). But, again, when each has to make an individual decision, each prefers the hard sell approach (since his project gets either $10 m or $1 m that way, as opposed to either $5 m or nothing). Given this, we expect a tragic outcome: each will try the hard sell, with the result that each project ends up with less than it could have received if they had managed to coordinate their behavior.

There are two lessons here, one specific and one more general. The specific lesson is that game theory can explain tragedy even in situations where self-interest is not in play. Roughly speaking, the key features of the tragic situations seem to be:

(a)   the success of each actor in achieving his or her aim depends in part on what the other actors do;
(b)   the aims of the actors are moderately at odds, in the sense that they cannot all achieve the best possible result in terms of their aim;
(c)   each actors' individual pursuit of his or her aim results in a less successful outcome for that aim than would be secured by coordinated pursuit;

but

(d)   adequate institutions to support coordination are not available.

But none of these assumptions mandates self-interested aims.

The more general lesson is that, in Derek Parfit's terms, there are many circumstances under which each individual's pursuit of a given aim can turn out to be collectively self-defeating.[9] The key point is that the structure of people's values, even when those values are in some sense shared, can undermine the collective pursuit of those values. When the value is self-interest, then the potential for conflict is clear. But self-interest is just one core example. Others arise when the values have a self-referential, or a time-indexed component. Suppose, for example, that everyone values the happiness of children, or world peace. Still, if this concern is always predominantly for the happiness of *one's own* children (or the children of *our* community), or for peace in *our* time—rather than for the happiness of children as such, or peace as such—the possibility of moderate conflict arises.[10]

On the face of it, this general lesson seems relevant to the perfect moral storm. Surely—the suspicion goes—the global and intergenerational settings are such as to give wide license to self-referential and time-indexed motivations. If each person's concern is with *their own* family, *their own* social class, *their own* country, and *their own* generation, scenarios in which certain kinds of action become collectively self-defeating seem plausible.

If the game theoretic models invoked by the perfect moral storm need not assume self-interest, what are the appropriate motivational assumptions? In a moment, I will sketch my own favorites for climate change. But before doing so, I want to emphasize that the perfect storm model does not stand or fall with these. Others may believe that alternative motivational assumptions—either stronger or weaker than the ones I propose—drive the climate storm. For example, we have already seen that Neo-Hobbesians would be comfortable with very strong egoistic assumptions. Similarly, some contractarians and communitarians might emphasize values that are both relative to specific communities, and perhaps have a limited time-horizon of only a small number of generations.[11] Both camps would accept starker versions of the model than I will suggest. Hence, deciding between rival motivational assumptions will turn out to be an important task within the perfect storm paradigm (and answers may differ across cases).

9. Parfit 1986, 55–6, 95–110.

10. In philosophy, a distinction is sometimes made here between agent-relative and agent-neutral reasons. See Nagel 1980, 1986, Parfit 1986.

11. Heyd 2009; de Shalit 1995.

Here, then, are my own favored, and very limited, assumptions for the case of climate change. I suspect that, given current institutions, there is a natural default position for human action: first, the main driver of the problem is the consumption behavior of agents (especially individuals) in the global economic system; and second, such consumption is largely prompted by factors with a very limited temporal and spatial horizon.

The basic thought is this. Suppose we take the consumption decisions of individuals as a leading cause of emissions growth. Then, assume that such decisions are overwhelmingly driven by the judgments those individuals make about the short- to medium-term consequences for themselves, their families and friends, and (perhaps) their local communities. More specifically, suppose that when most people go to the grocery store, to the gas station, or to the mall, or when they buy houses and vehicles, or decide to go on vacation, their choices are dominated by the implications here and now, for themselves and those close to them. As it happens, I suspect that "here and now" means a timeframe of no longer than ten years, and a spatial horizon that does not extend much further than the actors themselves and their families. But, for the sake of argument, we could be more generous and extend this to say that, at the very most, the factors that dominate most people's consumption decisions are those which play out over roughly the timeframe of their own lives, understood as the expected duration of their generational cohort, or just a little longer. (If so, we can speak of their concerns as governed by "generation-relative" reasons or motivations.) Either way, we see the prominence of the kind of self-referential and time-indexed motivations that generate tragic structures of agency.

Two quick remarks may make the status of these claims clearer. First, in saying that this is the "natural default position" for action on climate change, I am (emphatically) not asserting that there is anything inevitable about the dominance of such motivations in human life, or even that they deserve any privileged position. Instead, I mean only that, if nothing is done to address the situation, such motivations will hold sway. In other words, given the status quo of existing institutions and motivations, then, other things being equal, we should expect the future to be shaped by such forces (e.g., the consumption decisions of individuals driven by their short- to medium-term concerns). Second, while it is true that, according to the default position, I am making some kind of appeal to narrowly economic motivation, in context, this appeal is not a very bold one. Moreover, it has some empirical support behind it. As we have seen from the discussion of political inertia, the world has been aware of the climate problem for a while (two decades at the time of writing), and yet has allowed a rapid increase in emissions in that period. This is largely because it has permitted consumption of fossil fuels and the goods that depend on them to continue unchecked, ignoring the dangerous climate externalities.

No doubt the claim that individual consumption is the primary driving force behind climate change is much too simplistic. Nevertheless, the basic idea can easily be extended to other important arenas of decision making, such as business and politics.[12] First, and most obviously, consider the situation of business. When energy companies and other large corporations make their decisions about future investment and marketing, it is reasonable to assume that the considerations that dominate are also narrow in scope and time-horizon. For example, it is plausible to think that the focus is on short- to medium-term profits, market power, and reputation. Again, the sphere of concern is not likely to extend much beyond a decade or so, if that. But the basic point would remain even if we were more generous and said that the time-horizons of a given set of managers, shareholders, and employees extended across their working lives.

Second, and almost as obviously, consider governments. It is plausible to think that when they make decisions, their concerns are skewed towards the consequences for the next two or three election cycles. Moreover, they are selected partly on this basis: when people vote for their leaders, their choices are largely driven by their expectations for what will happen to them, their families, and to their local and national community in the immediately foreseeable future.

In conclusion, my key motivational claim is that, other things being equal, the decisions that cause the climate change problem are driven by concerns with a very limited spatial and temporal horizon. Unfortunately, this assumption (applied to individuals, businesses, and governments)

12. For example, some might argue that business is responsible for creating many of the preferences that drive individual consumption, and for driving government policy in many nations. I do not take up such matters here, since I am much more interested in uncovering underlying structural patterns of agency than in the question of the relative contributions of different agents, or the causal influences operating between them.

seems both perfectly realistic in the world in which we live, and more than sufficient to generate the perfect moral storm. Still, it falls far short of any assertion that people are, or ought to be, exclusively self-interested. Indeed, so far the analysis has taken no position on whether consumption decisions driven by such factors are *in any way* in the interests of those concerned. In fact, no mention has been made of "self-interest" at all. (For all that is said to this point, it may turn out that consumption of this sort is predominantly bad for individuals, and that they should retreat to an ascetic life.) For such reasons, the key motivational assumption of the perfect storm can be much weaker, broader, and (I hope) more compelling than that of narrow self-interest.

Given this, and considering also the wider theoretical points made above, I conclude that the perfect moral storm analysis can employ game theoretic models without endorsing problematic assumptions about the content of self-interest, or the normative status of egoism. Still, we should not neglect the self-interest model completely. Often, it will be appealing to say that individuals, businesses, and governments do act in what they *perceive* to be their own self-interest, and that this perception is narrowly or dominantly economic. Hence, we should keep both the very weak and the stronger motivational assumptions in mind.

3. On Effects

What of the third concern? Does awareness of game theoretic analysis have bad effects? Does it obstruct ethical solutions to policy problems by casting a (false) veil of legitimacy over morally bad behavior? Does exposure to game theory actually encourage selfishness? If so, do such concerns undermine the perfect moral storm analysis? In a moment, I shall argue that the analysis remains intact. Still, it may be worth noting that even if exposure to game theory does have morally bad consequences, this need not imply that the perfect storm analysis itself is mistaken. Of course, if general awareness of the perfect storm would have very bad consequences, perhaps some (friends of future generations and the world's poor, for example) would want to suppress the account, and in particular prevent it from reaching the corridors of power, or the populace at large. They would, of course, need an argument for doing so, which should be assessed. But even a successful argument would not show that there is anything mistaken about the analysis itself. (Sometimes the truth hurts.) Moreover, it is hard to see what a good argument for suppression would look like. After all, even on my limited assumptions—where the driver for the storm is short-term consumption—the analysis mainly seeks to describe what it is already going on. Given the magnitude of the current problem of political inertia, it seems unlikely that sharing a philosophical analysis of it will make matters appreciably worse.

Fortunately—and more importantly—we should not readily concede that exposure to the perfect moral storm analysis will have bad consequences. There are two reasons. First, my way of fleshing out the motivational assumptions does not imply that they are insurmountable. On the contrary, their limited nature suggests a potential avenue for solutions. If the climate problem is caused by the fact that certain kinds of motivations and institutions dominate current decision making, then one remedy would be to call on other motivations, and work out how to generate institutions that would make them operative. In particular, suppose that it is short-term, consumption-oriented motivations, as registered through the market system, that cause the climate change problem; then, the solution might be to engage motivations with a longer time-horizon and wider purview, including moral motivations such as those for intergenerational justice and respect for nature. Nothing in the assumptions of the perfect moral storm says that such motivations do not exist, nor that they are inferior to their rivals. Instead, the main point seems to be that if they do exist, these motivations have not yet been made manifest in decision making, or at least sufficiently manifest to challenge their competitors. Given this, on my understanding, the initial roots of the perfect moral storm lie not in deep egoistic assumptions about human nature, but rather in much more specific claims about the limitations of existing institutions for adequately registering important human concerns. If this is correct, awareness of the perfect moral storm analysis—knowing what the problem is—may play an important role in encouraging solutions. If we are alerted to the intergenerational storm and the prospects for moral corruption, we can be on our guard. Sometimes, "sunlight is the best antiseptic."[13]

Second, even if one were to employ a stronger set of motivational assumptions, and argue that self-interest considered as such does drive

13. Shue 1980, 341.

much of the behavior that causes the perfect moral storm, it is not clear that such assumptions would be morally undermining. For one thing, the claim that self-interest is an obstacle to ethical behavior is commonplace. Hence, it would be strange if this observation alone undermined efforts to be moral. For another, the analysis ought to have, and is intended to have, a positive normative impact. Corruption by self-interest is not only a problem for the irredeemably wicked; it applies equally to the otherwise decent, especially in cases of moral complacency. This, I think, is the current situation (see chapter 9 and the case of John Dashwood). Moreover, it is particularly easy to be complacent when one is told that the problem is "uncertain," or that something is already being done; and particularly easy to believe this when it is strongly in one's (perceived) interest that it be true. In addition, this kind of corruption leads to others. For example, it motivates one not to look too hard for evidence that one is behaving badly, and to overlook or explain away such evidence when it appears. Game theory can help here. In some circumstances, it can elucidate the exact structure of our wanting to look the other way, and so serve as a guide to help us escape hypocrisy. This, I hope, is the normative impact of the current analysis.

It should be clear from these remarks that I do not want to assume that people or states are exclusively self-interested in a narrow economic sense. Far from it. If there is to be a solution to the severe moral problems I identify, then we need to call on other motivations, and in particular moral motivations provoked by recognition of the injustice we might otherwise do the future, and our moral failure more generally. Indeed, the aim of my analysis is just that kind of provocation.[14]

In summary, the perfect moral storm model retains its bite if, instead of assuming self-interest, we claim only (1) that much of the actual (perhaps unreflective) consumption behavior of individuals is based on their own relatively short-term or generation-relative concerns, (2) that these concerns are often made manifest in ways that are narrowly economic, and (3) that it is such behavior which drives much energy use (especially in the rich industrialized countries), and so much of the

---

14. Even when discussing the factors that explain the behavior of countries in climate change negotiations, I am not necessarily attributing bad conscious motives to either individual leaders or citizens. Much of what I have in mind concerns those deep facts which structure "political reality" for such people, and thereby frame their ideas of what is possible, and determine the nature of the agreements they are able to reach.

problem of climate change. Such minimal claims are sufficient to show the relevance of the perfect storm analysis to climate change. Moreover, if these claims are reasonable, then the use of more robust terms such as "perceived self-interest" or "generation-relative incentives" in modeling the climate problem is not seriously misleading. For the role of such assumptions is simply to suggest (a) that, *if nothing is done to prevent it*, this kind of behavior will dominate action, (b) that this leads to tragedy, and so (c) that some kind of intervention (e.g., by governments, or individuals and firms themselves) is necessary to avoid a moral disaster.

III. A GREEN ENERGY REVOLUTION?

Despite all of these concerns, there are reasons not to disavow the language of self-interest completely. As mentioned above, one is that some game theoretic models, like the prisoner's dilemma and tragedy of the commons, show that certain behavior can be bad even on self-interested grounds. Another is that in the real world agents are often distracted from, or confused about, what their real interests consist in. Sometimes the problem is not that people are too self-interested, but that they are not self-interested enough.[15] Given this, attention to self-interest can often help to bring about better policy.

One thought along these lines gives rise to a possible criticism of the perfect storm analysis. In the public debate, the presence of the storm is often obscured even by those most in favor of action on climate change. This is because many of these are social and technological optimists. They believe that there is a win-win scenario: it is possible for us to do right by future generations in particular (and perhaps even the poor and nature more generally) without making any serious sacrifices ourselves. In this vein, most politicians who support action tell us that a green technological revolution around energy will not only solve the climate problem, but also make both us and the future better off at the same time. At the very least, they claim that such a revolution will not make us worse off. Given this, their position seems to be that any self-interested

15. Butler 1983.

objection that the current generation (or the world's rich) might have against action is mistaken. "Green" is good for everyone.[16]

On the face of it, the notion of a green energy revolution poses a basic challenge to the analysis of climate change as a perfect moral storm. First, and most obviously, if the transition to green energy is best for our generation and for the future, then there is no conflict between the interests of these groups, and therefore no intergenerational storm. Hence, the rationale for intergenerational buck-passing disappears. The current generation can pursue its own aims and benefit the future at the same time because the good that most matters—green energy—is mutually beneficial for all concerned.

Second, similarly, the green energy revolution appears to benefit nature. It is, after all, assumed to be "*green*," and so environmentally benign. Moreover, there is a presumptive case for this. Presumably, whatever else is true of them, alternative energy technologies such as solar and wind do not have the main drawbacks of burning fossil fuels. They do not produce greenhouse gases and so cause climate change, and they do not result in other familiar kinds of pollution, such as poor urban air quality.

Third, it is sometimes said that the green energy revolution will benefit the world's poor, at least indirectly. An initial objection to the switch in energy sources is, of course, cost, and many of those who oppose action on climate change emphasize that green energy is a luxury that the world's poor will not be able to afford. Still, some green revolutionaries argue that costs will fall dramatically as investment in research and the scale of deployment of green technology increases, making such energy at least reasonably accessible to the poor. In addition, there is the (admittedly vague) assurance that the developed countries will assist the developing countries in clean development through the new technologies. Of course, this assurance is slightly in tension with a further claim

---

16. There is good evidence that the pursuit of energy efficiency and renewables can bring down emissions substantially (see, e.g., Pacala and Socolow 2004, US Department of Energy 2008, and the discussion in Shrader-Frechette 2011). Whether it can do so quickly enough, without having negative economic effects, and without serious social change, is less clear, but I remain cautiously optimisitic, if we could muster the political will. My concerns in this section are with what we are morally entitled to assume in making policy, and with the demand that we must be persuaded that the current generation will benefit before considering change.

often made by green revolutionaries, that particular developed countries stand to gain a major competitive advantage from pursuing green industry early. But on a charitable interpretation, this may be just another fortunate feature of the win-win scenario. Perhaps the advantage is merely an additional benefit to the developed nations that facilitates more general prosperity in "a rising tide that lifts all boats."

This grand positive vision of the green energy revolution is, of course, an attractive one. (Solving all of one's current problems and becoming better off at the same time always is attractive.) Still, we must not be too quick to embrace the vision and declare the perfect storm analysis dead. Before confronting the issue directly, let me make two preliminary points.

The first point is that we should remember that climate change is only one aspect of the global environmental tragedy. Hence, even if the perfect storm analysis turned out to be false for climate change because the prospects for green energy were so very bright, this need not diminish its wider interest. Perhaps we just got lucky in this case. This would not license us to be complacent about other environmental tragedies. Other problems might yet emerge to test us; and it would be rash to assume that human ingenuity is unlimited and always fast enough to avert disaster, or that technological fixes are always clean and perfect solutions. (See chapter 5 on the invisible hand argument.) After all, particular societies have floundered before. Think of the cases documented by Jared Diamond in his well-known book, *Collapse*.[17]

The second preliminary point is that the green energy solution might be genuine in theory, but the perfect storm still hold sway in practice. Perhaps some politically powerful groups will block the revolution because they believe (perhaps rightly) that although green is better in general, it is not better for them. In other words, perhaps action in climate change is good for humanity as a whole, but not for the vested interests. If so, the perfect storm analysis may offer a persuasive account of what is going on, even if the green revolutionaries are technically correct about the possibility of a win-win scenario. Here we might note that the energy revolution has not already happened, despite some noble efforts on its behalf over several decades. Hence, there must be some limit to the win-win scenario. The perfect storm analysis may do a good

17. Diamond 2004.

job of describing the practical problem when we are faced with such a limit, even if it does not hold more generally.

With these preliminaries in mind, let us confront the objection more directly. My central response is that the green revolution objection applies only to some versions of the perfect storm analysis. For example, it would apply to a Neo-Hobbesian version, couched in terms of narrow self-interest. But it need not affect my consumption-based version. As mentioned above, it would be compatible with that analysis to claim that we are already not acting in accordance with (a correct account of) self-interest. Instead, we are making the relevant decisions on very narrow short-term or generation-relative grounds that may be in conflict with genuine self-interest. On that view, the availability of a realistic green revolution option would only make our failure more spectacular. But perhaps it is.[18]

If true, this diagnosis would have further moral consequences. On the one hand, to fail in one's moral duty and inflict serious risks on others when success would also be better for oneself may suggest that selfishness is not the problem, and so make the moral situation in one way better. Still, on the other hand, selfishness is not the only vice, and probably not the worst. Suppose, for example, that you are in extreme distress, but I will not aid you even though to do so would also benefit me. Then, I may be worse than selfish. For example, perhaps I exhibit an extreme form of moral indifference, or even malevolence. If something like this is going on with climate change, then the possibility of a green revolution may make our moral failure deeper. (See also section IV below.)

Even though the green revolution claim need not undermine the intergenerational storm, there are reasons to be concerned about it. Most notably, the call for a green revolution tends to obscure much of what is at stake, morally speaking. Consider three examples.

The first emerges when we distinguish between different versions of the green revolution hypothesis. One might be called the "lucky for us" view. It holds that we have a serious intergenerational obligation to

---

18. The green revolution claim might be strengthened so as to come into conflict with my assumptions. For example, it might be claimed that the revolution can neutralize our consumption-based reasons for emitting too much. In principle, this might be true. But if so, it is not yet affecting our actual consumption decisions because the infrastructure is not in place to make the revolution relevant at that level.

address climate change; but asserts that fortunately facts about alternative energy, new technologies, and so on make it the case that fulfilling this obligation will also be good for us, or at least not very onerous. As it happens, I have some sympathy for this view. (I certainly *hope* that it is true.) Nevertheless, it differs sharply from another version of the green revolution thesis, which we might call the "only game in town" view. This asserts that unless some kind of energy revolution is forthcoming that makes going green more beneficial for our generation than the alternatives, then action on climate change is unwarranted. I suspect that the "only game in town" view is implicit in much of the public and political debate. Unfortunately, in my opinion, it is also a manifestation of a severe form of intergenerational buck-passing, and therefore morally indefensible. In not distinguishing between these two views, the focus on green revolution often hides this fact.

A second worry about how the green revolution claim obscures what is at stake morally speaking is less obvious. Notice that the scenario described by the revolutionaries is a highly optimistic one, even in the "lucky for us" version. So, one important question is whether *we* are entitled in our deliberations to assume that it is available, so that there are no trade-offs to be made. This seems dubious. If the assumption turns out to be false, the costs of our making it are potentially disastrous, and would tend to fall on the poor, future generations and nature, rather than us. Hence, strong moral justification would be needed for taking such risks. Moreover, in the context of the perfect moral storm, we have every reason to fear immoral justifications. Simply assuming that there will or could be a green revolution, so that solving the climate problem presents a win-win scenario, offers a rationale for not allowing our own standards of living to go down. This is highly convenient for the current generation, and especially the world's rich. So, the threat of moral corruption is high.

A third way in which the call for a green revolution obscures matters concerns how it shifts our attention away from the moral dimensions of the problem, and especially towards technocratic, economic, and lifestyle issues. Suddenly the pressing questions become: "Which alternative energy technologies are most promising? How cheap are they? What kind of vehicle will I be able to have? Will I still be able to go on overseas vacations?" This, of course, captures much of the recent debate.

Some argue that such a shift is beneficial for motivating action[19]; but I have serious doubts. One reason is that it is easy (all too easy, given the storm) to get bogged down in the details of technocratic and economic issues, and lose interest in the wider problem. Hence, I fear that engaging with the issue at this level publicly tends to lead to stagnation and an eventual loss of interest. A second reason is that the lifestyle issue can quickly become contested. Although initially many people probably simply assume that a shift in energy supply would just allow things to carry on exactly as before, this is unlikely to be the case. Given this, choices between technologies, and sketches of the implications of such choices, quickly become value laden, provoking suspicions of "green conspiracy," and handicapping attempts to address the problem.[20]

More generally, the current focus on the green energy revolution rationale puts pressure in the wrong place. The dominant reason for acting on climate change is not that it would make us better off. It is that not acting involves taking advantage of the poor, the future, and nature. We can hope that refraining from such exploitation is good (or at least not too bad) for us, especially in terms of current lifestyles and those to which we aspire. But such hope is and should not be our primary ground for acting. After all, morally speaking, *we must act in any case.* If it turns out that we can do so and still do well ourselves, then this is to be welcomed as a fortunate empirical fact, and no more.[21] Given this, incessant hand-wringing about whether, how, and to what extent we might benefit from action is at best a side issue, and at worst just another vehicle for procrastination and moral corruption.

For such reasons, I suspect that calling on altruistic and distinctively ethical motivations is not only necessary, but also has significant strategic advantages. The green revolution claim runs the risk of obscuring what is at stake in climate change, and in a way that undercuts motivation. The key point is that we should act on climate change even if doing so does not make us better off; indeed, even if it may make us significantly worse off. If we hide or dilute the moral issues, then this important truth is lost, and the prospects for ethically defensible action diminish.

19. Nordhaus and Shellenberger 2004, 2007.
20. Lomborg 2001, 320–22.
21. That being said, the green revolution argument would give us additional ethical reasons to act. Not only may action actually be good for us, but (as mentioned above) a refusal to pursue the benefits of a green revolution when the other arguments for action are strong may seem even more morally outrageous.

IV. CONSUMPTION AND HAPPINESS

Let us now return briefly to the issue of how we should think about self-interest. Again, I agree with the spirit of some of the criticisms of traditional game theory. In my view, further investigation of the notion of "self-interest" would be both useful and appropriate. In particular, if it could be shown that action on climate change or other environmental problems is compatible with the living of richer human lives, this would help to remove a substantial obstacle to change. Moreover, ethics has something to contribute here. How to conceive of human well-being is a traditional philosophical topic, and one with a rich and sophisticated history.[22]

Naturally, I cannot attempt such a contribution here. Still, to illustrate its potential importance, it may be worth making two preliminary points. First, the link between the consumption behavior that drives much of the climate problem and human well-being is complex. For example, it is by now well-known that a body of empirical research in psychology shows that people's own reports of their happiness do not crucially depend on their own per capita income, but rather are, beyond some threshold, largely insensitive to income.[23] What is perhaps less appreciated is that, given this research, much of the contemporary political practice of evaluating societies and policies in terms of economic output and growth is called into question. This has important implications. If standard methods of evaluation are much too simplistic, it is not clear that we have good reason to resist social change solely on the grounds that they may have negative impacts on such criteria. In particular, the uncoupling of raw income and well-being seems to open up an important possibility: *perhaps there are ways of preparing for the future that involve less economic output (as traditionally understood), but are still better for all.*[24] Such claims deserve further investigation, and substantive ethical theory has a role to play here.[25]

The second preliminary point is that game theory might also help. Specifically, problematic incentive structures such as the prisoner's

22. Recent contributions include Griffin 1989, Kraut 2007.

23. See, for example, Layard 2005.

24. Given this, we might need a better economics, based on a different or wider moral theory. See chapter 7.

25. For further discussion and a nice review of the some of the relevant literature, see Andreou 2010.

dilemma, tragedy of the commons, and intergenerational buck-passing can presumably arise with respect to lifestyles as well as elsewhere. Hence, if there are opportunities to reorganize the ways in which we live that overcome such structures, and so make everyone better off, then— other things being equal—these seem to be worth pursuing.

As an illustration, consider the following thought. Many environmentalists claim that an obsession with consumption and accumulation makes everyone worse off. Yet, still we pursue them. Perhaps this implies that the environmentalists are wrong. But it might also imply something more profound. Perhaps western consumerist lifestyles themselves involve elements of the prisoner's dilemma, or similar puzzles. Suppose, for example, that collectively we would acknowledge that all of us would be better off if we did not work quite so hard and consume so much stuff. Still, thinking as individuals, each of us says, "If I have the opportunity to earn extra money and buy more things, I will do so"; therefore, we all do. Since we all reason in the same way, everyone ends up worse off than they might have been. This situation is tragic. If these activities also harm the poor, the future, and nature (e.g., because they involve carbon emissions), there is a double tragedy.

These are disturbing thoughts. But they might be pressed even further. It is one thing if each individual's dogged pursuit of her own (perceived) self-interest ends up being self-defeating. But surely everyone has had the suspicion at some point or another that matters might be much worse than this. At the extreme, some patterns of consumption behavior can start to look *absurd*. For example, what if people spend longer at work, and away from family and friends, earning money in order to buy gifts for those same people that no one really wants, needs, or has space to store? Or what if some fancy neighborhoods are filled with enormous houses heated all day and night at a constant 72 degrees while their owners rarely do anything but sleep in them because they are working all hours to pay the mortgage? Hasn't something gone wrong here?[26]

The implications of this more extreme line of thought are startling. First, if we seriously harm ourselves, the poor, the future, and nature through behavior that on reflection seems seriously absurd, our collective problem seems not to be driven by deep and intractable values

---

26. One account involves the phenomenon of conspicuous consumption (Veblen 2008). But there are others.

(as traditional game theoretic analyses tend to suggest), but rather by a bizarre (and arguably vaguely stupid) superficiality. This is genuinely tragic—but might also be seen as somewhat pathetic. (Why can't we just get over it?)

Second, such charges (of absurdity and superficiality) may color our moral assessment of ourselves in new ways. On the one hand, it may make our behavior seem less blameworthy. Far from consciously taking advantage of others, what we do is against our own interests too, and so looks less directly reprehensible. Meaningless self-indulgence often seems morally less problematic than cold-hearted buck-passing, even if both are vicious and so to be deplored. On the other hand, if we are concerned not just with what we do, but also with what kind of people we are, learning that we impose high risks on others through absurd behavior may actually increase our dismay. It is more blameworthy to be ruthlessly selfish and unjust, to be sure. But to be told that one is *merely* "superficial, incompetent, and unjust" is in some ways worse, because it seems to raise a more basic challenge to agency. Who wants to appear "pathetic"? This worry signals a distinct evaluative perspective on the problem posed by climate change, which on some approaches to ethics will be especially disturbing. Though I cannot develop this thought here, it may add a crucial dimension to climate ethics, and indeed intergenerational ethics more generally.[27]

V. CONCLUSION

This chapter clarifies some assumptions of the perfect moral storm analysis. Most centrally, it argues that the analysis need neither rely on controversial egoistic assumptions, nor denigrate the role of self-interest in forging a solution. In the case of climate change, my suggestion was that the model can appeal to a very limited claim about the role of consumption in contemporary life, and that this allows for substantial criticisms of current behavior from within theories of self-interest. In addition, I suggested that game theoretic models can illuminate some of the problems that environmentalists see with contemporary lifestyles,

27. See chapter 10, Gardiner forthcoming, Bendik-Keymer forthcoming.

and so help to promote a more nuanced approach to the global environmental tragedy. If so, we need not fear their role in moral analysis, provided we are clear about our assumptions and their limitations. Finally, I suggested that a more substantive approach to the ethics of well-being may well be crucial. If the roots of our behavior are more superficial than self-interested, then this casts a different light on our moral predicament.

PART B

The Global Storm

CHAPTER 3

Somebody Else's Problem?

Now we can go home and look our children in the eye and be proud of what we have done.

—Margot Wollstrom, EU Environment Commisioner (quoted in Brown 2001)

Kyoto is simply a miserable precursor of the global regime intended to deliver genuine climate stablization—and was never expected to be more.

—John Schellnhuber, Potsdam Institute for Climate Impact Research (Schellnhuber 2007)

Having sketched the perfect moral storm analysis and clarified some of its assumptions, I now turn to a more detailed account of each of its main components. I begin with an exploration of the spatial dimension of climate change, and the extent to which it constitutes a "global storm." Again, although climate change is the focus of the discussion, this is just because it constitutes an especially important, and currently relevant, example of a more general phenomenon. In my view, just as with Hardin's tragedy of the commons, the basic shape of the account has wider import.

Climate change is often seen as a paradigmatically global problem. This is because human activities produce greenhouse gas emissions everywhere people live, and once emitted, carbon dioxide—the main anthropogenic greenhouse gas—quickly spreads though the atmosphere, affecting temperature globally, and potentially causing impacts anywhere and everywhere.

In light of this spatial dispersion, solving climate change is usually thought of as a problem of bargaining between the main political units in the current international system, nation states. On this assumption, two basic analyses of the situation are influential: one optimistic and one pessimistic. In this chapter and the next, I explain these models, and their application to past climate policy, as exemplified in the Kyoto regime and the recent search for its successor (in Bali and Copenhagen). Initially, I shall claim that the pessimistic model is the better of the two, because it takes seriously the scale of the international problem. However, ultimately, I will argue that even it is too generous. One reason is that it fails to appreciate the intergenerational dimension of the perfect moral storm. In my view, this dominates in the case of climate change, and this helps to explain the policy experience.[1] A further reason is that the pessimistic model neglects issues of international fairness and skewed vulnerabilities. Implicitly, it assumes either that the background circumstances of different countries are such as to make an agreement based on international bargaining fair, or else that fairness is not important. These assumptions are unwarranted. In addition, they undermine our appreciation of the real climate challenge.

Despite their general inadequacy, I shall argue that the usual models remain relevant. In a perfect moral storm, we should expect "shadow solutions" to the problem at hand that reflect only the limited concerns of those with the power to act. Such "solutions" are morally problematic. Not only are they typically inadequate as a matter of substance, but they also create the dangerous illusion of real action, and this serves as a distraction through which continued buck-passing can be perpetrated. Unfortunately, this account is highly plausible in the climate case.

This chapter explores the optimistic analysis of the global storm. Section I briefly recounts the history of international climate policy. Section II introduces the optimistic ("battle of the sexes") model of international policy-making, according to which successfully addressing climate change requires the participation of only a limited number of key players. Section III argues that this model fails, both in theory and in practice, so that we should be more pessimistic about international agreement. Chapter 4 explores this pessimism in light of the likely outcome of Kyoto,

1. Note that the intergenerational storm would remain relevant even if it did not have predictive or explanatory power in this sense. After all, it might have turned out that humanity quickly rose to the climate challenge. In that case, the perfect storm analysis would still have a role to play in showing why this was a great victory. Failure merely makes the problem more perspicuous.

and the more recent Copenhagen experience. It argues that a degenerate version of the optimistic analysis may still have a role to play.

I. PAST CLIMATE POLICY

Let us begin with a brief history of international climate policy.

1. The Kyoto Experience

In Bonn in July 2001, and in a subsequent clarificatory meeting in Marrakesh in the following November, 178 of the world's nations reached agreement on measures to combat global climate change brought on by anthropogenic emissions of greenhouse gases. Despite the notable omission of the United States, representatives of the participants, and many newspapers around the world, expressed elation. After the Bonn meeting, Michael Meacher, Britain's Environment Minister, said, "Climate Change is the single greatest threat to the human race. This agreement is a historic day that all of us will remember."[2] His sentiments were echoed by Pete Hodgson, New Zealand's Energy Minister, who claimed, "We have delivered probably the most comprehensive and difficult agreement in human history."[3] Commenting after the later meeting in Marrakesh, David D. Doniger, director of climate programs for the Natural Resources Defense Council, called it "by far the strongest environmental treaty that's ever been drafted," with compliance conditions that are "as good as it gets in international relations."[4] Margot Wollstrom, the Environment Commissioner for the European Union, went so far as to declare, "Now we can go home and look our children in the eye and be proud of what we have done."[5]

The Bonn-Marrakesh agreement emerged in three main phases.[6] The first encompassed most of the twentieth century, and came to fruition at the Rio Earth Summit of 1992. Awareness of the possibility that humans

2. Brown 2001.
3. Brown 2001.
4. Revkin 2001d.
5. Brown 2001.
6. Jamieson 2001; Barrett 1998; Weart 2003.

might alter the climate through industrial activity had been present since the late nineteenth century, in the work of Gustav Arrenhius and John Tyndall. Initially, it was thought that such change would probably be benign. But by mid-century the idea that it may constitute a significant threat began to be taken seriously. Presidential briefings took place as early as the Johnson Administration, with a 1965 report concluding, "Man is unwittingly conducting a vast geophysical experiment."[7] By the seventies, the concern was making front-page news, with the *New York Times* declaring: "Scientists Fear Heavy Use of Coal May Bring Adverse Shift in Climate."[8]

Nevertheless, it was not until the late 1980s that the concern began to have real traction. Most notably, in 1985, a major meeting of meteorologists in Villach, Austria, declared it a matter of international consensus that by the middle of the twenty-first century humanity could experience a rise in global mean temperature greater than at any time in its history, and suggested that governments take action.[9] Three years later, a World Conference on the Changing Atmosphere in Toronto concluded that "humanity is conducting an unintended, uncontrolled, globally pervasive experiment whose ultimate consequences could be second only to a global nuclear war," and advocated reducing carbon emissions by 20% by 2005.[10]

In response to such claims, the United Nations Environment Program and the World Meteorological Association created the Intergovernmental Panel on Climate Change (IPCC), and charged it with the task of providing member governments with state of the art assessments of "the science, the impacts, and the economics of—and the options for mitigating and/or adapting to—climate change."[11] The IPCC issued its first report in 1990. This asserted that the atmospheric concentration of greenhouse gases were increasing due to human activity, and projected that this would result in increases in global temperature of 0.3 C per decade (with an uncertainty range of 0.2–0.5 C). In addition, it noted that observations supported the claim that

7. President's Science Advisory Committee 1965, 126.
8. Waert 2003, 96.
9. Waert 2003, 151
10. Suzuki 2009.
11. IPCC 2001a, vii.

there had been warming over the previous century (of 0.3–0.5 C) that was consistent with climate models. However, it also said that it would likely take another decade or more for an unequivocal signal of man-made warming to emerge.[12] This was primarily because of the difficulty of separating out the background "noise" of natural variability during the early period of global warming.

On the basis of the first IPCC report, the countries of the world went to the Rio Earth Summit and committed themselves to the United Nations Framework Convention on Climate Change (UNFCCC). This required "stabilization of greenhouse gas concentrations in the atmosphere at a level that would prevent dangerous anthropogenic interference with the climate system," and endorsed a principle of "common but differentiated responsibilities," according to which, the richer, industrialized nations[13] would take the lead in cutting emissions, while the less developed countries would pursue their own development, and take significant action only in the future.[14]

Initially, in line with the Framework Convention, many of the rich countries (including the United States, the European Union, Japan, Canada, Australia, New Zealand and Norway) announced that they would voluntarily stabilize their emissions at 1990 levels by 2000. Unfortunately, as the decade progressed, it became clear that merely voluntary measures would be ineffective. Most of those who had made declarations did nothing meaningful to try to live up to them, and their emissions continued to rise without constraint. (The United States, for example, saw an increase of more than ten percent for the decade.) The only exception, the European Union, looked likely to succeed only because, by a fortuitous coincidence, the United Kingdom and Germany posted sharp reductions in emissions for economic reasons unrelated to climate change.

Thus, a second phase ensued. Meeting in Berlin in 1995, the parties decided that they should set binding constraints on their emissions, and these constraints were subsequently agreed in Japan in 1997, with the negotiation of the Kyoto Protocol. This took place against the background of the second IPCC report of 1995, which repeated the future projections

12. IPCC 1990.

13. These are listed under "Annex I" in the agreement, and known as the Annex I countries.

14. UNFCCC, Articles 2 and 3.1. This treaty was later ratified by all the major players, including the United States.

but also claimed that a signal was beginning to emerge ("the balance of evidence suggests a discernible [human] influence on climate").[15]

The Kyoto agreement initially appeared to be a notable success, in that it required the Annex I countries to reduce emissions to roughly 5 percent below 1990 levels between 2008 and 2012. But it also involved a couple of significant concessions on the goal of reducing emissions in individual rich countries. First, Article 3 of the Protocol stipulated that carbon "sinks" would be counted towards meeting a country's obligations as well as reductions in direct greenhouse gas emissions. Second, Article 17 allowed countries to trade their rights to emit under their emissions targets, so that rich countries could buy credits from other countries in order to acquire more than their own initial allotment.

The Kyoto Protocol was a historic step. But matters soon took a turn for the worse. In the Hague in November 2000, a subsequent meeting to thrash out details broke down without agreement, and amid angry recriminations. Then, in March 2001, after initially saying it would support Kyoto, but faced with an imminent meeting in Bonn to agree on compliance mechanisms, the Bush Administration dramatically withdrew U.S. support. Condoleeza Rice, the U.S. National Security Adviser at the time, voiced the view of many when she pronounced the Protocol thereby "dead."[16] Ironically, these events coincided with a hardening of the science. In January 2001, the IPCC released its third assessment, repeating its long-term projections, but also asserting that change was becoming more evident on the ground: "most of the observed warming over the last 50 years," it said, "is likely to have been due to the increase in greenhouse gas concentrations."[17]

In the end, the declaration of Kyoto's demise turned out to be premature. The process did not collapse in Bonn. Instead, a third phase began in which a full agreement was negotiated among the remaining parties, with the European Union, Japan, and Russia playing prominent roles.[18] By the end of 2001, at a subsequent meeting in Marrakesh, the final details had been thrashed out, including the thorny issue of a compliance

15. IPCC 1996, cited by Houghton 2004, 105.

16. Borger 2001.

17. IPCC 2001a, cited by Houghton 2004, 106.

18. The latter two countries won substantial concessions on their targets, resulting in a further weakening of the overall goal.

mechanism, and the Kyoto Protocol was sent out to participating governments for ratification. By 2003, almost all of the major players, including the European Union and Japan, had ratified, and it needed only ratification by Russia to meet the threshold of support—at least fifty-five countries responsible for at least 55 percent of emissions— necessary to pass into international law. After a period of substantial uncertainty, Russia ultimately endorsed the Protocol in November 2004, and it went into effect in February 2005.

2. The Road to Copenhagen

The Kyoto Protocol was intended to be the first in a series of substantive agreements to implement the Framework Convention on Climate Change, with its provisions covering the period up until the end of 2012. Given that the process from Rio until Kyoto's ratification in 2005 had taken 13 years, the next agreement would need to be fully ratified in roughly half of the time to be in place when Kyoto expired. Negotiations towards a second commitment period began in late 2005. Initially, progress was very slow, but new momentum was added in 2007, when the IPCC released its fourth report. This concluded that across the century the best estimate for a low emission scenario would be 1.8°C (likely range 1.1°C to 2.9°C), and for a high emission scenario 4.0°C (likely range 2.4°C to 6.4°C). In addition, the report stated that the warming trend was now unequivocal, and "very likely" (meaning a probability of 90% or more) due to human activity.[19] Given that a robust international effort seemed necessary to get close to the low emission scenario, the issue of the stalled negotiations became urgent in the eyes of mainstream scientists. The head of the IPCC, Rajendra Pachauri, captured the mood when he declared, "If there's no action before 2012, that's too late. What we do in the next two to three years will determine our future. This is the defining moment."[20]

Politically, matters reached a head at the annual conference of the parties in Bali, Indonesia, in December of the same year. Prior to the meeting, the UN Secretary general, Ban Ki-Moon, observed of the IPCC

---

19. IPCC 2007a.
20. Rosenthal 2007.

report: "The world's scientists have spoken, clearly and in one voice. In Bali, I expect the world's policymakers to do the same."[21] Against the widespread perception that the United States, under the Bush Administration, was holding back the process, and a dramatic plea from a representative for Papua New Guinea ("If for some reason you're not willing to lead, leave it to the rest of us. Please get out of the way"[22]), the meeting finally delivered a "roadmap" for a new agreement, formally known as the Bali Action Plan. According to this document, the nations of the world would work aggressively over the next two years in order to reach a full and binding agreement on a new treaty in December 2009, at a meeting in Copenhagen. This was already less than some parties had wanted.[23] But 2009 was salient for two main reasons. First, many participants thought progress would be facilitated by a change in administrations in the United States after the 2008 presidential election. Second, 2009 was widely believed to be the very latest feasible deadline for formal agreement of a treaty, if it was to be formally ratified by national governments and implemented before Kyoto expired.

Despite the roadmap, progress after Bali was again very slow. By December 2008, the next annual conference of the Parties, in Poznan, Poland, very little had been achieved. As an article in the *Washington Post* reported "the core questions—how much industrialized countries will slash their emissions, what they expect in return from major emerging economies, and what they will do to help poorer countries pursue low-carbon development—remain untouched."[24] Nevertheless, with a new U.S. president, Barack Obama, due to take office in January 2009, hopes for a new agreement had begun to rise. Initial reports of high-level dialogue with China on the topic, and the drafting of a new climate change bill in the U.S. Congress, added to an air of optimism in the first part of 2009. However, the mood started to shift as the year went on. Domestically, the obstacles on Capitol Hill began to appear formidable, and many were disappointed by the limited aspirations of

21. Rosenthal 2007.

22. Revkin 2008.

23. German Environment Minister Sigmar Gabriel had previously said that the Bali conference would be meaningless without targets. "I do not need a paper from Bali in which we only say,'O.K., we'll meet next year again,'" Gabriel said. "How we can find a roadmap without having a target, without having a goal?" (Adam 2007)

24. Eilperin 2008b.

the emerging Waxman-Markey bill; internationally, expectations for Copenhagen began to be downgraded. By the fall, a full treaty was already being said to be no longer possible there. But UN officials still held out hope for an agreement on the "political essentials" that would frame a treaty, so that it could be quickly formalized in 2010.

In December, the conference of the parties finally convened in Copenhagen for two weeks of negotiations. Still, diplomatic progress was elusive, and conflict soon broke out about a perceived attempt by the Danish hosts and the rich countries to circumvent the UN process, and abandon the architecture of Kyoto. As world leaders began to arrive for the last two days of the talks, very little had been achieved since Bali. Finally, after many closed door meetings between leaders of key nations, a document entitled "The Copenhagen Accord" emerged from the United States, China, India, Brazil, and South Africa. It called for nations to limit global temperature rise to 2 degrees Celsius, and to submit individual targets for 2020 by January 31, 2010. This hastily drafted text was then "noted" by the full conference—not "welcomed" or endorsed—and the leaders departed.

As we shall see in chapter 4, initial perceptions of this result differed markedly. But the public pronouncements of the main architects of the Accord seemed cautiously optimistic. The United States called the outcome "meaningful," while acknowledging that much more needed to be done. The head of the Chinese delegation said, "The meeting has had a positive result, everyone should be happy."[25]

II. SOMEBODY ELSE'S BURDEN?

An international climate policy regime must be built by an international coalition of countries that are willing to undertake action to reduce . . . emissions. According to game theory, the size of the coalition will be determined by the so-called marginal country.

—Wytze van der Gaast (Van der Gaast 2008)

It is tempting to be optimistic and believe that climate change might be solved by something like the Bonn-Marrakesh agreement even given the

25. BBC 2009.

withdrawal of the United States, or something like the Copenhagen Accord even given its initial endorsement by only a small group of large countries. The optimism begins with a basic theoretical thought.[26] Climate change is caused by an increase in the total global emissions of greenhouse gases; therefore, what is needed to address it is a cut in this total. But this suggests that, from the strictly physical point of view, the distribution of reductions across countries is irrelevant. From the point of view of the climate, it does not matter where the cut occurs.

As an illustration, suppose one were trying to achieve a global cut in carbon dioxide emissions of roughly twenty percent (as many scientists had suggested that Copenhagen should try to achieve by 2020). In theory, this could be achieved unilaterally, by the United States or China acting alone.[27] Since each of these countries currently accounts for around twenty percent of global emissions, either could achieve the objective by cutting their own emissions to zero.[28] Similarly, the reduction could occur through more modest cuts made by a group of less polluting nations acting in concert. For example, the European Union (with roughly a 15% share of the current global total), Russia (with a 5% share), and Japan (with a 5% share) could each cut their emissions by half and achieve a global cut of more than 10%; if either China or the United States did the same, the 20% cut would be achieved.[29] On the optimistic analysis, then, it seems plausible to think that a comprehensive climate agreement, involving cooperation and cuts by all countries, is not necessary to solve the climate problem. In principle, a smaller group of committed nations acting in concert can get the job done.

One initial obstacle to this analysis is that it seems to face a motivational problem. Why would some countries consider acting, when others will not? Why would they take on the costs and allow others a free ride? These are good questions, but—initially at least—they seem to have answers.

---

26. A version of the optimistic analysis, invoking this thought, is put forward by Waldron, unpublished. See also Mabey et al., 1997, 356–59, 409–10; Barrett 1998, 36–7; Oleson et al. 2009.

27. Marland et al. 2008. Of course, as we saw in chapter 1, such draconian cuts would not be desirable, since they would likely cause humanitarian catastrophes.

28. See Waldron, unpublished.

29. These numbers—like the 20% cut—are for illustrative purposes only. However, they have a general grounding in the numbers for 2004 in Marland et al., 2008.

1. Pure Public Goods

One answer draws on a concept prominent in public economics, that of a pure public good. Pure public goods are such that, once created, they benefit everyone, and no one agent's consumption of the good diminishes the benefits to others.[30] Take the standard example of a lighthouse. Once built, it benefits all sailors who travel in that area: everyone can see the rocks, and so can avoid them. Moreover, my benefiting from being able to see the rocks has no negative implications for your being able to do the same thing, and vice versa. Each of us can see the rocks without getting in the way of the other, or using up something that the other wants.

How does one bring about the provision of a pure public good? Suppose that the lighthouse does not yet exist. Concerned about this, a group of sailors gets together and issues a call for contributions to pay for building one. A natural suggestion is that all who would benefit should contribute. But suppose some refuse. Still, the project may not fail. Those who are willing to contribute may find it worthwhile to cover the shortfall. They would, of course, prefer it if they did not have to take on a greater share of the costs. They may even have a grievance against those who refuse to contribute, but who will still enjoy the benefits. (If they could, they would make them pay a share of the costs, or else exclude them from the benefits.) Nevertheless, they also really want to be able to see the rocks. Given that they can secure this with an extra contribution, they are willing to do so.

The pure public good analysis has important implications. It suggests that under at least some circumstances—those relevantly similar to the building of the lighthouse—the motivation problem can be solved and the good can be secured even without the full cooperation of the beneficiaries. If the stakes are high enough, and the costs are not crippling, some will find it worthwhile to contribute even if others free ride. Moreover, this is so even if everyone accepts that there is something unreasonable or unfair about the arrangement. If the good is important enough to the contributors in relation to the costs, they may put up with others taking advantage of them.

---

30. More formally, this is a good whose consumption is both nonexcludable (once it is available to some, others cannot be prevented from consuming it) and nonrival (one person's consumption does not limit or inhibit another person's consumption).

Is dealing with climate change relevantly analogous to the lighthouse example? At first glance, it seems so. For one thing, if the aim is to reduce or eliminate the risk of catastrophic climate change by securing a cut in global emissions, this seems to be a pure public good. It benefits all countries, regardless of whether they contribute, and the benefit provided to one country does not diminish that available to another. For another thing, given the theoretical point above about the global character of the climate problem, it seems plausible to think that motivations are in play that are structurally similar to those in the lighthouse example. Just as it might be in a particular sailor's interest to contribute to the costs of a lighthouse even if some others will not, so it may be in a particular country's interest to participate in a global warming treaty and cut its own emissions even if some other countries do not. This may be so even if the participating country has to take on extra costs, and believes (rightly) that this is in some sense unfair or unreasonable.

If correct, what are the implications of this argument for climate policy? Both the lighthouse example and the optimistic analysis involve two crucial features. The first is that the problem they confront is resolvable even with less than full participation of the parties involved. As long as a large enough coalition can be found, the problem can be successfully addressed. (Call this claim *partial cooperation*.) The second feature is that each model assumes that members of the cooperating group do not require any additional, outside incentives to cooperate. The benefits of cooperation alone are sufficient to secure their participation, even given the costs such participation involves, and that others free-ride. (Call this *internal motivation*.) These features are of political importance. They suggest that solving the climate problem might be easier than one might otherwise have thought. If one can assemble a suitable "coalition of the willing," then the job can be done, and this is so even if the willing regard the actions of the unwilling as unfair.

2. The Battle of the Sexes

The lighthouse example is a useful illustration, but climate change need not be a pure public good for the optimistic analysis to succeed. Instead, the crucial features of partial cooperation and internal motivation can be found in a wider range of cases. This can be seen by invoking a further model from game theory, the battle of the sexes.[31] *(Those uninterested in the technicalities may safely skip this subsection.)*

The term "battle of the sexes" comes from the standard (unfortunately sexist) example used to elucidate situations with this structure.[32] Suppose Ben and Emma are deciding where to go for a date. Ben would prefer a boxing match; Emma a ballet. But each prefers going to the other's favored event (and thereby preserving the date) over not having the date and going to their own favored event alone. (In other words, Ben would prefer to go to the ballet with Emma than to go to the boxing match alone, and Emma would prefer going to the boxing with Ben over going to the ballet alone.) This yields the following set of preferences:

TABLE 3.1

		Emma	
		Boxing	**Ballet**
Ben	**Boxing**	1st, 2nd	3rd, 3rd
	Ballet	-, -[33]	2nd, 1st

31. Waldron, unpublished.

32. I take the example from Luce and Raiffa 1957, 91. It is worth noting that, in texts on game theory, the term "battle of the sexes" is used to describe a number of distinct but related scenarios. All of them share the idea that the two parties prefer a different venue for the date, but also prefer to be together rather than alone. In some scenarios, the parties have already arranged the date but cannot remember where they agreed to go, and cannot communicate to clear up the confusion. So, each has to make a decision on where to go based on their knowledge of their own preferences and those of the other. In other scenarios, they are actually negotiating the venue for the date (and so can communicate).

Such variations make a difference to how one describes the less preferable scenarios. In the former case, where there is a knowledge and communication problem, all the combinations are in play: it is possible for each to end up at their favored event alone, or at the others' favored event alone. In the latter case, where the venue is not set and the parties are able to negotiate, the worst-case scenario is presumably not in play: the default position is either to go to one's own favored event alone, or else stay at home. Matters are made even more complicated by different assumptions about the status of the relationship. Some writers assume that the parties are a married couple; others that it is a first date. This may make a difference. For the former, the whole relationship is not (usually!) at stake, whereas for the latter, it might be. This makes some difference to how we understand the readiness to concede or hold out; but it also affects whether the less preferred scenarios are really in play. (For example, for the first date, it is less likely that they are.) I mention this because background views on the norms and anxieties surrounding dating and marriage play a significant role in interpretation.

In such a situation, both parties want to avoid the noncooperative outcomes (both want the date to happen), but there is no natural equilibrium position (it is not clear whether boxing or ballet will be chosen). Hence, there is a coordination problem.

According to the standard account in game theory, this coordination problem has interesting features. First, under favorable circumstances, it is relatively easy to resolve. For example, there is a solution if either Ben or Emma believe that things will turn out better if they let the other person have their way than if they dig their heels in and insist on their own favored event.[34] Second, just as in the case of a pure public good, the collective action problem may be resolved without the need for any change in payoffs or motivation on the part of the players.

33. In the above scenario, this option is not on the table. In the version of the story where the venue is prearranged and the parties have forgotten, this would be 4,4. In some sources, it is labeled 3,3. But I assume that Ben and Emma would each prefer going to their favored event alone over going to their nonfavored event alone.

34. In reality, this is likely to bring in factors external to the game. Consider just two examples. First, the parties are likely to assume that the game is to be repeated. If so, they may make the natural assumption that whoever concedes this time will get to choose on the next occasion, so that it does not matter very much who concedes now. Second, one of the parties may think it better in the long run to concede in conflicts like this, because to do so is likely to bring other benefits. In particular, they may believe that being too insistent (especially on the first date) would undermine the prospects for a longer term relationship. Similar factors seem relevant to international relations and climate change. But this complicates the claim that climate change is a battle of the sexes with strictly internal solutions.

Given such concerns, a better analogy than the "battle of the sexes" story might be the following. Imagine two strangers, John and Paul, who meet at a conference in an exotic vacation spot. Each has a free afternoon and would like to get out and enjoy the local environs. Each prefers to have company, but they want to do different things. Assume also that the strangers are from different walks of life and different continents, so that the background motivation of the date in the battle of the sexes—the long-term aspect—is missing. What are the implications? It seems reasonable to suppose that internal solutions are still possible, but the prospects for agreement more fragile. For example, if it is a question of canoeing or kayaking, then for many people resolution will not be that difficult. But if it is sky diving or ice fishing, then the company has to be really worth having. The key difference here is that in the traditional battle of the sexes example we tend to assume that the parties place a high background value on being together, but in the case of the outing, we need not. The point is that the latter case might be more parallel to climate change, especially given the background presence of the intergenerational storm. (We could also alter our background assumptions about the battle of the sexes. Perhaps I should realize that going to the boxing match won't save the relationship: He's a meathead and I just need to get rid of him.)

Since both parties want the date to happen, even if it means going to the event they don't favor, there is no motivational obstacle to finding a solution.[35]

The battle of the sexes structure becomes even more interesting and relevant when it occurs in problems involving more than two parties. To illustrate this, consider *the rugby game*. Suppose that a group of fifty enthusiastic rugby fans is trying to organize a game of rugby. They need two teams of fifteen players each. Unfortunately, even though everyone wants the game to be played, each person would prefer not to have to be one of the players. (Each fan likes watching rugby far more than playing it. It is, after all, a rough, physical game.) In short, though each person supports the establishment of the team, each also tries to avoid being part of it, hoping to free-ride on the participation of the others.

Under some circumstances, the fans' reluctance to play will be fatal to the cooperative venture; but under others it will not. Suppose, for example, that each of the fans would prefer to play rather than see the match abandoned; then, the cooperative venture should not fail. Rather, it is to be expected that the least unwilling will volunteer, while the others free ride.

The rugby case and the lighthouse example have similar features. On the one hand, less than full participation is required. In other words:

(Partial Cooperation) There is a number M (such that M < N) which is the minimum number of players whose cooperation is necessary if some situation, which is dispreferred by all, is to be avoided.

On the other hand, on the assumption above, there is internal motivation that supports the formation of the group:

(Marginal Cooperation) If the number of others who are willing to cooperate is just short of M, then a given party prefers to cooperate, since each prefers to

---

35. The good at stake—the date—is not completely nonrival in consumption. Each prefers having the date at their favored venue, so each must give up something if the date is elsewhere. So, this is not a situation involving a pure public good.

enjoy the benefits of cooperation and pay a share of the costs than to forego the benefits altogether.[36]

In addition, it is implied that the group is protected from outside interference. For example, none of the noncooperators proposes a game of tiddlywinks or a trip to the sports bar instead. More formally:

> (Passive Cooperation) Once the cooperating group is formed, the noncooperators prefer that it remain so, and succeed in its task. Hence, although they will not take on the costs of cooperation, they will also refrain from disrupting the efforts of the cooperating group.

Under such conditions, then, one expects the multi-person battle of the sexes problem to be rationally resolvable, and again without the need to change payoffs.

Now, the basic battle of the sexes analysis is of practical importance, since it seems likely that at least some environmental problems take this form. Consider, for example, the charitable organization The Nature Conservancy in the United States. This group purchases plots of land and

---

36. Waldron characterizes the global warming problem as follows:

(a) There are more than 2 players. Call the number of players N.

(b) There is a number M (such that M < N) which is the minimum number of players whose cooperation is necessary if some situation, which is bad for all, is to be avoided.

(c) If M players cooperate, all N players benefit.

(d) Each player prefers the situation in which M players cooperate but he is not one of them, to the situation in which he is one of the M co-operators. In other words, cooperation is costly.

(e) The greater the number of cooperators, the smaller the cost to each of cooperating. Thus each prefers that, if he is a cooperator, that the number of cooperators be as large as possible.

(f) If any cooperate, and the number of cooperators is less than M, then the cooperators suffer the cost and enjoy none of the benefits of cooperation. Each would prefer not to cooperate than to be in this situation.

(g) If the number of others who are willing to cooperate is just short of M, then a given party prefers to cooperate, since he is better off enjoying the benefits of cooperation and paying his share of the cost than he is in the situation where not enough people cooperate.

So, I have picked out his (b) and (g). (Waldron unpublished, 34–35.)

protects them from human exploitation. To do so, it solicits donations from individuals. Suppose everyone agrees that such action is desirable, and would be willing to make a contribution to make sure that it happens. Still, there may be an incentive to free-ride. Perhaps the resources required to purchase the necessary land could easily be provided by only some of those willing to contribute. For example, suppose 50 million citizens would be willing to contribute $10 per year (giving a potential fund of $500 million), but only $200 million is required, so that only 20 million contributors are needed. In that case, some can have their concern met by relying on others to pay the necessary costs. Nevertheless, even knowing this, those who do contribute may continue to find it worthwhile to do so. (The land is acquired, after all.) Moreover, the internal motivation means both that noncooperators would rally to the cause if the original cooperating group lost critical mass (i.e., they would contribute funds if they needed to), and the passive cooperation claim implies that they will not interfere with the activities of the cooperators (e.g., by bidding up the value of the land themselves).

3. A Climate Battle?

If the battle of the sexes analysis looks compelling for some environmental problems, does it also hold for climate change? There are two reasons for thinking that it does. The first is the original theoretical point from above. Severe climate change threatens all with disaster, and what is needed to address it is a cut in global emissions. Since from a strictly physical point of view, it does not matter where the allowed emissions (and therefore the cuts) occur, the geographical distribution of cuts across countries is irrelevant. Hence, it seems possible for some large country or group of countries to solve the problem without global participation. If true, this would be a very important result, and one likely to have a substantial effect on the geopolitics of the problem. It suggests that, even without the United States or some other major producers, the rest of the countries of the world could effectively combat climate change.

The second reason is that, initially, the political events of 2001 and 2009 might appear to support an optimistic reading of the two agreements. Consider first three aspects of the Bonn-Marrakesh deal. First, there is the behavior of the noncooperators. At the time of these events, it was widely assumed that the United States stood to gain the least from action to combat climate change.[37] If this were correct, one would expect it to remain outside the cooperating group, since it would benefit least from being the marginal cooperating player; and, of course, it did so. Similarly, developing countries maintained (plausibly) that they faced other, more pressing issues, and so refused to agree to binding emissions targets. This makes sense on the optimistic reading, since such countries could plausibly claim to have the highest costs of participation.

Second, there are the concessions made to the marginal players. Most obviously, in the wake of the United States's withdrawal from the Kyoto agreement, Wallström is reported to have said that the European Union was "fully aware of the fact that we will have to look at how to keep Japan on board in order to keep the Kyoto process alive"; and as things developed, Japan was reported to have won concessions that effectively reduced its reduction target from 6 to 1 percent.[38] (Similarly, much effort was expended in obtaining Russian ratification.) Less obviously, prominent noncooperators (the United States and the developing countries) encouraged the cooperating group to form. Indeed, the United States even seemed to expend some effort to support Japan's participation, and so forestall Kyoto's collapse.[39]

37. Sometimes this was based on analysis. Some (e.g., Mendelsohn 2001) argued that the economic benefits of global warming would marginally outweigh the costs in the United States. Sometimes, however, it seemed simply to be inferred from the U.S. stance in negotiations (e.g., Mabey et al., 408; and Nitze 1994, 189–90). In both cases, there is a serious problem in coming up with realistic assessments of possible costs (see chapter 7.) For a more complex analysis from the same period, see National Assessment Synthesis Team 2000. More recently, reports have made the more limited claim that the United States (and perhaps China) has relatively less to lose than many other nations (Mendelsohn et al. 2006 and Cline 2007, cited by Posner and Sunstein 2008). On this basis, it is sometimes suggested that other nations should make side payments to the United States (and China) in order to induce their cooperation (Posner and Sunstein 2007, 2008).

38. Barrett 2005, 371–72. The situation with the other marginal player, Russia, fits less neatly into this picture, as it appeared to involve external incentives. Although Russia was already allowed to increase its emissions substantially from then-current levels, and also stood likely to gain from selling permits to nations with genuine reduction targets, its participation in Kyoto became linked with the issue of its joining the World Trade Organization. See *Pravda* 2004.

39. In the immediate aftermath of the United States' withdrawal from the Kyoto agreement, the U.S. president and Japanese prime minister agreed to high-level bilateral talks on areas of common ground on climate change. Shortly after Japan started to express reservations about ratification in January 2002, the second round of talks took place in Tokyo. Japan ratified later that year.

Third, although the 2001 agreement on compliance conditions contained penalties for those who did not ultimately meet their targets, all of these were internal to the agreement itself. In particular, there was no link to other issues, such as trade. This suggests that the benefits of cooperation alone were sufficient incentive for the parties to comply with the agreement; and this fits with the optimistic analysis. (More on this later.)

Consider now the Copenhagen Accord. Procedurally, this was agreed behind closed doors between the United States, China, India, Brazil, and South Africa, with the presumed tacit consent of the European Union, and then offered to the wider conference for support. The idea seemed to be one of setting the overall goal of limiting climate change to two degrees Celsius, pinning down commitments from a number of key players, and then inviting others to join in. This would make sense on the thought that the key nations could deliver all or most of the cuts needed, and then count on other marginal players to rally to the cause.

III. AGAINST OPTIMISM

At first glance, then, it seems plausible to think that the climate change problem is a battle of the sexes problem, and so be optimistic about the international negotiations. But this would be a mistake. The optimistic analysis is flawed both in theory and in practice.

1. Practice

Let us begin with the practice. First, neither Kyoto nor Copenhagen is really designed to achieve an overall cut in global emissions. Most notably, neither agreement contains any commitment by any particular country or group of countries to deliver or enforce a global ceiling. Kyoto calls only for individualized, short-term, and national targets for the specific countries that participate. Copenhagen at least mentions an overall objective of limiting climate change to two degrees, and recognizes the need for deep cuts in emissions to achieve this goal. But it draws no conclusions about how much can be emitted globally in the second commitment period, or how these emissions should be distributed. Instead, it merely invites countries to submit commitments on their own emissions. More generally, "There is no headline global target for emissions cuts. National targets must be taken on trust. There are no incentives for countries to pollute less and no sanctions on those that pollute more. Many commitments are to be enacted 'as soon as possible'—not a phrase with much authority in international law."[40]

Second, the national targets that initially emerged appear to make an extremely minimal contribution towards solving the problem. Consider first Kyoto. On the one hand, as those opposed to action on climate change have often pointed out, even if the original Kyoto deal were extended indefinitely into the future (i.e., beyond its current expiry date of 2012), it would have only a negligible effect on global emissions by 2100, amounting to a mere six-year delay in reaching those atmospheric concentrations anticipated under "business-as-usual."[41] On the other hand, since many major emitters are either outside the regime (like the United States), or else not committed to reductions (like China, India, and Russia), overall global emissions were projected to continue to rise significantly over the first commitment period. Indeed, as we saw in chapter 1, they had already risen by around thirty percent by 2007, and were then rising at between two and three percent per year, a much faster rate than in the 1990s, and beyond the high end of expectations even as recently as 2000.[42] In short, as a matter of practice, there was no question of those countries making commitments under Kyoto solving the climate problem for the rest of the planet.

Consider now Copenhagen. Procedurally, as the deadline for submissions of national commitments under the Copenhagen Accord approached in January 2010, climate convention head Yvo de Boer described it as "soft," and added that countries were now in a "cooling off period" before thinking about their approach to the next conference of the parties, scheduled for Cancún in December 2010.[43] More substantively, those commitments that did come in on time were widely seen as disappointing: only fifty-five countries made pledges; those of the main players were the same as they had offered in Copenhagen; and these efforts were projected to allow increases in global temperature of

40. Guardian 2009.
41. Lomborg 2001, 304.
42. Marland et al., 2008; Moore 2008.
43. Black 2010.

3 degrees or more.[44] Clearly, the major emitters fell far short of solving the problem for the rest of the planet.

2. Theory

Even if Kyoto and Copenhagen do not follow the logic of the optimistic analysis, some may argue that this is a criticism of these agreements, rather than the analysis. Perhaps a successful approach still *should* conform to the battle of the sexes structure, so that this model remains appropriate for future agreements. For example, perhaps the problem with Kyoto was simply the omission of both the United States and China from the cooperating group, and perhaps the problem with Copenhagen was simply a failure of ambition on the part of the leading nations, or a problem caused by political constraints at home. If such difficulties could be overcome, some may insist, the relevance of the battle of the sexes model would be restored.

In my view, this approach is mistaken. The optimistic analysis is false in theory as well as practice. This is because partial cooperation and internal motivation are false. Let us begin with partial cooperation.

a. Partial Cooperation

As it turns out, it would be virtually impossible for a group of countries to deliver a global ceiling on emissions without the cooperation of the others. The reason is that the global warming problem occurs in a dynamic context. The potential "cuts" we have been talking about are calculated against totals for current emissions. But the potential gains from greenhouse gas emissions have not yet been exhausted. Therefore, for any stable policy, what really needs to be assessed is whether a group of nations could deliver a ceiling in the face of the *potential* emissions of noncooperating countries. And this seems seriously unlikely.

Consider the following (rough) calculations. Total global emissions from fossil-fuel burning, cement manufacture, and gas flaring in 1990

44. UNEP 2010: Gray 2010.

were 6.164 billion metric tons of carbon.[45] This would correspond to a global per capita emission rate of 1.16 tons. But in 2005, the U.S. population emitted at a rate of 5.32 tons per capita. If the rest of the world were to follow suit, this would amount to nearly 32 billion tons, or a 417% increase. (If we factor in an increase in world population to 9 billion—that expected by mid-century—the number rises to nearly 48 billion tons, or a 677% increase.) In light of this, suppose a group of countries were to try to ensure a global ceiling at the level of a twenty percent cut on 1990 emissions. This would amount to a cut of 1233 tons per year, and set a global ceiling at a total of 4931 million tons. How might this ceiling be broken? The answers are stunning.

First, imagine that the world consisted only of people emitting at the current American rate.[46] How many people could be accommodated without breaking the ceiling? The answer is a mere 927 million. In other words, if either the Chinese or the Indians (with populations of over 1 billion people) emitted like Americans, they would easily break the ceiling *all by themselves, even if the rest of the world cut its emissions down to nothing.* Similarly, if they emitted at current American levels, all of the available emissions could be consumed by a coalition of medium-sized countries that included Brazil, Pakistan, Bangladesh, Nigeria, Russia, and Japan. In other words, even if China, India, Europe, the United States, and the rest of the world emitted nothing, this group could break the ceiling all by itself.

Second, consider a slightly more realistic scenario. Suppose that when the twenty percent cut were put in place, most of the countries outside of the cooperating group did not cut their emissions at all, but rather continued to emit at their current levels. In other words, suppose that most of the noncooperators adopted a passive "holding pattern" on their own emissions, and so implicitly aided the cooperators in the task of enforcing a global ceiling at the level of a twenty percent cut. What kind

45. The following figures are drawn from Marland 2008. Emissions are sometimes reported as tons of carbon dioxide, rather than carbon. This gives higher numeric values (as CO_2 is heavier), but the same qualitative results.

46. Arguably, the U.S. rate is not a good benchmark, since it is anomalously high even among the rich countries. Still, similar results would emerge even if one used the much lower rate (of around 3 tons per capita per year) characteristic of many other developed nations. The basic lesson is that according to the science humanity at large cannot emit at such rates without causing severe environmental damage and perhaps catastrophe.

of defection from this norm would be sufficient to erase the cut? In other words, how feasible would it be for a small group of countries outside of the initial cooperating group to break the ceiling even if most noncooperators stabilized their own emissions at current levels? The answer is: very feasible. As an illustration, if they increased their per capita emissions to current American levels, *Pakistan and Bangladesh could manage it all by themselves.* Here are the numbers. In 2005, Pakistan had a population of 165 million people, and per capita emissions of 0.24 tons; Bangladesh had a population of 158 million people and per capita emissions of 0.08 tons. If both countries increased their per capita emissions to current U.S. levels, this would amount to a net increase of more than 1660 tons, which is nearly a third more than is needed to break the ceiling.[47]

In my view, such results are breathtaking. Still, they may underestimate the size of the problem for the optimistic analysis. First, it is not clear that the current U.S. per capita rate exhausts the potential interest in increasing energy consumption, and therefore (given current technology and prices) extra carbon emissions. One indication of this is that, prior to the 2008 election, even the United States was planning a 30 percent increase in energy use over the next few decades, mainly fueled by coal and oil. Other things being equal, this would push the American per capita emission rate up to nearly 7 tons per year.[48] Second, world population is projected to increase by 2 to3 billion people (roughly 30–50%) in the next fifty years. This substantially increases the number of people to be accommodated under the cap. Hence, it makes potential cuts much more vulnerable to undermining. Third, the current scientific consensus is that a global cut of twenty percent is only relevant as a short- to medium-term target (for one or two decades) at best. By 2050, a global cut of the order of 50–80% appears to be needed. To put this into perspective, an 80% cut corresponds to a total carbon budget of only 1233 million tons. But Brazil could break this all by itself if Brazilians emitted

47. Marland 2008.

48. Other things may not be equal. It is true that the per capita emission rate in the United States has remained in the range of 5.25–5.60 tons from 1988–2005, and that the per capita rates from other high emitters such as Australia and Canada have also stayed in a (slightly lower) range during that period. So, perhaps the per capita rate can stabilize at a high rate. Still, as we have seen, this is not comforting given the large reductions in global emissions that are necessary given the science.

at current U.S. per capita levels (again even if the rest of the world emitted nothing). More realistically, if all were to emit equally under an 80% cut, the global average for emissions would have to be a mere 0.2 tons per capita for 6 billion people, and 0.14 tons per capita for 9 billion people. In other words, on average each citizen of the world would have to emit significantly less than the average Pakistani does now.

In context, then, the optimistic scenario is untenable. Any small or medium-sized group formed to combat the problem could not achieve its goal without wider cooperation, and would probably absorb astronomical costs even in trying. The claim that a limited coalition of countries could effectively address climate change is therefore false or, at best, deeply misleading. Combating climate change requires the cooperation of at least all countries of significant size.[49] Partial cooperation is false for climate change.

b. Internal Motivation

The internal motivation claim also faces a serious challenge. In particular, of its two components, passive cooperation appears to be false, and this undermines marginal cooperation as well. The core problem facing a small group of countries trying to deliver a global ceiling is that there are strong incentives for noncooperators to undermine the cooperative effort. Consider the following. The relevant costs and benefits to the different parties are three: the public good of having a ceiling on emissions (shared by all); the costs of having a ceiling (borne only by the members of the cooperating subgroup); and the marginal economic benefits of breaking the ceiling (open to all). From the point of view of the noncooperators, then, there is competition between enjoying the public good and the potential marginal benefits of breaking the ceiling. But, in the circumstances of climate change, it seems highly likely that the benefits for noncooperators of breaking the ceiling will exceed those of maintaining it. If this is right, the

49. The countries that might not be needed are only those with low emissions and small populations. Moreover, even this claim is fragile. If fossil fuels became very cheap because most of the world was not using them, who is to say that a small nation would not find reasons (and/or technology) to consume at what currently count as astronomical levels, and so break the ceiling in that way?

noncooperators will be motivated to undermine the efforts of the cooperators and break the ceiling.

Why would noncooperators be motivated to break the ceiling? Allow me to clarify this point by considering two possible objections. *(This section may be skipped by those uninterested in such technicalities.)*

The first objection maintains that, since they are simply following their business-as-usual emissions, the noncooperators are already emitting as much as is economically beneficial to them, so there will be no incentive for them to increase their emissions at the margin. Thus, passive cooperation is true after all.

The basic problem with this objection is that it suggests that the economies of most countries are already in an equilibrium state with respect to emissions. This seems false. First, currently, the main constraint on the energy consumption of most countries is budgetary: countries consume as much energy as they can afford. Hence, other things being equal, as they get richer, countries will consume more. Moreover, there is a positive feedback. On standard economic assumptions, energy consumption is strongly linked with economic growth, and fossil fuels are a very cheap source of energy. So, in general, as countries consume more energy and emit more carbon dioxide, they get richer, and as they get richer, they consume more. In short, given current economic realities, so long as they pursue economic growth, individual countries have a strong interest in additional energy consumption and so in emissions. Thus, there is an initial presumption against passive cooperation.[50]

Second, there is good reason to believe that an agreement by some countries to limit emissions might shift the incentives for the others further away from passive cooperation. This is because the relative costs of carbon emissions to those outside the cooperating group seem likely to go down

---

50. Moreover, there is no end in sight. As we saw above, given that most countries are far from American (or even European) levels of per capita emissions, they are far from achieving even the current (perceived) gains from the cheap energy associated with high emissions. Furthermore, even those with high per capita emissions rates do not think that they have exhausted the gains from energy consumption. We might add to this that the gains from emissions are tangible, immediate, and accrue directly to those consuming, whereas the costs of extra consumption—the increased risk of negative climate impacts—are intangible, deferred, shared across all countries, and accrue disproportionately to the world's poor and future generations. Given this, growth in emissions is a natural default position.

with an agreement. For one thing, sources of carbon emissions (such as coal and oil) might become relatively cheaper as demand for them in the cooperating countries subsides in light of regulation; for another, industries which use fossil fuels intensively will be motivated to migrate away from the cooperating countries to places where they can emit more cheaply, without having to pay taxes (or for permits) for their emissions.[51] Under such scenarios, there would be strong incentives for noncooperators to increase emissions beyond their previous business-as-usual projections.

The second objection to the claim that noncooperators will be motivated to break the ceiling relies on the idea that the emissions ceiling might be a threshold good, so that breaking it would undermine the public good completely. In other words, suppose the atmosphere were just below an important concentration of carbon dioxide, the breaching of which would result in a global catastrophe, such as a sudden reversal of the thermohaline circulation. Suppose also that the cooperators would continue to maintain their total emissions at the level which would be required to stay beneath the threshold if the noncooperators were not to increase emissions, but they would not try to offset additional emissions by the noncooperators. Then one might have a subsidiary game between the noncooperators. With such a rigid threshold, each noncooperator would have to weigh the high costs of breaching the threshold (losing the public good) against those of emitting more (gaining the marginal benefits of extra consumption). Under some circumstances—for example, if breaching the threshold involved real catastrophe for each noncooperator—there would be a strong case for passive cooperation.[52]

There is something to be said for this analysis of at least part of the climate change problem. In particular, if one assumed that individual countries really did represent the interests of their citizens across generations, then it would be reasonable for them to engage in passive cooperation with respect to critical climate thresholds.[53] Still, there are

51. Barrett 2005. The technical term here is "leakage."

52. Note that if "noncooperators" did stick to their pre-agreement emissions profiles, this would amount to an implicit (and self-regulating) agreement amongst them to help maintain the emissions ceiling. Thus they would, in effect, turn into tacit cooperators. The only differences would be (a) that they would not be making the deeper cuts made by the original cooperators, (b) that they would not be making explicit "cuts" against their previous emissions, and (c) that they would be acting outside the agreement (albeit in concert with it).

53. Of course, under such circumstances, the relevant game may not be the optimistic one of the battle of the sexes, but the much more pessimistic one of playing chicken.

reasons for caution. One reason, of course, is that, given the intergenerational storm, the assumption of intergenerational representation is highly optimistic when it comes to the real world. (More on this in chapter 5 and 6.)

A second reason for caution is that the scenario is highly specific. First, each country would have to know exactly where the thresholds are, and how their contribution is likely to contribute to a breaching of one. Second, for each country the costs of losing the public good of maintaining emissions below the crucial threshold would have to outweigh the potential gains. (This matters because if, for example, the negative effects of an abrupt change were regional, countries outside the region might not be concerned about the breach.) Third, each country would have to believe that they could rely on the others to come to similar conclusions and act accordingly. There would be no point in maintaining one's own emissions in accordance with a given ceiling if someone else will cause the threshold to be broken anyway.

As it turns out, these circumstances seem empirically unlikely for climate change. Currently, our best grasp of the relevant thresholds is qualitative and vague. At the global level, if there are such tipping points, we do not know where they are, how many of them there are, or what it would take to break any one of them. Moreover, threshold breaking is likely to have different consequences for different countries, but these are unknown. Hence, countries lack the information relevant to fine-grained strategic calculations around possible thresholds.

A third reason to question the threshold objection is that an exclusive focus on tipping points seems inadequate to the problem at hand. For one thing, the incremental effects of climate change are serious enough to justify substantial action without calling on catastrophic abrupt changes, so this account of the problem would seem to leave out much of what is at stake. More importantly, as we shall see in chapter 6, this account ignores the large time lags involved in breaking any climate thresholds.

In summary, internal motivation appears to be false for climate change. Noncooperators seem to have strong reasons to be tempted by defection. This undermines passive cooperation, and also puts marginal cooperation under severe pressure. Given that partial cooperation also appears to be false, internal solutions to the climate problem seem unlikely. Hence, the battle of the sexes analysis is implausible.

IV. CONCLUSION

This chapter introduced an optimistic analysis of the global storm, and fleshed out that analysis by appeal to a simple public goods model and a simple game theoretic model, the battle of the sexes. It argued that in its usual form the optimistic analysis fails both in practice and in theory. In practice, neither Kyoto nor the Copenhagen agreement corresponds to the model of a small group of cooperators trying to enforce a ceiling on emissions, and so supply the public good of climate stability for themselves and others. In theory, none of the main claims of the broader battle of the sexes model—partial cooperation, internal motivation, and passive cooperation—seems likely to be true of climate change. The scale of the problem is simply too large, and the incentives to undermine an agreement too great, at least under current assumptions about energy consumption. For such reasons, I conclude that we should look elsewhere for a compelling account of the shape of the global storm.[54] Hence, in the next chapter, I turn to two more pessimistic approaches.

Cancún Update (December 2010): The Cancún meeting occurred too late for an update of the main text. However, some sense of the meeting can be taken from a few key quotations. The *Guardian* reported: "Most observers think the Cancún agreement kept the UN show on the road and made some progress on the principles of how to tackle global warming, while leaving the really difficult, concrete decisions to next year in Durban". Bolivia was the lone dissenter. Its ambassador, Pablo Solon, was reported to be unmoved by the cheering in the plenary hall, claiming: "This is a hollow and false victory that was imposed without consensus, and its cost will be measured in human lives. . . . They are thinking like politicians. The experts that know about climate change, they know that we are right. This agreement won't stop temperature from rising by 4C and we know that 4C is unsustainable." Christopher Huhne, the British climate minister, dubbed the Bolivians "radical outriders" with "an unrealistic level of ambition". However, *The New York Times* quoted Jeffrey D. Sachs, the Columbia University economist, as saying: "Nature doesn't care how hard we tried. Nature cares how high the parts per million mount. This is running away." (See Carrington 2010a, 2010b; Gillis 2010.)

---

54. See chapter 4 for two ways in which the optimistic analysis may remain useful.

CHAPTER 4

A Shadowy and Evolving Tragedy

*Pessimistic souls assume that the international response to climate change will go
the way of the prisoner's dilemma.*

—*The Economist* (drawing on Liebreich 2007)[1]

This chapter continues our investigation of the global storm. If the
optimistic analysis fails for climate change, what are the alternatives? In
particular, what might explain the last two decades of climate policy,
and so provide a better model of the problem for future discussion? One
obvious option is to invoke the prisoner's dilemma and the tragedy of
the commons. These models are ubiquitous in describing environmental problems, and climate change is no exception. On this view, the
climate crisis is a rather "common" tragedy.

This chapter explores the strengths and weaknesses of this account.
Section I considers the standard prisoner's dilemma model, and argues
that climate change deviates from it in significant ways. Section II claims
that these deviations reflect important differences between the prisoner's dilemma and the tragedy of the commons metaphors. Climate
change is an evolving tragedy, and this suggests further ways that it
might be resolvable. Section III explores some issues raised by this
analysis. First, climate change lacks the features that make resolution
empirically likely. Second, the analysis neglects the vital issue of fairness,
and so is likely to underestimate what is at stake. Third, and most
importantly, even the evolving tragedy account neglects the problem of

---

1. Citing the *Economist* piece, the Wikipedia entry on prisoners dilemmas states: "In
environmental studies, the Prisoner's Dilemma is evident in crises such as global climate
change . . . therefore explaining the current impasse."

intergenerational buck-passing. These issues threaten to undermine the analysis. Section IV asks whether the evolving tragedy model can be revived by appeals to either normative nationalism, or to the relevance of shadow solutions to the perfect storm. Section V argues that both Kyoto and Copenhagen make the shadow solution account plausible. Hence, both the battle of the sexes and tragedy of the commons models remain relevant to climate change, albeit in degenerate forms.

I. CLIMATE PRISONERS?

1. An Initially Plausible Case

The prisoner's dilemma analysis demonstrates that in some situations individuals reasoning purely on the basis of their own values can be led to make decisions that are suboptimal in terms of those values. Chapter 1 introduced the standard prisoner's dilemma model and suggested that the problem can be (roughly) characterized in terms of two core claims:

> (PD1) It is *collectively rational* to cooperate: each agent prefers the outcome produced by everyone cooperating over the outcome produced by no one cooperating.
>
> (PD2) It is *individually rational* not to cooperate: when each agent has the power to decide whether or not she will cooperate, each (rationally) prefers not to cooperate, whatever the others do.

Are these claims true of climate change? Initially, this seems plausible. For example, at first glance it is attractive to interpret the situation facing individual members of the current generation, or particular firms, as a multi-agent prisoner's dilemma.[2] Assume for the moment that the members of the current generation and individual firms accept PD1. Suppose, for example, that they care sufficiently about themselves, future generations, animals, and nature that they do not want catastrophic climate change ever to occur. Hence, they prefer that everyone cooperate to prevent climate change rather than that no one cooperates. Still, there may be powerful

2. I consider the extension to countries below.

incentives to defect, so that PD2 also looks plausible. On a standard view of what is at stake not overpolluting (with greenhouse gas emissions) tends to involve either a reduction in energy consumption, or else an increase in energy costs. But both involve sacrifice on the part of individuals and firms. In the case of individuals, the sacrifice is of consumption goods, ways of living to which people are attached, and (again, on a standard under-standing of things) self-interest more generally.[3] In the case of firms, on the standard assumptions that it is cheaper to overpollute than not, and that cheaper energy is a comparative advantage when one is competing in the market place, the sacrifice is of competitiveness.

On such assumptions, it is plausible to think that individuals and firms in the current generation have the following preference structure:

1st preference: I overpollute, you don't.
2nd preference: No one overpollutes.
3rd preference: Everyone overpollutes.
4th preference: You overpollute, I don't.

But this, of course, is a prisoner's dilemma preference structure. It sug-gests that, other things being equal, when left to their own devices each individual and firm will chose a strategy of overpolluting, even though this gives each agent only their third preference, and not their second.

Assuming the prisoner's dilemma model appears to have additional practical benefits. Recall that the main appeal of classifying climate change as a battle of the sexes was that such problems have internal solutions. In other words, they may be resolved by appealing to fairly narrow considerations, without having to change the incentives facing the parties.[4] Given this, such problems seem relatively easy to address. But if climate change is a prisoner's dilemma, internal solutions are not available. Hence, in that case, it seems that we must seek external solutions, such as payoff changes.[5] However, this leads to an important

3. For a more nuanced view, see chapter 2.

4. Notice the "may" here. Internal solutions may require the identification of a salient rallying point. In the case of climate change, this is made difficult by the complex nature of the problem.

5. One might also engage moral motivations. Ultimately, I suspect that this is necessary. But here I am comparing the usual two models under standard assumptions about motivation.

point. External solutions can resolve *both* prisoner's dilemma and battle of the sexes problems; hence, if we are unsure about whether a given problem is one or the other, but are nonetheless determined to solve it, then employing external solutions appears to be our best strategy. In other words, if there is reasonable doubt about whether a given situation is a prisoner's dilemma or a battle of the sexes, there is a presumption in favor of employing solutions which apply to both: if one tries only the internal methods appropriate to the battle of the sexes, then one might fail.[6] Hence, if in doubt, there is a practical reason to go with the prisoner's dilemma interpretation. This reason is especially pressing when there are strong reasons to believe that failure to solve the problem would be catastrophic, as there are in the case of climate change.

2. Deviations

On standard assumptions then, the prisoner's dilemma analysis seems plausible, and we have practical reasons to favor it in the case of doubt. The core features of that analysis—PD1 and PD2—appear to carry over to a central aspect of the problem, the way in which it is driven by the consumption decisions of individuals and firms. Hence, we might say that these agents accept I&F1 and I&F2, where these claims are identical to PD1 and PD2.

At this point, however, we may notice that the climate problem also diverges from the standard story of the prisoners in some very significant ways. Suppose we begin by simply extending the standard story

---

6. There is an additional reason to favor external solutions. Even if the intragenerational problem were a battle of the sexes, the relevance of this fact would be undermined by the background presence of the intergenerational problem. So far, we have simply assumed that problem away in this section, but in practice it will likely corrupt the presence in the current generation of concerns for the distant future. Similarly, localized variants of the intergenerational problem occur within the present generation. For example, governments and businesses are typically headed by elites whose time-horizons are extremely limited. They have a strong incentive to ignore altogether, or at least defer action on, problems whose solutions demand high costs to be instituted on the present set of voters and other politically influential groups for the sake of benefits to those who do not currently have any political power.

from two to many prisoners. If we do so, the prisoner's dilemma seems to have the following additional features:

(PD3) Each agent must make only one decision. (Whether or not to confess.)

(PD4) The decision is "all or nothing" and there are no intermediate options. (The options are "confess or not confess.")

(PD5) A single defection is decisive: it is enough to render the cooperation of other parties completely ineffective. (Confession by one prisoner is sufficient to doom the others.)[7]

(PD6) The decision must be made without any information about what the other agents have actually done. (The decisions are simultaneous.)

(PD7) There are no independent considerations to be taken into account. (The only topic at issue is jail time.)

By contrast, a natural reading of the climate problem facing individuals and firms generates sharply different claims:

(I&F3) Each agent must make multiple decisions. (They must decide how much to pollute for a range of purposes and over a period of time.)

(I&F4) The decision at a particular time need not be all or nothing, since there are intermediate options. (In addition to overpollute or not, the agent may decide on the level of overpollution.)

(I&F5) At a particular time, neither the defection of any one agent, nor even that of all agents, is decisive. Even so, such noncooperation does progressively erode the cooperative outcome. (The longer overpollution continues, and the more people contribute, the worse the situation gets.)

(I&F6) Each agent could make future decisions in light of information about what others have done in the past. (The decisions are multiple and spread out in time.)

(I&F7) There are independent considerations to take into account. (For example, one's wider social and economic relations with other actors.)

What difference do these divergences make? Do they undermine the point of the prisoner's dilemma analysis? I think not. To see why, let us turn to the other familiar model, the tragedy of the commons.

---

7. This is the most natural extension of the two-person case. As we shall see, this assumption is not made in the tragedy of the commons metaphor.

II. AN EVOLVING TRAGEDY

The Tragedy of the Commons captures the logic of a whole spectrum of envi-
ronmental disasters that we have brought upon ourselves . . . . We pump carbon
dioxide into the atmosphere as though there were no tomorrow.

—Ken Binmore (Binmore 2007, 67)

In chapter 1, I described the tragedy of the commons as a prisoner's dilemma involving a single common resource. As we shall now see, this description was too simplistic. Interestingly, while the parable of the tragedy of the commons shares the core features of the prisoner's dilemma, it also accommodates the divergences just mentioned.

Let us begin by rehearsing again the classic story. A group of herdsmen graze their animals on common land. Each aims to maximize his own profit, and asks himself whether he should add further animals to his herd. Weighing matters, he realizes that the main benefit of each extra animal (the price fetched at market) accrues directly to him, but the main cost (the degradation of the commons) is shared by all herdsmen. Moreover, he sees that his own share of the cost is easily offset by the benefits of the sale. Hence, the herdsman faces a strong incentive to add extra animals, and this is true for all herdsmen, since they face the same situation. Thus, all add animals, and this leads to a systematic overgrazing of the commons that is ruinous for all.

The central features of the tragedy of the commons are identical to those of the prisoner's dilemma. On the one hand, each herdsman prefers the commons to remain intact rather than go to ruin. So, each prefers that all maintain a sustainable herd rather than increasing the size of their herds indefinitely. Thus, roughly speaking:

(TC1) It is *collectively rational* to cooperate: each agent prefers the outcome produced by everyone cooperating over the outcome produced by no one cooperating.[8]

On the other hand, when each has to decide, each herdsman chooses to add to his herd. Hence, roughly speaking:

---

8. In the example, each herdsman prefers the commons to remain intact rather than go to ruin. So, each prefers that all maintain a sustainable herd rather than increase the size of their herds without limit.

(TC2) It is *individually rational* not to cooperate: when each individual has the power to decide whether or not she will cooperate, each person (rationally) prefers not to cooperate, whatever the others do.[9]

In essence, the paradox familiar from the prisoner's dilemma is repeated. Since each herdsman has the power to decide whether or not he will cooperate, then, given TC2, no one cooperates. (Each adds animals to his herd.) But this means that each ends up with an outcome that he disprefers over an alternative outcome that is available. For according to TC1, each prefers the cooperative over the noncooperative outcome. (Each prefers that the commons remains intact.)

So far, so good. However, now we must note that, despite their fundamental affinity, the parable of the commons diverges from the prisoner's dilemma in important ways. Most prominently, Hardin's description of the case suggests that each herdsman faces a *marginal* decision: whether to add one animal, and then another. He says:

> As a rational being, each herdsman . . . asks, "What is the utility to me of *adding one more animal* to my herd?" . . . the rational herdsman concludes that the only sensible course for him to pursue is to *add another* animal to his herd. *And another* . . .[10]

We can make sense of this claim if we consider the following (I assume common) interpretation of the story. Suppose that at the outset the commons is at or close to its optimal carrying capacity. Then, the herdsmen make a sequence of marginal decisions to add extra animals that begins to erode the land, presumably by diminishing the amount and quantity of good grass available. This process ultimately results in a collapse of the pasture by removing the grass altogether. Hardin himself does not specify the precise mechanism by which this collapse comes about. But suppose we assume that every month each herdsman goes to market and decides to add one more animal, with the result that all herds increase at a steady rate. In this scenario, if the common is large, the number of herdsmen small, and the amount of erosion caused by each extra animal limited, ultimate collapse will likely take some time to result.

9. In the example, when each has to decide, each herdsman chooses to add to his herd.

10. Hardin 1968, 307, emphasis added.

This interpretation of the classic story leads us to the first two divergences. Each herdsman seems to confront neither a single decision (PD3), nor one that is all or nothing (PD4). He does not ask himself about the *maximum* number of animals that he could add, and then decide whether to add *this amount or none at all*. Nor does he contemplate adding all of those he would like to add *at the same time*. Instead, he considers only whether he should add an extra animal at the margin. However, having made the decision to add one animal this month, he then faces the same question next month, and so on. Hence, there are multiple decisions to be made (i.e., TC3 and TC4 mirror I&F3 and I&F4).

This leads to the third divergence. In our interpretation of the story, although each particular herdsman's decision to add an animal contributes to the ongoing degradation of the commons, none is sufficient to bring on complete disaster all by itself, at least in the early stages. In other words, no single defection is decisive. Unlike the case of the prisoners, where the confession of one is sufficient to doom the rest (PD5), the effect of any herdsman's defection is itself marginal. It *erodes* the collective good—making the full collectively rational outcome unattainable—but does not make further cooperative efforts pointless. The tragedy of the commons is an *evolving* one. It is the cumulative effects of marginal decision making that result in collective ruin (i.e., TC5 mirrors I&F5).[11]

If a commons scenario evolves, this raises some important issues. One is that it becomes possible for some features of the situation to change over time. Consider, for example, the fourth divergence. The herdsmen (unlike the prisoners) may have the opportunity to make later decisions in light of further information. Suppose, for instance, that there are marginal impacts each time the herdsmen all add one more animal. For example, in response to everyone's monthly purchase, the grass gradually becomes less available, and what remains of lower quality, so that the animals are noticeably less well fed. This may have implications. First, it may alert the herdsmen to the effects of their behavior. Second, other things being equal, it will affect the incentives they face. Some component of the cost-benefit calculation for adding

---

11. Philosophers will notice the similarity between the evolving tragedy and paradoxes of choice such as the sorites, and the puzzle of the self-torturer. I cannot pursue these matters here. For some observations about their relevance to environmental affairs, see Andreou 2006, 2007.

yet another animal is altered, and presumably for the worse. Third, the evolution of the problem may give rise to new options. If the common has not yet crashed, more limited goals may be achieved even in the face of some defection (PD4 again). For one thing, agents who have failed to cooperate for some period may change course in order to preserve what is left of the commons. Degradation may be stabilized at a particular level, or even reversed. For another, in the absence of this, even if some subset of agents cannot prevent disaster all by themselves, they may be able to have an effect on the speed at which it comes about. Hence, for example, they may be able to buy time for further efforts to secure cooperation.

It is easy to miss these potential features of the commons situation, since Hardin himself assumes that each marginal decision has exactly the same answer ("Add one more!") so that the logic of the commons grinds remorselessly on despite the divergences. Given this, in Hardin's tragedy, the sequence of marginal decisions has the same cumulative effect as if all of the extra animals had been added at once (namely, disaster for all). However, this is simply an assumption on Hardin's part, and does not follow from the other characteristics of the commons story. This is important because when we consider real world scenarios, we must ask whether the assumption holds in practice. After all, this may make a considerable difference to whether and how the situation can be addressed.

It seems clear that the general claim of marginal decision making is important to the logic of the commons. So, why make it? Why not claim instead that each herdsman decides how many total animals to add to his herd, and comes to the conclusion that he should add infinitely many? Two reasons come readily to mind. The first is that in the real world, herdsmen will face other constraints, and especially a budget constraint. Indeed, the size of their existing herds probably already reflects such constraints. Given this, any real herdsmen would be making decisions at the margin based on, for example, the limited availability of extra funds. The second reason is that there will be some number at which the environmental costs of an increase in herd size would become so large even for a single herdsman that they outweigh the benefits. For example, under normal circumstances, even a very wealthy herdsman, facing no relevant budget constraint, would not consider adding a million animals to his local village common.

This would be simply self-inflicted disaster. The magnitude of the change would be sufficient to destroy all of his own animals, even though he also "spreads the costs around" by ruining the commons for others as well. Given this, there is presumably some limit to the incentive to add one more animal.

I note these reasons for a marginal approach because they have the potential to make a considerable difference to how one understands the tragedy of the commons model. Each of them constitutes a constraint on the application of TC2, the claim about individual rationality. This is important in theory and in practice. If such constraints are operative, they might forestall the rush to disaster.

Consider first the budget constraint. In principle, its presence may buy time. This can be helpful if the time is well-used. For example, in the case of climate change, global emissions are currently much less than they might be if everyone were as well off as the citizens of the United States and the European Union. As we saw in chapter 3, per capita emissions in the United States are roughly five times those in China, and fifteen times those of India. In China, of course, they are rising quickly. But the fact that the Chinese and other low emissions populations cannot instantly leap to U.S. per capita levels buys some time. If we can use that time to develop alternative energy sources and effective mitigation technology—as many hope—then perhaps we can alter the incentives so that the logic of the commons is undermined.[12]

Second, consider the notion that there might be some limit to the incentive to add extra animals. Under some conditions, this may give rise to a natural stopping point on the road to disaster. Although things can get bad, perhaps there is some floor to the level of degradation. In many settings this might constrain the corrosive effects of the core claims, and so reduce the magnitude of the problem to something less than complete disaster (but see also chapter 6).

Still, third, we should note that there are situations in which the evolving tragedy itself corrodes natural stopping points. For example,

---

12. This point can also aid the optimistic analysis discussed in chapter 3. If the time period of a given agreement is short enough, and noncooperators cannot increase their emissions fast enough, then an attempted global cut pursued by a group of major polluters may buy some time.

suppose that some herdsmen are not profit maximizers, but do have a strong concern for at least maintaining their current income. (Call them *satisficers*.) On a plausible understanding of the situation, the addition of animals by others makes this more difficult. As there is more grazing on the common, each animal gets less (or lower quality) food, and so is less valuable than before. Hence, in order to maintain their incomes, even the satisficers must add extra animals. Degradation of the commons by some provokes further degradation by others, even if they were content with the original status quo. Moreover, the worse it gets, the stronger these incentives become. In essence, through these undercutting feedbacks, the erosion of the commons becomes a dramatic *race to the bottom*.[13] Unfortunately, this effect may be manifest in the case of climate change. Costs can be deferred across generations, so that many initially salient "floors" (such as nasty climate "tipping points") cease to be salient to those making the relevant decisions. Moreover, the effect of reaching disastrous thresholds may be strongly counterintuitive: it can actually make matters worse for the further future, and even set off the equivalent of an intergenerational arms race (chapter 6).

Given this discussion, it is easy to see the appeal of the pessimistic analysis of climate change. On common assumptions, the two core claims shared by both the prisoner's dilemma and tragedy of the commons seem to fit the situation facing individuals and firms. Moreover, the tragedy of the commons analysis does well in explaining the nature of the climate problem as an evolving tragedy. The decisions to be made are marginal, multiple, and subject to new information, budget constraints, possible floors, and undercutting feedbacks. This adds an extra layer to the analysis that is helpful. Some of these features (such as possible floors and budget constraints) offer prospects for solution, and others (such as the possibility of a race to the bottom) reveal deeper threats. Each makes clear that when approaching a particular real world problem, we should not simply rest with the basic prisoner's dilemma/tragedy of the commons claim, but press harder. As I have emphasized from the outset, a correct

---

13. The phrase "race to the bottom" is associated with U.S. Supreme Court Justice Louis Brandeis, Ligget Co. v. Lee (288 U.S. 517, 558–9), 1933.

understanding of the problem can be a vital first step on the path to solutions.[14]

III. BEYOND PESSIMISM

Most who have described climate change as either a prisoner's dilemma or a tragedy of the commons make three further assumptions that must be discussed.[15] They suppose (1) that climate change is primarily an international problem, and so (2) conceive of the relevant actors as individual countries, who (3) represent the interests

14. A further alternative to the prisoner's dilemma model is the stag hunt or "assurance problem" (see Skyrms 2001, 2004). The two are often conflated, but the stag hunt has a more promising structure. In the standard example, individual hunters must decide independently whether to hunt stag or hare. Hare they can get alone; stag hunting requires cooperation. Getting hare is okay, but the rewards are greater hunting stag. There are two stable equilibria(all hunt stag or all hunt hare) but all would prefer stag. (I thank Aaron James for pressing me to address this model.)

Is the global storm an ongoing stag hunt? At first glance, it seems not. Consider three key differences between this and my evolving tragedy of the commons. First, the cooperative outcome is stable. There is no threat of defection from all hunting stag. Second, the dispreferred outcome is also stable. There is no threat of a race to the bottom. Third, the dispreferred outcome is not tragic. All can survive hunting hare. On standard assumptions, none of these claims seems plausible in the case of climate change. Instead, defection is a realistic threat that escalates the problem, and catastrophic climate change would be a tragedy for all.

Despite this, there may be a place for the stag hunt analysis. A fourth key difference between the models is that in the stag hunt what it is best for one party to do depends on what the others actually do (whereas in the prisoner's dilemma they are better off defecting no matter what the others do). Hence, if one could really assume away the intergenerational storm, then perhaps it is plausible to claim that nations representing the interests of all their citizens across time would not defect from the cooperative solution once it was in place. This may be correct. Unfortunately, it is hard to say in advance because successfully "assuming away the intergenerational storm" may radically transform the global situation, and so make many different accounts of the remaining intragenerational problem plausible (see section 5.IV).

15. The assumptions are commonplace. For a few academic examples, see Soroos 1997, 260–1; Danielson 1993, 95–6; Barrett 2005, 368; Sandler 2004, 58–9; Binmore 2007, 67; Helm 2008, 234; Harris 2010, 86.

of their people in perpetuity. Initially, this extension looks appealing. First, a plausible case can be made that the core claims hold. On the one hand, presumably no country that genuinely represents the interests of its future citizens would want severe climate change, as this would have bad, and possibly catastrophic, consequences in the long term. Hence, each would prefer the outcome produced by everyone restricting their emissions over the outcome produced by no one doing so (i.e., TC1). However, on the other hand, since noncooperation is likely to mean relatively cheap energy, there are (it is assumed) very large economic incentives to defect from any agreement. Hence, given the chance to decide, each country might prefer not to restrict its own emissions, no matter what the others do (i.e., TC2).[16] Second, the tendency to defection highlighted by the tragedy of the commons analysis appears to be reflected in the political history. As we have seen, international climate change policy has been characterized by voluntary commitments made and broken, agreements to reduce emissions without any corresponding action, and significant attempts to free-ride.

Despite its initial appeal, the extension of the pessimistic analysis to countries does not so easily explain the persistence of the climate problem. This is for the surprising reason that it is not pessimistic enough; instead, it sharply underestimates the problem at hand. Let me now offer three justifications for this claim.

1. Standard Solutions

The first justification emerges from the fact that in the real world, situations that resemble the tragedy of the commons are not usually irresolvable. For one thing, since all parties to such situations can see that their individual actions leave everyone worse off than they would otherwise be, all should be motivated to seek an agreement. For another, there are circumstances in which stable agreement should be possible.

---

16. In my view this claim applies better to a given generation than to a given country viewed as existing in perpetuity. This undercuts the tragedy of the commons analysis as a general account of the climate problem, but it still retains a more limited relevance. See the next section.

For example, solutions can often be achieved when parties are involved in repeated interactions, and when broader concerns are at stake.[17] Moreover, importantly, such circumstances ought to obtain in the climate case.[18] Not only must countries make repeated agreements on greenhouse gas abatement over time, but they do so in a context where global cooperation on other issues—the global economy, security, and other environmental issues—must also take place.[19] Given all this, if global warming really were most fundamentally a tragedy of the commons, and if the countries of the world were serious about it, we would expect a truly comprehensive global agreement on greenhouse gases, involving strong links to other cooperative issues, such as trade and security. But we have now had nearly two decades without much interest in either. What might explain this?

One factor is that on closer inspection climate change lacks many of the characteristics that make solving traditional commons problems easier. For example, Elinor Ostrom has shown that local communities are capable of resolving (and often do resolve) commons problems under certain conditions.[20] Specifically:

> Effective commons governance is easier to achieve when (i) the resources and use of the resources by humans can be monitored, and the information can be verified and understood at relatively low cost . . . ; (ii) rates of change in resources, resource-user populations, technology, and economic and social conditions are moderate . . . ; (iii) communities maintain frequent face-to-face communication and dense social networks—sometimes called social capital— that increase the potential for trust, allow people to express and see emotional reactions to distrust, and lower the cost of monitoring behavior and inducing rule compliance . . . ; (iv) outsiders can be excluded at relatively low cost from using the resource . . . ; and (v) users support effective monitoring and rule enforcement.[21]

Unfortunately, such claims are not very encouraging when it comes to climate change. First, the features that encourage cooperation seem

17. Axelrod 1984; Ostrom 1990.
18. Liebreich 2007.
19. Ward 1996, 850–71.
20. Ostrom 1990.
21. Dietz, Ostrom and Stern 2003, 1908.

largely absent.[22] On the one hand, climate change lacks the characteristics listed above. From an international perspective, social capital is weak, not everyone supports regulation, excluding noncooperators from emitting carbon is very difficult (if not impossible), emissions are difficult to monitor, and the rate of change in emissions in at least some economies is considerable (e.g., China is building new power plants every month). On the other hand, additional factors relevant to the international context also appear to be lacking. In the international relations literature, we are told that cooperation is more likely when there is recognition of a shared threat, leadership by a dominant nation, and a sense of sufficient mutual self-interest.[23] But in past climate negotiations each of these has been hard to come by.

Second, as we saw in chapter 1, such deficiencies are exacerbated by a number of further technical and political issues. For one thing, a shift away from fossil fuels, the main anthropogenic source of greenhouse gas emissions, may have profound social consequences. At the very least, such a shift would require considerable technological advances and large investment, and may threaten powerful private interests, such as those of the multinational energy companies. But it also has the potential to significantly (perhaps dramatically) change existing social and economic arrangements. In addition, scientific uncertainty about the precise magnitude and distribution of impacts, especially at the national level, complicates action. Politicians and their populations face real difficulties in trying to forecast the implications of any given magnitude of climate change for their own countries. Last, but not least, any actual allocation of greenhouse gas emissions to different countries will raise fundamental issues of international fairness and have large, and potentially radical, implications for the distribution of social and economic benefits.[24]

Third, in any case the most salient level of the problem is (arguably) not local, but global. As the Stern Review put it, climate change (like other global environmental issues) "cannot be resolved through local community action" but requires cooperation between governments, because it "require[s] choices to be made between

22. Stern 2006, 512; Dietz, Ostrom and Stern 2003.
23. Stern 2006, citing Sandler 2004.
24. See chapter 11 and Baer et al. 2007.

clear and immediate local incentives and diffuse, long-term global benefits."[25]

2. International Fairness

The second justification for the claim that the extended pessimistic analysis underestimates the climate problem is that it neglects basic issues of international fairness. Though this is standard in game theoretic thinking, in this case it undermines the project of understanding the basic problem. As usually understood, the tragedy of the commons analysis of the climate problem diagnoses the difficulty as one of securing cooperation between self-interested states through a normal political bargaining process ("mutual coercion, mutually agreed upon").

25. Stern 2006, 512; Wiener 2007. Recently, Ostrom has cautioned against seeing climate change as exclusively global, and emphasized the multiple levels at which action can occur. Hence, she advocates a "polycentric" approach "where many elements are capable of making mutual adjustments for ordering their relationships with one another within a general system of rules where each element acts with independence of other elements" (Ostrom 2009, 33; quoting Vincent Ostrom 1999, 57). In addition, she claims that empirical support for conventional approaches to collective action is weak, and that "a surprisingly large number of individuals facing collective action problems do cooperate." Hence, her message is that we should not be too pessimistic in our motivational assumptions, or underestimate the potential for normal motivation to drive solutions.

There is much to be said for Ostrom's approach. Still, I doubt that it undermines our analysis. One reason is that the main drivers of her solution are reciprocity and the presence of (positive) externalities of cooperation at different scales (e.g., the health benefits to individuals of cycling versus driving). The first faces difficulties construed intergenerationally (Gardiner 2009a). The second faces two challenges. Intragenerationally, if it were easy to marshal such co-benefits, then there remains a mystery about why more is not being done, which is what we are currently trying to explain. Hence, more needs to be said. Intergenerationally, it is not clear that such benefits exist, or if they do, that they are sufficient to overcome the intergenerational storm (see chapter 5).

A second reason is that Ostrom regards trust and fairness as crucial to a solution. Hence, her view is compatible with the claims (1) that if agents are motivated only by self-interested or generation-relative concerns, this poses an ethical problem, (2) that (therefore) resolving the global storm is likely to require moral motivation, and (3) that to the extent that action is not taking place, this is some evidence that the ethical challenge is not being met.

Implicitly, this assumes either that the background circumstances of different countries are such as to make bargaining between them fair, or that fairness is not important. But both assumptions are unwarranted, and morally problematic.

The first assumption is highly questionable for two reasons. The first is that there are *skewed vulnerabilities*. Those countries that have made the biggest contributions to the problem are the industrialized countries. But these countries are (perceived to be) much less vulnerable to the impacts of climate change, at least in the short- to medium-term. This is partly because of their industrialization, and the wealth and infrastructure it has given them, and partly because of their geographical location in the temperate zones. By contrast, the countries most vulnerable to climate change are those who have emitted least. These are those poor nations which have not yet industrialized and have very weak infrastructure for dealing with shocks. These are disproportionately located in the tropical and subtropical climate zones where the greatest climate impacts are likely, at least in the short- to medium-term. In short, those likely to be the biggest victims of climate change are also those least responsible for the problem.

The second reason has to do with the background state of global justice. Many people believe the existing world system to be seriously unjust, especially because of the history of colonialism, currently pronounced global poverty and inequality, and the role of rich nations in structuring existing transnational institutions.[26] If this is correct, then it complicates the attempt to model the problem of climate change as a bargaining situation confronting existing countries under their present circumstances. There are real worries that such a model merely facilitates what Henry Shue calls a *compound injustice*: powerful countries taking further advantage of those already exploited by the current structure. Moreover, Shue identifies a specific reason for this worry in the case of climate change. Existing discussion in the developed countries and international settings is almost exclusively focused on mitigation. Though mitigation is vital, the pronounced neglect of other concerns that are equally pressing for the less developed countries, but not for the developed—such as adaptation and

26. Shue 1996; Pogge 2002.

compensation—suggests a strong bias away from the concerns of those most vulnerable to serious climate impacts.[27]

It is worth noting that the problems of skewed vulnerabilities and compound injustice are obscured by the tragedy of the commons analysis in concrete ways. First, the analysis is essentially forward-looking. It considers only future costs and benefits, not past contributions to the problem. Hence, it ignores historical responsibilities.[28] But many believe such responsibilities to be of profound moral importance. Second, in applying the tragedy of the commons model, it is too easy to assume that all parties face identical costs and benefits from cooperation and noncooperation. (All are herdsmen with similar herds.) But this is unlikely to be true, at least in the short- to medium-term. The poor are much more vulnerable to catastrophic impacts than the rich. Moreover, this is not just true at the level of countries. Poor people are disproportionately vulnerable wherever they live, and this especially true of the world's poorest people, who live in conditions barely imaginable to most middle-class citizens of the developed countries, and whose basic survival depends on factors that are fragile, and which climate change is very likely to undermine.[29]

The fact that the tragedy of the commons analysis obscures many issues of fairness is of independent importance in the perfect moral storm. We should notice that a focus on that model facilitates the neglect of considerations that would, other things being equal, impose stronger burdens on the better off. At first glance, it is unfair for any agreement to ignore the disproportionately large contributions of the rich to causing the problem, the greater vulnerability of the world's poor to its worst impacts, and the issue of aiding and compensating its victims. When matters are obscured in this way, the problem of moral corruption looms large.

---

27. Shue 1990. Although both the UNFCCC and the Kyoto Protocol incorporate mechanisms for adaptation and the need for technological assistance for the developing nations in meeting mitigation targets, these mechanisms have received little attention and funding over time. See also Vidal and Adam 2009.

28. The approach is not alone in this. Some welfarist approaches, such as conventional cost-benefit analysis, also do so. See Posner and Sunstein 2008.

29. IPCC 2007c; Ebi 2008.

Against all of this, some may claim that the tragedy of the commons model remains intact because, in their view, fairness is not important. However, this claim is also dubious. First, and most obviously, the idea that fairness, or justice more specifically, is not an important value seems both false and, in the present context, probably self-defeating. I cannot defend the first view here, and so will simply assert it, hoping that most will find it plausible on its face. But it may be worth saying something about the second. One of the primary reasons to be concerned about climate change is that it has the potential to visit extreme suffering on innocent people. In my view, if we ignore such values, we neglect concerns *right at the heart* of the climate change problem, concerns that make it the kind of problem that it is. If this is correct, the idea that we would try to understand the climate issue, and yet deny that concerns about fairness and harm to the world's poor matter, is self-defeating. To neglect these concerns is to refuse to admit a central part of the challenge that faces us.

Second, and less obviously, given the need to secure genuinely global cooperation—the participation of at least all countries of significant size in a climate agreement—the idea that fairness can be neglected seems seriously unrealistic. Other things being equal, countries are unlikely to accept agreements that they deem to be seriously unfair to them. Moreover, not all of the poorer nations are desperately so, and some of those nations who have contributed least to causing the problem to this point (such as China and India) do have serious political power, and could easily undermine any agreement that they perceive to be unfair to them. Part of the task of crafting an effective global agreement on climate change will thus involve paying due respect to fairness.[30]

Of course, this need not imply that a complete background understanding of international justice is required, especially just to get started. One reason comes from historical precedent. Thomas Schelling argues that our one experience with redistribution of this magnitude is the post–World War II Marshall Plan. In that case, he says, "there was never a formula . . . there were not even criteria; there were 'considerations' . . . every country made its claim for aid on whatever grounds it chose," and the process was governed by a system of "multilateral reciprocal scrutiny," where the recipient nations cross-examined each other's claims until they came to a consensus on how to divide the money allocated, or faced

---

30. Athanasiou and Baer 2002.

arbitration from a two-person committee. Though not perfect, such a procedure did at least prove workable.[31] Given the urgency of our current problem and the large theoretical issues involved in devising a perfectly just global system, this is an encouraging thought. Perhaps a vaguely fair system can see us through in the short- to medium-term, even if over time the pressure for something better can be expected to grow.[32]

Unfortunately, of course, such claims suggest a further obstacle to action mentioned earlier in chapter 1. Pressing forward on climate change creates a moral risk for the developed nations, since it may embody a recognition that there are international norms of ethics and responsibility, and reinforce the idea that international cooperation on issues involving such norms is both possible and necessary. This may encourage attention to other moral defects of the current global system, such as global poverty and inequality, human rights violations, and so on. But if the developed nations are not ready to engage on such topics, this creates a further reason to avoid action on climate change. Indeed, it puts pressure on the claim that there is a broader context of interaction within which the climate problem can be solved. If some nations believe strongly that it is not in their interests to engage with issues of global justice, and they assume that creating a climate regime leads down this path, then this lessens the incentive to cooperate.

I conclude that the basic tragedy of the commons model is, at best, seriously incomplete. The model's neglect of differences in vulnerability, and especially the plight of the global poor, means that it obscures vital features of the problem at hand. This is so even considering only the spatial dimension that is supposed to be the focus of the model. But matters become much worse when one considers the temporal dimensions of climate change.

3. Intergenerational Ethics

The third, and most serious, reason that the pessimistic analysis underestimates the problem is the intergenerational storm (introduced in chapter 1). In chapter 5, we shall examine this challenge to ethical action

---

31. Schelling 1997; Miller 2009.
32. Cf. Buchanan 2006.

in more detail. But here I simply assume it, and ask what difference its presence makes for how we understand the global storm as such.

Let us begin with a quick reminder of the shape of the intergenerational storm, and its relevance to climate change. This storm arises because of a pronounced temporal dispersion of causes and effects. In the case of climate change, this is caused mainly by the long atmospheric lifetime of the main greenhouse gas, carbon dioxide, and by the fact that some of the basic physical systems influenced by the greenhouse effect (such as the oceans) are subject to profound inertia, so that changes play out over centuries and even millennia.[33] This is important because it suggests that whereas fossil fuel emissions have immediate and tangible benefits for present people, many of the most serious costs are likely to be substantially deferred to future generations. Hence, there arises the possibility of intergenerational buck-passing: the current generation can consume with some level of impunity, passing a major portion of the costs of its behavior on to the future. Worse, the problem is iterated: each new generation finds itself in the same position. Moreover, it threatens to arise at various levels of analysis. Intergenerational buck-passing is possible not only for whole populations, but also on a smaller scale, for entities such as social classes, business elites, and political administrations.

The possibility of intergenerational buck-passing is relevant to the global storm because it places pressure on the background assumption (made by both the optimistic and the pessimistic analyses) that governments can be relied on to represent the interests of their countries' citizens in perpetuity. If a particular generation of government leaders sets its political priorities predominantly by considering the consequences during its own tenure, or if a particular generation of voters selects its leaders primarily by considering the likely effects during their own lifetimes, then the background assumption is false. In the real world, of course, this seems highly plausible. Thus, the presence of temporal dispersion threatens to undercut the very motivation of countries to act on a problem like climate change. This poses a much more severe public policy challenge than would an ordinary tragedy of the commons; and in my view this is the real global warming tragedy.

33. IPCC 2001a, 16–17; Archer et al 2009.

IV. LINGERING TRAGEDY

Given the intergenerational storm, the tragedy of the commons analysis fails as a *general* account of the problem posed by global climate change. But is it still relevant? In this section and the next, I consider two reasons for thinking that it is.

1. Normative Nationalism?

The first arises if one thinks that the background assumption that governments represent the interests of their countries' citizens in perpetuity *ought* to be true. In that case, the tragedy of the commons analysis might contribute to our understanding of the climate problem by showing what that problem would look like if countries and their leaders were appropriately motivated. I do not want to reject this suggestion outright. But I do have reservations.

The first is that, if the intergenerational storm is serious—as I think it is—simply stipulating that countries should think intergenerationally is an audacious move, and one that has the effect of assuming away a big part of the problem. This would be worrying in any setting, but it is more so when there is a threat of complacency. Given the lurking problem of moral corruption, we should beware "solutions" that tend to push the intergenerational problem to one side.[34]

My second reservation concerns the fact that the "in perpetuity" assumption simply takes for granted that the intergenerational problem should be solved *domestically*, by each country looking after the interests of its own citizens. Again, this is a bold claim, and appears to be unmotivated. In particular, it is far from clear that intergenerational responsibilities in general arise only in the domestic setting. These days most political theorists accept international norms of basic human rights, and believe both that these constrain what states can legitimately do, and impose duties on them to protect and aid citizens of other nations.[35] It is highly plausible to think that these or similar duties are relevant to

34. Moreover, representing the interests of one's own citizens in perpetuity is left unanalyzed. This is troubling given the theoretical storm.

35. Rawls 1999; Miller 2007.

the present case.[36] In particular, it is widely thought that climate change threatens the basic human rights of many future people.[37] Why then should we simply assume that the intergenerational responsibilities of states end at their own borders?

My third reservation concerns the further implicit assumption that a successful solution to the intergenerational storm will both leave the traditional account of the state more or less intact, and justify turning over whatever is left of the global storm to such states for bargaining. Given our current theoretical naïveté, such assumptions seem unwarranted. For example, several influential views in contemporary political philosophy are based on a highly cosmopolitan individualism: they assume that what matters primarily in global ethics is the individual. For such views, addressing intergenerational justice may already require looking past states and their traditional roles in radical ways, and generating new institutions. But if such reforms were implemented, why would we assume that the best way to address any problems that remain would be to revert back to the old model of bargaining between traditional nation states? Would there even be any such states, according to the radical cosmopolitans? (If not, why reinvent them for this purpose?) Would there even be any remaining problem for the old model to deal with? If one already had new institutions to deal with intergenerational justice, perhaps they would either already address the problem, or else radically transform how it should be understood.[38]

My final reservation about the assumption that governments should represent the interests of their countries in perpetuity is that if one truly makes it, the tragedy of the commons analysis may not apply. In favor of the analysis, it is still very plausible to think that idealized governments who represent the interests of their people in perpetuity would prefer the outcome produced by every country cooperating to solve the climate problem over the outcome produced by complete

36. In addition, since nations do not last forever, one might wonder whether existing countries ought at least to represent the interests of any successor nations or political groups that might occupy the same territory.

37. Caney 2010.

38. Note that I am not arguing for a radical cosmopolitan view here, nor am I assuming that some such view must be true. I am merely trying to show that the assumption that the tragedy of the commons model would still be relevant after the intergenerational storm is dealt with is contentious.

noncooperation. (In short, TC1 remains plausible.) However, against the analysis, it is not at all clear that idealized national representatives would accept that, when each country can decide, it is in the *intergenerational* interests of their own citizens not to cooperate, no matter what the other countries do. (In other words, TC2 is in doubt.) This part of the tragedy of the commons analysis seems somewhat plausible if one is looking only at the interests of an individual generation, because it can overconsume emissions and pass the worst risks of its own behavior on to the future. But it is not clear what would justify the intergenerational version of such a claim. Why, from an atemporal perspective, would it be in the interests of a particular country—that is, in the interests of all or most of its citizens from now into the indefinite future—to overconsume carbon emissions no matter what every other country does?[39] Presumably, a country with genuine intergenerational concern would not want catastrophic climate change to hit any of its generations. Indeed, it may well believe that it would be much better for most of its future citizens if the world acted quickly and decisively to address the threat and moved to prepare its infrastructure for a post-carbon, alternative energy future, even if this imposed significant costs on the current generation.

These reservations raise significant questions about the true shape of the global storm if it is understood as nested within the intergenerational storm. Specifically, if the intergenerational dimension could really be set aside, it is far from clear either that the intragenerational dimension of climate change would resemble a tragedy of the commons, or that the relevant actors would remain nation states as we conventionally understand them. Solving the intergenerational problem might transform the intragenerational situation. Since we do not yet know what it would take to solve that problem, we cannot rule this out from the outset. Despite this, there is reason to persist with the tragedy of the commons analysis. Absent a solution to the intergenerational storm, this (and the battle of the sexes) seems relevant to understanding shadow solutions.

---

39. One answer would be if there were undercutting feedbacks that facilitate a race to the bottom. But we should ask if there is a significant incentive for any country to defect when it considers the matter intergenerationally, and whether other countries who think intergenerationally might have strong incentives to punish such defection.

2. Shadow Solutions

Once one identifies the intergenerational storm, it emerges that any given generation really confronts *several versions* of the global storm. Three are particularly perspicuous. The first is the one highlighted in the literature. It assumes that each generation of a given country takes on the task of representing the interests of all of its citizens in perpetuity. This version of the global storm is genuinely cross-generational, and so assumes away the intergenerational storm. (Call this the "cross-generational global storm.") The second version is less familiar. It assumes that each generation of a country takes itself as predominantly representing only the interests of its *current* citizens. This storm is merely intragenerational, and this has important implications. Suppose that we assume that the interests of any current generation of a nation's people will be predominantly concerned with benefits and burdens arising *during their limited generational horizon* (as discussed in chapter 2). Then, the second global storm will focus on how to distribute just this limited set of benefits and burdens among the current generation of the world's people. Plausibly, it will simply fail to recognize, or at least to adequately consider, the claims of future generations. (Call this the "current generation's global storm.") A third version of the global storm is an even more degenerate form. In it, the current generation of the world's political and economic leaders represents their own interests, focusing on the next few election or business cycles. (Call this the "governmental global storm.") This sharply reduces the range of considerations taken as relevant.

Now the existence of different versions of the global storm gives rise to an obvious problem. Collectively rational solutions to these distinct commons problems may be very different. For example, with climate change, it is probable that the current generation's global storm calls for much less mitigation of greenhouse gas emissions than the cross-generational global storm. Moreover, each problem also probably calls for different kinds of action. For example, other things being equal, in the case of climate change, we would expect a policy motivated by the current generations' concerns to be biased against mitigation, which has a long-term time-horizon, and towards efforts such as geoengineering and military investment, which may be more useful to current people (see chapters 6 and 10).

One upshot of all this is that even if a particular generation of decision makers or the public appeared to resolve *some version* of the global storm—say by generating some kind of global agreement—we could not infer from this that they have really succeeded in confronting the perfect moral storm. Perhaps it is only the current generation or governmental global storm that has been confronted, when the cross-generational version is really the most morally relevant form. In practice then, any actual agreement to act on climate change may represent what I shall call a *shadow solution*. It may indeed constitute significant action, but without actually responding to the true nature of the moral problem. Instead, it might address only those aspects of the problem that affect the concerns of present political and economic leaders, the current generation more generally, or the affluent, narrowly construed. This is an important thought. With it in mind, let us now turn back to climate politics.

V. CLIMATE POLICY IN THE SHADOWS

The worry about shadow solutions gains substantial support from the history of climate policy. In general, the overall pattern of procrastination, delay, and false promises between 1990 and early 2010 suggests the prevalence of the current generations' or governmental global storms (see chapter 3). More specifically, I shall now argue that even the most high profile attempts at action, the Kyoto Protocol and Copenhagen Accord, seem beset by shadows. In essence, it is highly plausible to believe that, at best, these efforts tried only to do something limited to protect the interests of the present generation, narrowly defined, and that, at worst, they served merely as a cover for business-as-usual. Either way, they did almost nothing to aid future generations, or the planet more generally.

1. Kyoto's Achievements

Let us begin by examining what commitments Kyoto actually contained for particular countries and regions after the renegotiation of 2001. First, and most prominently, the *United States was absent*. This is to be explained most directly by the intervention of politically powerful industries who produce or are heavily reliant on energy.[40] But there are other reasons as well. It was widely said that the U.S. faced very high marginal costs as a result of its past energy practices and future energy policy.[41] It also seemed likely to benefit considerably from migration of dirty industries and a lower international price for oil. Moreover, it appeared to suffer least in the medium term from the impacts of warming given its geographical location and the economic resources potentially at its disposal for adaptation, and of all major countries it seemed to have the least grassroots political interest in global warming.

Second, consider the *less developed countries*. Though formally included in the Kyoto agreement, these countries were not expected to make substantial reductions in either current or projected emissions. Instead, their development "needs" were seen as paramount during the commitment period.

Third, of the other major players, many agreed to the Protocol in exchange for incentives that undermined its effectiveness. For one thing, Russia consented partly because its emissions were already much lower than its 1990 benchmark because of the economic collapse following the end of the Soviet Union. Hence, its "target" imposed no constraint on its own activities, and it hoped to receive revenue from the sale of its excess carbon credits to other countries. (See below.) For another, Japan and Canada lobbied hard for increases in their allocations based on already existing carbon sinks (especially forests). Moreover, these and many other countries expected to meet some of their targets by buying unused capacity from Eastern Europe and the countries of the former Soviet Union.

Finally, consider *Europe*, on the face of it the most concerned party. Even there, the European Union planned to meet its obligations as a block, and so had an easier time because of gains made in the 1990s by the largest emitters, Germany and the United Kingdom, for unrelated economic, not environmental, reasons. So, even the European Union's projected "cuts" were not as large as they initially seemed.

40. Three days after a front-page story in the *New York Times* reported that the administration was planning to cut carbon dioxide emissions, intense lobbying by conservatives within and without lead to a sharp about-turn by President Bush. This involved not only withdrawal from Kyoto, but a commitment to produce 1,300 new power plants over twenty years, and so significantly *increase* emissions. See Revkin 2001a, 2001b, 2004; McKibben 2001, 37–8.

41. Victor 2001.

These sharp limitations on the global commitment to reduce emissions were apparent even at the time that the Kyoto and Bonn-Marrakesh agreements were being negotiated. Indeed, they gave rise to sharply conflicting estimates of how much those agreements could achieve. The original 1997 protocol intended to impose a 5% cut on 1990 levels for the Annex I countries. This was clearly weakened by subsequent negotiations, especially in Bonn and Marrakesh, but by how much? This was unclear, but two initial suggestions captured the extremes.

The more optimistic suggestion, prevalent in the immediate aftermath of the Bonn and Marrakesh meetings, was that the revised Kyoto deal would represent a 2% cut over 1990 levels for participating Annex I countries. A 2% cut can be viewed in two ways. On the one hand, considered from a static perspective, it seems unimpressive. For one thing, since the early nineties climatologists have been maintaining that a reduction in anthropogenic carbon emissions of the order of 60–80% from 1990 levels was ultimately needed to maintain climate instability at its current level. So, 2% seems a paltry contribution to the ultimate goal. For another, talk of a shift from a 5% (Kyoto) to a 2% (Bonn-Marrakesh) cut obscures matters in an important way. In terms of the total *volume* of emissions for the industrialized countries, a 2% cut without the United States is, of course, drastically less than a 5% cut that includes the United States. In short, this was not truly a loss of 3%. For the original proposal, "in absolute terms, the cutback for the United States from 1995 levels [until 2012] accounted for *more than half* of that required for the OECD overall and almost exactly [equaled] the increase allowed to Russia."[42] Hence, since the Bonn-Marrakesh deal did not involve the United States, and required very substantial extra concessions to Russia, it both lost the country responsible for much of the initially projected cutback and increased the effective allocation to the country with the greatest increase. In other words, the overall volume of emissions allowed increased dramatically with the new deal.

On the other hand, from a dynamic point of view, a 2% cut even by only some industrialized countries looks considerably more important. If one considers what would be achieved against *projected* emissions under business-as-usual, it is clear that if the participating Annex I countries really reduced emissions by 2% from 1990 levels, they would

42. Grubb et al. 1999, 161–2.

be making substantial cuts by 2008–2012, on the order of 10–15%. Still, it should be said that even looked at in this way, the net effect of Bonn-Marrakesh would not look impressive from a global point of view. A 2% net reduction in two decades from only a few countries seems a pretty weak response to the global storm, especially in a context where world-wide emissions from 1990 to 2012 stood to increase by more than 30%. This hardly seems a stellar achievement given that by 2012 we will be "celebrating" the *twentieth* anniversary of the Rio Earth Summit and the Framework Convention.

Sobering as this analysis is, even at the time some analysts suggested that the idea that the revised agreement provided for a 2% cut over 1990 levels for the participating countries was wildly optimistic, because the changes to the Protocol between Kyoto and Marrakesh were even more dramatic than initially recognized. One prominent study suggested that the revised agreement merely limited the growth of participants' emissions to *9% above 2000 levels* (rather than imposing a cut on the much lower 1990 levels). Moreover, it added that under (the then-current) slow economic growth, this might amount to no cut at all, since business-as-usual emissions would be lower than the constraint.[43] If this projection turned out to be correct, then at best Kyoto-Marrakesh would do very little to reduce emissions, and at worst it would do absolutely nothing.

How then did matters turn out? At first glance, the picture looks rosy. According to the United Nations, by 2006 the emissions of the industrialized nations taken together had fallen to 4.7% below 1990 levels.[44] Given this, the original Kyoto goal of a 5% reduction seemed easily within reach.[45] Moreover, if one ignores U.S. emissions, this collective reduction would become an impressive 17%. On the face of it, this seems like a notable achievement, and produced newspaper articles with headlines such as "World Emissions on Target to Meet Kyoto Cuts, says UN Climate Chief" (the *Guardian*), and "World Ahead of Kyoto Emissions Targets" (*New Scientist*).[46]

---

43. Babiker et al. 2002, 202. They also claimed that most of any reductions that might occur would be in non–carbon dioxide gases.

44. UNFCCC 2008; Adam 2008.

45. EEA 2008. This was partly because of anticipated offsetting projects in developing countries.

46. Adam 2008b. In their main texts, both articles register some of the concerns given below.

Unfortunately, this rosy facade conceals vital facts. Most prominently, it focuses on the wrong numbers. First, and most importantly, almost all of the decline in the industrialized countries' collective emissions is due to the economic collapse in the former Soviet bloc following the fall of communism. By 2006, emissions in these "economies in transition" (as they are known in the agreement) were indeed down by 35% from 1990 levels. However, elsewhere in the industrialized world, they had *increased by almost 10%*.[47] Indeed, beyond the former Soviet bloc, only six of the twenty-three industrialized Kyoto countries had cut emissions since 1990.[48] So, the impression of widespread progress in cutting emissions created by the overall UN numbers is seriously misleading.[49]

Second, the comparison with 1990 masks more recent growth. From 2000–2006, emissions actually increased even in the former Soviet bloc countries, by 7.4%, and in the industrialized nations more generally by 2.3%. Hence, it would be a mistake to think that there is any kind of collective downward trend; on the contrary, emissions are rising in the industrialized world as a whole. This is concealed by the rosy picture because of the magnitude of the earlier crash.

Third, by 2006, many of the individual nations who were supposed to make significant cuts under the Kyoto arrangements were struggling. Emissions in Japan were up by 13%, in Canada by 26%, and in New Zealand by more than 30%.[50] In the EU, there were also problems. By 2005, Italy was up 12%, Austria 18%, Ireland 25%, Portugal 40%, and Spain 52%.[51] Nevertheless, overall the EU seemed on track when taken as a block, since these rises were compensated for by the stability and even slight reduction of German and British emissions since the mid-nineties. Still, even this achievement may be chimerical. Some economists say that "it is reasonable to assume that the outcome would not have been markedly different" had Kyoto not occurred, and that the numbers "flatter the true underlying position" since the EU targets do not include aviation and shipping which have

47. Adam 2008a. I thank Paul Baer for help in confirming these numbers.

48. Zarembo 2007.

49. This is not a criticism of the UN documents themselves, which have clear graphics to show some of these trends. See UNFCCC 2008.

50. Marland 2008.

51. Helm 2008, 219.

"risen strongly since 1990," cause greater damage, and are more than sufficient to "undermine the limited reductions claimed as directly caused by the Kyoto Protocol targets."[52] Beyond this, of course, emissions in those countries outside of the agreement were left unchecked. In the developing world, both China and India's emissions roughly doubled between 1990 and 2005; in the developed world, U.S. emissions rose by 20% from their already high level. More generally, as we have seen, global emissions were up by nearly 30% during the period from 1990–2006, and by 2007 were growing at an even faster pace than before. Given such facts, we should surely acknowledge, as a columnist in the *Los Angeles Times* did in 2007, that Kyoto "has been a failure in the hard, expensive work of actually reducing greenhouse gas emissions."[53]

Such results are surely disturbing. However, there is more to be said, because there is a sense in which the misleading initial impression of success is no accident. Recall that Kyoto was originally negotiated in the period 1995–97. But by then it was already evident that emissions in the economies in transition had dropped by around a third, that this amounted to a 5–7% reduction from 1990 for the industrialized world as a whole, and that a further drop in the former Soviet bloc countries was probably to be expected. It was such facts that made the benchmark of 1990 and the figure of 5% salient. As it turned out, the hit taken by the emerging economies would have reduced total emissions from the industrialized world by 10% in 2006 (rather than 4.3%) had not the other nations increased their emissions over the period.[54] In light of such numbers, it is tempting to conclude, as an article in the Associated Press did in 2008, that "the collective Kyoto target was always going to be reached."[55] If so, then what was the point? Unfortunately, the perfect moral storm provides an answer. Giving the *impression* of meaningful action without actually acting might be highly convenient for those in its grip. Sometimes shadow solutions are to be expected.

52. Helm 2008, 214.
53. Zarembo 2007.
54. Michael Grubb points out that even if the United States had been included in the original "5% cut," the original Kyoto agreement would have involved at best only stabilization of emissions at the then-current level for the industrialized countries, and likely some increase, given the concessions on sinks. Grubb et al. 1999, 155.
55. Bloomberg 2008.

2. Kyoto as a First Step

Kyoto's enthusiasts typically object to such complaints by stressing that the 2008–2012 targets were intended only as the first round in an ongoing schedule of such measures. Once it is up and running, the thought goes, the international climate regime can be strengthened so as to make a serious contribution to addressing global warming. This position was ubiquitous in the immediate aftermath of Bonn-Marrakesh, but has also been echoed more recently. In December 2008, Yvo de Boer, executive secretary of the UN climate secretariat, said the following in answer to the question "Has Kyoto worked?":

> In terms of emission reductions achieved, the answer would be no. A 5% cut is a pretty small step on what will be a long and arduous journey. On the other hand, Kyoto has had great success in putting an architecture in place. Monitoring and verification systems, carbon markets, technology transfer, and funds for adaptation have all been mobilised by Kyoto. I think this is a fabulous architecture that we can build on the road to Copenhagen.[56]

There is something to this argument; but there remain several reasons to be cautiously skeptical. First, it is not obvious that Kyoto has done very much to further the cause of an eventual regime.[57] In fact, the basic architecture has left many of the central issues for subsequent agreements to sort out (see below and chapter 3). This is disappointing given the goals of the Framework Convention, and the fact that it was ratified in the early nineties. Perhaps Kyoto is a foundation; but if so, it is a very limited one with respect to the scale of the problem.

Second, it is not clear that small and slow steps are best. Optimism about Kyoto seems to rest largely on a charitable interpretation of the motivations of those countries, such as Germany and the United Kingdom, who appeared at least to try to provide real global leadership by to some extent going it alone, and showing that something can be done. This understanding may indeed be plausible for at least some leaders, governments, and organizations, and it has precedents in global

---

56. Adam 2008.
57. Eilperin 2008b.

environmental policy, such as with the Nordic countries' attempt to deal with acid rain and the United States's efforts to address CFCs.[58] Still, such efforts usually have only a limited time-horizon. If they do not provoke wider support fairly quickly, they tend to break down.[59] Hence, we should not be complacent about the pace of change. Indeed, the struggles of many countries to contain emissions growth should sound a note of alarm.

The third reason for skepticism about the "first step" analysis is the history of the climate policy. Given the false promises of the past and the difficulties of securing even the weak Kyoto agreement, we should not just blithely assume that international climate policy will be transformed (and soon) into a more meaningful program (e.g., that targets will be tightened, developing countries will agree to emissions ceilings in future periods, and the United States will come on board in a serious and decisive way). Moreover, even if these things do happen, we should not presume that they are motivated by, or reflect, the interests of future people. Why assume that action in the future will be easier than in the past? In many ways, the most testing times for international climate policy may be yet to come. As we shall see below, progress towards a second commitment period has been far from encouraging.

Fourth, with this in mind, even on an optimistic reading of what has occurred, we must also consider a shadow explanation for limited action, that actors are really endorsing a moderated wait-and-see policy. Faced with significant evidence of warming, perhaps some countries are concerned primarily with the possible short- to medium-term impacts on their present populations and so see it as in their interests to try to *slow down* the rate of increase of emissions during that period, in particular by not committing themselves to long-term capital investments that increase the risks. This would explain why some may be willing to take small, cautious steps that can be reviewed on a decade-by-decade basis. Perhaps taking low-cost measures to slow down the warming (as opposed to arresting it) is perceived to be in the interests of those who may be around for another twenty to forty years, and so a solution to the current generations' global storm (see also chapter 10).

58. Soroos 1997, 226.
59. Ibid.

3. Shadow Compliance

Some support for this skepticism comes from the limited structure that Kyoto did bequeath, the current narrow focus of climate policy, and the subsequent experience of Copenhagen. Let us begin with Kyoto's much-lauded compliance regime.

According to Bonn-Marrakesh, parties who do not meet their targets in a given period are to be assigned penalties in terms of tougher targets in subsequent periods (subject to a multiple of 1.3 times the original missed amount) and to have their ability to trade emissions suspended.[60] Initially, these penalties seem reasonably serious. But two considerations cast doubt on this appearance.

First, the sanctions appear substantial because it is natural to assume that permit trading will be a major way in which parties meet their obligations, that permits will be costly, and that the 1.3 multiple is punitive. But the latter two claims are questionable. Some have argued that the price of permits will be extremely low absent U.S. participation, and that the 1.3 multiplier is equivalent merely to "a borrowing provision with an interest rate of 5 percent per annum."[61] This suggests that the costs of noncompliance are small and the deterrent effect therefore minimal.

Second, even if the penalties were in themselves serious, it is not clear that they could be made to stick. Not only is there the obvious, general problem of the lack of an effective enforcement mechanism in international relations, but there are also three specific obstacles to compliance. To begin with, if tightening the future emissions target of a country that has missed its current target ratchets up the costs of compliance in the next period, this might make it impossible for the country to remain in the regime. Given that countries want others to remain in the regime, there is some incentive to avoid punishing transgressors, provided that they are at least somewhat cooperative. In addition, since subsequent targets are not necessarily set prior to the knowledge that the existing target will be missed, the procedure is open to corruption. Future targets can be relaxed so that compliance sanctions do not actually bite. Finally, and most importantly, the sanctions themselves are easy to evade. The background protocol structure contains two major opt-out clauses. On the

60. Marrakesh Accords 2001.
61. Bohringer 2001; Babiker et al. 2002, 197.

one hand, while Article 18 of the Kyoto Protocol requires that the enforcement of compliance rules be approved by amendment to the Protocol, Article 20 stipulates that such an amendment is binding only on those parties that ratify the amendment. Hence, any party can escape compliance penalties simply by refusing to ratify the amendment necessary to punish it.[62] On the other hand, Article 25 of the FCCC specifies that any country can leave the regime at one year's notice, three years after the treaty has entered into force for it. Hence, all countries know that they can evade future penalties for current failure to comply with the treaty merely by exiting it at some appropriate point. They also know, given the fragility of the existing coalition, that other countries will not want this to happen; and that, since future targets are yet to be negotiated, there is an easy way to avoid this: one can simply be more generous with future emissions targets in order to offset the influence of any penalties.

The second reason to worry about a shadow solution concerns the limited focus of current climate policy. Recall the two basic questions of climate policy mentioned in chapter 1: where to establish a global ceiling, and how to divide emissions between nations. In practice, under the Kyoto system the latter question became primary, and the former was quickly pushed into the background. Moreover, the main political method for resolving disputes about national allocations was to allow recalcitrant nations extra emissions, and so drive up the global total. Given the possibility of shadow solutions, these developments are deeply suspicious, and may manifest corruption. If we are to resolve the intergenerational storm, the question of where to set the global ceiling over time appears to be of at least equal importance to that of how to distribute national commitments at a time. But the presence of that storm also makes it perfectly explicable why the current generation might tend to marginalize the intergenerational question, focus on issues of intragenerational allocation, and then tend to drive up even the very modest short-term global targets.

Interestingly, a focus on limited intragenerational aims may also help explain the usefulness of the battle-of-the-sexes models in accounting for the behavior of countries in addressing climate change. If only very limited action is wanted—a modest experiment in reducing emissions, say, or in investing in alternative energy or geoengineering—then a small group can achieve this. Given this, a degenerate version of the optimistic analysis

62. Barrett 2005, 384; 2007, 209.

of climate change (discussed in chapter 3) still has relevance. It can explain the shape of the governmental or current generation's global storms, even if it cannot explain the persistence of the more general climate problem.

I have more to say about how shadow solutions might evolve in chapter 10. For now, let us conclude this section with some discussion of how the search for Kyoto's successor also provides support for skepticism.

4. A Crisis in Copenhagen?

The Kyoto Protocol expires at the end of 2012, and negotiations have been ongoing since 2005 in search of its replacement (see chapter 3). These negotiations have yielded the Bali Action Plan, and now the Copenhagen Accord. The original intent of the Bali plan was to deliver a full and comprehensive agreement that could be accepted as a treaty in Copenhagen and then immediately sent off to national governments for ratification in order to meet the 2013 deadline. In advance of the meeting, this expectation seemed clear. For example, in 2008, Yvo de Boer, the UN's chief climate official, said:

> Copenhagen, for me, is a very clear deadline that I think we need to meet. And I'm afraid that if we don't, then the process will begin to slip . . . . one deadline after the other will not be met, and we sort of become the little orchestra on the *Titanic*.[63]

Even in late 2009, after the prospect of a full treaty had receded, British Prime Minister Gordon Brown stated: "Our aim is a comprehensive and global agreement that is then converted to an internationally legally binding treaty in no more than six months. . . . If by the end of next week we have not got an ambitious agreement, it will be an indictment of our generation that our children will not forgive. . . . Sometimes history comes to turning points. For all our sakes, the turning point of 2009 must be real."[64] Lars Løkke Rasmussen, Prime Minister of Denmark and host of the conference, cautioned: "We cannot do half a deal in Copenhagen and postpone the rest till later," adding that the agreement should be "precise on specific commitments" and "provide for immediate action."[65]

63. Monbiot 2009.
64. Brown 2009.
65. Lean 2009.

As it turned out, Copenhagen failed to deliver on these expectations. The Accord announced a goal of limiting the rise in global average temperature to 2C, as scientists had suggested, but offered no route to get there. Moreover, nations were simply invited to make their own pledges for action, and the document itself had not been endorsed (merely "noted" and not even "welcomed") by most of the world's nations. Even those who thought of the Accord as a "step forward" acknowledged that "much of the hard work lies ahead ... [and it] leaves a long list of issues undecided"[66], and U.S. president Barack Obama conceded that the Copenhagen commitments would "not be by themselves sufficient to get to where we need to get by 2050 ... and ... we're going to have to take more aggressive steps in the future."[67]

Many, however, were much more scathing. For example, in its editorials, the *Guardian* declared the Accord a "sham," stated that "a considered reading ... reveals that it is not just inadequate but in fact utterly empty," and concluded: "only two years ago, the world's leaders swore this would be the summit to build a new carbon order. ... It is a sad tribute to collective failure that the all-important question at the end of Copenhagen is: what happens next?" Such responses were far from unusual. Environmentalists labeled Copenhagen "breathtakingly unambitious," a "spectacular" and "utter failure."[68] George Monbiot, the columnist and climate campaigner, went so far as to say: "it would be hard to conclude that this is not the end of the process, because once you've lost your diplomatic momentum, once the red carpets have been rolled up and the cutlery has been cleared away, it's just very hard to regain it."[69] Such worries gained momentum after the original deadline for submitting national targets for 2020 (January 31, 2010) was declared "soft," and fewer than half of the countries participating at Copenhagen registered commitments. In contrast to the official goal of limiting global temperature rise to 2C, a UN analysis claimed that even if met the Accord's remaining commitments would likely raise global temperatures by more than 3C.[70] De Boer commented, "the window of opportunity

66. Fuqiang Yang, Director of Global Climate Solutions, World Wildlife Fund. Quoted in Guardian 2009.
67. Eilperin and Faiola 2009.
68. McKibben 2009; Bryony Worthington, quoted in Guardian 2009; Ward 2009.
69. Goodman 2009.
70. Gray 2010.

we have to come to grips with this issue is closing faster than it was before."[71] Shortly thereafter he announced his resignation.

VI. CONCLUSION

After the Bonn meeting, Margot Wollstrom, the Environment Commissioner for the European Union, declared: "Now we can go home and look our children in the eye and be proud of what we have done."[72] Over the last two chapters, I have argued that we cannot. From the theoretical point of view, climate change just does not look like the kind of problem that is well understood in terms of the optimistic or mildly pessimistic models with which we are most familiar in international relations. Though those models remain relevant in a degenerate form, the explanations they offer fail to highlight the crucial ethical dimensions of the perfect moral storm. From the practical perspective, it is difficult to interpret the Kyoto Protocol or its successor the Copenhagen Accord as sincere global initiatives to protect the interests of future generations from a serious threat, however well-intentioned some of their supporters may have been. As bad as this news is, there may be worse to come. Although international climate negotiations may be having very little effect on emissions, they do achieve *something*. Talk of historic and "meaningful" agreements creates the comfortable illusion that serious progress is being made, and this itself is a substantial obstacle to overcoming the climate challenge.[73] Sadly, the perfect moral storm provides an explanation. The twin specters of moral corruption and shadow solutions loom large.

These conclusions suggest that the global storm is only one aspect of global environmental tragedy. In addition, in cases like climate change, it is not the most important. The intergenerational storm frames the global, and ultimately determines much of its shape. This storm is much less appreciated. To it we now turn.

71. Black 2010.
72. Quoted in Brown 2001.
73. Arguably, the negotiations have also "stifled discussion of alternative approaches" and tied up the energy of many people of goodwill by becoming the "only game in town" for more than a decade. See Prinz and Rayner 2007.

PART C

The Intergenerational Storm

CHAPTER 5

The Tyranny of the Contemporary

The politicians in Copenhagen have the power to shape history's judgment on this generation: one that saw a challenge and rose to it, or one so stupid that we saw calamity coming but did nothing to avert it.

—Editorial run by 56 newspapers worldwide prior to the Copenhagen Meeting
(the *Guardian 2009*)

I'll be frank with you. I don't spend a lot of time really worrying about short-term history.
I guess I don't worry about long-term history, either, since I'm not going to be around to read it.

—Former U.S. President George W. Bush, on leaving office
(quoted by Eggen 2008)

We turn now to the intergenerational storm. I believe that the distant future poses a severe moral problem, the nature and extent of which has not yet been adequately appreciated. This problem is in some ways analogous to the problem of the tyranny of the majority that has historically played a large role in political theory. Hence, I call it the "tyranny of the contemporary." This tyranny can take many forms. The main aim of this chapter is to give a brief, initial account of its most perspicuous form by describing the central problem of intergenerational buck-passing and its main features.

I will also argue for three claims about the status of the central problem. First, it is the core concern of distinctively *intergenerational* ethics. It explains both why conceiving of the ethics of the future in terms of generations makes moral sense, and what is distinctive about generational issues.[1] Second, it occurs in a pure, long-term form manifest across human history and global populations, but also in degenerate forms that apply to shorter time periods and to social institutions. Third, it is manifest in the real world. In practice, it is neither rendered inert by fortuitous circumstance, nor overwhelmed by other future-oriented difficulties. I illustrate this through a discussion of our leading example, global climate change.

The chapter proceeds as follows. Section I posits several serious challenges to the idea that it makes moral sense to think in terms of generations. Section II introduces the central problem as a way of overcoming these challenges, using a playful example I call *the fairy tale*. Section III explains why this intergenerational problem has a particularly difficult structure; and section IV describes its features in more detail. Sections V–VII consider various obstacles to the application of the model, including the fact of intergenerational overlap among humans, the possibility of an invisible hand mechanism that drives social progress, and the philosophical nonidentity problem.

---

1. My position contrasts with that of Bryan Norton. Norton says:

> The philosophical problem of what we owe the future is not a single, monolithic problem, but rather an inter-related cluster of problems. For convenience, we group these sub-problems into three categories and give them somewhat descriptive names. They are: (1) *the distance problem*—how far into the future do our moral obligations extend? . . . (2) *the ignorance problem*—who will future people be and how can we identify them? And, how can we know what they will want or need, or what rights they will insist on? . . . and (3) *the typology of effects problem*—how can we determine which of our actions truly have moral implications for the future? (Norton 1998, 123–4. See also, Norton 1995.)

I do not want to claim that the problem of future generations is monolithic, nor would I deny that Norton's perceptive classification of sub-problems is useful. But I do think that none of the sub-problems Norton identifies is exclusive to the future, and that even collectively they fail to make clear why (at least some) ethical issues concerning the future should be conceived of in *generational* terms. My account, on the other hand, explains why there is a distinctively intergenerational problem about the future. Writers who may see the fundamental issue in terms close to my own include Goodin 1999, 247–54, and O'Neill 1993, 46–50. In the last section of the chapter, I explain why Norton's sub-problems do not overwhelm the issue I identify.

I. PROBLEMS WITH "GENERATIONS"

Ethical issues concerning future people are usually conceived of as problems of future generations. But this practice requires defense. For it makes two important assumptions: first, that it is both possible and useful to divide all of those who will exist into groups of contemporaries; and second, that this is the morally salient way of conceiving of them. But neither of these claims is obviously correct.

Consider first the attempt to divide humanity as a whole into generations. This faces a significant prima facie objection. Individuals do not come into and out of existence as temporally discrete classes. On the contrary, there is a continuum of entry and exit, a revolving door of births and deaths. In addition, even if one agrees that humanity should be so divided, the presence of the continuum raises difficult questions about exactly how and where generations should be individuated. Consider just three central issues.

First, there is the matter of determining the size of a generational unit. For example, some people define a generation in terms of replacement (e.g., the amount of time it takes for children to take the place of their parents); others do so in terms of the possibility of mutual interaction (e.g., future people are those whom people presently alive will not live to meet); and still others take a generation to be all those currently alive (so the relevant excluded group is those not yet born). This discrepancy is important in itself. After all, which unit should we choose? But it is also important because the choice of generational unit makes a great practical difference: the first definition suggests new generations at intervals of about 30 years[2], the second roughly 200 years, and the last about 100.

The second central issue is that, whatever the unit, there is the question of determining an appropriate starting point for each generation. To begin with, this choice can have a crucial impact on how—or even whether—a problem is seen in intergenerational terms. For example, say that one takes the position that a new generation appears every 30 years, and that one is trying to describe the

2. Notice that much depends on what replacement is taken to consist in. Thirty years assumes a Western model. But if to replace is simply to provide a net income to the family rather than a net loss, in some societies this will occur in late childhood, and a generation may be a mere 8–15 years; whereas if to replace is to become (say) a village elder, a generation may be much longer (50–70 years).

bulk of the twentieth century in these terms. Suppose then that one is trying to decide whether to start the generational scheme in 1901, 1911 or 1921[3], and that one takes this to yield three relevant generational streams:

TABLE 5.1

	1st Generation	2nd Generation	3rd Generation
Stream 1	1901–1930	1931–1960	1961–1990
Stream 2	1911–1940	1941–1970	1971–2000
Stream 3	1921–1950	1951–1980	1981–2010

Then, the choice of stream may make a very significant difference. For example, Stream 1 puts the cultural revolution of the 1960s in one generation (1961–1990), and WWII in another (1931–1960); but the second puts them together (1941–1970).[4]

More generally, there is the question of how one goes about choosing one starting point over another. In practice, much actual talk of generations seems to be indexed to major historical and social events or experiences, such as World War II, and the so-called baby boom. But it is not immediately obvious either why any particular event or experience should be chosen over another to define a generation, or, more importantly, why we should think that such divisions are morally relevant. Presumably, it would be odd to start speaking of "the Nixon goes to China generation," or "the Gilligan's Island generation." So, what makes "the baby boom generation" better? In demography the divisions between different generations are apparently often based on individuals' self-reports of the major historical events occurring during their own lifetimes.[5] However, to be relevant to intergenerational ethics, this practice would require further justification. Do we really want goods and opportunities to be allocated to people on this basis? If so, why?

3. Of course, there are infinitely many other possibilities: 1907, August of 1908, 24th December 1909 at 5 p.m., and so on.

4. The example works best if one is talking about the United States, since it became embroiled in World War II in November 1941, with the attack on Pearl Harbor. But, of course, nothing much depends on the example.

5. See, for example, Schuman and Scott 1989.

 The third central issue concerns what to say about intergenerational overlap. For one thing, on most definitions of the generational unit, one generation may be physically present during the "time" of another generation and affected by what occurs. For example, the baby boomers did not simply disappear when generation X first arrived on the scene on or around 1965, when they began to reach the age of replacement in 1995, or even with the election of the first post-baby boom president (Barack Obama) late in 2008.[6] But, given this, how do we deal with these "lingering generations"? Similarly, individuals have different life spans, so that while some people's entire lives may occur within a single generation, others may overlap with three or four generations. So, there is a question about whether we should treat the "persistent lingerers" differently.

These three issues imply both that any concrete proposal for a generational division requires specific defense, and that in many contexts this will make a great deal of difference to how and whether one conceives of a given problem in intergenerational terms. This already puts pressure on distinctively intergenerational ethics. But there is also a second, more general worry. Is it even morally desirable to make such divisions? Clearly, some rationale is needed for seeking to divide humanity into temporal classes in the first place. We must ask why might it be useful to speak of ethical obligations to future people in generational terms. For example, why not theorize purely in individualist terms, speaking only of future persons and how they are affected as such? Or, alternatively, why not focus on the overall long-term interests of a particular group (e.g., one's family, community, or nation)? Such divisions are familiar from normal political theorizing. So, why not leave it at that?

My proposal is that the use of the concept of a generation to structure talk of ethics and the future can be made sense of indirectly. Talk of "generations" gains its point from the need to confront a certain kind of severe moral problem that is best conceived of in generational terms. Given this, an account of intergenerational justice is one that provides an answer to the severe problem, since that is the point of a distinctively intergenerational theory. One advantage of this approach will be that it

---

6. There is some doubt among those who classify in this way as to whether President Obama really counts as a baby boomer, a member of generation X, or something in between. But the general point remains.

can explain and accommodate the use of intergenerational language across divergent temporal settings. Since the intergenerational problem can arise for groups of different temporal sizes and over different timeframes, it makes sense to be flexible about what one is willing to count as a generation.[7]

II. INTERGENERATIONAL BUCK-PASSING

To motivate this way of thinking, let us begin with an admittedly flippant example, which I shall call *the fairy tale.*[8]

1. The Fairy Tale

The fairy tale proceeds as follows:

> Once upon a time, there was a generation that confronted great challenges and survived them. It struggled through a time of global financial collapse, defeated a frightening, destructive, and evil enemy, and ostensibly made the world safer for freedom and democracy for generations to come. This generation inherited a mess, but cleaned it up and passed on a better world to the future. It earned the moniker, "the most splendid generation."
>
> The most splendid generation was succeeded by another generation, "the bloopers." This generation had a reputation in its youth for grand visions and

7. In this book, I am focusing on future-oriented difficulties: how earlier generations may act badly with respect to later generations. But the model is also relevant for past-oriented problems. If earlier generations have legitimate interests in what happens after their members are dead, and if later generations have some moral reason to take those interests into account, then if the later generations ignore these reasons, they may be taking advantage of temporal asymmetry in a morally reprehensible way. (See later footnote on overlap.)

8. The label reflects the fact that the example is intended to amuse, rather than accuse. Though it uses terms that bear some relation to the real world, this is only to bring out the intuitions I want to discuss. Some will detect a grain of truth in the example, but we should be cautious about thinking that it is anything more than a grain. Real intergenerational relations are complex, with much good and bad being done by each generation. (See, however, Willetts 2009.)

moral seriousness ("peace, love, and understanding"); however, when it actually came to hold the reins of power, it became more consumed by the pleasures of the moment, and self-aggrandizement ("sex, drugs, and reality TV"). Given this, it paid scant attention to the concerns of the future, and indulged in whatever activities it could that brought it soft comforts and profit in the short term, regardless of the long-term consequences. For example, the bloopers deregulated the financial markets, leaving the world vulnerable to a Great Depression–like crash; they provoked an international arms race and allowed the proliferation of weapons of mass destruction, making future wars more likely and more destructive; they polluted the natural environment with wild abandon, undermining the future integrity of the world's climate system and food supply; and so on. In short, the blooper generation lived fast and loose, caring little whether others suffered greatly and died young because of it. (Indeed, succeeding generations quipped that one of the bloopers' favorite anthems should have been reworded: "I hope I die before you get old.")

As things turned out, serious harms were indeed inflicted on the following successive generations (call them the Xmen, the yurts, and the zeds) as a direct result of the behavior of the bloopers. These generations really did see global financial collapses, horrific wars, environmental catastrophes, widespread famines, and so on. Like the most splendid generation before them, it was left to them to clean up a mess.

What should we say about the fairy tale? Does it have any moral import? Are there any lessons about intergenerational ethics to be learned from it? The obvious answer is that there are. Our hypothetical bloopers are a profligate generation. They squander their inheritance and the hard work of their predecessors, and they inflict serious harms on their successors. Moreover, they do all of this for the sake of cheap pleasures, and the comforts of easy living. Such a generation would receive harsh criticism from both the future and the past, and this criticism would be well deserved. Indeed, they should be ashamed of themselves. They fail to discharge their intergenerational responsibilities. Too much goes wrong on their watch, and too much of this is self-inflicted. Who would want to be a member of such a generation? Who would want to be implicated in its behavior?

The fairy tale is a useful hypothetical case. Moreover, it suggests the beginnings of a more serious analysis of intergenerational ethics. Presumably, the bloopers do wrong for many reasons. One is that they fail the past. They let down their predecessors (i.e., the most splendid and presumably at least some of those who came before them) by undermining the legitimate efforts of these earlier generations in favor of the further future. This is perhaps a controversial reason, and one whose shape is difficult to explain philosophically. After all, many will refuse to concede that there could be obligations to those who are now dead, as some previous generations are. Nevertheless, in my view, it is an important part of the explanation of why what the bloopers do is wrong.

Still, I will leave this consideration aside here in order to focus on a set of reasons that are arguably more central and easier to explain. The bloopers also go wrong because they inflict serious harms on their successors, and without adequate justification for doing so. (They cause real suffering on others for the sake of easy pleasures and comparatively trivial comforts.) Moreover, they are able to do this only because they take advantage of those who are extremely vulnerable and cannot defend themselves: those in the future who are not yet born, and those not yet old enough either to understand what is being done, or to do something about it.

2. The Central Problem

In my view, we can make sense of these reactions to the fairy tale by invoking a more general analysis. This begins with a sketch of the problem in its starkest and most abstract form. Consider the following schematic example.

The pure scenario

Imagine a world that consists of a sequence of groups of inhabitants over a length of time. Suppose that the membership of the groups does not overlap (i.e., no member of one group is also a member of another), and that each group is temporally distinct (in the sense that they inhabit the world at different times and not contemporaneously). Suppose also that the only causal influence of one group on another is forward-looking: earlier groups can affect later groups in the sequence, but no later group has any causal impact on any earlier group. Add to this that each group has preferences that are exclusively concerned with events that happen during the timeframe of its own existence. In other words, it cares only about what takes place while it is around, and not at all about later events.[9] Finally, suppose that each group has access to goods that are temporally dispersed. In particular, consider two types of such goods.[10] The first are such that their benefits accrue to the group that produces them, but their costs are substantially deferred, and fall on later groups. (Call these *front-loaded goods*.) Goods of the second type are such that their costs accrue to the group that produces them, but their benefits are substantially deferred and arise to later groups. (Call these *back-loaded goods*.)

What is likely to happen under the pure scenario? Let us begin with a simple (but core) case, focusing on the kind of activity engaged in by the bloopers.[11]

The core example

Suppose that we are dealing with front-loaded goods of a particular kind. They give modest benefits to the group that consumes them (and only to them), but impose very high costs on all later groups. Under the conditions of the pure scenario—where each group is only concerned with what happens while it is around—consumption of these goods is to be expected. We would predict that earlier groups will chose to consume the modest benefits available to them and thereby impose very high (and uncompensated) costs on later groups. We might also expect that those further along in the sequence would receive escalating burdens, since the costs will be compounded over time. Later generations bear the costs passed on to them by each one of their predecessors, and the later a generation is, the more predecessors it has.

Consider a simple numerical illustration. Suppose that the sequence of groups is ABCDE. Then, if each group consumes front-loaded goods that benefit it by X but cost each later group 10X, then the overall impacts on each group are:

---

9. In some situations, we might make the narrower assumption that each group is exclusively self-interested, and this is often useful for motivating the general idea. For more on this issue, see chapter 2.

10. Other types of temporally dispersed goods will also be relevant. I focus on these two for purposes of explanation.

11. This example is parallel to that of the bloopers in many respects, but also worse in important ways.

TABLE 5.2

	Benefits to Each Group	Costs to Each Group
A	X	0
B	X	10X
C	X	20X
D	X	30X
E	X	40X

In short, A absorbs no costs, C takes on 20X, and E must confront 40X. Moreover, if the practice were to continue, matters would only get worse. For example, if it went on to Z, it would be 260X; if there were 100 groups, the 100th would have to cope with 990X.

Intuitively, the core example poses a moral problem. Other things being equal, it is hard to see how the practice it portrays could be justified. There are perhaps different ways of describing what has gone wrong. It seems highly plausible to say that the infliction of high costs on later groups for the sake of modest benefits for oneself is at least unfair or unjust.[12] Depending on the case, one might also want to add (or substitute) that it is thoughtless, reckless, selfish, cruel, or callous (to mention but a few options[13]). Still, that there is a moral problem of some kind seems clear enough. This is especially so if the costs passed on are actual physical harms (such as suffering, disease, and death), or if they are catastrophic for some future group (e.g., by rendering their homeland uninhabitable), and if the benefits appear to be luxury items (e.g., exotic vacations on the other side of the planet) or comparatively trivial (e.g., the extra comfort and status provided by an unnecessarily large and inefficient vehicle). Then, the moral problem seems severe.

The core example describes an especially clear case of intergenerational buck-passing. There are several reasons for its basic appeal. One is presumably the inequity suggested by the trade of modest benefits for

12. Suppose we assume that fairness requires some kind of impartiality between affected parties. The world envisioned violates impartiality by allowing for costs to be visited on future groups for the benefit of earlier groups, even when there is no compensation, and where the benefits are small and the costs large and potentially catastrophic.

13. For example, under some circumstances, it may also manifest exploitation and domination. (See Bertram 2009; Nolt 2011.)

very high costs. This already suggests that the profligate generation is making a moral exception of itself, unfairly favoring its own interests over those of others. But when the costs rise to the level of catastrophic evils (such as mass starvation and death), and the benefits are minor (such as bigger cars and cheaper, more exotic vacations), this becomes an especially serious kind of moral wrong, showing that one group has little or no regard at all for others, and far too much regard for itself.

Another reason for the appeal of the core example is the infliction of very high costs on others per se. (Note that there is no mention of compensation or consent.) Such inflictions often violate negative duties not to harm others, and these are usually regarded as especially stringent moral duties. In particular, many people believe that violations of negative duties not to harm are much more serious, from the moral point of view, than violations of positive duties to aid. They say that a failure to help, though often morally serious, is just not as bad as an intentional infliction of harm.

For such reasons, the core example presents an especially compelling case of moral concern. (It is not difficult to see it as a tyranny of the contemporary over its successors.) Still, it seems plausible that the basic problem can be generalized to include the other kinds of temporally dispersed goods included in the pure scenario. Let me first sketch this extension and then try to clarify it through a response to some questions.

Here is the extension. In the pure scenario, each group is exclusively concerned with events that happen during the timeframe of its own existence. Hence, we expect each group to *oversupply* front-loaded goods and *undersupply* back-loaded goods quite generally. That is, we predict that in general each group will engage in what we might call "buck-passing behavior." Each will secure benefits for itself by illegitimately imposing costs on its successors, and avoid costs to itself by illegitimately failing to benefit its successors. The core example captures one central case of this, but the underlying problem is much more general, albeit with similar implications. For one thing, each group in the sequence of groups faces the same incentive structure when it has the power to act; hence, we expect the buck-passing to be iterated. Given the opportunity, every group in the sequence will engage in it. For another, given the iteration, the buck-passing is likely to have cumulative effects. The negative impacts will be worse for more distant groups than for those who come earlier in the sequence, since the costs passed on to them are likely to be compounded.

· I propose that we give this problem two names. The first is descriptive. In my view, the generalized version of the buck-passing problem nicely captures the central form of the tyranny of the contemporary. This is so even though its direct application is sharply restricted, especially by the fact that it assumes no generational overlap, and considers only goods with a simple distributive profile (i.e., the front-loaded and back-loaded goods). This is because degenerate forms of the problem remain even in the presence of generational overlap and more complex temporally extended goods. For this reason, I propose that we call the problem "the central problem of intergenerational buck-passing" (CPIBP or "the central problem").

The second name makes a claim about the status of the central problem. In my view, this is also the core problem of distinctively *intergenerational* ethics.[14] First, it explains why it is important to think specifically in terms of generations. If we are worried about the kind of ethical problem constituted by buck-passing in a temporal sequence, generations are morally relevant groupings, since isolating them helps to reveal that problem. Second, it can account for the wide disparities in the way the term "generation" is used. Since the collective action problem can arise in many contexts, and over very different periods of time, it is easy to see why the scope of a generation varies dramatically in different contexts, from hundreds of years, to just a few. For these reasons I also call the central problem "the pure intergenerational problem" (PIP).[15]

14. To say that the buck-passing problem is the central problem of distinctively intergenerational ethics is not by itself to claim that it is the core problem of the ethics of the future, or of intertemporal ethics more generally (including the past, present, and the future), since there may be intertemporal issues that are not best seen in generational terms. Nevertheless, I do believe that it is at least one core concern of such ethics, and that the global environmental tragedy makes it especially prominent, and pressing.

15. Why do I insist on having two labels for the same problem? (Isn't this a bit extravagant? Can't I just make up my mind?) The answer is that although in general, I prefer the PIP label, I recognize that the claims about its status may be contentious. Thus, the more descriptive CPIBP label is available for discussing the problem without having to assert that it has this status. Again, I am trying to prevent tangential theoretical squabbles from undermining the main analysis.

3. Clarifications

In the next section, I will go on to describe why the central problem is so challenging. But before doing so, some clarifications are in order. In the remainder of this section I will offer some quick responses to four natural questions about the analysis.

The first is as follows. In describing the central problem, why do I speak of the *over*supply and *under*supply of certain goods, and the *illegitimate* imposing of costs and failures to benefit? Such words seem to presuppose some background normative benchmark against which actual distributions are to be assessed. But why presuppose that? Indeed, doesn't it amount to begging the question in an important way?

This query is correct in its claim that the central problem presupposes some normative benchmark. The reason for this is that I do not want to assume that there ought to be no consumption of temporally diffuse goods under any circumstances. Presumably, there are some costs that it is justifiable to pass on to the future, and some things that earlier generations ought to do for posterity. A full theory of intergenerational ethics would, I assume, tell us what these requirements are. Acting in accordance with such requirements would not count as buck-passing, since the term already includes the idea of something illegitimate. Hence, a correct theory of intergenerational ethics would not be vulnerable to the central problem; on the contrary, it would solve it.[16]

This point is important because it implies that intergenerational buck-passing is not a completely general problem. In particular, it does not arise for theorists who deny that genuine questions can be raised about the intergenerational distribution of goods, or claim that any current generation is morally permitted to do completely as it pleases with temporally diffuse (and other) goods. Such positions are, no doubt, worthy of philosophical discussion. Still, I shall ignore them here. In my view, they are in serious conflict with some basic moral intuitions, and remain very much minority opinions. Hence, for present purposes, it is safe to leave them aside. I do not think that this amounts to begging the question against any major opponent. In practice, the fact that the

16. Of course, it may also have to solve other problems. Though I claim that the CPIBP is the core problem of distinctively intergenerational ethics, I do not assert that it is the only problem, or that other issues that are not essentially generational in form are not relevant to a full theory.

central problem arises for all positions that accept *any* substantive claims of intergenerational justice renders it highly relevant for philosophical and political discussion. In short, my view is (first) that though the central problem makes some moral assumptions, most people will think that these are very minimal, and (second) that the burden of proof is clearly on those who doubt this to make their case.

The second natural question is: Why do I make the central problem so broad? In particular, why include both back-loaded and front-loaded goods? Why not focus on just one kind of front-loaded good—that discussed in the core example, where one generation inflicts very high costs on future generations for the sake of modest benefits for itself? Given what I say about inequities and negative duties above, doesn't the core example give us a more compelling account of the *central* problem of intergenerational ethics?

In reply, I agree that the core example presents an especially perspicuous kind of intergenerational problem (that's why it is core, after all), so I admit that I am somewhat tempted by the proposal to restrict the scope of the central problem.[17] Still, overall, I am comfortable extending the claim about centrality to include both other kinds of front-loaded goods and back-loaded goods under the general umbrella. There are two main reasons.

The first is that some failures to benefit future generations seem so egregious as to be on a par with many inflictions of harm. Suppose, for example, that the correct theory of intergenerational justice requires a given generation to aid its successors by providing them with a modestly priced asteroid detection system. Assume that this generation is aware of the obligation; but also that it takes a while to build the system, so that it cannot benefit. Suppose then that the earlier generation fails to supply the detection system because it has some relatively trivial pet project of its own that it wants to pursue instead (e.g., a massive millennial fireworks display). As a result, the next generation is decimated by an asteroid collision that might have been avoided if the system had been active. This looks like a plausible example of a central intergenerational failure to me, and so seems to warrant inclusion.

The second reason to broaden the claim about centrality is theoretical. On reflection, I suspect that further work needs to be done to grasp the central wrongs gestured at by the core example and these extensions, and

---

17. Indeed, I often focus on the core example myself in presenting the PIP.

that this will require taking more substantive positions in moral and political theory. Given this, for present purposes it seems wise to cast the net widely, but without prejudging too many normative questions. Going further would move us beyond our aim of stating the problem and into developing solutions. But this is a task for another occasion.[18]

The third, and perhaps most serious, question of clarification also concerns terminology. Why do I use the term "intergenerational" to describe the problem, when the scenario contains no mention of their being a *genetic*, *political*, or *social* connection between the successive groups? (For example, why not speak of "the problem of sequential buck-passing," or "the central predecessors problem," or something like that?) This question gets its force from a linguistic claim. The thought is that to be a real generation, a later group must be *produced by*, or *emanate from*, a corresponding prior group in some relevant sense, of which literal biological reproduction is the core example. Without such a connection, the thought suggests, we should not speak of "generations" at all.

Much might be said in response to this query. One approach would be just to concede the point and move on. Hence, it might be said that, in practice, the main subjects of the buck-passing analysis will turn out to be groups that are in fact socially, politically and/or genetically related to at least some extent: nations, institutions, firms, families, and so on. Hence, one might say that, even if we should restrict the scope of the label "the central problem of *Intergenerational* buck-passing" to apply only to generations in this richer sense (and so not to groups without the deeper connections), it may still be a very important problem, and central to intergenerational ethics.[19] Alternatively, another approach would be to claim on independent grounds that the right kind of special relation does exist in all cases. So, for example, one might assert that the generations relevant to any particular problem can always be appropriately interlinked by virtue of being members of some larger group, such as (say) humanity, rational agents considered as such (e.g., Kant's Kingdom of Ends), or the community of living beings.

18. However, see chapters 8 and 11, and Gardiner 2011a, forthcoming.

19. In other words, the central problem would refer only to a specific type of predecessor problem. I suspect that some would also then want to deny that many other predecessor problems are genuine moral problems considered simply as such. For example, some staunch communitarians or nationalists might say this, since the connections they see as morally relevant do not hold outside of specific relationships.

These approaches are, I think, relevant. Still, as a first move, my own inclination is to say that it is both permissible, and indeed common practice, to use the term "generation" in a more minimal sense than the question suggests. We often speak, for example, of "the next generation" of cars or computers or movies (and so on) without presupposing that this will be in any sense *produced by* the same people who make the current crop of cars or computers or movies (and so on), or by those who are genetically, politically, or socially related to them. Similarly, with regard to people, we refer to "future generations" of campers, students, or Wimbledon champions, even if these groups are otherwise unrelated. (Suppose, for example, that the next generation of Wimbledon champions all turn out to be from the planet Vulcan. It is not clear that this fact alone would disqualify them.) But if we can do all of this, why can't we use the term "generation" in a minimal way to refer to a group in a temporal sequence like that sketched in the pure scenario? (Isn't that roughly what we'd be doing anyway in the case of the extraterrestrial Wimbledon champions?) After all, extending the term "generation" to the pure scenario requires only that we are willing to speak of those who inhabit a common world over time in generational terms; and this seems to me unexceptionable.

More importantly, I suspect that the main reason to deny that the language of generations should be used to describe the groups in the pure scenario would be if one had some independent theoretical axe to grind. Perhaps the thought is that in practice the deeper "generational" relations (of production, or social, political, and genetic connection more generally) will be sufficient to resolve or forestall the central problem. In other words, the intuition is that the problem simply will not arise for true "generational" groups in the richer sense, and so the central problem will lose its claim to be the core problem of intergenerational ethics. This seems to me an important position. Nonetheless, it is one best assessed independently, on its merits, rather than by definitional fiat. Moreover, later in the chapter—in the section on overlap—I will say something about why I am not swayed by it.

4. Summary

In this section I have introduced the central problem of intergenerational buck-passing, and made two main claims about it. The first claim was that, other things being equal, it seems to pose a moral problem. This is clearest in the case of the core example, and perhaps front-loaded goods more generally, because it seems unethical for an earlier generation simply to foist large costs on a later generation for the sake of modest benefits for itself. But it is also relevant for back-loaded goods. On the (modest) assumption that, other things being equal, any given current generation has an obligation to engage in at least some back-loaded projects (e.g., some with extremely low present costs and extremely high future benefits), then each generation will fail in its duties to the future if it fails to invest in such projects.[20]

The second claim is that, under some circumstances, the problem may become very serious. For example, in some cases the impacts imposed on future generations may be extremely large. Sometimes this will be because the impact of a single generation's behavior is great; more often perhaps it will be because of the substantial *cumulative* effects of the behavior of many generations. In other cases, the impacts passed on may be of an especially pernicious kind. Most obviously, they might erode the fundamental preconditions of human life and society in ways that might easily have been avoided.

Most people would, I think, accept both that the central problem is a genuine moral problem, and that sometimes it may become very serious. Moreover, given this, they would maintain that we have a moral reason to limit the impact of our generation-relative preferences.[21] The

20. Perhaps there would be no moral problem if each generation were to consume to the same extent, so that each takes from the future only as much as has been taken from it by the past. But even this claim is questionable. First, such a situation may be highly inefficient, and immoral for this reason, if intergenerational justice requires some level of efficiency. Second, the response looks best if the relevant costs and benefits are simply passed on from one generation to another. But this raises two obvious issues. For one thing, it seems too neat a picture: many effects of overconsumption are likely to be spread out over many generations, and also to be cumulative. For another, when sanitized in this way the model starts to mimic theories of intergenerational justice that rely on indirect reciprocity across generations. But, of course, it would be no surprise to find that distributions that satisfy a (correct) theory of intergenerational justice are not prey to the CPIBP. Third, it is not clear that distribution is the only thing that matters. For example, if Sammy takes Fred's lunch and Fred takes John's lunch and then John takes Sammy's lunch, they all end up with an equal share (one lunch). Nevertheless, none has his own lunch, and each has a legitimate complaint against one of the others.

21. Such a limitation might take a number of different forms. For example, perhaps we should subject our generation-relative preferences to certain direct constraints. Alternatively, perhaps we should seek to engage other, and especially intergenerational, preferences that we either already have or ought to develop.

question then becomes how and to what extent such a limitation is to be achieved. To answer this question, we need a theory of intergenerational ethics.

Unfortunately, this leads us to a further problem, which is that we are not currently well placed to offer such a theory. This is part of the theoretical storm discussed in Part D of this book. The remainder of this chapter explores intergenerational buck-passing in more detail, in order to better understand the problem's import, limits, and wider theoretical context.

III. INTERGENERATIONAL BUCK-PASSING VS. THE PRISONER'S DILEMMA

One reason why the central problem (or PIP) is so important is that it has a peculiarly harsh structure that makes it unusually difficult to resolve. These facts can be brought out by comparison of a specific form of the problem with the more familiar prisoner's dilemma and tragedy of the commons.[22] As we have seen, the familiar collective action problems share the two core claims of the prisoner's dilemma:

(PD1) It is *collectively rational* to cooperate: each agent prefers the outcome produced by everyone cooperating over the outcome produced by no one doing so.

(PD2) It is *individually rational* not to cooperate: when each agent has the power to decide whether or not she will cooperate, each (rationally) prefers not to do so, whatever the others do.

These claims are paradoxical because given the first it is better for all parties to cooperate than to defect, but given the second the structure of the situation undermines their doing so. In particular, the second claim makes it the case that individuals acting rationally in pursuit of their aims collectively undermine those aims.

If we are to compare the PIP with the more familiar collective action models, we need to do some translating. To begin with, the PIP makes no mention of "collective rationality" or "cooperation," but speaks instead in more general terms of the oversupply and undersupply of goods relative

---

22. Some of the material in this section is drawn from Gardiner 2001a.

to some background theory of justice.[23] Hence, we must be willing to convert talk of buck-passing into these terms. Fortunately, there is good initial reason to do this, at least as a heuristic. The guiding thought is that at least some departures from what the usual models term "collective rationality" or "cooperation" are likely to be almost universally regarded as ethically problematic. Most notably, if all prefer a certain outcome, behavior that seriously undermines that outcome is likely to be morally lamentable. Given this, if we focus on departures from collective rationality, we highlight a form of buck-passing that almost all moral and political theorists will want their theories to overcome. Hence, accepting the translation can form part of our strategy of couching the general worry about intergenerational storm in minimal terms, by prejudging as few normative questions as possible.[24]

Suppose then that we envision a paradigm example of intergenerational buck-passing, a case where earlier generations inflict serious and unjustifiable pollution on later generations. How might collective and individual rationality function here? How might this parallel the core claims of the prisoner's dilemma and tragedy of the commons? As we saw in chapter 1, my suggestion is that we consider as a paradigm the following kind of case:

(PIP1) Almost every generation prefers the outcome produced by all generations restricting their pollution over the outcome produced by everyone overpolluting.

(PIP2) When each generation has the power to decide whether or not it will overpollute, each generation prefers to do so, whatever the others do.

In working out a paradigm case, the second claim seems clearly suitable. PIP2 parallels PD2 and highlights the incentive for intergenerational

---

23. This seems to be to the advantage of the central problem. There is a live worry that the terms "collectively rational" and "cooperation" may be too theoretically loaded, and in particular that ultimately we may not be able to describe the correct approach to intergenerational ethics in these terms. (See, for example, Gardiner 2009a and Kumar 2009.)

24. Here we might refer again to the core example, where it is assumed that for one generation to impose high costs on others merely for the sake of modest benefits for itself is prima facie a serious case of injustice. More specifically, the idea is that if the cooperative outcome is undermined (by PIP2), so that the good acknowledged as collectively rational (in PIP1) is not achieved, something has gone wrong from the point of view of ethics.

buck-passing. The first claim, however, is more contentious. PIP1 constitutes an optimistic assumption about the mutual compatibility of the aims of different generations. However, perhaps there is no sense of "collective" rationality in many intergenerational cases, or perhaps the sense is much weaker than that suggested by PIP1. For example, in some cases of buck-passing it may be that a significant number of generations are prepared to suffer the high costs inflicted by their predecessors so long as they retain the ability to pass on even higher costs to their successors. In such cases, PIP1 would be false, but there is still likely to be a serious ethical problem. [25]

Since PIP1 constitutes a very generous reading of the paradigm pollution problem, more pessimistic interpretations of the buck-passing problem compete both with the familiar models and with the analysis I will consider. Nevertheless, it is worth focusing on the model that includes PIP1. One reason is that it seems highly relevant to an ethical analysis (see below). But a second reason is that even though it contains optimistic concessions to the familiar models, it still creates major difficulties. It is to these I now turn.

If we generalize from the pollution example, we can complete the translation as follows:

> (PIP1*) It is *collectively rational* for most generations to cooperate: (almost) every generation prefers the outcome produced by everyone cooperating over the outcome produced by no one cooperating.
> (PIP2*) It is *individually rational* for all generations not to cooperate: when each generation has the power to decide whether or not it will cooperate, each generation prefers not to cooperate, whatever the others do.

What are the implications of this conversion?

Despite the optimism of PIP1*, this version of intergenerational buck-passing is notably worse than the prisoner's dilemma and tragedy of the commons. There are two reasons. One is that its constituent claims are worse. Consider first the claims about individual rationality. PIP2* is

---

25. The flexible definition of "generation" under the PIP can help with some cases where the cooperative claim is weaker. For example, suppose that the time-lag between cause (e.g. emissions) and effect (e.g. climate impacts) is long enough that a number of generations can pass on costs to the future without having to absorb costs from their predecessors. The earlier sequence of asymmetrically powerful groups may count as a first generation in this longer-term PIP.

worse than PD2 because the underlying rationale for it is more intractable. PD2 typically arises because there are contingent obstacles to coopera-tion. For example, the parties in the prisoner's dilemma lack the ability to come together to make a contract, and also the coercive power to enforce any contract that they might make. Hence, PD2 might be rendered false by removing such contingencies. (Cooperation is easy if both are mem-bers of the mafia and their mafia lawyers tell them that the "family" wishes them to cooperate.) But the reasons for PIP2* are not contingent. If a collective agreement is in the interest of a given group, it is because it does not want to suffer the ill-effects of the activities of its predecessors. But at the point that each generation has the power to cooperate, it is no longer subject to action by its predecessors—by definition, they no longer exist,[26] and have already either cooperated or not.

Consider now the claims about collective rationality. PIP1* is also much worse than PD1. In PD1, everyone prefers complete cooperation over complete noncooperation. But in PIP1* this is not the case. First, cooperation is not preferred by the first group in the sequence. It is being asked to refrain from noncooperative activities it prefers simply for the sake of future groups. Hence, if it is motivated purely by self-interest or generation-relative concerns, it will not cooperate. Second, this implies that the preference of later groups for cooperation is fragile. Coopera-tion is preferable for any given group if and only if the groups that pre-cede it also cooperate. But the asymmetrical position of the first group threatens to undermine subsequent cooperation. If the first group does not cooperate, then it makes it the case that the second group has nothing to gain from cooperation, and so (under egoistic or generation-relative motivational assumptions) will itself not cooperate. But then the third group has nothing to gain from cooperation, and so on, for all the other groups in the sequence. In other words, the problem of the first group seems likely to become iterated.

The second reason that the optimistic version of the PIP is worse than the prisoner's dilemma and tragedy of the commons is that it resists standard solutions. Typical remedies for the prisoner's dilemma involve appeal to the broad self-interest of the parties, or to some notion of reciprocity. But these solutions do not work for the PIP. For one thing, appeals to broad self-interest characteristically make reference to a wider

---

26. We have assumed that each group is temporally distinct.

context of interaction where mutual advantage is possible. But there is no such wider context under the pure scenario. For another, the possibilities of mutual benefit or reciprocity (as normally understood) are ruled out by the casual circumstances.[27]

IV. THE FEATURES OF THE PURE INTERGENERATIONAL PROBLEM

We have established that the PIP is a hard problem, even in its most optimistic varieties. Still, the conditions for its manifestation appear to be stringent; hence, it is likely to be rarely (if ever) instantiated in a pure form. Despite this, I shall argue that the PIP remains useful as a paradigm, since the basic structural ideas have force even under some common deviations from the idealized conditions. To show this, and to give a more robust account of the problem itself, I will now analyze its features in a little more detail.

The first feature is *temporal asymmetry*. The PIP envisages groups of people who can be represented as a sequence of temporally distinct classes. As we have seen, categorization in terms of such groups grounds the use of the term "generations" in the PIP.

The first feature of the PIP does not yet justify using the language of generations to describe *our* problems with the future. For, as we have already noted, human beings do not pop into and out of existence in distinct, fully-formed, temporal groups.[28] Hence, for human situations,

27. These considerations imply that the PIP is worse than the prisoner's dilemma in a further way. Historically, the most influential accounts of fairness or justice have relied crucially on ideas of mutual advantage or reciprocal exchange. But the PIP challenges both forms of analysis. Hence, it poses a fundamental challenge to some kinds of political theory. See, for example, Barry 1978, and Gardiner 2009a.

28. After writing the paper on which this chapter is based, I came across an article by Tim Mulgan which describes a situation which resembles the PIP in having rigid temporal group differentiation because the beings involved are mayflies. In light of this example, Mulgan proposes as a minimal test for political theories that they justify at least some obligations to future generations in the Mayfly Case (Mulgan 2001.) This is in the spirit of the PIP, and suggests that the problem might be relevant to nonhuman political communities with a certain biology even if different biology meant that it could be overcome in the human case (see also Steiner and Vallentyne 2009).

we need some other account of group differentiation. This account emerges from the second and third characteristics.

The second feature of the PIP is *causal asymmetry*. Earlier groups have the power to impose costs on later groups (including severe costs affecting their basic life circumstances),[29] whereas future groups have no causal power over them. Causal asymmetry is the central feature from the point of view of describing the phenomenon as *generational*: it plays the role of individuating generations, and so makes talk of generations appropriate.[30] Given this, whether the PIP has any application depends not on whether people come in temporally distinct classes—they clearly do not—but whether there are causal asymmetries of the relevant type[31] between groups in the temporal sequence. In other words, causal asymmetry is the primary notion. On this account, a generation is a group which has a place in the temporal sequence and which stands in the basic causal relations with predecessors and successors described by the causal asymmetry.

This account of generations has an important implication. It suggests that the basic problem of fairness persists even if the relevant asymmetries cannot be assigned to rigidly separated groups, because the passage from generation to generation is more fluid. Consider the following. In the pure model, groups have constant membership over time and there is no overlap. But these conditions might be relaxed in various ways without altering much of the central causal structure of the problem. For example, a relevantly similar asymmetric causal relation may hold between groups whose core members remain the same, even if at the margins both add and shed members, in some cases to other groups

29. There is also the power to decide whether future generations exist and which individuals will constitute them. I defer discussion of this problem until the final section.

30. Initially it might appear that causal asymmetry simply follows from the temporal asymmetry, given the temporal closure of the past. In this case, temporal asymmetry would be the primary theoretical notion. But it is not. A generation is not just any randomly chosen group from within the temporal sequence. It must satisfy a further criterion. Causal asymmetry provides this criterion.

31. There may be other interesting causal asymmetries. Some will count as degenerate cases of the PIP; others will not. I leave such questions aside here, since the point of the present chapter is not to provide a taxonomy of either intergenerational problems or group dynamics more generally.

(as when the older members of the first join the second). Given this, the problem of the continuum (mentioned in section I) need not imply that the PIP has no application to the human case.[32]

The third feature of the PIP is *asymmetric independence of interests*. Though later groups have a substantial amount to gain from earlier groups, the reverse is not true: the interests of earlier groups are independent of the interests of groups which succeed them. In particular, on standard assumptions, earlier groups have nothing to gain or lose from the activities or attitudes of later groups (though later groups have a substantial amount to gain from earlier groups). This feature is important because it seems to rule out the possibility of intertemporal exchange for mutual advantage.[33]

In the PIP, asymmetric independence of interests is an independently posited feature. However, it is tempting to think that this might be unnecessary, because perhaps one can claim that asymmetric independence follows directly from causal asymmetry. Two reasons for this claim spring to mind. First, the main cause of independence is presumably the lack of potential for direct reciprocity through exchange of goods. But this depends on the causal asymmetry: if there can be no causal effects of later on earlier groups, then the later groups are unable to reciprocate in any way. Second, one might think that reciprocation is impossible for a more pragmatic reason: there is nothing that the later groups could give that the earlier could not take in any case.

However, the connection between causal asymmetry and asymmetric independence is less tight than the above account suggests. First, relationships characterized by reciprocity and mutual advantage narrowly conceived are not the only kind possible between different temporal groups. One possibility would be that groups pass on benefits through a scheme of indirect reciprocity—the first benefits the second, the second the third, and so on. Another is that earlier generations pass on benefits as gifts to the future, with the prospect of "receiving" gratitude in return. Neither requires backwards causation. Second, it is not strictly true that there is nothing that later groups can offer which the earlier are not in a position to take. Some goods are time-dependent: they are not available until later,

32. See also section V.
33. For a detailed analysis of contractarian attempts to deny this, see Gardiner 2009a.

and essentially so. Examples might include the respect or approval of future groups, or the continuation of projects and a group history.

These exceptions to the extent that causal asymmetry implies asymmetric independence are of practical importance. They imply that asymmetric independence is likely to be false, strictly speaking, in the real world. Still, it is questionable whether the assumption of asymmetric independence is *substantially* false, in the sense that it simplifies in a way which undermines the point at issue. What is important for the PIP is that the present interests of the current generation—that is, those interests that they can secure for themselves by overconsuming—dominate any benefits they might expect to receive from the future and which depend on their not overconsuming. This still seems empirically likely. Hence, a degenerate form of the PIP is likely to have application.[34]

To see this, consider a paradigm case, energy conservation. On the one hand, the benefits to the present generation from energy consumption are likely to be large, secure, tangible, and immediate, whereas the benefits from abstaining for the sake of the esteem of future generations are likely to be relatively small, uncertain, intangible, and deferred. On the other hand, some benefits of reputation will not depend on the present generation not overconsuming. For example, some of the uses of energy consumption might be for cultural or scientific projects which themselves endear the present to the future in some respects.

The fourth feature of the PIP is its *motivational assumption*. In the pure scenario, the assumption is that each group has preferences that are exclusively generation-relative: concerned with events that happen during the timeframe of its own existence. This initial assumption is stark. However, degenerate forms of the PIP need not go so far. As we have seen in previous chapters, the motivational assumption can be made stronger or weaker for specific purposes, or in response to additional background beliefs. A popular stronger version of the assumption

---

34. It is not clear that it would be desirable for things to be different. For example, suppose some course of action could ensure a large and long-lived reputational gain for the present generation. This would likely be only for some correspondingly large project. But this would imply large investment (e.g., in the building of pyramids, a major space program, etc.). We could perhaps devote ourselves to these but it would probably be to the detriment of the welfare of both current and future people. So, it is not obviously desirable. Furthermore, later people might be able to do such things better, and more cheaply, in any case.

would be that each group is exclusively self-interested; a weaker version is Hume's claim that although people are not self-interested, they do tend to be much more concerned with those close to them (friends, family, those in their immediate community) than those more distant. A weaker version still (suggested in chapter 2) is that the members of the group are largely motivated by short-term considerations when they make the consumption decisions that drive some serious intergenerational problems.[35] It seems plausible to say that the concerns of generational groups will often reflect those connections. In my view, it is a virtue of the PIP analysis that it allows for a variety of motivational assumptions, and especially that it need not rely on controversial (and probably false) claims about the hegemony of self-interest. In particular, we will want to allow for altruistic and other motives if the PIP is to have a practical solution. On my preferred interpretation of the PIP, the key problem is that such motives are not adequately registered by current institutions.[36]

The fifth feature of the PIP is that it involves *temporally diffuse goods*. The focus on such goods is designed to illustrate the problem in its most uncontroversial form. This has practical application in the case of climate change, since the phenomenon is subject to such a large time-lag that climate stability is clearly a temporally extended good. Nevertheless, some deviations from this make little difference to the basic intergenerational issue. Most obviously, generations may have obligations to save current (nondiffuse) goods or resources for future generations. Suppose, for example, that an earlier generation has good reason to believe that a certain mineral deposit or vaccine would be of great use to a particular future generation. Then they may be obliged to preserve a sufficient amount for them. But if their preferences are solely generation-relative, they may fail to live up to this obligation, and so may the intervening

35. We might also say that some overconsumption has little to do with "interests" per se. Arguably, much overconsumption is caused by desires to indulge or amuse, such as relatives show towards children. Indeed, it may be that it is easier to persuade people to give up overconsumption on their own behalf rather than that on behalf of others. I thank Leslie Francis for discussion on this issue. See also chapter 2.

36. We might note that this could be a severe problem even if the issue arose in only a fraction of relevant cases. Buck-passing by the current generation on 10% of serious intergenerational issues might still cause tragedy in the end and serious burdens along the way. I thank Rachel Fredericks for discussion on this point.

generations. (For example, the first ten generations may each take 10% of the amount that should have been saved for the eleventh.)

The final feature of the PIP is its *sequential* aspect. Its most obvious manifestation comes when the first group in an intergenerational sequence lacks a generation-relative incentive to cooperate, and so does not, with the result that the second group also lacks the incentive, does likewise, and so on. This feature of the PIP can also accommodate deviations. First, buck-passing is a problem even in the absence of iteration. Hence, two generations are sufficient to raise the basic moral issue. Second, groups do not need to be temporally proximate to each other in a continuous sequence for the problem to occur. Instead, buck-passing may skip some generations. Imagine, for example, a progression of causally asymmetric groups ABCDEF, each of which is temporally proximate to the previous one. Given the right causal facts, the generational sequence relevant to the PIP may be ACE or ADF, rather than ABCDEF.

V. APPLICATIONS AND COMPLICATIONS

This discussion of the basic features of the PIP and the extent to which they can accommodate deviations has necessarily been preliminary and incomplete. Still, it suffices to show that cases with structures close to the PIP are likely to arise in practice, so that the PIP may be a serious problem in the real world. In this section, I suggest three schematic areas where we might expect to see degenerate forms of the PIP. These areas correspond to three different understandings of the length of a generation.

First, the closest approximations to the pure form of the problem are likely to be found if one adopts the widest definition of future generation mentioned earlier: that future generations are the future people whom those presently alive will not live to meet.[37] Such situations seem to arise in a number of real world cases. One prominent set of examples would be certain long-term implications of climate change. Suppose, for example, that our excessive emissions over the next fifty years set in motion processes that in a thousand years or so cause the sudden release of massive amounts of methane hydrate currently stored under the

---

37. This should be unsurprising, since the wide definition of future people is the one that approximates most closely to the causal asymmetry condition of the PIP.

oceans. Some scientists believe that such a release once caused the biggest extinction of all time, the end of the Permian era 251 million years ago, when ninety percent of species were suddenly lost.[38] Clearly, a change of this kind would be catastrophic. A *New York Times* columnist aptly referred to it as "the Big Burp Theory of the Apocalypse."[39] If our generation (on the wide understanding of the term) causes such an apocalypse through reckless activity, then we will have done a grave wrong. Indeed, in my view, this is one of the worse things that we could have done.

Still, most issues usually described as intergenerational do not fit the wide definition. Hence, for the PIP to be central to our problems with future generations it will also have to address narrower definitions of "generation," and so deal with cases of temporal overlap between different groups. The application of the PIP is less clear in situations where there is overlap. Nevertheless, I believe that degenerate forms still persist in such cases.

Let me begin by distinguishing two kinds of overlap. The first is related to a usage of "future generations" mentioned earlier, where future generations are those generations whose members have not yet been born. This use allows for a weak kind of overlap, namely cases where present people will exist at the same time as future people, but those future people are not yet present. The second kind of overlap is stronger. It allows for members of one group to be present alongside members of another when relevant decisions are being made. This corresponds to the use of "generation" to mark the period needed for effective replacement of parents by their children.

The simultaneous physical presence of different generations naturally requires some distinction of groups based on factors other than temporal isolation. But here the PIP model is on firm ground. For the causal asymmetry feature both provides and explains that distinction. First, in the weak overlap case (where members have not yet been born), the present generation retains the strong form of causal asymmetry of the PIP until the first group of future people arrives on the scene. (Then it reverts to the strong overlap case.) Second, even with strong overlap (where members of one group are present alongside members of another when relevant decisions are being made), there is a relevant causal

---

38. Berner 2002; Barry 2005, 260.
39. Kristof 2006.

asymmetry. For parents (and adults more generally) retain a strong power over their children until they grow up and achieve some kind of independence. Indeed, this is presumably what gives the narrower definition of generations its point. "Replacement" means taking on the rights and responsibilities of adulthood, and that requires coming to approximate causal parity.[40]

So far, then, the PIP seems useful in explaining the degenerate cases. It can distinguish a succession of groups even in overlap cases, and these distinctions are morally relevant. But perhaps we should consider whether the peculiar features of overlap undermine the overall application of the PIP. If they are to do so, this will presumably be through their effects on the relationship between the generations (narrowly conceived). The two main factors here seem to be potential reciprocity and personal attachment, both of which are thought to be impossible in the PIP. Hence, let us briefly consider each of these factors in turn.[41]

The PIP explicitly rules out the most obvious forms of reciprocity, through the assumption of asymmetric independence of interests, which ensures that earlier generations have nothing to gain from their successors. But this assumption is unlikely to be true in cases of both strong and weak overlap. Given this, for most real world situations it is presumably true that the potential for reciprocity makes some difference, and that this difference increases with the extent of overlap.

Still, we must be careful not to overstate matters. First, many overlapping future people will have limited opportunities to benefit us much: for example, they will still be too young; we will be too old. (This is especially so in weak overlap cases.) It may also be true that though there is overlap, this is not when the problem is bad, or when complaints can be made. Perhaps we're harming our grandchildren now, by bringing on an abrupt change that will hit them in 2100. But we have not met our grandchildren yet, they'll be young when we do, and we'll be dead by the time the problem arises.

Second, there are at least two kinds of scenarios in these cases, and this makes a difference. In the first, the later group will eventually attain

---

40. Indeed, without this account, it is difficult to grasp either the meaning or the importance of "replacement" as a criterion for generation-individuation.

41. The following discussion does not consider a number of specific strategies that have been offered, especially within the literature of contractarian political philosophy. I address such strategies in Gardiner 2009a.

causal symmetry, and then be able to subject the earlier group to reprisals. This would presumably have some effect on the behavior of earlier groups. Still, it is not clear that it would actually pay the later group to withhold cooperation for the sake of past bad treatment once it actually achieves causal parity, when this withholding might damage its interests still further.[42] So, the effect may be limited. In the second kind of scenario, the later group may eventually attain a *reversed causal asymmetry*, where they have the upper hand. Here, earlier groups know that they will eventually be at the mercy of their successors.[43] Now, this presumably has some influence when it occurs, and insofar as it does, it may limit the application of the PIP.[44] Still, it is doubtful to what extent it characterizes many contemporary relationships between generations. So, the PIP will remain relevant in a range of cases.

Third, important though these factors are, they are limited by the fact that earlier groups can determine many of the circumstances within which the choices of later groups will be made. Manipulation is obviously a concern. But even without this, the general circumstances for later groups will almost necessarily include the fact that at least some of the behavior of earlier towards later generations will have been beneficial. (For example, some nurturing behavior is necessary to their very survival long enough to gain significant causal power.) Hence, future groups will necessarily have at least mixed views about their relationship with their predecessors, and so be correspondingly reluctant to take punitive action against them for their transgressions.

In conclusion, then, it seems that by itself reciprocity will not automatically solve the problem. There are many reasons to suspect that actual overlap cases will retain much of the driving structure of the PIP.

The second main complicating feature of overlap is the possibility of personal attachment. The idea here seems to be that attachment can ground strong concern for later generations with the power to override (or modify) self-interest or generation-relative aims. Still, even if this is right, there are several problems in this case. For one thing, the model

42. It may, of course, pay to pretend earlier on that this is what one will do, in order to extract benefits.

43. The fading of this is, no doubt, one of the reasons why some intergenerational problems are becoming more visible and pronounced. In earlier times the old were extremely dependent on the young. But they are much less so in many countries now.

44. For more, see Gardiner 2009a.

seems to presume that attachment occurs only on contact; but contact might be a long time coming, and so too late. (If contact is not required, then "personal attachment" must be carefully distinguished from moral motives which imply direct concern for the future individuals. Such motives must presumably be part of any solution to the PIP and its manifestations.) For another, it is not clear that attachment would give concern with the necessary emphasis on the long-term prospects of the future person, rather than on her short- to medium-term well-being. There is no reason to assume that concern is an all-or-nothing affair. Instead, what seems likely is that it is graduated. On the one hand, we are generally less concerned with those whom we will never meet than with those not yet alive with whom there will be overlap, and less concerned with these than with people currently around. But, on the other hand, even when there is overlap, and we care about the well-being of at least some of the people who remain after we are dead, that concern tends to be less than our concern for individuals around now (even when the same people are at issue) and to decline over temporal distance.

We can conclude that issues of reciprocity and attachment complicate the relevance of the PIP to the human case. However, it is far from clear that they undermine it completely. Rather, they seem to suggest that the crucial issue with overlapping generations is not *when* those who will live when we have gone appear, but the extent of our *present* concern for their well-being. Thus, the PIP remains relevant. Merely to assert that reciprocity and personal attachment are possible does nothing to show that they are actual, that they are present now, or (most importantly) that they are strong enough to overwhelm the competing influence of self-interested or generation-relative concerns.

This point can be made more vivid with a particular kind of example. The relevance of degenerate forms of the PIP is perhaps most stark in one area where there is quite strong overlap. Institutions are often set up so as to produce a temporal sequence of groups with asymmetrical power over others and extremely limited time-horizons. This is especially noticeable with some of the most important institutions, such as national governments and large corporations. Here, the presence of the second factor (extremely limited time-horizons) is obvious. Governments are often focused on their impacts over limited terms of office, particularly as they affect their ability to win the next election; corporations are often focused on the dividends likely to be produced in the immediate years ahead, not the further implications of their actions. But the first factor (asymmetrical power over others) is also present because such institutions are typically headed by elites, who are predominantly people in their mid-forties to mid-sixties. The time-horizons during which the impacts of their policies on their institutions or people has significant effects is often much longer than the time they will be around to experience those effects.[45] Furthermore, even within these groups, there is diminishing institutional loyalty, and much moving around. Hence, often what is important is to make a good, highly visible, short-term impact at a given institution, as a way to move on. And this results in an incentive to ignore the long-term implications of policy.

The relevance of the PIP to institutions with strong overlap is important for a number of reasons. One is that the analysis may have explanatory power in many real world cases. Consider, for example, problems such as the financial deregulation that led to the current global economic crisis, and the attempts at appeasement in the 1930s. Were these caused by intergenerational buck-passing? At first glance, it seems possible. More importantly, the relevance of the PIP to such cases shows that it cannot be dismissed merely with the observation that human beings do not exist in rigid generational cohorts. We see the threat of intergenerational buck-passing even when there is strong overlap and relatively quick generational turnover. If it can happen there, isn't it even more likely in less friendly settings, such as the long-term impacts of climate change?

VI. MITIGATING FACTORS

If I am right about the centrality and pervasiveness of the PIP, why has it not been emphasized before? There seem to be two main reasons: first, it has not

45. An example might be the Canadian ratification of the Kyoto Protocol. One journalist claims that this had more to do with the then-Prime Minister's wish to pose a difficult problem for his successor, a political rival, than any policy conviction: "The internal politics are treacherous. . . . So why the rush? Why anger the provinces? Why forge ahead without preparation? The simplest explanation is that Chrétien won't be around to implement the Protocol. . . . His heir apparent is his arch-rival and former finance minister, Paul Martin. . . . He is the one who will have to cope with any economic fallout from ratifying Kyoto. . . . Much of Chrétien's energy in the past few years has been devoted to sticking it to Martin." (McClroy 2002)

seemed pressing in practice; second, other significant theoretical problems tend to obscure its presence. This section briefly addresses these matters.

1. The Invisible Hand

One response to the PIP is to claim that, assuming continued economic growth, people in the future will already be better off than the present generation, so that there is no immediate danger of affecting them for the worse. The basic idea here is that current economic activity tends to result in improved capital stock and infrastructure which are then passed on to the next generation. So, the self-interested consumption behavior of the present generation actually has good results for future people. There is *an invisible hand.* In addition, it is often claimed that these effects are so large over long time periods that they dwarf any damage that we might do to the future through climate change (or anything else). If the world economy continues to grow at the current rate, it will be more than thirty times larger by 2100 than it is now. Given this, the thought goes, the temporal dispersed good of current emissions is actually modest benefits to us now, followed by massive benefits to future people later. In particular, future people will not thank us for restricting economic growth (the engine of their prosperity) in order to save them from climate costs; such a rich future can surely buy its way out of trouble.

There is something to the invisible hand argument. But we must be cautious about its import in this context. Most importantly for our purposes, it relies on a set of bold empirical claims. The core example of the PIP posits temporally diffuse goods which bring modest benefits for the present generation but impose high costs on future generations. But the invisible hand argument asserts that *overall* human activities are temporally diffuse in a different, very beneficial way. They have long-term benefits as well as short-term benefits, and the long-term benefits are persistently larger, so that the future is always better off overall.[46]

---

46. The argument presumably also assumes that the long-term benefits cannot be converted into short-term benefits for the current generation—otherwise we would need to account for why they do not do so—or that the long-term benefits can be achieved without specific attention to the PIP.

Now, if the empirical claim of the invisible hand argument were true, this would generally be a good thing from the point of view of intergenerational justice. Moreover, if one focuses on the volume of economic goods, there are good reasons to think that it has been substantially true, at least in the recent history of the more developed nations. Still, we should not get overly carried away by this thought. For it seems unlikely that the empirical claim holds to the degree necessary to undermine the relevance of the PIP.

First, the mere assertion of an invisible hand is not enough to dismiss the PIP. Suppose that at least some goods are temporally diffuse in the PIP sense. On the one hand, it is possible that buck-passing will occur with respect to these goods even if the overall pattern of an earlier generation's behavior is beneficial to the future. Perhaps it is just less beneficial than it ought to be; or perhaps the goods subject to buck-passing are one's to which future generations are separately entitled (e.g., decent air quality or the absence of a highly toxic environment).

On the other hand, some temporally-diffuse goods, such as climate security, may be so important that the presence of buck-passing in these areas has the potential to overwhelm other (and purely economic) gains. A truly catastrophic abrupt climate change, for example, could wipe out decades, or even centuries, of economic growth. This is a serious worry. It suggests that the invisible hand might really be so only from a limited intergenerational perspective. Imagine, for example, that rapid industrialization fueled by fossil fuels produces significant net benefits only for the first ten generations, but is then very costly for those who come after because of its adverse environmental impacts. The short-term invisible hand of economic growth could then turn into the longer-term "invisible boot" [47] of environmental catastrophe. This is not an outlandish suggestion; after all, we know that invisible boots are possible. The prisoner's dilemma and tragedy of the commons also point out ways in which they can occur.

Second, even if there is a very strong invisible hand (so that the difficulties just mentioned disappear), the PIP remains relevant. In particular, it seems probable that, to the extent that it is present, the invisible hand operates only under certain advantageous background conditions. It is not a law of nature, or an inevitable fact of economic life.

---

47. I take this term from Brennan and Pettit 2004.

In particular, it seems to require a social structure partially constituted by a well-functioning legal and moral framework. But the presence of such a structure hardly characterizes all countries and all periods of the world's history. Hence, if we favor the invisible hand (and in part because it discharges our intergenerational responsibilities), we presumably have obligations to maintain such a framework. Part of my claim is then that the possibility of the PIP will play a role in explaining the form and import of those obligations. So, again, the PIP analysis is not undercut. [48]

2. Future Uncertainty

The second reason why the PIP tends to be obscured is *future uncertainty*. In particular, we do not know the technology, the general circumstances, nor the preferences of future people. Some writers seem to regard these problems as both definitional of future generations problems and fairly crippling. They also seem to undermine the manifestation of the PIP. If it is impossible to know what will count as a cost in the future, then it is equally impossible to tell when the present generation is generating the relevantly temporally diffuse goods.

The uncertainty problem seems to me overstated. First, the importance and extent of technological changes is easily overemphasized. While it is true that the Internet, mobile phones, and other luxury goods may not even have been conceivable in the late nineteenth century, it is also the case that basic human needs for food, water, shelter, and health remain both largely unchanged and under threat in many parts of the world, in ways depressingly reminiscent of earlier centuries. We should not forget that even in the early twenty-first century, billions of the world's people continue to live in conditions of subsistence barely

48. A further challenge to the invisible hand argument is that ethical concern for future generations ought not to be understood solely in economic terms. Other things, such as, say, stable political institutions and environmental quality ought also to be considered, and we should not assume that more economic resources can always compensate for these (see chapter 8). In addition, evidence about growth says nothing about the distribution of wealth. So, we cannot tell, for example, whether growth will ultimately benefit mainly some future elite in one part of the world at the expense of future (or present) people in another part. Notice that the United States, for example, has experienced substantial growth over the last twenty years and yet middle class incomes have remained relatively stagnant.

removed from those well-known for millennia.[49] Second, the uncertainty issue is not essentially, or even characteristically generational. We already face large problems with uncertainty with much shorter time-horizons (e.g., in our own lives, in assessing what our long-term preferences might be, and in public policy, with the use of biotechnology in agriculture); still, we can and do act. Third, the most worrying problems involving future people—those of large-scale environmental degradation and resource depletion—do not seem to be swamped by uncertainties about future preferences or technologies. For example, it is difficult to believe that the people of 2100 or 2200 will prefer climate instability to stability, or even that they will be in possession of an adequate and completely benign climate stabilization device. More importantly, it seems clear that we would not be justified in basing current inaction on the assumption that they will.

3. Creation

The third complicating issue is that *we determine the very existence of future generations*. This suggests that the present generation can assert some control over the obligations it is under. Not only can it determine whether there is anyone to have such obligations *to*, but it can also influence the extent of those obligations. For example, if it manipulates the number of future people, it might control which goods really count as temporally diffuse in the relevant sense.

I cannot attempt a full analysis of such complications here. Instead, I will make three brief comments, and then turn to a specific worry posed by the infamous nonidentity problem.

The first comment is that, in practice, cases where earlier generations are tempted to manipulate the future in this way are likely to arise only rarely. Consider just two points. On the one hand, at the global level at

---

49. These facts tend to be obscured by both the theoretical focus (in economics and elsewhere) on particular preferences, and the fact that we tend to have the preferences of affluent Westerners for luxuries in mind when invoking future generations. Attention to broader measures such as capabilities would show more consistency, and make it clear that what is needed to confront future uncertainty is flexible strategies for discharging obligations to the future.

least, such intervention is likely to be very difficult to achieve. World population, for example, is subject to many complex drivers, few of which are likely to be substantially altered on the kind of time scale likely to be useful to the current generation in manipulating its obligations to the future. As it stands, we have reasonable projections of global population for the next fifty years or so, and a reasonable grasp of the underlying trends. These suggest that world population for the next century or so will be substantially above that of the present. Other things being equal, this would increase our obligations to the future. But it is not clear that there is much that the current generation can do about that. On the other hand, if the current generation wants to manipulate its obligations to the future, it has other, less dramatic means at its disposal. For example, it can try to manipulate the values and preferences of its successors so as to facilitate its own buck-passing. Given the control it has over the upbringing of the next generation, this seems a highly feasible strategy.

Second, in circumstances where there is a threat of manipulation, one salient question is whether the present generation has any obligation to bring a certain number of future people into existence. The PIP analysis attempts no answer to this question. But if the answer is "yes," the PIP might help to explain why either too many or too few people are created.

Third, most creation issues are not specifically generational, and those who believe that they pose large ethical problems nevertheless tend not to think that they undermine our ethical obligations to the future. They will therefore still be concerned about the impact of the PIP on those obligations. With this thought in mind, I turn to a more specific concern involving creation.

4. The Nonidentity Problem (A Brief Aside)

Some people believe that the most important intergenerational problem is what Derek Parfit calls "the nonidentity problem" (NIP). The NIP might seem to threaten the PIP analysis in a specific way. (*This section may safely be skipped by those uninterested in such technicalities.*) Consider Parfit's classic example, "depletion."[50] Parfit imagines an earlier

---

50. This is not the only nonidentity case that he considers, but it is the one most relevant to climate change. See Parfit 1986, Schwartz 1978.

generation contemplating two environmental policies. The first, "conservation," increases quality of life for more than 200 years, and then stabilizes at a high level thereafter. The second, depletion, involves a slightly higher increase in quality of life for 200 years, but then makes the subsequent quality of life much lower, though still such that life is worth living. Parfit regards it as obvious that depletion is the worse choice. But he points out that there is a problem with the normal explanation for this, that it harms future people.

The problem can be illustrated as follows. Suppose that the choice between the two policies has dramatic social effects. Imagine, for example, that depletion is akin to business-as-usual and conservation is tantamount to a radical green revolution, so that the social infrastructure produced by each policy is very different. As a result, people live, work, and play in very different ways under each policy. Given this, assume that over time the choice will lead people to make different reproductive decisions. They will have children at different times, and perhaps also with different partners, under depletion than under conservation. Suppose also that the identity of a particular child depends crucially on its genetic makeup as determined by the particular sperm and egg from which he or she develops. On this view, even children born to the same parents are different individuals if they emerge from a different sperm and egg. (Children from different parents are of course different.) Hence, the choice of policy will make a difference to which individuals are born. After 300 years or so, Parfit thinks that the difference will be so profound that no individuals who would exist under depletion also exist under conservation, and vice versa. Hence, the two groups are entirely distinct. Call those who exist 300 years into the future under conservation group A, and those who exist under depletion, group B. Suppose then that depletion is chosen. Is anyone harmed? Parfit argues that they are not. On the one hand, members of group A are not harmed, since they do not come into existence. On the other hand, members of group B are not harmed, since their lives are worth living, and since without depletion they would not have existed at all. So, no one is harmed, and the natural explanation for what is wrong with depletion is defeated.

Parfit goes on to offer an alternative explanation of what is wrong with depletion. But the issue of what to say about the NIP is not our concern here, so I will leave it aside. Our concern is with the threat to the PIP posed by the NIP. The threat is this. Proponents of the NIP may claim

that it implies that one of the PIP's central claims is often false. PIP1*
states that it is *collectively rational* for most generations to cooperate. In
other words, almost every generation prefers the outcome produced by
everyone cooperating over the outcome produced by no one cooperating. But in nonidentity cases, future people who are the "victims" of noncooperation by their predecessors (e.g., group B in depletion) may not
prefer the cooperative outcome. After all, they may prefer to exist rather
than not exist, given that their lives are still worthwhile.

If PIP1* is false, the optimistic analysis of the buck-passing problem
fails to apply, but in an interesting way. Although PIP1* is rejected, suggesting a more pessimistic version of buck-passing, the claim of the NIP
is that this pessimism does not give rise to a moral complaint. Still, we
should not be too quick to assume that the PIP is in real trouble. There
are three reasons. First, Parfit's nonidentity cases are only a subset of
those to which the PIP might be applied. So, the relevance of the PIP
does not stand or fall with what is said about such cases. For one thing,
in identity cases, where the generation produced by noncooperation is
the same as that produced by cooperation, PIP1* remains plausible. In
addition, for nonidentity cases where the lives of future people are not
worthwhile, PIP1* also retains its force. This especially relevant when we
are considering cases such as climate change where there is a real prospect of global catastrophe. It suggests that the NIP only troubles the PIP
(and the climate problem more generally) in the less severe cases.

Second, if the PIP fails in some nonidentity cases, notice that it fails
in an interesting way. The claim that vanishes is the one that implies
that noncooperation is a moral or prudential problem. Thus, if it
defeats the PIP, the NIP seems to justify what initially seems problematic (as it does in the case of depletion). If we retain the sense that
something has gone wrong in such cases, we may be more inclined to
resist the NIP than the PIP.[51]

Third, in any case, it is far from clear that the NIP does undermine
the PIP. Although I cannot give a full response here, a few brief remarks
may be helpful. The complaint against the PIP rests on the idea that in

51. Note that Parfit himself does not think that intergenerational ethics is undone by
the NIP. His view is that the problem makes no practical difference. Instead, it makes
only a theoretical difference to which kinds of moral theories we should accept. Moreover, nothing he says there suggests that the PIP analysis should be rejected.

nonidentity cases some prefer to exist under noncooperation rather than not to exist at all. The problem is with group B. Under the NIP, the claim is that B will prefer noncooperation, since their existence depends on it. Hence, group B appear to undermine PIP1*. But matters here are more complicated·than they first seem.

To begin with, even if group B would prefer noncooperation, group A would prefer restricting pollution, since it allows them to come into existence in a situation where there is no unfairness to them. Hence, group A do not dissent from PIP1.* This is not enough to make PIP1* true—since the claim requires a strong consensus—but it does complicate the picture.

In particular, since PIP1* actually refers to the preferences of *generations*, the dispute between A and B brings into focus the issue of what is to count as a distinct generation. Are A and B *considered together* (perhaps with others) a generation? Or does each count as a *separate* generation? The nonidentity-based objection to PIP1* looks best of one assumes that they are separate. If B is a distinct generation, then PIP1* might be straightforwardly false. But is B a distinct generation? Arguably, it is not, and the PIP analysis itself gives strong grounds for saying so. Suppose that a generation is a group that occupies a specific temporal period and is in a given causal relationship to its predecessors and successors, as the PIP suggests. This seems to yield an account of a generation as (roughly) *those who might be alive* at time t, and are affected by the decisions of the present generation. But this includes both group A and group B.

If the morally relevant "generation" includes A and B, then it seems that we need a way of forming a joint attitude of that generation towards PIP1*. It is not clear how one is to do this. But we can make two important observations. First, the fact that it needs to be done suggests that it is not obvious that the NIP casts doubt on PIP1*. Second, there seem to be some possible ways of forming the joint attitude that favor PIP1*. Consider the following example. Suppose that one is sympathetic to Rawlsian accounts of fairness. Then, the relevant question to ask B (and A) might be whether they would prefer noncooperation from behind an appropriate veil of ignorance where they do not know who they will be or which policy is to be chosen. But if this is the question, then PIP1* looks more appealing. Intuitively, possible members of a later generation whose actual constitution will be determined by the choice between depletion or conservation, but who don't know whether they will exist or not, would have strong reason to choose conservation. If so, PIP1 may be true for that "generation."

Now, I want to be careful about the point I'm making here. I am not claiming that Rawls's own approach succeeds; indeed, I am implicitly invoking a distinct model.[52] Nor do I claim to have shown that my invocation of this model decisively resolves the nonidentity problem. (Though something like it might, these are matters for another occasion.[53]) For current purposes, the crucial point is merely that the PIP *need not be undermined by the NIP*. There is logical space through which it may escape its clutches.

In conclusion, in this brief aside I have considered the claim that the PIP is undermined by another intergenerational problem, the NIP. I have argued that it is not. First, not all intergenerational cases are Parfitian. Not only are some identity cases, but others involve making people worse off than some moral minimum, and these are relevant to global environmental tragedies such as catastrophic climate change. Second, if there is a conflict between the PIP and the NIP, it is not clear that we should preserve the NIP. Third, the sense of "generation" underwritten by the PIP is not obviously vulnerable to nonidentity objections, and may even provide the beginnings of a response to such objections.

VII. CONCLUSION

This chapter has argued for five main claims. First, there is a core moral problem—the problem of intergenerational buck-passing—that constitutes the central challenge of distinctively intergenerational ethics, and so deserves the label "the pure intergenerational problem." Second, this problem can accommodate and justify the standard variations in our usage of the language of "generations." Third, it is not overwhelmed by the presence of other difficulties often thought of as distinctively

52. For some doubts about Rawls', see Gardiner 2009a and Gardiner 2011a.
53. These points originally appeared in Gardiner 2003, note 10. More recent discussions of the nonidentity problem seem to be in a similar spirit (e.g., Reiman 2007; Kumar 2003; see also Woodward 1986).

intergenerational. Fourth, the problem can manifest itself in a variety of impure forms in the real world—including in some of our most serious environmental problems, such as climate change. Fifth, the problem has an especially challenging structure, and one that makes it more resistant to solution than similar problems, such as the prisoner's dilemma and tragedy of the commons.

The PIP is clearly a difficult problem to solve. But we should not be downcast. The aim of this analysis is not to undermine ethical behavior towards the future, nor to show that it is impossible. Rather, the hope is that the identification of the pure intergenerational problem will motivate further theoretical investigation of our obligations to future people, and remind us that in practice present generations are vulnerable to corruption, in virtue of their asymmetric causal power and time-dependent interests. The central problem of vulnerability captured by the PIP is easy to grasp, even if the nature and extent of the challenge it poses has not yet been adequately appreciated. Moreover, this is a case where a good diagnosis may contribute substantially to a cure. Understanding that one is engaging in intergenerational buck-passing is morally uncomfortable. As Rawls himself says: "It does not follow [from the severity of the theoretical problems] ... that certain significant ethical constraints cannot be formulated. . . . it may often be clear that a suggested answer is mistaken even if an alternative doctrine is not ready to hand."[54] (See also chapter 11.)

54. Rawls, 1999, 253.

CHAPTER 6

An Intergenerational Arms Race?

We are all used to talking about these impacts coming in the lifetimes of our children and grandchildren. Now we know that it's us.

—Martin Parry, co-chair of Working Group II of the IPCC (quoted in Adam et al. 2007)

If things get bad enough, then with any luck everyone will play the game.

—*The Economist* (Economist 2007)

The previous chapter describes the pure intergenerational problem in very abstract terms. This chapter fleshes out that description by responding to an obvious challenge to the application to climate change. Perhaps severe change is coming much sooner than we think, and to us.

This challenge has some initial plausibility. In recent years, scientific discussion of climate change has taken a turn for the worse. Traditional concern for the gradual, incremental effects of global warming remains; but now greater attention is being paid to the possibility of encountering major threshold phenomena in the climate system, where breaching such thresholds may have catastrophic consequences. As recently as the 2001 report of the Intergovernmental Panel on Climate Change (IPCC), such events were treated as unlikely, at least during the current century.[1] But some recent work tends to suggest that these projections

1. IPCC 2001a [Science]. The 2007 Report is equivocal. For example, Working Group I tried to avoid the topic of rapid ice sheet collapse, and was criticized by some scientists for doing so, while Working Group II highlighted the possibility (IPCC 2007a, 2007b [Impacts]; Dean 2007; Adam 2007). The Synthesis Report charted an intermediate course, saying that it projected linear sea level rise, but more rapid change "cannot

are shaky at best. As the United States National Research Council has warned us, climate surprises are "inevitable."[2]

This paradigm shift may alter how we understand the moral and political challenges posed by climate change, and in particular the current problem of political inertia, in a number of ways. In this chapter, I will examine two suggestions. The first is that abrupt climate change undermines political inertia, in part through undercutting three common explanations for it, based in economic, psychological, and intergenerational factors. The second suggestion is that the shift in focus to abrupt (as opposed to gradual) change aids positive action more directly. On the one hand, it supplies strong motives to the current generation to do what is necessary to tackle the climate problem on behalf of both itself and future generations; on the other hand, failing this, it acts as a kind of fail-safe device, which at least limits how bad the problem can ultimately become.

These suggestions are initially plausible. However, I will argue that they turn out to be largely mistaken, for two reasons. First, the possibility of abrupt change tends only to reshape, rather than undermine, the usual concerns; hence, the intergenerational storm persists. Second, paradoxically, the possibility of abrupt change may make appropriate action more (rather than less) difficult, and exacerbate (rather than limit) the severity of the problem. Worst of all, if the change is severe, it may provoke the equivalent of an intergenerational arms race.

I. ABRUPT CLIMATE CHANGE

The debate on global change has largely failed to factor in the inherently chaotic, sensitively balanced, and threshold-laden nature of Earth's climate system and the increased likelihood of abrupt climate change.

—Robert Gagosian (Gagosian 2003)

---

be excluded." More generally, it stated: "Anthropogenic warming could lead to some impacts that are abrupt or irreversible," and mentioned high levels of species extinction as an example. (IPCC 2007c [Synthesis], 13.) For a more recent assessment, see Lenton et al. 2008.

2. U.S. National Research Council 2002.

Until recently, scientific discussion of climate change has been dominated by what I shall call "the gradualist paradigm." Researchers tended to assume[3] that the response of natural phenomena to increases in greenhouse gas concentrations would be mainly linear and incremental, and this assumption tended to result in analogous claims about likely impacts on human and nonhuman systems. Hence, for example, the original IPCC report projected a rise in global temperature at an average of 0.3C per decade in the twenty-first century[4], and typical estimates of the economic costs of impacts ran at around 1.5–2% of gross world product.[5]

Such results are hardly to be taken lightly, and much of the first three IPCC reports were taken up with showing how and why they are matters of serious concern. But recent research suggests that they may underestimate the problem. This is because there is increasing evidence that the climate system is much less regular than the gradualist paradigm suggests. In particular, there may be major threshold phenomena, and crossing the relevant thresholds may have catastrophic consequences. Scientists have been aware of the possibility of such thresholds for some time. But recent work suggests that the mechanisms governing them are much less robust, and the thresholds themselves much closer to where we are now, than previously thought. This suggests that we need an additional way of understanding the threat posed by climate change. Let us call this "the abrupt paradigm."[6]

Where might this paradigm be instantiated? Three possibilities are especially well-known. The first is ice sheet disintegration, accompanied

---

3. One scientist suggested to me that they were right to do this, since standard methodology says that we should consider the null hypothesis before exploring "more exotic" possibilities. This claim implies that the paradigm shift may have *procedural* roots: the standard methods of science encourage a focus on the linear before the abrupt. If true, this raises questions about whether such a procedure is desirable. Perhaps under some circumstances—such as the threat of catastrophe—society might want to put a stronger priority on investigating nonlinear possibilities.

4. IPCC 1990a; cf. Brown 2002, 18–19.

5. Houghton 2004, 184.

6. For explicit mention of "a new paradigm," see U.S. National Research Council 2002, 1. The Council offers the following scientific definition of an abrupt change: "Technically, an abrupt climate change occurs when the climate system is forced to cross some threshold, triggering a transition to a new state at a rate determined by the climate system itself and faster than the cause." However, recognizing that what is important from the point of view of policy is the societal and ecological impacts, it also suggests that an abrupt change is "one that takes place so rapidly and unexpectedly that human or natural

by a major rise in sea level. In the past, such change has occurred very abruptly: as much as "an average of 1m of sea level rise every 20 years" for four hundred years.[7] Furthermore, the current potential for change is substantial. Melting the mountain glaciers and Greenland alone would lead to a sea level rise of around seven meters, and adding the West Antarctic ice sheet would boost the total to twelve meters.[8] Moreover, it is easy to see why such melting might be catastrophic. Even a total rise of over two meters "would be sufficient to flood large portions of Bangladesh, the Nile Delta, Florida, and many island nations, causing forced migration of tens to hundreds of millions of people."[9] Indeed, since "a large

---

systems have difficulty adapting to it" (p. 14). I have two concerns about these definitions. First, it is not clear that being unexpected ought to be essential to the second definition: if we could reliably predict that we were just about to cross a major climate threshold, this would not lessen the policy concern. (More on this later.) Second, and more importantly, there is some tension between the definitions: since the policy definition makes no mention of thresholds and new states, it seems that a perfectly regular but high magnitude change might count as abrupt on the second definition but not the first. (For an improved technical definition that appeared later, see Lenton et al. 2008.)

These points help to bring out my reason for using the language of "paradigms." Since our primary policy concern is with the impacts of climate change, the relevant difference between gradual and abrupt change appears to be one of degree, rather than kind. Suppose, for example, that on the gradualist paradigm the climate system turned out to be very sensitive to even quite small alterations, so that the increments of uniform and regular climate change were large. Then, the linear change envisioned by gradualism might turn out to have results that mirror severe abrupt change in their phenomenology and impacts. Conversely, if a sudden and irregular change were only of modest magnitude, then it might resemble the typical gradualist changes in its effects. Under such scenarios, the issue of whether the underlying change was scientifically regular or abrupt would not be of much interest to policy makers, since it is only if the impacts of gradual and abrupt change diverge substantially that the distinction becomes important. This suggests that we need terms that will help us to focus in on the most salient impact scenarios. With this in mind, I have characterized the irregular change in the abrupt *paradigm* in terms of catastrophic outcomes, thresholds, and proximity. Clearly, we might encounter catastrophic outcomes quickly even under linear change (e.g., if the magnitude of such change were considerable), and if that were the case, much of what is said about the abrupt paradigm below would apply equally to this kind of gradual change. Still, given prevailing gradualist views, it seems safe to say that the usual gradualist *paradigm* is not of this form. My claim then is that the abrupt and gradualist paradigms are good focal points for discussion. This can be the case even if both are a little caricatured.

7. Hansen 2005, 269.
8. Oppenheimer and Alley 2004, 1–10; UNEP 2007, 64.
9. Hansen 2005, 274.

portion of the world's people live within a few meters of sea level, with trillions of dollars of infrastructure,"[10] James Hansen has stated that such a rise would "wreak havoc with civilization,"[11] making the issue of sea level "the dominant issue in global warming" and one which "sets a low ceiling on the level of global arming that would constitute dangerous anthropogenic interference."[12] Given this, it is clearly a matter of concern that the Greenland ice sheet has recently been said "to be shrinking by 50 cubic kilometers per year," and that this might prime the ice sheets for a sudden, "explosive," and irreversible disintegration.[13]

The second possibility is a weakening of the ocean conveyor of the North Atlantic, which, among other things, supports the Gulf Stream to Western Europe. Again, paleoclimatic evidence suggests that the system is vulnerable to abrupt change, and there is little reason to doubt that such change could be catastrophic, at least to some countries.[14] Given this, it is sobering to see that substantial effects on ocean circulation are projected by climate models, and some scientists reporting that the conveyor may already be showing some signs of disruption.[15]

10. Hansen 2004, 73.

11. Hansen 2005, 275.

12. Hansen 2004, 73.

13. Schiermeier 2006, 258; Hansen 2006. See also Lenton et al 2008, 1789.

14. Gagosian 2003; Alley 2004, 68; Stouffer et al. 2006; Vellinga and Wood 2002, 251–67; Lenton et al 2008.

15. See, for example, Bryden et al. 2005. Of course, many facets of this work remain controversial. Though most agree that the past events occurred and were accompanied by a slowdown, there is disagreement about the extent of the climatic impacts, how they might be relevant to predicting future climate change, and whether we are indeed seeing signs of such change already. Still, much of this controversy concerns *when* we might expect a change, not whether there will be one if global warming continues well into the future. Models do predict a point "beyond which the thermohaline circulation cannot be sustained" (Schiermeier 2006, 257). But there is a disagreement about what conditions are necessary to trigger this. On the one hand, many scientists apparently believe that it requires warming of 4–5 degrees Celsius, and that we will not experience that this century (IPCC 2007; Schiermeier 2006, 257). On the other hand, some say that the range goes lower, to 3–5 degrees, and that some simulations "clearly pass a THC tipping point this century" (Lenton et al. 2008, 1789–90). From an ethical point of view, we should note that even a small chance of collapse this century is a matter for concern, and (more importantly) that it is not clear why we should put so much emphasis on whether it may come before or after 2100.

A third, less understood, possibility for abrupt change is that "vast stores of methane hydrate—a super-greenhouse gas—that are currently frozen under the oceans will, when global warming has reached some point, rise to the surface and dissipate themselves into the atmosphere."[16] This is "the Big Burp Theory of the Apocalypse" referred to in chapter 5.[17] Again, there is precedent. Such a release is said to have caused the biggest extinction of all time, the end of the Permian era 251 million years ago, when ninety percent of species were suddenly lost.[18] Clearly, a change of this kind would be catastrophic.

These three examples are of serious interest in their own right. However, it may be that the most important thing about them is the support they lend to the abrupt paradigm. This is because perhaps our greatest uncertainty at the moment concerns how good we are at identifying catastrophic risks. In other words, it is reasonable to believe that our current grasp of the possibilities is seriously incomplete, and that "it seems wise to assume that we have not yet identified all potential policy-relevant tipping elements."[19] This may be the most crucial fact from the point of view of policy.

If there are abrupt thresholds, where might they be? Recent work suggests that some are in the area of projected emissions, and of these, some may be close by. According to the IPCC, the preindustrial atmospheric concentration of carbon dioxide was around 280 parts per million (ppm), and the current concentration is around 380 ppm. Based on a range of model scenarios making different assumptions about rates of technological change and economic and population growth, the IPCC projects atmospheric concentrations of carbon dioxide of 535–983 ppm, and an increase in surface temperature of 1.1–6.4° Celsius (best estimate, 1.8–4.0°C) by the end of the century.[20] Estimates of where the relevant thresholds might be include: 1°C for the disintegration of the Greenland ice sheet; 2°C, 450 ppm CO_2 or 2–4°C, 550 ppm for the West Antarctic ice sheet; and 3°C in 100 years,

16. Barry 2005, 260.
17. Kristof 2006.
18. Berner 2002; Barry 2005, 260.
19. Lenton et al 2008, 1792; Alley, "Abrupt," 69.
20. IPCC *2007a*.

700 ppm CO_2 for a shutdown of the thermohaline circulation.[21] Clearly, we are in dangerous territory.

II. THREE CAUSES OF POLITICAL INERTIA

Society may be lulled into a false sense of security
by smooth projections of global change.

—Timothy Lenton (Lenton et al. 2008)

Still, perhaps the news is not all grim. It has been suggested that the possibility of abrupt change may help us out of our current problem of political inertia. Plainly, there is a mismatch between the apparent seriousness of the climate issue and our collective institutional response. No doubt there are many possible explanations for this, more than one of which may play a contributing role. To see the initial appeal of the idea that the abrupt paradigm might help, let us consider three of these explanations.[22]

1. Economics

One explanation for political inertia is that people believe that action is not justified. Such arguments are often couched in economic terms.[23] The benefits of action, we are told, do not justify the costs. It is better to allow the global economy to continue to grow using fossil fuels under a "business-as-usual" scenario, and then use the resources created to adapt to climate change, than to risk forestalling growth by cutting back on

21. Oppenheimer and Petsonk 2004. More recent work gives similar estimates: 1–2°C for Greenland, 3–5°C for the West Antarctic and 3–5°C for the thermohaline (Lenton et al. 2008).

22. Important suggestions not considered here include scientific uncertainty, media bias, misinformation campaigns, and cultural barriers to change. I do not wish to deny the importance of such considerations, nor that of a more general account of political inertia. I assume, however, that the three considerations I do consider are important enough to deserve separate treatment (Lomborg 2001, 2007; Oppenheimer 2006; Gardiner 2004b).

23. Some, of course, argue that the science is not compelling. Others add that there is some kind of conspiracy afoot. For current purposes, I will set such views aside. For discussion see Brown 2002, Gardiner 2004a and chapter 11.

carbon emissions. As we shall see in chapter 8, such claims are dubious even under the gradualist paradigm. But the abrupt paradigm appears to undercut them even more decisively.

The central problem is that severe abrupt changes threaten the general idea of following a business-as-usual path, as well as the more specific claim that we can rely on projections of past economic growth as reliable predictors of future performance across the next few centuries. This is obvious with the most catastrophic possibilities, such as the massive methane hydrate release (the apocalyptic "Big Burp"). But it is also relevant to the less dramatic possibilities. Consider, for example, a substantial temperature drop in Europe caused by a major change in ocean circulation in the North Atlantic. This would presumably have a large impact on global society. As an illustration, a report commissioned by the Pentagon speculated that the regional impacts of a shutdown in the thermohaline circulation would be "a world where Europe will be struggling internally, large numbers of refugees washing up on its shores, and Asia in serious crisis over food and water," such that "disruption and conflict" would be "endemic features of life."[24] It went on to say that "in the event of abrupt climate change, it's likely that food, water, and energy resource constraints will first be managed through economic, political, and diplomatic means such as treaties and trade embargoes. Over time though, conflicts over land and water use are likely to become more severe—and more violent. As states become increasingly desperate, the pressure for action will grow."[25] Under this kind of scenario, it seems unreasonable to assume that business-as-usual projections are much of a guide to what would unfold. To say the least, such changes would presumably have a profound effect on relative prices globally, the productivity of investment, and the possibility of intergenerational saving.

In short, a severe abrupt change would surely undermine the reliability of existing cost-benefit analyses of climate change. Hence, there is at least one respect in which the possibility of a catastrophic abrupt climate change does seem to help with the problem of political inertia. It appears decisively to undermine the appeal of the standard economic arguments for inaction.[26]

24. Schwartz and Randall 2003, 14.
25. Schwartz and Randall 2003, 22.
26. One way out of this might be to add geoengineering to the standard package (e.g., Carlin 2007.) I briefly address this approach in chapter 10.

2. Psychology

A second prominent explanation for political inertia is psychological. Elke Weber, for example, claims that political inertia is not surprising, since neither peoples nor their governments have (yet) become alarmed about climate change, and this has meant that they have not (yet) become motivated enough to act.[27]

Why aren't people alarmed? A full explanation would no doubt be very complex. But Weber's account suggests that the outline is accessible enough. In short, human beings have two processing systems, the affective and the analytical,[28] and these two systems are influenced in different ways and by different kinds of inputs. Moreover, in cases involving risk and uncertainty—such as climate change—the affective system is dominant.[29] This gives rise to a number of general problems. First, the two systems can, and often do, offer different judgments for the same cases.[30] Second, the reasons for these differences seem shallow. In particular, the two systems acquire information in different ways: the affective tends to rely on personal experience, whereas the analytical favors statistical descriptions, with the result that "ostensibly [the] same information can lead to different choices depending on how the information is acquired."[31] Third, for reasons we shall see in a moment, the interplay of the two mechanisms gives rise to a systematic bias in decision making: "low-probability events generate less concern than their probability warrants on average, but more concern than they deserve in those rare instances when they do occur."[32]

To make matters worse, these problems interact badly with some related psychological phenomena surrounding risk. For one thing, Weber claims that there is a "finite pool of worry": people have a limited

27. Weber 2006, 103. See also Leiserowitz 2005, 1438 & 1440; 2004, 27. Broader psychological, institutional, and political explanations are canvassed in Oppenheimer 2006 in the papers by Baron, Bazerman, Leiserowitz, and Sunstein. I focus on Weber's account because it has the most direct relevance to the distinction between the abrupt and gradual paradigms.
28. Weber 2006, 104.
29. Weber 2006, 104.
30. Weber 2006, 104.
31. Weber 2006, 106.
32. Weber 2006, 102.

capacity for the kind of worry that motivates action, so that an increase in concern about one risk tends to reduce concern about others.[33] For another, there is an analogous limitation in people's responses to problems even when they are motivated to act. Decision makers have a "single action bias," such that they are "very likely to take one action to reduce a risk that they encounter and worry about, but are much less likely to take additional steps that would provide incremental protection or risk reduction." Moreover, this bias persists even if the single action taken is neither the most effective, nor suitably coordinated with other actors, since a single action alone is enough to reduce worry.[34]

These two tendencies have a number of implications. First, the presence of a finite pool of worry suggests that we can expect political inertia even when people appreciate that a particular problem exists, if concern for that problem is "crowded out" by other issues that seem more pressing. Second, given its dominance, failure to engage the affective mechanism is likely to result in a particular problem's being marginalized by other—perhaps objectively less important—concerns that do so engage.[35] Third, even successful engagement is not enough, given the single action bias. Hence, in cases where piecemeal, incremental policy making is unlikely to work, it is vital not only to take major action when an issue has succeeded in grabbing the political spotlight, but also then to take all (or most) of the action necessary.

The relevance of these general claims to climate change seems clear. First, most of the available information comes from science and is both abstract and statistical. Hence, it engages the analytical system. However, given the dominance of the affective system, such engagement is liable to be ineffective by itself. Second, it is difficult to engage the affective system in the case of climate change because within that system "recent personal experience strongly influences the evaluation of a risky option"[36] and "personal experience with noticeable and serious consequences of global warming is still rare in many regions of the world."[37] Third, given this, we

33. Hence, for example, "increases in the concern of the U.S. public about terrorism post 9/11 seem to have resulted in decreased concern about other issues such as environmental degradation or restrictions of civil liberties" (Weber 2006, 115).

34. Weber 2006, 115.

35. Weber 2006, 105.

36. Weber 2006, 103.

37. Weber 2006, 108.

should expect a communication problem. Weber claims that statistical information has a different impact on those who are used to employing their analytical systems and those who are not. Hence, she claims, there is likely to be a mismatch between the reactions of scientists and lay-people to the same information.[38] Finally, concerns about the psychological limits of attention and action seem pressing. For one thing, empirical work suggests that many people see climate change as a real problem, but also rank it below many other concerns, particularly when it comes to voting behavior.[39] For another, many political communities do seem to have suffered from a kind of attention-deficit disorder when it comes to climate change. Moreover, those efforts that have been made tend to be predominantly piecemeal and incremental. Even the current Kyoto agreement is routinely defended as merely a necessary first step. But these may be dangerous tendencies given the single action bias.

What are the implications of all this psychology? Weber suggests that we must find a way of engaging the affective system, "perhaps by simulations of [global warming's] concrete future consequences for people's home[s] or other regions they visit or value."[40] However, then she adds that invoking the gradualist paradigm is unlikely to work:

> To the extent that people conceive of climate change as a simple and gradual change... the risks posed by climate change would appear to be well-known and, at least in principle, controllable ("move from Miami to Vancouver when things get too hot or dangerous in Florida"). While some of the perceived control may be illusory, the ability or inability to take corrective action is an important component of vulnerability.[41]

Instead:

> It is only the potentially catastrophic nature of (rapid) climate change (of the kind graphically depicted in the movie *The Day after Tomorrow*) and the global dimension of adverse effects. . . that have the potential for raising a visceral reaction to the risk.[42]

38. Weber 2006, 108.

39. See references in Jamieson 2006, and the ongoing work of the Yale Project on Climate Change.

40. Weber 2006, 103.

41. Weber 2006, 112.

42. Weber 2006, 113–14. (More on the full version of this passage later.)

In short, Weber claims that the abrupt paradigm has the capacity to engage the affective system in a way sufficient to motivate action. Given this, the growing scientific support for that paradigm is indeed good news in one respect, for it offers a potential way out of psychologically induced political inertia.[43] Of course, Weber herself wants to go even further than this. For she asserts that *only* abrupt climate change—and truly global and catastrophic instances of it at that—can help.

3. The Intergenerational Analysis

The third explanation of political inertia is, of course, the perfect moral storm, and in particular the dominance of the intergenerational storm.[44] On the gradualist paradigm, intergenerational buck-passing looks especially likely, because of the long timeframe over which climate change plays out. But might the abrupt paradigm help? Initially, it appears so, since the potential proximity of the relevant thresholds appears to undercut the intergenerational aspect of climate change. Consider, for example, the following statement by former British Prime Minister Tony Blair:

> What is now plain is that the emission of greenhouse gases, associated with industrialisation and strong economic growth from a world population that has increased sixfold in 200 years, is causing global warming at a rate that began as significant, has become alarming and is simply unsustainable in the long term. And by long term I do not mean centuries ahead. I mean within the lifetime of my children certainly; and possibly within my own. And by unsustainable, I do not mean a phenomenon causing problems of adjustment. I mean a challenge so far-reaching in its impact and irreversible in its destructive power, that it alters radically human existence.[45]

Blair's main claim appears to be that the impacts of climate change are both extremely serious, and coming relatively soon. (He does not mention abrupt climate change explicitly, but it is reasonable to assume

43. Weber does point out that there is some concern that abrupt climate change may "crowd out" other legitimate policy concerns. (See my later remarks about the intergenerational arms race.)

44. We have already seen that it is plausible to believe that this is manifest in the global politics of climate change, and more will be said in chapter 8.

45. Blair 2004.

that this is what he has in mind.) If this is right, it seems to give current people powerful reasons to act. Again, the abrupt paradigm appears to extinguish a major source of political inertia.

III. AGAINST UNDERMINING

At first glance, then, it appears that the abrupt paradigm undercuts all three of the major explanations for political inertia we've considered. However, I shall now argue that in the case of the last two explanations, this appearance is deceptive. Instead, it is plausible to think that the possibility of abrupt climate change will actually make the intergenerational problem worse, rather than better, and that the psychological problem will add to this sad state of affairs.

Let us begin with the intergenerational problem. Blair suggests that some impacts of climate change are serious enough to "[alter] radically human existence," "within the lifetime of my children certainly; and possibly within my own." A rough calculation suggests that this means possibly within the next 26 years, and certainly within the next 75 (or 58).[46] At first glance, such claims do seem to undermine the usual intergenerational analysis. But this is too hasty. For the notion of proximity is complicated in the climate change case by the considerable time lags involved—the same lags that give rise to the possibility of intergenerational buck-passing.

Let us remind ourselves of what was said in chapter 1. First, the atmospheric lifetime of a typical molecule of the main anthropogenic greenhouse gas, carbon dioxide, is often said to be around 200–300 years. This introduces a significant lagging effect in itself, but obscures the fact that around 25% remains for more than a thousand years.[47] Moreover,

46. Blair's four children were born between 1984 and 2000. If we assume an average lifespan of 80 years, then he is claiming with certainty that there will be radical impacts no later than 2080. Since Blair himself was born in 1953, he is also claiming that radical impacts could come before 2033. Moreover, on the reasonable assumption that he intends to suggest that abrupt climate change would have profound effects on the course each of their lives (rather than simply being observed by them right at the end of their lives), Blair presumably envisages timeframes notably closer than these outlying dates.

47. Archer 2005, 5.

many of the basic processes set in motion by the greenhouse effect continue to play out over thousands of years. Second, these facts have implications for the shape of the climate change problem. For one thing, the problem is *resilient*: once the emissions necessary to cause serious climate change have been released it is difficult—and perhaps impossible—to reverse the process. For another, the problem is *seriously backloaded*: at any given time in the foreseeable future the current impacts of anthropogenic climate change do not reflect the full consequences of emissions made up to that point. Finally, this implies that the full effects of current emissions are *substantially deferred*. Even if the current generation is to reap some of what we sow, *we* will not reap all of it.

These points suggest that it is worth distinguishing two kinds of proximity: temporal and causal. When Blair claims that the impacts of climate change are coming soon, he means to speak of temporal proximity: the impacts are near to us in time. But claims about causal proximity are different: here the idea is that the point at which we effectively commit the earth to an abrupt change by our actions is close at hand. Given the presence of resilience, serious backloading, and substantial deferral, temporal proximity does not always imply causal proximity, and vice versa. This fact has important implications, as we shall now see.

1. Domino Effect

Consider first a scenario where we are in a position to set in motion a chain of events that will commit humanity (and other species) to a catastrophic abrupt impact, but we won't suffer that impact ourselves because it will be visited on future generations. In this case, there is causal, but not temporal proximity. Call this scenario *the domino effect*. Several of the most worrying impacts currently envisioned seem to fit this scenario. For example, even very rapid ice sheet disintegration is presumed to take place over centuries, such that its impacts are intergenerational;[48] similarly, the limited work that has been done on deposits of methane hydrate in the oceans suggest that the associated impacts would not arise for several centuries, if not millennia.[49] Hence,

---

48. Hansen 2005.
49. Lenton et al. 2008; Archer and Buffett 2005; Harvey and Huang 1995, 2905–26.

the real concern in these cases is with causal proximity: the worry is that by our actions we may commit future generations to catastrophic climate changes.[50] However, such a scenario clearly raises, rather than undermines, the intergenerational analysis. So, we will have to look elsewhere for a challenge to the intergenerational storm.[51]

2. In the Cards

A second kind of scenario would involve temporal but not causal proximity. Suppose, for example, that we are already only a few years from crossing a major climate threshold, and that at this point we are already committed to doing so. The most obvious reason why this might be the case would be because, given the time lags, our past emissions make breaching the threshold literally inevitable. But it might also be that we are already committed because there are emissions that we are morally no longer going to be able to avoid (for example, because avoiding them would impose intolerable costs on current people and their immediate descendents). Call this scenario *in the cards*.

If it turned out that in the cards characterized our situation, and if we knew that it did so, then the implications of the abrupt paradigm for political inertia would be more mixed than the basic objection to the intergenerational analysis suggests. First, and most obviously, the in the cards scenario might simply reinforce inertia. Suppose, for example, that a given generation knew that it would be hit with a catastrophic abrupt change no matter what it did. Might it not be inclined to fatalism? If so, then the temporal proximity of abrupt change would actually enhance political inertia, rather than undercut it. (Why bother?)

Second, and less obviously, in the cards may provoke action of the *wrong kind*. For example, assume, for simplicity, that the two main policy responses for climate change are *mitigation* of future impacts through reducing the emissions that cause them, and *adaptation* to minimize the

50. For this reason, Hansen describes the ice sheets as a "ticking time bomb" (Hansen 2004, 275). I prefer the analogy of a domino effect, since the central issue is that one generation is in a position to initiate a chain of events that will be very difficult (though not impossible) to stop.

51. Blair himself mentions both a mismatch in timing between cause and effect, and the intergenerational dimension, suggesting a sensitivity to the PIP.

adverse effects of those impacts that can or will not be avoided. Then, the following may turn out to be true of in the cards. On the one hand, the incentives for the current generation to engage in mitigation may at least be weakened, and might disappear altogether. This is because, if a given abrupt change is, practically speaking, inevitable, then *it* appears to provide no incentive to a current generation with purely generation-relative motivations for limiting its emissions. Perhaps the current generation will still have reasons to engage in some mitigation, since this might help it to avoid further impacts (including abrupt impacts) after the given abrupt change. But the given abrupt change does no motivational work of its own. Hence, its presence does not help future generations. On the other hand, the incentives for the current generation to engage in adaptation might be substantially improved. If big changes are coming, then it makes sense to prepare for them.[52] In itself, this appears to be good news for both current and future people. But there are complications. For it remains possible that the current generation's adaptation efforts may be unfair to the future. This point is important, so it is worth spending some time on it.

Let us consider three ways in which the improved motivation for adaptation provided by the in the cards scenario may come into conflict with intergenerational concerns. First, considering only its generation-relative preferences, a current generation aware of an impending abrupt change will have an incentive to overinvest in adaptation *relative* to mitigation (and other intergenerational projects). That is, given the opportunity, such a generation will prefer to put resources into adaptation (from which it expects benefits), rather than mitigation (which tends to benefit the future).[53] Moreover, even within the category of adaptation, the current generation will have an incentive to prioritize projects and strategies that are more beneficial to it (e.g., temporary "quick fixes") over those that seem best from an intergenerational point of view. In short, we should expect shadow solutions.[54]

52. Alley 2004; U.S. National Research Council 2002.

53. This incentive is likely to be augmented by the possibility of greater opportunities for "double counting" and "no regrets" policies within adaptation (as opposed to mitigation) projects. For example, suppose that one adaptation strategy involved building up emergency response capabilities. Such a strategy would presumably bring with it benefits for dealing with nonclimate as well as climate-related disasters.

54. See chapters 4 and 10.

Second, this problem is likely to be exacerbated by psychological effects. For example, Weber claims that proximity which brings with it engagement of the affective mechanism often leads to an overreaction: "low-probability events generate . . . more concern than they deserve in those rare instances when they do occur."[55] Hence, those in the grip of an abrupt change are likely to overinvest in their adaptive responses.

Third, and most importantly, the proximity of the abrupt change may actually provide an incentive for *increasing* current emissions above the amount that *even a completely self-interested generation* would normally choose. What I have in mind is this. Suppose that a generation could increase its own ability to cope with an impending abrupt change by increasing its emissions beyond their existing level. (For example, suppose that it could boost economic output to enhance adaptation efforts by relaxing existing emissions standards.) Then, it would have a generation-relative reason to do so, and it would have this *even if* the net costs of the additional emissions to future generations far exceed the short-term benefits. Given this, it is conceivable that the impending presence of a given abrupt change may actually *exacerbate* intergenerational buck-passing, leaving future generations worse off than under the gradualist paradigm (or than they would be if the earlier generation had not discovered the falsity of that paradigm). Furthermore, just as in the original PIP, this problem can become iterated. That is, if the increased indulgence in emissions by earlier generations intent on adapting to a specific abrupt climate change worsens the situation for a subsequent generation (e.g., by causing a further threshold to be breached), then the later generation may also be motivated to engage in extra emissions, and so on. In short, under the in the cards scenario, we may see the structural equivalent of an intergenerational arms race surrounding greenhouse gas emissions. Abrupt climate change may make life for a particular generation hard enough that it is motivated to increase its emissions substantially in order to cope. This may then increase the impact on a subsequent generation, with the same result. And so it goes on.

At first, the possibility of an intergenerational arms race may seem outlandish, in at least two ways. For one thing, it may seem to envisage an impossible, or at least very remote possibility: that the proximity of abrupt climate change could motivate even more greenhouse gas

55. Weber 2006, 103.

emissions than are currently being generated. For another, it may seem to attribute to a generation a hopelessly immoral (and therefore utterly unrealistic) outlook.

The first objection seems to me implausible. Consider, for example, a substantial change in the ocean conveyor brought on by climate change. If the physical impacts in Europe were anything like the magnitude of the past events mentioned by oceanographers, then the social and economic impacts would likely be very large, and negative.[56] Is it implausible to think that such impacts would cause a sharp change in energy and industrial policies in Europe? Is it unlikely that a Europe facing shortages of food, water, and fuel (as the Pentagon report predicted) would abandon high energy taxes and clean burning technologies, seeking whatever aid additional energy could give it in fighting such problems?[57] Moreover, is it likely that the rest of the world, witnessing such impacts, would stand by and stoically refuse to aid those in distress? Would they not relax their own standards, burning their own oil and coal in whatever ways might be helpful in alleviating such a tragedy? Such actions seem entirely natural. Moreover, they are likely to be exacerbated by the psychology of risk. If Weber is right that there is a finite pool of worry and a single action bias, one would expect a current generation to be consumed with the immediate tragedies of a severe abrupt change at the expense of other, more long-term worries.

This brings us to the second objection. However likely people might be to act in these ways, wouldn't they have to be grossly immoral to do so? I'm not so sure. As the above scenario suggests, there may be something admirable about the actions of such a generation, even if there is also something tragic, in that such actions predictably harm future people. Indeed, such a generation may be *morally justified* in its actions. Considering a similar situation, Martino Traxler likens the case to one of self-defense:

56. Some people may regard the possibility of such impacts as itself outlandish. But that will not help here. For here we are considering arguments that use such possibilities in their main premises. The question is, *if* such impacts are possible and likely close by, does this undermine the intergenerational problem? My answer is that it does not.

57. Note that California's widely lauded recent climate change legislation includes an explicit "safety valve" clause, such that the governor may delay or suspend regulations "in the event of extraordinary circumstances, catastrophic events, or threat of significant economic harm." See California Assembly Bill 32 (2006), section 38599.

Where the present harm from not emitting is conspicuous enough, we would be unrealistic, unreasonable, and maybe even irrational to expect present people to allow present harm and suffering to visit them or their kith and kin in order that they might avoid harm to future people. In these cases, we may with good reason speak of having so strong or so rationally compelling a reason to emit that, in spite of the harm these emissions will cause to (future) others, we are excused for our maleficence.[58]

We seem then to have uncovered a way in which abrupt climate change may lead to a form of the PIP that is actually worse in several respects than the one suggested by the gradualist paradigm. First, abrupt climate change might increase the *magnitude* of intergenerational buck-passing, by increasing the presence of front-loaded goods. If a current generation can protect itself more effectively against an abrupt change through extra emissions that harm the future, then it has a reason to do so.[59] Second, a severe abrupt change may make taking advantage of such goods not simply a matter of self- or generation-relative interest (which might be morally criticized), but morally justifiable in a very serious way. Hence, abrupt change may make buck passing even harder to overcome.[60]

3. Open Window

The in the cards scenario shows that it is possible for abrupt change to make matters worse. But perhaps that scenario is too pessimistic. Hopefully, even though there is a sense in which the climate thresholds are close, it is not true that we are already committed to crossing one.[61] Interestingly,

58. Traxler 2002, 107. See chapter 11.

59. Of course, such a scenario may arise under gradual change as well, even given the modest rate of change posited by the gradualist paradigm. It is simply more likely to arise, to arise quickly, and to swamp intergenerational concerns under the abrupt paradigm.

60. It is worth noting that the presence of an intergenerational arms race with a bias towards adaptation might easily result in an economic argument for inaction predicated on the premise that unfettered economic growth is the best adaptive strategy. In many cases—though not always—this may manifest a form of moral corruption.

61. More weakly, perhaps we are committed only to crossing some thresholds and not others, and the abrupt climate change to which we are not yet committed is, on balance, worth avoiding, even for our own sakes.

this thought reveals a tension in the proximity claim that is supposed to undermine the intergenerational problem: to be successful, the threatened abrupt change must be temporally close enough to motivate the current generation, but distant enough so as not yet to be in the cards. This tension suggests that the argument against the intergenerational analysis presupposes a very specific scenario: that there is an abrupt change that would affect the current generation, to which the planet is not yet committed, but to which it will become committed unless the current generation take evasive action very soon. (Call this scenario *open window*.)

Several issues arise about open window. The first, obviously enough, is whether there is such a window, and, if so, how big it is. These are empirical questions on which our information is sketchy. Still, the preliminary estimates are not particularly encouraging. First, two parameters loom large. At the present time, scientists often say that there is a further temperature rise beyond that which the earth has yet experienced but which is "already in the system." Estimates of this commitment typically range from 0.5–1.0°C, suggesting that a fair amount of climate change is already literally in the cards. The vital issue then becomes how much more is *in effect* in the cards, since we cannot stop the world economy (and so the current trajectory and level of global emissions) on a dime. Barring a sudden technological miracle, the answer to this question would also seem to be "a substantial amount." These facts suggest that we are already committed to any abrupt changes likely to arise in the short- to medium-term. Thus, the in the cards scenario has substantial relevance.

Second, preliminary calculations suggest that our ability to avoid a more substantial commitment is limited. Consider, for example, the common call for limiting the global temperature rise to 2°C in order to avoid dangerous climate change. The origins of this target are a little unclear,[62] but according to one recent analysis, its policy implications are sobering:

> To have a high probability of keeping the temperature increase below 2C, the total global 21st century carbon budget must be limited to about 400 Gigatonnes . . . A budget of 400 GtC is *very* small. To stay within this budget, global emissions would almost certainly have to peak before 2020 and decline fairly rapidly

62. Barry 2005, 265; Oppenheimer and Petsonk 2004.

thereafter. If emissions were to continue to grow past 2020, so much of the 400 GtC budget would be rapidly used up that holding the 2C line would ultimately require extraordinary rates of emission reduction, rates corresponding to such large and historically unprecedented rates of accelerated capital-stock turnover that, frankly, it's difficult to imagine them occurring by virtue of any normal, orderly economic process. Time, in other words, is running out.[63]

Given the ongoing growth in global emissions, stabilization in just over ten years is a very ambitious target. According to the authors of the analysis, the 400 Gt budget is so tight that even if the developed nations were to reduce their emissions to *zero* by 2028, it would require serious reductions by developing countries starting in 2030. Obviously, absent some technological miracle, the antecedent of this claim is politically (and morally) impossible. But the consequent is almost as *implausible*, given that projections indicate that in 2030, the developing nations will still be quite poor.[64]

It is thus unclear whether the 2°C target is feasible. Hence, if meeting that target is really necessary for avoiding any catastrophic abrupt impacts for the current people,[65] the prospects for motivating action on those grounds appear slim. Much would then depend on how many other impacts that are still causally proximate are temporally close enough to have notable effects on the current generation. This remains an empirical question. But the projections suggest that we are now dealing with a very limited subset of the impacts of climate change. In short, for a generation interested only in impacts that affect its own concerns, the window may be closed, or at best, only slightly ajar.

Hopefully, the projections just cited will turn out to be unduly pessimistic.[66] Hence, it is worth making some observations about the importance of intergenerational buck-passing even if there is an open window for the current generation. Our second issue then is whether, if the window is open, this undermines the relevance of the PIP. One concern is that generations might care less about the end-of-life abrupt climate change than earlier-in-life ones. Another is that even an open window

63. Kartha et al 2005, 4.

64. Kartha et al. 2005, 10.

65. Some, of course, believe that 2°C is too high (e.g., Barry 2005, 267); See also chapter 11.

66. Notice, however, that even if that is the case, they may enter into the present reasoning of the current generation, and so corrupt its decision making.

severely restricts the relevance of future people's concerns. For the open window scenario to be effective, there have to be enough effects of present emissions that accrue within the window to justify the current generation's action on a generation-relative basis. But this ignores all the other effects of present emissions—including those that accrue to other generations. So, the PIP remains. Moreover, in light of the PIP, there is a realistic concern that solutions that avoid a particular abrupt climate change will be judged purely on how they enable a present generation to avoid that change arising during their lifetime, not on their wider ramifications. For example, each generation might be motivated simply to *delay* any given abrupt climate change until after it is dead. So, it may endorse policies that merely postpone such a change, making it inevitable for a future generation. Finally, sequential concerns may arise even under the open window scenario. Considering the PIP, it would be predictable that earlier generations tend to use up most of any safety margin left to them. Given this, it may turn out that some later generation cannot help pushing over a given threshold, and using up most of the safety margin for the next.

4. The Self-Corrective Argument

If all of this is the case, the potential for the abrupt paradigm to undermine the intergenerational problem appears to be slim. But before closing, it is worth addressing one final argument. Weber suggests that the psychological problems she identifies may eventually take care of themselves:

> Failing these efforts, the problem discussed in this paper is ultimately self-corrective. Increasing personal evidence of global warming and its potentially devastating consequences can be counted on to be an extremely effective teacher and motivator.[67]

The basic idea seems to be that, once realized, the impacts brought on by inaction on climate change are of a sort to engage the affective mechanism. Of course, as Weber recognizes, this may only happen once

67. Weber 2005, 116.

a substantial amount of damage is already done, and the planet is committed to significantly more.[68] Still, the claim is that at least there is some kind of limit to inertia provided by the phenomena of climate change themselves.

Does the abrupt paradigm impose some limit on how bad climate change can get? Perhaps. But again the intergenerational problem rears its ugly head. If climate change is resilient and seriously backloaded, the effects on a present generation that experiences an abrupt change and knows these facts are unclear. If further bad impacts are already on the cards, or if the open window is only slightly ajar, then, if the present generation is guided by its generation-relative preferences, we may still expect substantial intergenerational buck-passing, and therefore more climate change. Experience of abrupt impacts may not teach and motivate, precisely because for such a generation the time for teaching and motivating has already passed, at least as far as its own concerns are implicated. Moreover, we should expect other factors to intervene. If a generation experiences a severe abrupt change, we might expect long-term concerns (such as with mitigation) to be crowded out in the finite pool of worry by more immediate concerns. We might also expect such a generation to be morally justified in ignoring those concerns, to at least some extent. In short, we might expect something akin to the beginnings of an intergenerational arms race.[69]

IV. CONCLUSION

This chapter has considered three theses: that the possibility of abrupt change undermines the usual economic, psychological, and intergenerational causes of political inertia; that it provides the current generation with positive motivation to act; and that it implies that there is some kind of fail-safe system that will limit humanity's ongoing infliction of

---

68. In the sentence immediately following the quoted passage, she says: "unfortunately, such lessons may arrive too late for corrective action." On the face of it, this remark appears to contradict the "self-corrective" claim. But this is an uncharitable reading. I provide a better one immediately below in the main text.

69. These remarks are not criticisms of Weber herself, since she envisions that the motivation will be intergenerational. See next section.

climate change on itself and other species.[70] Against these claims, I suggested that although the real possibility of abrupt change does tend to undermine economic explanations for inertia (which were, however, not very strong anyway), it does not undercut either its psychological or intergenerational roots. Instead, the abrupt paradigm threatens to make climate change an even worse problem than the gradualist model it is supposed to augment or supersede. Abrupt climate change may actually increase each generation's incentive to consume dangerous greenhouse gas emissions, and may even cause at least some generations to have a moral license to do so.

I conclude that we should not look to the disasters of abrupt change—either the actual experience of them, or increasing scientific evidence that they are coming—to save us. One implication of this is that we should not waste precious time waiting for that to happen. If severe abrupt climate change is a real threat, the time for action is now, when many actions are likely to be prudentially and morally easier than in the future.

Still, how effectively to motivate such action remains a very large practical problem, about which the psychologists have much to teach us. In my view, if we are to solve this problem, we will need to look beyond people's generation-relative preferences. Moreover, the prevalence of the intergenerational problem suggests that one set of motivations that we need to think hard about engaging is that involving moral beliefs about our obligations to those only recently, or not yet, born.[71] This leaves us with one final question: can the abrupt paradigm assist us in this last task? Perhaps so: for one intriguing possibility is that the prospect of abrupt change will engage intergenerational motivations. Indeed, Weber explicitly suggests as much in the full version of a passage quoted earlier:

70. Taken together, these claims are comforting in at least two ways. First, they suggest that the way to overcome political inertia is simply to make current people aware of the possibility of abrupt climate change, through personal experience or relevant simulations of that experience. Awareness ought to be enough, the thought goes, because the current generation does appear to be vulnerable to such change, and the magnitude of it is sufficient to engage the right affective mechanisms. Second, the three claims imply that if, for some reason, this does not work, at least there is a limit to how bad it can get before the problem of political inertia finally goes away.

71. We need also to think about duties to nonhuman nature. But since this is, at best, a far more difficult case to make, I leave it aside here. For the view that this is the only strategy likely to work, see Jamieson 2010.

It is only the potentially catastrophic nature of (rapid) climate change (of the kind graphically depicted in the movie *The Day after Tomorrow*) and the global dimension of adverse effects *which may create hardships for future generations* that have the potential for raising a visceral reaction to the risk.[72]

If Weber is right that concerns about the potential effects of abrupt change on future people can cause the needed psychological effects,[73] then the psychology of abrupt climate change might turn out to be of profound importance after all, even taking the intergenerational problem into account. Still, this would now be because such change helps to underwrite a solution to the pure intergenerational problem, not because it undermines its application. Hence, such a result would fit well with the main aim of this chapter, which has been to show that a solution to the intergenerational problem is still required, and that, given this, these psychological and philosophical questions are the right ones to be asking.

72. Weber 2006, 113–14.

73. Leiserowitz may disagree. He claims that "climate change is unlikely to become a high-priority national issue until Americans consider themselves personally at risk," and though he may be taking a broad view of the "personal" in this passage—probably intending to refer to "impacts on themselves, their family or their local community"—this is still likely to be too narrow to capture the kind of intergenerational concern needed. See Leiserowitz 2005, 1437–8.

PART D

The Theoretical Storm

CHAPTER 7

A Global Test for Contemporary Political Institutions and Theories

If political leaders have one duty above all others, it is to protect the security of their people. . . . And yet our long-term security is threatened by a problem at least as dangerous as chemical, nuclear or biological weapons, or indeed international terrorism: human-induced climate change.

—Sir John Houghton, former head of the IPCC (Houghton 2003)

"The minimum that is scientifically necessary [to combat global warming] far exceeds the maximum that is politically feasible.

—Al Gore (early 1990s, quoted in McKibben 2001, 38)

Parts B and C argue that climate change puts us in the grip of global and intergenerational storms, and that the intergenerational aspect dominates. In the face of such threats to ethical action, it would be nice if we had robust general theories to guide us. In particular, it would be helpful if our theories were internally well-developed, externally well-defended, and appropriately specific to guide policy over the long term. This would allow us both to set a firm course, and to resist the countervailing forces of the first two storms.[1]

Unfortunately, this is not our situation. Instead, even our best moral and political theories are poorly placed to deal with many of the issues characteristic of long-term global problems such as climate change. These include (but are not limited to) intergenerational equity,

---

1. On the important role of more modest theoretical work, see chapter 11 and Vanderheiden 2008a.

international justice, scientific uncertainty, persons whose existence and preferences are contingent on the choices we make, and the human relationship to animals and the rest of nature. When such issues coincide they deliver the third component of the perfect moral storm, the theoretical storm. In essence, the problem is that traditional approaches seem largely "inept," in the nonpejorative sense of being "unsuited" for, poorly "adapted" to, "inappropriate" for, or lacking the necessary skills and basic competence to complete, the task.[2]

In this book I will not attempt to justify the claim of theoretical ineptness by trolling through the literature, but simply regard it as highly plausible on its face.[3] Nevertheless, I will try to motivate the background concern in two ways. This chapter argues that the climate problem brings on a global test for political institutions and theories that they currently (in the wake of Kyoto, Bonn-Marrakesh, and Copenhagen) seem to be failing. Chapter 8 offers as an example of theoretical failure the most influential theoretical approach of the day in public policy, cost-benefit analysis.

The claim that global environmental change in general, and climate change in particular, poses severe theoretical difficulties is subject to an immediate challenge. Some might say: "Why aren't these just normal political problems, perplexing in their scale perhaps, but not of a fundamentally different kind than most other problems in domestic and international affairs? Why isn't the political problem, insofar as there is one, simply that certain actors have behaved badly, for the usual political reasons?"[4] This chapter offers one central answer to such questions by advancing a minimal global test for social and political institutions and

2. The former phrases are taken from OED; the latter from Encarta Word Dictionary. In saying this, I have no wish to denigrate the efforts of those who have contributed. The charge of theoretical ineptness has more to do with the intrinsic difficulty these areas, and their relative neglect by the wider community, than with the quality of the limited work done so far. For useful contributions specifically related to climate change, see Gardiner et al. 2010 and Page 2006.

3. This is partly because it is difficult to provide strong evidence of absence, and partly because such a discussion would be of limited interest in a book of this kind. For some general support of the claim, see Broome 2005; Gardiner 2009a, 2011a, forthcoming; Jamieson 1992, 2009; Palmer 2011. Intergenerational ethics provides a prime example, where much of the best work uncovers problems rather than resolving them (e.g., Parfit 1985).

4. These are questions that I am often asked, but I am grateful to Stephen Macedo for pressing them most forcefully.

theories, and then suggesting that conventional versions of both may fail in the case of climate change. If this argument is correct, then the climate problem poses a major challenge to global systems.[5] Among other things, this implies that the current (almost exclusive) focus on scientific and economic questions is a dangerous mistake.

Section I introduces the global test and provides some general reasons for believing that it may apply to climate change. Section II states more precisely what is so worrying about climate change by identifying two challenges to institutions and theories that it may bring on: the *hard landing* and *crash landing* scenarios. Section III advances the conjecture that existing global systems are poorly placed to handle such scenarios, and argues that humanity's initial response to the climate crisis appears to confirm this conjecture. Section IV identifies some basic difficulties for evaluating political theories in this setting, and tried to address them by pointing out some vices such theories may have. Section V illustrates the relevance of these vices through a brief discussion of utilitarianism and cost-benefit analysis. Section VI illustrates our theoretical predicament by a comparison with the evolution of another area of political concern, the moral and political status of women.

It is perhaps worth emphasizing at the outset that, although the argument of this chapter is primarily negative, the motivation is not to disparage contemporary institutions and theories—many of which have been very useful for other purposes—but to advance them. The thought is that the climate change case helps us to see ways in which our systems (of action and thought) may need to be reoriented. As global ethics emerges as a major concern in both political philosophy and the world at large, this is an important task.

I. THE GLOBAL TEST

In July 2003, Sir John Houghton, former co-chair of scientific assessment for the United Nations Intergovernmental Panel on Climate Change (IPCC), published an open letter to U.S. President George

---

5. For convenience, I will sometimes use the phrase "a global system" to refer to a set of global social and political institutions (including states and other subnational institutions) and the philosophies that support them.

W. Bush and British Prime Minister Tony Blair in the British press. Frustrated with the lack of action on climate change, Houghton accused the two leaders of neglecting their fundamental political duty towards their citizens in "an abdication of leadership of epic proportions."[6]

Houghton's charge is remarkable. First, this is a very serious accusation for a senior public figure to make, especially when the accusing is done in such a public way. This is important in its own right, since it suggests that Houghton regards the stakes as very high.[7] Second, Houghton's language clearly suggests the belief that there is something special about the threat posed by climate change. He is not, it seems, regarding climate change as a "normal" kind of political problem. Instead, in couching his complaint in terms of the fundamental duty of political leaders, he implies that there is something deep and basic about it.[8]

Houghton's charge has intuitive appeal. Still, one might doubt whether he himself pushes it far enough. On the surface at least, Houghton seeks only to put climate change on a similar footing to issues such as international terrorism and the spread of weapons of mass destruction. These are serious problems. Yet many people, including some mainstream politicians, want to say that climate change is preeminent among them. Moreover, the scope of Houghton's charge also seems too narrow. Focusing on Bush and Blair makes the complaint appear personal, and so isolated from any wider political context. But even if these two individuals should take some (central) responsibility for past international neglect of climate change,[9] surely there are other contributors. In particular, not only had the issue been around for much longer than their administrations, but many political leaders seemed to have agreed with Al Gore's statement, from

6. Houghton 2003.

7. One might also note that it is a very surprising intervention for a leading scientist.

8. This is not conclusive. Perhaps Houghton does think that climate change could have been solved by normal political means if just Bush and Blair would get their act together. If so, the complaint against them would be especially serious, since they alone would be responsible for the global failure.

9. Blair, of course, became much more active in trying to address climate change after 2003.

early in his term as vice president of the United States, that "the minimum that is scientifically necessary [to combat global warming] far exceeds the maximum that is politically feasible."[10] In essence, the complaint is that the inaction of our leaders merely reflects wider political realities. If this complaint is justified, then the concern that Houghton identifies runs deeper than he himself implies. In short, the worry arises that the charge of fundamental failure can be leveled not just against particular leaders or administrations, but also more generally, against current social and political institutions, and the mainstream moral and political theories that support them. This idea may seem radical, but is in fact mainstream. Recall former Danish Minister for Climate and Energy Connie Hedegaard's remark in the run up to the Copenhagen meeting: "If the whole world comes to Copenhagen and leaves without making the needed political agreement, then I think it's a failure that is not just about climate. Then it's the whole global democratic system not being able to deliver results in one of the defining challenges of our century. And that . . . should not be a possibility."[11]

Such worries motivate the following thought. Suppose that human life on this planet were subject to some serious threat. Moreover, suppose that this threat was both caused by human activities, but also preventable by changes in those activities. Add to this that the existing social and political systems had allowed the threat to emerge, and then shown themselves to be incapable of adequately responding to it.[12] Then ask two questions: Would such failure license a criticism of the existing social and political systems? If so, how serious a criticism would this be?

Suppose that the fact of global failure would indeed count as a criticism of existing systems, and that such a criticism is potentially fatal. Moreover, assume that the charge of global failure can be applied not only to social and political institutions, but also to the philosophies that stand behind them. Under these assumptions, we seem to have identified an important global test for social and political institutions and

---

10. McKibben 2001, p. 38.

11. Von Bulow 2009.

12. The systems might be incapable even though humanity as such is not. As mentioned later, under an expanded version of the test, humanity itself might fail.

theories:[13] if either does not respect the claim[14] that failure to address a serious global threat is a criticism of it, and a potentially fatal one, *then it is inadequate and must be rejected.*[15]

On the face of it, this is an important claim. The global test functions as a condition of adequacy on institutions and theories; it sets a constraint on their acceptability. How then should we understand the test?

One point to notice is that to say that the global test is one constraint on the acceptability of social institutions and theories is not to claim that it is the only such constraint, or even the dominant one. Indeed, this seems unlikely. After all, the test itself is narrowly conceived (e.g., because it deals only with self-generated threats), and there are other important areas of social and political concern, such as individual rights, distributive justice, intergenerational justice, the preservation of communities, our relationship to nature, and so on. Though these concerns may often be implicated in the global test, we need not assume at the outset that they can always be simply subsumed under it, nor need we assume that if there are conflicts, the global test always takes precedence.

In my view, these caveats do nothing to diminish the import of the test. For one thing, clearly the key assertions remain: the global test is one kind of constraint, and a serious neglect of it can be fatal to our

13. The term "a global test" I take from Senator John Kerry, who invoked it in the 2004 presidential election in a criticism of President George W. Bush. Kerry had in mind the need to consult with other countries about security matters, and to convince them of real threats, as a way of maintaining American influence in world affairs. The President subsequently ridiculed the Senator's claim, arguing that the basic security of the United States should not be made conditional on the opinions of other nations. The test I have in mind here is different. It does, however, tend to suppose that the security of any state is dependent to some extent on the security of the global system of which it is part, and that this implies that state sovereignty *may* not be absolute.

14. By "respect the claim," I mean roughly that the system must acknowledge and seek to address the criticism.

15. This claim has some structural similarity to Dryzek 1987. But it differs from Dryzek's in several respects, including its scope (his concern is exclusively with ecological problems; mine is wider), its targets (his are social choice mechanisms; mine include political theories), its critical diagnosis (he blames "instrumental rationality"; I take no position), and its framework for solutions (he claims that we must move to more discursive and decentralized decision-making institutional bodies; I emphasize theoretical change and make no institutional claims here).

assessment of a global system. Hence, the test has an important status. For another, work needs to be done to fill in the details of the test, and such work may conceivably toughen its requirements. In short, perhaps on closer examination, the test will be more central and demanding than the caveats allow. This is work for another occasion. For current purposes, I simply assume without argument that there is something initially compelling about the test, something that those who would resist it would have to take on a significant burden of proof to undermine.

A second point to notice is the high initial level of abstraction of the test. This may seem a failing. But it is useful for our purposes, for two reasons. The first is that the abstract statement of the test leaves some latitude for competing traditions and political philosophies to offer different interpretations of its crucial terms. This is important because it reduces the risk that the basic formulation begs the question against some particular approach. The second reason is that, even when expressed in extremely abstract terms, the test retains some intuitive bite. There seem to be clear cases where almost everyone would agree that the global test is violated; and this suggests that it can be useful even when its precise details are left unexplored.

The third point builds on this. At first, stated baldly and at this high level of abstraction, the test may appear so obvious and unexceptional as to be barely worth mentioning. But, as we shall now see, this appearance would be deceptive. First, the test is highly relevant to current concerns, since a strong prima facie case can be made that climate change fulfills the basic conditions suggested in the schematic example, and so constitutes a case of global failure. Second, so far mainstream discussion of the climate problem—in politics, academia, and society at large—has largely ignored the test. Instead, the discourse is dominated by scientific, economic, and short-term geopolitical concerns, and comparatively little has been said about the adequacy of existing social and political systems. In short, the concern highlighted by the test is conspicuous by its absence. Third, this fact should give us pause. As we shall see, one way of failing the test is to be oblivious, complacent, or even evasive about its concerns. In our current setting, this is a real worry. Earlier we saw that Sir John Houghton accused President Bush and Prime Minister Blair of "an abdication of leadership of epic proportions." Is it possible that our institutions and theories are vulnerable to the same charge?

II. SCENARIOS

The perfect moral storm surely invites this question. In the theoretical storm, cases such as climate change involve the intersection of a number of characteristics that conventional approaches to public policy are not well-equipped to handle, such as uncertainty, the very long-term, and the creation of different preferences and persons. Moreover, it integrates them in a mutually reinforcing way. Given this, it is not surprising that climate change exposes some weaknesses of current orthodoxy. The general theoretical storm is a serious one.

Still, the idea of the global test suggests something more specific. After all, other policy problems may involve similar convergences and reinforcement. For example, if a society is designing an appropriate set of family leave policies for parents of babies and young children, it will face choices that have uncertain effects, and involve long-term consider-ations and creation issues. Indeed, perhaps this is true for almost all large-scale projects with long time-horizons. Still, such projects do not (normally) pose a challenge to political practices of the form I want to discuss here.[16] Instead, Houghton's remark suggests that there is a more specific reason that climate change is theoretically important. There is something special about climate change that makes it raise fundamental questions about conventional social and political practices, something to do with security. This is why it makes sense to invoke the global test in this case, but not in many others with some of the same characteristics. Given this, it is natural to ask: Why is climate change special?

To answer this question,[17] we must first take a step backwards and attempt to clarify what we are discussing. One difficulty in talking about environmental issues in general, and climate issues in particular, is that both "environment" and "climate" are large "catch-all" terms. Hence, in

16. This is not so say that they *cannot* pose such challenges. For example, if a set of social and political institutions imposed a set of policies that were such as to eliminate people's motivations to have children (or render those motivations inert), then this could lead to a global failure that counted as a violation of the global test. Similarly, not all kinds of climate change are likely to run afoul of the global test. (See section III below.)

17. The answer presented here is not intended to be definitive, but to push in the right direction. A true response to the global test would require a much deeper answer in moral and political philosophy, which I do not attempt in this context, and would probably be incompatible with the aim of advancing only minimal ethical claims.

order to discuss the nature of the difficulty posed by the climate system, it will be helpful to begin by distinguishing different aspects of environmental and climate change.

Suppose we begin, somewhat roughly and artificially, with the idea that climate change (and environmental change more generally) is usually caused by inputs to physical and ecological systems which bring about alterations in those systems, and then cause impacts on humans, animals, plants, and places that they value. In the area of alterations of basic systems, change has a number of important dimensions. One dimension is the *magnitude of the increments* of change, which may be small, medium, large, or massive. A second dimension is *timing*. This includes matters such as the *speed* (e.g, slow, fast) and temporal *profile* of the alterations (e.g., even, bounded,[18] bumpy, abrupt).[19] At one extreme, change may be slow and involve evenly distributed physical effects. But at another extreme it may also be fast and abrupt: as for example, if there are significant thresholds in the climate system, the breaching of which causes significant disruption to normal processes. A third dimension is *scope*. The salient level of a particular climate change may be local, national, regional, or global; and the physical effects of such a change may also be predominantly realized at one or other of these various levels.[20]

18. By "bounded," I mean that at in any particular period the change is subject to upper and lower limits above and below some given point. Thus, the extent of change in a given period is constrained. However, note that this formulation does not exclude the possibility (which seems in fact probable) that the given point may itself change from one period to the next, provoking an associated shift in the limits. For example, suppose that the given point is a mean global temperature for a decade. Then, there might be upper and lower limits on the variation in average global temperature in any given year, or perhaps on the variation of regional temperatures. But this is compatible with gradually increasing average global temperatures in subsequent decades, accompanied by associated increases in the upper and lower limits in any given year or any given region.

19. The distinction between the timing of effects and of the change itself makes sense since we should not assume, for example, (a) that regular change implies even effects, or (b) that bumpy change implies uneven effects. For instance, suppose that we measure change in terms of the atmospheric concentration of greenhouse gases. We should not assume that an increase in atmospheric concentration of, say, 10 ppm per decade will mean a linear increase in effects of the same proportion.

20. For example, a collapse of the thermohaline circulation in the North Atlantic might be best understood primarily as a regional climate change even if it has significant effects on global physical processes (e.g., precipitation in some parts of Africa and Asia).

Integrating these three dimensions can help us to make some useful categorizations. For present purposes, let us isolate four especially salient types of physical change:

- *Creeping change*: Slow and even change in small increments that is local in scope.
- *Methodical change*: Moderately paced and bounded change in medium increments that is national in scope.
- *Dramatic change*: Moderately-paced and bumpy change in large increments that is global in scope.
- *Spectacular change*: Fast and abrupt change in massive increments which is global in scope.

In a moment, we will consider the importance of these different types of change. But before we do so, it will be useful to create a similar taxonomy for the impacts of climate change.

The main reason that we care about climate change is because of its potential impacts on humans and other forms of life. Although we may have some interest in the physical and ecological effects of climate change in their own right, we are predominantly concerned with their implications for humans, animals, plants, and places of special value to them.[21]

Given this, the fourth dimension of climate change worth noting is the *extent* of these impacts.[22] For one thing, their *magnitude* may range from very minor to significant, major, or extraordinary. For another, the *valence* of the impacts is important: the effects may be either positive,

---

21. For this reason, there would be some rationale for omitting the dimensions of the physical effects considered merely as such from the taxonomy, since many will say that their relevance depends exclusively on their implications for impacts. I have chosen to leave them in here for two reasons. First, much of the scientific work does still revolve around physical effects rather than impacts, and it is worth keeping note of the fact that any claim about the connection between these two needs to be established separately. Second, some people will be concerned about physical impacts for reasons other than, and in addition to, their concern for human (and even other forms of) life. For example, some will regard effects on particular places, or the transformative anthropogenic influence more generally, as something to be deplored (e.g., McKibben 1989).

22. The scope of impacts will also vary. For simplicity I assume here that this is approximately the same as the scope of physical effects. But this need not be true, given the complexity of global social and political systems (especially the economic system).

negative, or mixed. Because we are concerned with possible failures of the global test, negative effects—ranging from the merely inconvenient to the catastrophic—will be our focus here. But it is also true that some systems may have difficulty in dealing with some kinds of effect that are, considered in isolation, very positive. After all, it is possible that even a change that is, all things considered, a very good thing may impose high transition costs on society at large, or on some particular groups. This may be especially likely if the change is widespread and fundamental.

The fifth dimension concerns the *character* of climate change's impacts. Are they reversible, or irreversible? Are there readily available substitutes for what is lost, or is it nonsubstitutable? Are the costs of adapting to the new situations high or manageable? For convenience, I will lump these issues together under the heading "malleability." The idea here is that our concern is with how well we can accommodate the effects of climate change on human and nonhuman systems. For example, effects that can be easily and cheaply reversed, or softened through the availability of substitutes, exhibit high malleability; whereas effects for which reversal or substitution would be very expensive, or even impossible, exhibit low malleability.

The point of this classification exercise is to allow us to distinguish four especially salient change scenarios:

- *Soft landing*: Creeping change with significant, but highly malleable, negative impacts.[23]
- *Rough landing*: Substantial change with major, and moderately malleable, negative impacts.
- *Hard landing*: Dramatic change with severe, and poorly malleable, negative impacts.
- *Crash landing*: Spectacular change with catastrophic negative impacts with no malleability.

These scenarios are summarized in the following table: [24]

23. The label "soft" is not meant to trivialize the impacts associated with the soft landing scenario. For one thing, the taxonomy is primarily concerned with impacts at the macro level. This may obscure the impacts on specific individuals, which may be severe and even disastrous. For another, soft landing is characterized as involving substantial but reversible effects, but we should not assume that reversibility implies that such effects are not serious.

24. For a related scheme, see Tonn 2003, 301.

Salient Change Scenarios

TABLE 7.1

	Soft Landing	Rough Landing	Hard Landing	Crash Landing
Change	Creeping	Substantial	Dramatic	Spectacular
Size	Small	Medium	Large	Massive
Speed	Slow	Medium	Medium	Fast
Temporal Profile	Even	Bounded	Bumpy	Abrupt
Salient Scope	Local	National	Global	Global
Impacts				
Valence	Negative	Negative	Negative	Negative
Salient Scope	Local	National	Global	Global
Magnitude	Significant	Major	Severe	Extraordinary
Malleability	High	Moderate	Poor	None

III. A CONJECTURE

Identifying these different scenarios enables us to discuss different possible threats that may be posed by climate change. This is useful for a number of reasons. One reason is that a failure to make such distinctions often obscures what is at stake in debates about climate policy.[25] Still, the main purpose here is merely to allow us to put forward the following conjecture for consideration: even if we concede (for the sake of argument) that conventional institutions and theories might do reasonably well with addressing soft landing scenarios, as we move towards the hard and crash landing scenarios there is little reason for confidence.

The point of the conjecture is this. Remember that we were trying to understand why climate change might pose a special challenge to our political systems and philosophies akin to the fundamental failure Sir John Houghton attributes to our political leaders. I claimed that "climate change"

---

25. For example, now that outright scepticism about climate science is much less fashionable, those who oppose a substantial response to the threat often do so on the back of the assumption that the threat posed by climate change is of the soft landing sort, whereas those who are most concerned are usually thinking primarily of hard or crash landing scenarios.

(like "environmental change") is a large catch-all term, and that this meant that we would need to make some distinctions. So, now we have identified several different kinds of climate change (creeping, substantial, dramatic, and spectacular) and a variety of different threat scenarios that might emerge from these (soft, rough, hard, and crash landing). The conjecture then asserts that although soft landing scenarios might pose no special problem for conventional institutions and theories, the hard and crash landing scenarios do.[26] Suppose then that our ethical concern is primarily with hard landing, crash landing, and the varieties in between. If conventional political institutions and theories are poor at responding to such scenarios, the global test suggests that they are to be criticized for that. Moreover, if this problem is deep—for example, if it turns out that they *cannot* respond adequately—then they fail the test outright.

At this point, three clarifications may be useful. First, the varieties of change introduced so far are characterized in quite general terms, so that the conjecture need not be related specifically to greenhouse gas emissions. This reveals that there are really two claims in play here. The first, more general, claim is that current institutions and theories are poorly placed to deal with hard and crash landing scenarios considered simply as such, so that any real world problem that threatens to result in one of these scenarios will pose a challenge to such institutions and theories. (Consider, for example, abrupt changes to the earth's magnetic field.) The second, more specific, claim is that they are poorly placed to deal with climate change in particular, in part because it may turn out to have the form of a hard or crash landing scenario. As it happens, I suspect that both claims are true, so that climate change is just one instantiation of a more general problem for current institutions and theories. Nevertheless, the focus here is on the second claim alone.

Second, at this stage we should be careful not to make unnecessary or unwarranted assumptions about what might justify the conjecture. For example, initially it may be tempting to think of the conjecture in terms of a steady progression: to assume that things become gradually more difficult for conventional practices as one moves from the rough

---

26. The rough landing scenario is a difficult intermediate case for the global test. On the one hand, it does seem that existing institutions may be capable of some kinds of actions to address such problems; on the other hand, there are grounds for seeing their efforts as inadequate.

landing to the hard landing scenario, so that by the time we come to crash landing there is no reason for confidence, and every reason for skepticism, in the ability of conventional political institutions and theories to cope. But we should be careful. For example, it may turn out that extra speed is a practical advantage. For instance, perhaps crash landing is easier to act on than rough landing because societies find it easier to muster the political will to react to sudden disasters than to those with somewhat longer time-horizons (witness the initial international response to the Indian Ocean tsunami of 2004 compared with that to persistent global poverty). This is, of course, paradoxical: it implies that if the problem is worse in some significant respects, it may be easier to fix. But our existing systems may exhibit such a paradox.[27]

Third, it may be worth investigating whether the conjecture has explanatory power. Perhaps it could be shown that current global systems are better at dealing with soft and rough landing scenarios than with other kinds, and so tend to focus on these dimensions of global problems at the expense of others, perhaps even to the extent of tending actually to conceive of multidimensional problems in a selective way. This is an interesting suspicion. Still, assessing it would require a substantial research project in political science; so, here I leave it aside.

Why might one accept the conjecture? As it stands, it is quite general and applies regardless of the ideal strategy for dealing with the particular problem at hand. However, we might refine the discussion by considering a variety of strategies for dealing with change. Suppose, for simplification, that we assume that there are two basic ways of responding to a potential change: those that involve addressing the cause, and those that involve addressing the effect.

Consider first three basic strategies for dealing with the cause of a potential change.[28] First, one might try to eliminate the cause, so that the effect does not arise. (Call this *prevention.*) Second, one might try to reduce the magnitude or scope of the cause, in order to moderate the effects. (Call this *mitigation.*) Third, one might take no action on the cause, and so allow the effects to be realized at their full strength. (Call this *acceptance.*)

---

27. For discussion of how even creeping change may have the potential to cause major and widespread damages, see Glantz 1999 and Andreou 2006. For discussion of the possible psychological and political effects of abrupt climate change, see chapter 6.

28. In the real world, of course, problems often have multiple causes, and often more than one strategy can be employed with respect to any one of them.

Consider now four basic varieties of dealing with the effects of an impending change. First, one might try to eliminate the effect by taking preemptive evasive action. For example, if one is expecting a large sea-level rise in the twenty-second century, one might prohibit new building on the coastline during the twenty-first century. (Call this *avoidance*.) Second, one might put in place a plan for evading damages when the effect arises. So, for example, one might establish an infrastructure capable of responding very rapidly to extreme weather events. (Call this *preparation*.) Third, one may simply count on one's ability to manage any adverse event if and when it occurs. For example, one may assume that one's existing capacities for dealing with other kinds of problems, such as the general emergency service infrastructure, will be sufficient to the task. (Call this *coping*.) Fourth, one may acknowledge that existing systems are not up to the task, but be resigned to taking whatever happens as it comes: that is, one might decide to "weather the storm."[29] (Call this strategy *endurance*.)[30]

These strategies are summarized below:

Strategies for Dealing with Change

TABLE 7.2

	Response to Cause	Response to Effect	Implications for Negative Impacts
Prevention	Eliminate	------	Do not arise
Mitigation	Reduce	------	Moderated
Acceptance	Ignore	------	Full strength
Avoidance	------	Preemptive evasive action	Do not arise
Preparation	------	Plan for evasive action when effect arises	Moderated
Coping	------	Assume evasive action when effect arises	Moderated
Endurance	------	Absorb the costs	Full strength

29. Perhaps one has other priorities, such as poverty and hunger, that are so pressing that one cannot devote present resources to evading damages.

30. It may be worth making finer distinctions. For example, perhaps counterbalancing the cause with an opposing influence ("Offsetting"), and redirecting the effects in ways that are less harmful ("Deflection"), deserve their own categories, since they are useful when speaking of geoengineering.

The core issue regarding the global test is whether institutions and theories prove themselves incapable (or perhaps simply unlikely) of responding appropriately to specific kinds of change by choosing a reasonable strategy (or set of strategies). So, for example, it seems reasonable to describe the current global situation with respect to climate change as a combination of acceptance and endurance.[31] If so, and if a strong case could be made that there is a realistic threat of hard or crash landing, and that this makes the accept and endure strategy unreasonable, then this would count as a criticism of the existing global system and a failure of the global test.[32]

Note that we need not assume that any particular strategy (such as accept and endure) is always unreasonable. The core issue with respect to the global test is whether existing institutions and theories are capable of choosing whatever strategy is reasonable for cases of particular kinds. However, there will be something suspicious about systems which endorse only one strategy very generally—that is, as appropriate in a very wide variety of cases. And this worry does arise about the existing system with respect to the accept and endure strategies, and their close neighbors.

Suppose then that the situation is such as suggested above. In other words, in the case of climate change:

(1)   There is a realistic threat of a hard or crash landing.
(2)   The current global situation is best described as manifesting a strategy of accept and endure.
(3)   The accept and endure strategy is a product of the existing global system.
(4)   The nature of the threat makes the accept and endure strategy unreasonable.

31. These options are perhaps too limited. Catriona McKinnon suggests to me that "deny and ignore" may be a more appropriate description of the recent global response. To my mind, "exacerbate and obstruct" also has its merits.

32. The policy may be attributed either to an implicit endorsement by the global system or merely as the result of paralysis. The global test applies in either case.

Under such circumstances, there is strong reason to believe that the existing system is failing the global test.

Here I shall not try to offer a comprehensive argument for (1), (2), and (3). Instead, I shall simply offer a few considerations that suggest that they are initially plausible. First, (regarding (1)) the possibility of the hard and crash landing scenarios seems real enough, at least if one takes the perspective of several centuries. Observe, for example, that the IPCC's projections for temperature rise by 2100 under the more fossil fuel intensive ("business-as-usual") emissions scenarios is a best estimate of 3.4–4.0 degrees C (likely range of 2.0–6.4) above the 1980–1999 average, and 3.9–4.5 degrees C (likely range of 2.5–6.9) above the 1850–1899 average.[33] This is a very serious change. For comparison, the difference in global average temperature between us and the last ice age is roughly 5 degrees C (though, of course, in the other direction), and the last time the earth experienced such concentrations of carbon dioxide was 50 million years ago, during a period when crocodiles could be found at the poles. These facts prompt some scientists to say that the kind of change being projected would bring us essentially to a "different planet" than the one on which human civilization has evolved. Moreover, this change would be very fast by geological standards, occurring over one or two centuries, rather than many hundreds of centuries. Under such conditions, hard and crash landing scenarios start to look plausible.

Second (regarding (2)), the description of the recent (1990–2008) global strategy as one of accept and endure seems reasonable. During that time, progress on mitigation has been extremely small. Instead of stabilization or reduction, global emissions have risen dramatically, as have emissions in almost all major countries. Global emissions are up by more than 30%,[34] and emissions for the United States (for example) are

---

33. Scenarios A2 and A1F1. The preceding temperature rises are against a baseline of 1980–99. If one takes a baseline of 1850–99, an extra 0.5 of a degree is added (IPCC 2007, p. 7).

34. Global emissions were up by nearly 29.5% from 1990–2005 (Marland et al. 2008), and emissions grew at a more rapid rate in 2007 (Moore 2008).

up more than 15%.[35] Moreover, there has been no substantial progress on adaptation, and indeed efforts in this direction have been substantially thwarted by the richer nations.[36]

Third (regarding (3)), there seems little doubt that this strategy for addressing climate change has emerged from our current global institutions. Several attempts have been made to craft a better international response, but none have succeeded. In the end, Gore's pessimism has proven prescient.[37]

IV. THEORETICAL VICES

Suppose that the accept and endure strategy is unacceptable, and that this shows that existing institutions fail the global test. What might this reveal about contemporary political philosophy? Does this also fail? This question turns out to be more difficult to answer than one might think.

The first complication is the general one that the connection between theories and institutions is likely to be imperfect at best. Given this, the worry arises that one cannot infer much about theories from institutional failure. Fortunately, in the present case, this concern does not seem too serious. Initially, there is at least some plausibility to the claim that current political institutions are, by and large, supported by the mainstream political theories (such as economic utilitarianism, libertarianism, Rawlsian liberalism, and cultural nationalism) or, more accurately, by some combination thereof; and that these theories themselves are often reflective of, and generated in response to, those institutions. More importantly, it seems unlikely that a closer correspondence between theory and practice will make a radical difference. Concern

35. The numbers are against the baseline of 1990, rather than projected emissions. But the numbers for projected emissions are hardly more encouraging, since emissions are now at the high end of the IPCC's 1990 projections.

36. This is why it is tempting to speak of "exacerbate and obstruct," rather than "accept and endure."

37. Some would object to both this and the second claim on the grounds that there is an impressive system of global governance in place in the Kyoto Protocol. For my response, see chapter 4.

about our political theories is not merely derivative from worries about current institutions. Instead, the general imperviousness of most such theories to both environmental issues and the concerns of the global test more generally give us independent reason to be troubled.

The second complication is that a theory might fall afoul of the global test in a variety of ways. For example, it might simply be silent on some important global threat, and therefore *oblivious*. But it may also encourage inaction, or else impede or block specific solutions, so that it is *complicit* in failure. Finally, a theory might preclude success altogether, and so *guarantee* disaster.

Unfortunately, such complaints have at least some initial credibility. In particular, much contemporary political theory does seem to have the effect of prioritizing other political concerns over those connected with the global test. For one thing, it has, until very recently, been focused on the individual and state level, largely neglecting global and intergenerational concerns. This supports the charge of obliviousness. For another, current work tends to concentrate on institutions that emphasize the short-term, local, and national aspects of political affairs—such as democratic elections on three- to six-year cycles, market mechanisms, and the rights of current individuals. Thus, it is not crazy to think that it may be complicit in, or even go some way towards generating, global failure.

The third complication is that the assessment of rival political theories does not occur in a neutral evaluative setting. Recall that in the perfect moral storm theoretical inadequacies are of special interest because our choice of political theory might itself be corrupt. For example, if the intergenerational dimension—the fact that one generation can benefit from activities that pass serious costs on to its successors—dominates, then we might expect earlier generations to prefer political philosophies that facilitate such buck-passing. In such situations, where the temptation to moral corruption is high, we must take extra care that our evaluation of theories is not distorted.

One concern, of course, is that we will praise the wrong approaches. But another is that we will be too forgiving of error. For instance, in normal contexts obliviousness often seems a less serious shortcoming than other causes of failure. But in the perfect moral storm silence may be a fatal flaw. Consider, for example, future generations. Obliviousness to their concerns should not be taken lightly, since it may disguise a morally unacceptable indifference to the future, or a worrying blindness to one of the central concerns of the subject. For comparison, what would we think of a political theory that placed a (perhaps impressive) account of intellectual property at its center, but had little or nothing to say about basic rights and political legitimacy; or one that was obsessed with etiquette but silent on everything else? Such myopia would surely be criticized, and for good reason. So, why be indulgent of political theories that are largely mute on the issue of the global test? The worrying answer is that it is because they address our concerns, and leave aside those that we would rather not see addressed.

The fourth complication is the difficulty of successfully accusing contemporary political philosophy of *anything* in particular. (Call this *the Teflon problem*.) In particular, it is possible to characterize most theories at a very high level of abstraction, and at such dizzy heights most theories are so drained of content that they verge on vacuity. Suppose, for example, that one says that utilitarianism is ultimately about "bringing about the best," or that Kantianism is about "respecting" persons or treating them "as ends," or that rights-based theories are ultimately about "protecting the individual." At these levels of description, the content of each view is radically underdetermined.[38] But this suggests that charges such as "utilitarianism fails the global test" will always be met with derision, especially by partisans. Surely, the thought goes, there is some—perhaps hither to unimagined—version that will do the trick!

Given the Teflon problem, it is tempting to retreat to claims like the following: theories of general type X *in their current or dominant manifestations* are incapable of dealing with climate change. But should we retreat in this way? Such limited claims would be interesting in their own right, and might be sufficient for many purposes. So, we should not denigrate them. Still, they can seem a little weak. In particular, they invite the following objection: if all that is being said really is that approach X hasn't got it right yet, how interesting (ultimately) is that charge? Can't we just say that we already know that our theories are imperfect—and, that all the criticism really amounts to is "try harder"?[39]

---

38. Hursthouse 1996.
39. I am grateful to Justin D'Arms for discussion on this issue.

This last complication makes it tempting to give up on deploying the global test against theories. Perhaps the claim of failure is just too difficult to prosecute, and the payoff of such prosecution too elusive, to be worth the trouble. This temptation is powerful. Still, I believe that we should resist it. First, there is simply too much at stake. The concern raised by Houghton's complaint, and highlighted by the global test, is just too central to concede this easily. Indeed, ignoring it seems to amount to a serious abdication of theoretical responsibility. Second, in any case, the emphasis on successful *prosecution* of claims of failure seems misguided. Presumably, the main point of introducing the test is not to convict any particular political philosophy, but rather to provoke a more general shift in focus. After all, we are much less interested in scoring partisan points than in engaging with the problem, and with the general project of doing moral and political philosophy. In short, if the global test provides a genuine condition of adequacy for political theory, then fair-minded philosophers of all camps will want to take it seriously and try to make progress with it. In that case, we need not focus on successful prosecution as such: for example, on efforts to generate and then apply a set of necessary and sufficient conditions for inadequacy, or to pin down the criticism decisively for all comers, including potential zealots. Instead, it will be enough merely to show that there is genuine cause for concern, and for this we might be satisfied with lower standards of proof. For example, just as in civil (as opposed to criminal) trials, we might accept a preponderance of the evidence approach, rather than insisting that the existence of a problem be shown beyond any reasonable doubt before we can proceed. After all, given that the stakes are so high, the former seems more than sufficient to justify further investigation.

Let us return then to the Teflon problem. How are we to react to claims such as that a given theory must *somehow* be able to deal with climate change, that we already know that our theories are imperfect, and that all the global test amounts to is an exhortation to try harder? An obvious initial worry is that global failure is a serious matter, so that the response seems a little glib. For example, think of how we might react to the proponent of an etiquette-centered theory of morality who made the same claims about his approach's silence about anything remotely resembling basic human rights. In addition, some ways of "not getting it right yet" are surely suspicious. For instance, we would have good reason to be skeptical of any approach that claimed that it could *always* adapt itself to any "new" set of concerns, however distant from its traditional ones.

To elaborate on this thought, let us consider some circumstances under which too much malleability seems to be a bad thing, revealing a flaw or vice of a particular approach.[40] One ground for suspicion arises if a theory turns out to be *unduly reactive*: it can mold itself to whatever trouble comes from the world or from other theories, but that trouble has to come first. In the face of something as severe as a potential failure of the global test, being reactive in this sense seems to make a theory overly *complacent*.

A second, related flaw arises when an approach appears initially blind to concerns that are, or ought to be, morally fundamental. Both Houghton's claim and the global test suggest that some considerations have a certain kind of priority over others, and we might expect a political theory to wear such concerns on its sleeve rather than discover them late in the game in response to a specific threat. An approach that is initially blind in this way appears to be (at least) worryingly opaque and perhaps also oblivious.

Third, and more generally, if a theory turns out to be extremely malleable, we might wonder about its internal integrity. While it is true that we do not want our theories to be inflexible and dogmatic in the face of new information and unexpected challenges, complete malleability would also be a problem. For one thing, infinitely pliable theories run the risk of becoming *vacuous*, functioning only as convenient labels for whatever happens to be on our minds at the time. For another, even if it does not lead to vacuity, excessive malleability threatens to make theories too *evasive*. We expect political theories to play a role in guiding action and justifying institutions. If they are to do this effectively, then they must already (explicitly or implicitly) address the major challenges we face.

---

40. In invoking "vice," I mean merely to signal that in their exiting forms the approaches display a contingent but stable negative disposition.

V. AN ILLUSTRATION: UTILITARIANISM

If an approach to moral and political theory is oblivious, complacent, opaque, or evasive, then these are significant objections to it. Let us briefly illustrate and explore such concerns by focusing on a particular kind of moral and political theory, utilitarianism.[41] Generally speaking, utilitarianism holds that "we are morally required to act in such a way as to produce the best outcomes," where outcomes are usually evaluated in terms of human welfare.[42] Hence, as a distinctively political doctrine, it claims that social and political institutions should be arranged towards the same end. This is an attractive view, and has been deeply influential in philosophy, economics, and law for several centuries.

In an excellent recent paper, Dale Jamieson advocates a utilitarian approach to the global environmental crisis in general, and climate change in particular.[43] In doing so, he emphasizes an attraction that is of special interest to us:

> Utilitarianism has an important strength that is often ignored by its critics: it requires us to do what is best. *This is why any objection that reduces to the claim*

41. I emphasize at the outset that the point of this discussion is merely that, to illustrate and explore. In particular, the point is not to put forward a comprehensive or decisive objection to utilitarianism; indeed, though I do not take myself to be a utilitarian, I suspect that suitably sophisticated versions of the view probably escape the charges made below. In particular, I am sympathetic to Dale Jamieson's worry about the gap between conventional categorizations of utiltiarianism and the views of its most illustrious defenders. See Jamieson 2007, 169.

42. The quotation is from Jamieson 2007, 164. Jamieson does not include an appeal to welfare as part of his definition, but his subsequent remarks are otherwise in sympathy with it. Of course, many utilitarians, including Jamieson, would extend concern to non-human animals as well. However, it seems fair to say that such considerations are not normally at the forefront of utilitarian political theory, and indeed may pose a major challenge to such theory, as usually conceived. Hence, I leave that complication aside here.

43. Strictly speaking, Jamieson defines "utilitarianism" more broadly than I have just done, as "the theory that we are morally required to act in such a way as to produce the best outcomes." This is the view often called "consequentialism," and is broader than what I have called utilitarianism in that it does not focus on welfare. However, Jamieson's subsequent remarks indicate that he also assumes that welfare is central to his approach, even if not by definition.

> *that utilitarianism requires us to do what is not best, or even good, cannot be successful.* Any act or policy that produces less than optimal consequences fails to satisfy the principle of utility. Any theory that commands us to perform such acts cannot be utilitarian.[44]

In short, Jamieson asserts that utilitarianism is invulnerable to a certain kind of objection: if a theory leads to worse outcomes, then it cannot be utilitarian. Moreover, in explaining this claim, he emphasizes the extreme malleability of the approach: "Utilitarianism is a universal emulator: it implies that we should lie, cheat, steal, even appropriate Aristotle, when that is what brings about the best outcomes."[45]

Let us call the claim that a theory that leads to worse outcomes can't be utilitarian, "Jamieson's dictum." The dictum makes utilitarianism look good in the face of the global test, since it suggests that one virtue of the approach is that it cannot lead us to disasters like the crash landing scenario.[46] More generally, the dictum resonates with an important truth that matters to both utilitarians and most nonutilitarians: specifically, that the consequences of our behavior are extremely important, perhaps in some circumstances overridingly so.

There is an obvious sense in which Jamieson's dictum must be correct. If one takes utilitarianism as a thesis about the ultimate justification of social and political systems, then there are clear ways in which a genuinely utilitarian global system *could not* fail the global test. Still, Jamieson's emphasis on malleability should give us pause. It suggests that this defense of utilitarianism comes at a price. Given our discussion above, the appeal to malleability threatens to make utilitarianism an extremely *complacent* and *evasive* approach to political theory. The trouble arises

---

44. Jamieson 2007, 164; emphasis added.

45. Jamieson 2007, 182.

46. There are complications, of course. As usually understood, utilitarianism claims that the right thing to do is to maximize happiness. But this doctrine may lead us to some outcomes that other moralists would be inclined to view as disasters. For example, in principle, the view may sanction massive rights violations for the sake of greater happiness, or it may justify the otherwise premature extinction of humanity if the benefits to the present are high enough, or it may lead to what Derek Parfit has called "the repugnant conclusion" (Parfit 1986). But I leave aside these wider issues here. Given that Jamieson's definition of utilitarianism leaves the notion of "best outcome" opaque, he is not vulnerable to such worries.

because, even if we are secure in our knowledge that a global system that severely failed the global test could not *in the end* be a good utilitarian system, this information alone does not provide us with any guidance. In particular, we are no further along in knowing whether any particular system *currently* being advocated as utilitarian really is one. Utilitarianism becomes bulletproof, but only at the cost of *opacity*.

Let me illustrate this worry though a brief discussion of actual utilitarian thinking in climate change policy and more generally. As we shall see, utilitarianism can be cashed out in a number of different ways. However, the most influential version with respect to climate change has been the use of cost-benefit analysis (CBA) within a conventional economic framework.

This approach quickly raises some of the concerns listed above.[47] Consider first *opacity*. As we shall see in chapter 8, different economic assessments of climate change deliver very different answers. Moreover, there are good reasons for this. One is that projecting costs and benefits into the long-term future is a difficult, if not impossible, task. How are we to know precisely what the global economy will look like in fifty or one hundred years' time, given that we do not know exactly which technological and social changes will occur, and what the specific negative effects of climate change will be?[48] This problem is so severe that John Broome once claimed that CBA for climate change "would simply be self-deception."[49] In the perfect moral storm, this is a worrying thought. Still, the main point here is simply that even if in principle CBA could tell us what we should do, the correct CBA for climate change may be inaccessible to us at this point, and perhaps necessarily so. In short, appeals to Jamieson's dictum are of no help for the decisions that need to be made.

Second, consider *complacency*. Here the prime suspect is the standard way in which CBA deals with future generations.[50] As we shall see in chapter 8, economists typically assume that future generations will be richer than we are. But this assumption is threatened by the hard and crash landing scenarios. More generally, in conventional CBA the benefits and costs that accrue to future people are subject to a positive

47. Jamieson 1992 is an important article, raising similar criticisms.
48. Broome 1992, 10–11; Stern 2008.
49. Broome 1992.
50. CBA also has trouble dealing with the value of nature. See, for example, Sagoff 1988.

social discount rate. This means both that they count as less simply because they are in the future, and also (because of compounding) that impacts in the further future are worth dramatically less at current prices than current effects. On the face of it, this is a highly questionable and poorly justified practice that heavily favors the interests of current people.[51] Hence, there are real worries about moral corruption.

Third, CBA is prone to *vacuity* and *evasiveness*. Since there are no remotely secure numbers for either future costs and benefits or the social discount rate, the approach is extremely malleable, and in a way which threatens its internal integrity. The economist Clive Spash goes so far as to say:

> Economic assessment fails to provide an answer as to what should be done. The costs of reducing CO2 emissions may be quite high or there may be net gains *depending on the options chosen by the analyst*. The benefits of reducing emissions are beyond economists' ability to estimate so the extent to which control options should be adopted, on efficiency grounds alone, is unknown.[52]

This gives rise to the worry that a suitably motivated economist could essentially justify whatever result she wanted. Given the temptation of moral corruption, this is a disturbing state of affairs.

CBA also faces a deeper, and less often noticed, problem: it is not obviously the best way to implement utilitarianism. Worse, there are strong reasons to think otherwise. It is well-known in utilitarian circles that calculating the net benefits of courses of action on each occasion is often a very poor way of maximizing total benefits. There are a number of reasons for this.[53] But the crucial point for our purposes is simply that *it is far from clear that either utilitarians, or those with other moral views who share a concern for maximizing benefits, should support CBA.* In my

---

·   51. This is controversial. See chapter 7.

52. Spash 2002, 178. See also Azar and Lindgren 2003, 253.

53. One is that it is often impossible to predict the specific features of the future with any degree of confidence; another is that making calculations may itself involve high costs; a third is that acting on a calculations may undermine other social goods, such as personal relationships and bonds of community. Other reasons also arise.

view, it is hard to overstate the importance of this problem. Taken seriously, it threatens to undercut the basic rationale for the whole approach. At a bare minimum, it implies that the claim that CBA is a good method for maximizing net benefits ought not simply to be asserted or accepted without argument. This implication is important, but it should not be surprising. For one thing, it is just the flip side of Jamieson's claim about malleability. For another, independent evidence that conventional CBA must face such scrutiny comes from many of its (officially nonutilitarian) critics, especially within the environmental movement. They often seem to be arguing that CBA causes more harm than good (or at least than some alternative policy).

The deep problem suggests a more general worry about the abstract declaration that we should adopt the utilitarian approach. This emerges from the following story. There are many versions of utilitarianism, and CBA is most closely related to "act-utilitarianism," the doctrine that one should aim to maximize the net benefits of each of one's actions. In the recent history of moral philosophy, act-utilitarianism has been subject to two major objections. The first to emerge was the complaint that utilitarianism neglects the individual. In focusing on the total happiness, it was said, utilitarianism puts no weight on how happiness is distributed. This may lead to the violation of what we usually think of as individual rights, and also to highly unequal distributions. Utilitarians responded to this objection in a number of ways. Some simply denied that rights or equality are important moral and political values. But most tried to diffuse such concerns by arguing that respecting individual rights and promoting equality usually contributes to greater happiness, and so these concerns should be offered special protection on utilitarian grounds. In particular, in response to the objection, many utilitarians gave up act-utilitarianism and came to advocate "rule-utilitarianism," the doctrine that the right thing to do is to act in accordance with the set of social rules which would maximize happiness.[54]

A second standard objection to utilitarianism emerged later. It claimed that both act- and rule-utilitarianism neglect the role of

---

54. For a sophisticated recent version, see Hooker 2000.

individual agency in morality. Hence, Bernard Williams, for example, infamously complained that utilitarians do not take the integrity of agents seriously. In particular, they are committed to seeing agents as completely in the service of the impersonal demands of maximizing happiness, and so do not account for the role of the agent's own values and personal attachments in moral action. In response, many utilitarians argued that they could accommodate such concerns by focusing on the character traits and relationships characteristic of good utilitarian actors. In particular, some came to endorse an approach called "character (or virtue) utilitarianism," the doctrine that the right thing to do is to develop the set of character traits most conducive to maximizing happiness.[55]

The point of the story is this.[56] The shift in focus from acts to rules to characters raises a worry mentioned earlier. If utilitarianism merely reforms itself in response to any serious objection—molding itself to whatever trouble comes from the world or from other theories, but only when that trouble comes first—then it seems *unduly reactive*. This threatens its ability to play one of the main roles we might expect of a political theory, that of guiding us towards good social systems. If the approach is also oblivious, opaque, and evasive, this worry becomes even more serious.[57]

In short, even if Jamieson's dictum is correct——that a theory which claimed to be utilitarian but led us to catastrophe could not be the correct utilitarian theory—this obscures an important consideration. If standard utilitarian thinking leads us to catastrophe, then it will be cold comfort to the survivors to be told that, by the standards of Platonic heaven, it could not have been utilitarian after all. From the point of view of the global test, the questions that really matter are whether *we*—those who have to make decisions about climate change and other global environmental problems—should be utilitarians in our actions, policies, and institutions, or whether utilitarianism can tell us what we

---

55. See Driver 2001.

56. Even as a simplistic potted history, the story no doubt leaves much to be desired. Moreover, as I mention earlier, I am sympathetic to Jamieson's skepticism about some of these categories, and especially about their relation to the great utilitarian thinkers (such as Mill and Sidgwick). Still, even its superficial plausibility seems relevant.

57. CBA is, of course, subject to similar worries.

should be.[58] But the answer to these questions remains unclear.[59] Given this, standard utilitarian thinking (such as CBA) might well fail the global test. To continue to endorse it merely because of Jamieson's dictum would be a very dangerous form of complacency indeed.

The upshot of this discussion is that, Jamieson's dictum not withstanding, the utilitarian approach is vulnerable to the vices identified above, and so might fail the global test. This is so despite the illusion of invulnerability bought through an appeal to abstraction.

Now, before proceeding, I want to be clear about the import of the above argument. Specifically, it is not intended to be in any way partisan. First, I do not mean to single out utilitarianism as such for criticism. In my view, the same problem arises for many rival political theories, including libertarianism, Rawlsian liberalism, and nationalist communitarianism.[60] Clearly, proponents of such theories will be tempted to say that a global system that results in catastrophe cannot be good by their lights because its effects on their favored set of concerns—human rights, property rights, communities, and so on—are extremely negative. The point I'm making is that there is something genuinely suspicious about *all* such responses, and so we ought to expect more from our theories than this. If the global test constitutes a genuine condition of adequacy, then fair-minded theorists of all camps will want to take such vices seriously and seek to address them.

Second, I do not take myself to be offering a decisive objection either to utilitarianism or to those other theories (of the sort just mentioned)

58. Traditional debates over whether utilitarianism can function as an esoteric doctrine, or is self-effacing or self-defeating, lurk in the background here. I cannot take on these questions here; but I do not believe that the current point rests on an unduly controversial position on those issues. The question at hand is merely whether, as an approach to moral and political theorizing, utilitarianism escapes the global test. I claim that Jamieson's dictum is not enough to show that it does. This involves claiming that such approaches must play some role in guiding action. But this is not to claim that they cannot be self-effacing or esoteric. Indeed, Jamieson's own theory may have these features, and I claim below that it does not fail the global test.

59. Jamieson, of course, ultimately argues on utilitarian grounds that *we*—the ones having to act—should be virtue theorists. Hence, as I say below, his view is not vulnerable to this objection.

60. On Rawls, see Gardiner 2011a.

that share its concern about consequences. Instead, I am merely confronting attempts to dismiss criticisms of existing approaches based on the global test by appealing to their most abstract versions. My complaint is that such appeals are vulnerable to important objections that can become especially serious in a context where global failure is possible and moral corruption likely. In a perfect moral storm, complacency, evasiveness, and opacity are serious vices for a political theory to have.

Third, my quarrel is not with Jamieson himself. For one thing, I have admitted that considered as a thesis about ultimate justification, Jamieson's dictum must be correct: utilitarianism is, ultimately, bulletproof. What I would take issue with is the claim that this allows utilitarianism to escape the global test for political theories. In addition, I do not think that Jamieson's own utilitarian approach is vulnerable to these objections: it is neither complacent, nor evasive, nor opaque. Jamieson advocates that individuals cultivate a demanding set of green virtues that are not contingent on the behavior of others. The problem for him is whether he can show that such virtues are really justified on utilitarian grounds. But this is to take on the problem of malleability, not to avoid it.[61]

VI. THE STATUS OF THE COMPLAINT

Before closing, I want to address one natural objection to the concerns just expressed. Am I not asking too much of moral and political theories? Isn't it enough for a theory just to list the ultimate objects of moral concern and its basic logic and be done? Isn't the rest simply a matter of implementation (and perhaps not even really ethics at all)? Moreover, in

---

61. As it happens, it is not clear that Jamieson succeeds in this task. Walter Sinnott-Armstrong, another utilitarian, has recently argued for the contrary claim: that individuals should not be blamed even for engaging in self-indulgent environmentally destructive behavior—such as driving big SUVs just for fun. On his view, the appropriate obligations are at the political, not individual, level. This disagreement between Jamieson and Sinnott-Armstrong naturally raises worries about the opacity and evasiveness of utilitarianiam. See Sinnott-Armstrong 2005.

asking for more, aren't I going beyond my self-imposed restriction of making only minimal ethical claims, and covertly insisting on a particular vision of ethical theorizing?[62]

The basic objection is a serious one. Ultimately, it may turn out that I should concede that it is difficult to address fully without making at least some claims in metaethics that are potentially controversial. However, I think that we can go a long way towards diffusing the objection by more indirect means, by drawing an analogy.

Until around one hundred years ago, most social and political systems around the world were deeply and overtly biased against the interests of women. (Many, of course, still are.) Most fundamentally, they denied women even the most basic kinds of equality in law and social practices. Moral criticism of these systems is in one way very easy. One can simply say that women deserve equal moral status to men, and these systems deny that. This captures the core moral wrong, and so is in one way all that needs to be said. Call this first step *initial diagnosis*.

Despite this, we might think that ethical theorizing ought not to stop there. On the one hand, it might try to contribute to a deeper understanding of precisely what is wrong with patriarchal systems, and how they shape our ways of looking at issues in problematic ways, and so aid thought about how to do better. Call this second step *deep analysis*. On the other hand, it might have much to say about the project of improvement. It can consider what ideal social arrangements might look like, and how society might move closer to them. This might take the direct form of arguing for specific kinds of social institutions and practices, or the more indirect form of thought about how to influence the ways of thinking on which the problematic practices depend. Call this third step, *redemptive measures*.

Imagine for a moment that contemporary ethical theorizing about the situation of women were a lot less developed than it is. Suppose then that someone accused feminist ethical thought of not being theoretically robust. Would it be a good response for its supporters to claim, "No. There is no inadequacy here because we can say that women deserve moral equality"? I think not. For one thing, if all such thought could say were this, then we

---

62. I am grateful to Debra Satz for encouraging me to respond to such concerns.

would think it seriously underdeveloped. For another, those sympathetic to the project of women's emancipation would not be happy with the reply. They would fear that the project had become too complacent, opaque, and evasive in the face of the real plight of women in the world and the deeper aims of ethical theorizing. They would insist that those sympathetic to the cause and to philosophy ought to demand more.

Philosophy, and especially feminist philosophy, has not been nearly so complacent with respect to the moral equality of women. Indeed, it has progressed beyond the stage of initial diagnosis to serious deep analysis and proposals for redemptive measures. This is not to say that it has yet solved all of the relevant problems, let alone seen the kind of change it suggests in the real world. But the effort and the aspiration are clearly there, and it offers much guidance about how we might proceed.

The sense of the analogy is thus as follows. In my view, in the case of global environmental tragedy in general, and the perfect moral storm in particular, the relevant moral and political philosophy is much closer to the stage of initial diagnosis than this. We are still largely at the stage of saying, for example, that climate change is seriously unjust to the global poor, future generations, and nature, rather than at the stage of offering deep analysis of what exactly has gone wrong and what it would take to get it right. This is not to deny that important work is being done, nor to cast aspersions on its quality. (Indeed, those who contribute to this project should welcome the charge of theoretical inadequacy, as it underlines the importance of what they do.) It is merely to make a claim about where we are with that work in order to encourage its development. My point is that in the face of the threat, theoretical responses to the global test that either do not reach, or are content to stop, at the step of initial diagnosis seem overly complacent, opaque, and evasive, and these are vices that we should seek to avoid.

VII. CONCLUSION

In this chapter, I have proposed a global test for social and political institutions and theories, and suggested that current varieties of both appear to be failing that test. I have also disputed the claim that some theories do not fail, because they might—or even must—in principle be able to address the test. Against this, I claimed that theories can fall short in other ways, such as by being overly oblivious, complacent, opaque, and evasive. Moreover, I argued that such vices are both more likely and more damning in the presence of a perfect moral storm where there is serious risk of moral corruption.

The implication of all this is that climate change should be of serious concern to political philosophy. So far, this challenge has been largely ignored, in both academia and the public realm. Instead, scientific, economic and short-term geopolitical discussions fill the journals, newspapers, and airwaves. In the abstract, this is puzzling. How could we be so oblivious and complacent in the face of such a potentially catastrophic threat? Unfortunately, the perfect moral storm offers an unflattering answer to this question. We need to wake up to that fact if we are to pass the global test.[63]

63. See also Gardiner 2011a and forthcoming.

CHAPTER 8
Cost-Benefit Paralysis

Neither science in general nor economics in particular can resolve the fundamentally moral issues posed by climate change.

—Michael Toman (Toman 2006, 366)

We can disagree on the right ethical position to take, but there is no getting away from the fact that making policy towards climate change unavoidably requires one to take a stance on ethical questions.

—Sir Nicholas Stern (Stern 2009, 77)

In chapter 7, I argued that the third component of the perfect moral storm, the "theoretical storm," is manifest in the case of climate change. This charge of theoretical inadequacy is likely to meet resistance from at least one quarter. Outside philosophy, we will be told, there are robust theoretical methods for dealing with such problems. In academia and policy, conventional economics has standard methods for addressing the future. Moreover, this approach has already, and extensively, been applied to the climate problem, and yields a clear result: governments should take at best modest steps to address climate change now, but increase those efforts in the future. As the main populariser of this view, Bjorn Lomborg, puts it: "Economic analyses clearly show that it will be far more expensive to cut CO2 emissions radically than to pay the costs of adaptation to the increased temperatures," so that "we should do something, but our cuts should be rather small." [1]

In this chapter, I challenge this claim. If we scratch the surface, we see that matters are more complex, less uniform, and much more theoretically

1. Lomborg 2001, p. 318.

troublesome than Lomborg's remark suggests. In particular, there is deep disagreement within economics about how to analyze climate change. This has been the case for nearly two decades, but has recently been made more publicly visible by the vigorous work of the U.K. government's Stern Review of the economics of climate change.[2] More importantly, this disagreement does not revolve around narrow technical issues within economic theory, but rather around basic scientific, philosophical, and most prominently *ethical* claims that fill fundamental gaps in that theory.[3] As a consequence, a focus on economic analysis shifts the debate elsewhere, leaving it to the assumptions of the modelers. This gives rise to the worry that far from providing an escape from theoretical inadequacy, conventional economics simply conceals it behind closed doors.

Given this, and given the urgency of the climate problem, the theoretical storm seems very much with us. Worse, the continued focus on economic analysis is likely to facilitate continued buck-passing. In the absence of strong theory, a stable, theoretically respectable, and action-guiding consensus from economics is not to be expected, at least in the short- to medium-term.[4] Hence, a preoccupation with economics as such is paralyzing, and this is highly convenient for the current generation of the most affluent.

Of course, none of this implies that good work in economics is not being done, or should not be pursued. But it does suggest that we should be careful about how we assess such progress, and about the role we assign to conventional economics in guiding policy. As we shall see, climate change may have deeper implications for the future of economics than current economics has for the future of the planet.[5] This is a significant dimension of the theoretical storm.

2. For example, see Broome 1992; Cline 1992; Spash 2002; Stern 2007.

3. Stern 2007, Stern 2008, 2009. After the Stern Review, Lomborg states the claim slightly differently: "All major peer-reviewed economic models agree that little emissions reduction is justified" (Lomborg 2007, 37 and 135; Nordhaus 2009, 167). This claim is misleading. Though the Stern Review was not "peer reviewed" in the strict sense, the report was put together by some of the world's top economists, and plenty of their subsequent discussion of it appears in major peer-reviewed journals.

4. We might add that if it is reached, this is likely to be largely for independent reasons, based more on background assumptions in moral and political philosophy than on the technical apparatus of economics.

5. Aldred 2009.

The chapter proceeds as follows. Section I provides a quick introduction to the background theoretical setting. It discusses a set of standard criticisms of conventional economics, together with some typical replies. Sections II–VIII describe the more specific issues that arise in the case of climate change, and trouble even those who support the approach elsewhere. Specifically, sections II–III describe the wide divergence of economic views on climate change, and point to some background reasons for this divergence; sections IV–VI consider worries about the usual approach to future generations; and sections VII–VIII briefly address the claim that ultimately some kind of economic analysis simply must succeed.

I. COST-BENEFIT ANALYSIS IN NORMAL CONTEXTS

The underlying ethics of basic welfare economics, which underpins much of the standard analysis of public policy, focuses on the consequences of policy for the consumption of goods and services by individuals in the community. . . . the objective is to work out the policies that would be set by a decision maker acting on behalf of the community and whose role it is to improve, or maximize overall social welfare.

—Sir Nicholas Stern (Stern 2007, 28)

Much of conventional economics rests on a simple basic idea, that policy should aim at maximizing net social welfare, usually understood in terms of some sort of aggregation of individuals' satisfaction from consumption.[6] In theory, traditional economists favor employing market systems to achieve this aim. But in practice they acknowledge that in the real world markets do not always function as they do in theory, and that

6. The nature and variety of the aggregation methods also deserves comment, but I cannot pursue that here. See Stanton In Press.

in many contexts they are simply not present at all. Hence, in many circumstances, economists try to promote the general aim of maximizing welfare through other methods. Prominent among these is conventional cost-benefit analysis (CBA). This is a method for evaluating competing projects by directly assessing their net benefits. Those which produce net benefits are said to be worthy projects. If there are insufficient resources to undertake all worthy projects, then those with the highest net benefits are chosen.

The application of CBA to environmental issues has been controversial for some time. In a moment, I will briefly review some prominent criticisms made of the method in normal contexts, as well as some typical replies. My aim is to give a deeper sense of what CBA is about, and of the theoretical setting in which the climate issue arises. Since the status of normal CBA is the subject of deep (and, regrettably, sometimes bitter) controversy, I want to be clear about two points from the outset. First, in this section, I am trying only to signal what the main issues are, rather than to settle disputes about them. Hence, I do not take myself to be giving decisive arguments on either side. Second, and more importantly, the main argument of the chapter does not depend on these more general issues. The central worries about theoretical inadequacy that are my focus in subsequent sections are specific to climate change and similar global environmental problems. Moreover, these worries are shared by many who are enthusiasts for CBA in other contexts.

1. Standard Criticisms

The first criticism of CBA in normal contexts is that its appeal is largely superficial, because the method is easily confused with cost-effectiveness. Almost everyone is in favor of policies that take the least costly means to *independently accepted and justified ends.*[7] Suppose I decide that I want to buy a new Toyota Prius. Since there is no point in paying more for an otherwise identical car, it makes sense to shop around at various dealerships looking for the best price. In short, I aim to take the most *cost-effective* means to my prior end of buying a Prius.

---

7. Des Jardins 1998.

Cost-benefit analysis is different. As traditionally conceived, it is a method for choosing between two policies based on which one yields the highest net benefits. As the economist Robert Frank puts it in his introductory textbook: "The decision-rule we use is disarmingly simple: If $C(x)$ denotes the costs of doing x and $B(x)$ the benefits, it is: If $B(x) > C(x)$, do x; otherwise, don't."[8] This decision-rule has broader implications than one endorsing cost-effectiveness. Though it would advocate buying the cheaper Prius, it would also take a position on whether I should buy a Prius, a Hummer, a bicycle, a Jacuzzi, or anything else. It would advocate that I choose according to the cost-benefit criterion. Hence, CBA aims to tell me *which* ends I ought to pursue, whereas simple cost-effectiveness does not.

CBA is thus much more controversial. To see why, consider an example. Suppose a mother is contemplating buying a new iPod for her daughter for her birthday. Cost-effectiveness analysis could offer advice about where to buy the iPod. But CBA might also evaluate whether she should buy something nice for herself instead. Thus, if the mother were to employ CBA in making her decision, this might prove controversial in ways that cost-effectiveness would not. In particular, CBA appears to reduce all other constraints on choice (such as those implied by parenthood) to cost-benefit terms, whereas cost-effectiveness analysis does not.[9] Thus, CBA becomes highly controversial in contexts where values other than cost-effectiveness seem pressing. For example, opponents of the approach resist it when matters of individual rights, procedural and distributive justice, close personal relationships, and the value of nature are at stake.

The second standard criticism of CBA is that it is strongly partisan. It is, some say, a manifestation of a particular and controversial moral philosophy, utilitarianism. Utilitarians claim that the ultimate objective of morality is the maximization of net benefits, so it is easy to see a connection between their doctrine and CBA. But this gives rise to two objections. One is that utilitarianism is a controversial moral theory, which is often criticized precisely because it appears to ignore or downgrade other values, such as those mentioned above. Another objection (already signaled in

8. Frank 2005.

9. There are, of course, fancy ways in which one might try to avoid this. Still, there are realistic worries that these are ad hoc.

chapter 7) is that it is far from clear that CBA is a good utilitarian practice. Perhaps respecting rights, justice, and so on would result in more net benefits than trying to calculate costs and benefits in economic terms. If so, then good utilitarians should reject CBA. Moreover, most contemporary philosophical utilitarians seem to do just that. For they argue that the best utilitarianism is highly indirect, pursuing the end of maximizing (or improving) social welfare through intermediaries such as individual rights and democratic decision-making.

The remaining standard criticisms of conventional CBA result from its typical methods. In practice, CBA is usually limited in the kinds of costs and benefits it takes into account. Typically, practitioners try to work out what consumers would be willing to pay for this or that good or service if it were available in the market place. However, this seems problematic in many contexts.

To begin with, it makes CBA too narrow, and biased against some concerns. (This is the third standard criticism.) The focus on willingness to pay limits the benefits and costs that can be considered to those whose value can be expressed in economic terms, and skews the evaluation towards short-term, consumption and individualistic values, rather than wider concerns, such as those bound up with communal, aesthetic, spiritual, environmental, and nonhuman concerns. How, for example, would one set out to do a realistic CBA on the Grand Canyon or the Mona Lisa? Is asking how much each of us would be willing to pay out of our own budgets to see them really the right way to proceed?

The fourth standard criticism of CBA is that it rests on a fundamental confusion. In a classic work, Mark Sagoff argues that when conventional CBA attempts to reduce all issues of value to matters of preference as measured by market prices, it is guilty of a "category mistake." It confuses mere preferences, whose significance might perhaps be measured in terms of the intensity with which they are held, with values, whose import is usually understood in terms of the reasons that underlie them.[10] Just as we should not evaluate mathematical claims (such as $2 + 2 = 4$) by asking how strongly mathematicians feel about them, and in particular how much they would be willing to pay for the rest of us to accept them,

---

10. The attempts to separate preferences from values and to evaluate preferences in terms of willingness to pay are also questionable. Moreover, nothing said here should be read as denying that emotions cannot be the source of morally reliable information.

so (Sagoff says) we should not evaluate ethical claims in these ways. To do so misunderstands the point of both kinds of discourse.[11]

The fifth standard objection (also prominent in Sagoff) is that, despite initial appearances, CBA is an essentially undemocratic decision procedure. This is so for two reasons. First, in a conventional CBA each person's influence on the decision is a matter of their weight in the calculation: how much they would be willing to pay or accept for a given outcome. But this is profoundly influenced by the resources at their disposal. For example, Bill Gates is willing to give more to almost any cause he is interested in than I am even to my favorite.[12] Second, in practice, cost-benefit analyses are generated by "experts": people who amass market, survey, and other information, and then distill and interpret it for some audience or another. This means that actual citizens and their voices become far removed from the process. Among other things, this introduces the worry that there is plenty of leeway for corruption in generating a CBA. The analyst has the power to shape the outcome of a given study through a large number of decisions about its scope, the data that is collected, and how the results are integrated.

2. Standard Defenses

Each of these standard objections is subject to dispute.[13] Nevertheless, in theory many enthusiasts for CBA accept much of their spirit, but argue that CBA can be modified so as to avoid them. First, they propose that CBA should seek to be more thorough in capturing the relevant costs and benefits, and more explicit about what it excludes. Second, they claim

11. Sagoff 1988. This threatens the normative authority of CBA. Against the claim that, in the market place, people would tend to buy good X rather than good Y, one can always raise the questions, "but should they?" and "so what if they would?" For example, if it emerged that people would play more for condominiums along the South Rim of the Grand Canyon than they would for tourist accommodation there, what of it? Is this sufficient reason to close the National Park and sell it off to developers?

12. Of course, the analyst can always choose to weigh Bill's contributions differently from mine. Perhaps $1 million from Bill should be worth the same as $10 from me. But how would one decide on which weights are appropriate? A clutch of other assumptions in moral and political philosophy seem to be needed.

13. Turner 2007.

that CBA should be more modest in its ambitions. It ought not present itself as the exclusive method of practical decision making, but rather as only one essential ingredient in a broader political process.[14]

On the face of it, this call for modesty is appealing. Still, there are reasons for caution. One serious concern, of course, is that it is an open question to what extent these theoretical claims about what CBA should be actually manifest themselves in practice. But there are also more specific worries. First, the aspiration to full-cost accounting is admirable in theory, but problematic in practice. It is at least very difficult, and arguably impossible, to estimate the full consequences of any large-scale project, especially one that is likely to have transformative effects on a global scale for centuries to come, like climate policy. Hence, anyone carrying out CBA on a large project must decide which costs and benefits to include, and over what time-scale. They must decide what costs and benefits matter to the purpose, and which should be left out.[15]

Second, the decision maker presented with a given CBA must decide whether, and to what extent, the answer to these questions renders the CBA relevant to the decision to be made. Does the CBA provide vital central information, or is its relevance overshadowed by its omissions? This is an important question in its own right. Say, for example, that you are deciding whether to undergo brain surgery. A CBA that showed you only the cost of the scalpel would be next to useless. So, the decision on whether a given CBA is good enough to guide policy, and to what extent, is itself highly significant.

These two points can be pushed further. In particular, it seems likely that, for both the practitioner and the decision maker, the choices to be made will be shaped by ethics. For example, if one thinks that the only morally relevant factors are short-term economic costs and benefits, then CBA is often easy and almost always useful; but if, on the contrary, one believes that the morally relevant issues are almost always elsewhere, then on most occasions CBA is likely to seem certainly challenging, probably inadequate, and possibly futile. Moreover, and perhaps most importantly, we might expect there to be a disciplinary selection bias. Those who are sympathetic to the values captured by CBA will be drawn to practice it; those who are not will look elsewhere

14. Schmidtz 2001; for a different kind of defense, see section VIII.
15. Raffensberger and Tickner 1999, p. 2.

for ways to guide policy. Hence, there is reason to suspect that actual CBA will be shaped more by some kinds of values (and valuers) than by others. As above, there is a concern that CBA becomes a partisan enterprise.

Such concerns ought to resonate with supporters of CBA because they threaten to undermine its central rationale, which is said to be the transparency and accountability it brings to public decision making. This threat is made deeper when one considers other features of conventional CBA. On the one hand, there is a problem of opacity. The results of a given CBA are usually communicated to the public in terms of simple summary numbers, and the internal mechanics of CBA can make them highly technical and complex endeavors. This tends to mean that many of the deeper value assumptions are difficult to discern, especially from the outside (as we shall see below). On the other hand, there is a worry about salience. Why a decision maker takes a particular CBA (with one set of assumptions) as more relevant than another (with a different set of assumptions) is often a difficult question to answer, and merely showing the preferred CBA does not provide it. In addition, there is the more general question of why CBA is used to justify some decisions, and decisions in some areas of policy, but not others. The selective use of (selective) CBA is itself a serious threat to the values of transparency and accountability that advocates of CBA take to motivate the approach. Hence, even enthusiasts have reason to treat the actual practice of CBA with caution.

This brings us to a third standard defense of CBA. Even if the practice sometimes leads to bad decisions, it might be argued, surely it is better to conduct CBA than not. For through its insistence on transparency, CBA at least rules out the very worst abuses of political power. Some projects are so egregious that no CBA can be constructed to justify them; and surely this is a good thing.[16]

This defense is potentially promising, but incomplete. First, it does not follow from the fact that conventional CBA gets the right result in some cases that it is the best *general* method. After all, it may go wrong more often or more severely, and these mistakes might outweigh its successes. Given this, one would like to see some good

---

16. I thank Bill Talbott for raising this objection. Similarly, Kristin Shrader-Frechette claims that the burden of proof is on opponents to suggest a better approach (1991, 174).

evidence that conventional CBA can pass its own test—in other words, that a *general policy* of subjecting individual projects to CBA is better than rival approaches at maximizing social welfare—and that it does not lead to the systematic violation or neglect of other values. But anecdotal claims are not sufficient here. Moreover, since CBA can take considerable time and other resources, demanding that any project pass such a test itself incurs costs. Hence, there is some pressure on the other side.[17]

Second, there is a more specific worry in the current context. Assume for a moment (for the sake of argument) that conventional CBA is spectacularly successful in normal contexts (e.g., in stopping "pork barrel" projects). This would indeed be a major victory. However, if its application in wider contexts brought on a severe failure of the global test, then the victory would turn out to be hollow. Those in the grip of a crash landing scenario would be unimpressed even by a strong run of victories within the federal budget.

II. CBA FOR CLIMATE CHANGE

The status of CBA in conventional public policy is worthy of further discussion. In particular, it is tempting to try to accommodate the standard challenges by limiting the scope of CBA, and introducing specific parameters. If some kinds of CBA are useful in specific contexts under specific constraints, it would be worth knowing exactly what these kinds, contexts, and constraints are, and how to manage them. Unfortunately, I cannot pursue such issues here.[18] Instead, I focus on a separate set of challenges that arise when CBA is applied to climate change and similar long-term, large-scale, and potentially catastrophic global environmental problems.[19] These are serious enough to make even those who would vigorously defend CBA in normal settings skeptical about it in such contexts.

17. I thank Julie Nelson for this point.

18. There is an enormous literature on risk management. Prominent philosophical work includes: Cranor 1993, 2006; Shrader-Frechette 1991, 1993, 2002.

19. This section builds on several paragraphs in Gardiner 2004b.

1. Which Economists?

Several attempts have been made to model the economic implications of climate change. Politically prominent among these is the Dynamic Integrated model of Climate and Economy (DICE) proposed by the Yale economist William Nordhaus. The DICE model is an integrated assessment model. Such models combine elements of biophysical and economic models in an attempt to understand the impact of climate and economic policies on one another. Typically, they aim to find a climate policy that will maximize the social welfare function. And many give the surprising result that only limited abatement should occur in the next twenty to thirty years since the costs of current reductions are too high in comparison to the benefits. This result is surprising because physical and ecological scientists typically advocate that global emissions should peak in the next few decades in order to avoid "dangerous" anthropogenic interference with the climate system. Against this, Nordhaus argues that, based on economic costs, the developed world (and the United States in particular) should largely pursue adaptation rather than abatement. This is the position embraced by Lomborg, who cites Nordhaus and like-minded economists as his inspiration.[20]

Much could be said about this. But for our purposes, I shall make just a few general points. The first is that, even if Nordhaus's calculations were reliable, the costs of climate change mitigation do not seem unmanageable. As Thomas Schelling puts it:

> The costs in reduced productivity are estimated at two percent of GNP forever. Two percent of GNP seems politically unmanageable in many countries. Still, if one plots the curve of U.S. per capita GNP over the coming century with and without the two percent permanent loss, the difference is about the thickness of a line drawn with a number two pencil, and the doubled per capita income that would have been achieved by 2060 is reached in 2062. If someone could wave a wand and phase in, over a few years, a climate-mitigation program that depressed our GNP by two percent in perpetuity, no one would notice the difference.[21]

Lomborg agrees with this. For he not only cites the 2 percent figure with approval but adds, "there is no way that the cost [of stabilizing

20. For the suggestion that Lomborg is heavily biased in his citations, see Ackerman 2008, 438.
21. Schelling 1997.

abatement measures] will send us to the poorhouse."[22] His claim is not then that mitigation is prohibitively expensive in itself, but rather that the money could be better invested elsewhere. (See later.)

The second point is that we have reason to think that the estimates are not robust. Nordhaus's work is controversial even among mainstream economists, and several important analyses have produced diametrically opposed conclusions. This state of affairs has persisted since the early nineties.[23] But the dispute has become more evident and politically prominent in recent years because of the publication of a major review of the economics of climate change by the U.K. Treasury, led by Sir Nicholas (now "Lord") Stern, a former Chief Economist at the World Bank. In essence, the opinion of the Stern team was that "the benefits of strong and early action far outweigh the economic costs of not acting."[24] The report concluded:

> Using the results from formal economic models, the Review estimates that if we don't act, the overall costs and risks of climate change will be equivalent to losing at least 5% of global GDP each year, now and forever. If a wider range of risks and impacts is taken into account, the estimates of damage could rise to 20% of GDP or more. In contrast, the costs of action—reducing greenhouse gas emissions to avoid the worst impacts of climate change—can be limited to around 1% of global GDP each year.[25]

More recently, Stern has said that these estimates were likely too conservative, claiming that "the modeling of the Stern Review probably underestimated significantly the risks of high damages from [business-as-usual], perhaps by 50 percent or more."[26]

22. Lomborg 2001, p. 323.
23. Cline 1992, Costanza 1996, Woodward and Bishop 1997, De Leo et al. 2001, Spash 2002.
24. Stern 2007, xv.
25. Stern 2007.
26. Stern 2008, 22. Commenting on the difference between his results and those of Nordhaus and others, Stern claims that previous models "have given rise to a *powerful and unjustified bias* against strong and timely action on climate change," adding that "the question is not so much why the Stern Review's modeling obtained high damages . . . as why the earlier literature made assumptions that give such low results." Stern 2008, 21–2; emphasis added.

To get a sense of the scale of this dispute, we can look at the implications for regulation. Nordhaus's most recent estimate is that this should be equivalent to a tax of $34 per ton in 2010 rising to $202 in 2100, but he also claims that on Stern's assumptions about discounting his DICE model would yield a tax of $305 per ton in 2010 rising to $949 per ton in 2100.[27] Hence, the disparity between the model results varies from factors of three to an order of magnitude.[28] Moreover, this is not the end of the matter. Lomborg claims that Nordhaus's new proposal is politically unfeasible, and so recommends an initial price on carbon of $7 per ton.[29] Hence, his suggestion diverges from Stern's (on Nordhaus's account of it) by three orders of magnitude.[30] This is a very serious difference, especially from the point of view of those trying to make policy.

The wide discrepancy between the various analyses leads to the third point. Some economists are highly skeptical of the whole enterprise. One worry concerns the integrity of the results. Clive Spash, for example, asserts:

Economic assessment *fails to provide an answer* as to what should be done. The costs of reducing CO2 emissions may be quite high or there may be net gains depending on the options chosen by the analyst. The benefits of reducing emissions are beyond economists' ability to estimate so the extent to which control options should be adopted, on efficiency grounds alone, is *unknown*.[31]

27. Nordhaus 2009, 82–3. The Stern Review suggested a social cost of carbon of $85 per ton at 2000 prices. See Stern et al. 2007, 322.

28. See also Stern et al. 2007, 322–3.

29. Lomborg expresses his tax in dollars per ton of carbon dioxide, rather than per ton of carbon, hence he advocates for $2 per ton of CO2. See Lomborg 2007, 31, 152, and note 31 on 174. Ackerman criticizes Lomborg for basing this merely on the "personal guess" of Richard Tol (Ackerman 2008, 442).

30. Similarly, an interagency report in the United States recently endorsed a central estimate of $21 per ton of CO2 compared to $83 in a similar report in the United Kingdom. See Ackerman and Stanton 2010.

31. Spash 2002, 178.

A further worry concerns the underlying reasons for this. Some claim that the economic models are overly simplistic[32], both in themselves and relative to the climate models.[33]

These points suggest that the idea that existing economic analysis clearly shows anything—in the sense that there is a robust consensus in the discipline as to what should be done—is deeply suspect. What then is Lomborg talking about? The best explanation seems to be that when he speaks of "economic analysis," he means to refer only to those studies that employ very traditional assumptions, relying on current market prices and substantial discount rates (of the order of 5% or more). If we consider only such studies, then Lomborg may be right that there is wide agreement that abatement should be limited, at least in the short- to medium-term. It is certainly true that a number of economists using this methodology have come to such conclusions, including Lomborg's personal favorite, Nordhaus.

Nevertheless, this fact does not have the implication that Lomborg intends—that only very limited action on climate change is justified. One reason is that it is precisely these key features of traditional economic approaches that many argue make them inappropriate tools for assessing long-term impacts. A second, more important, reason is that the dispute about these and related issues is not narrowly economic, but rather concerns wider scientific, philosophical, and especially ethical issues. Spash puts the point this way:

> The ethical questions fail to disappear just because a market price and economic analysis are substituted for ethical debate and public discourse. . . . The contradiction

32. One commentator says of Nordhaus: "the model is extremely simple—so simple that I once, during a debate, dubbed it a toy model" (Gundermann 2002, p. 150–4). In addition, while many models (including Nordhaus's) do not take into account indirect social and environmental costs and benefits not associated with production, some claim that these benefits may outweigh the direct costs of abatement (e.g., De Leo et al. 2001, pp. 478–79).

33. This poses a serious paradox for some skeptics, since they are both very demanding in the standards they impose on climate models but not at all cautious about the power of economic models. This is surprising. For, without wishing in any way to be derogatory about contemporary macroeconomics, it has at least as dubious a status as a predictive science as climatology, if not worse. Hence, if one is going to be as critical of the IPCC consensus on climate change as some skeptics are, one should be even-handed in one's approach to the economic models (Gundermann 2002, p. 154).

is that [traditional mainstream] economics takes a very specific philosophical and ethical position and then ... tries to deny the relevance of ethics in economics.[34]

We gain some insight into these matters by looking at some of the complaints of those skeptical about the whole enterprise of CBA for climate change.

2. Costs

Recall from chapter 1 what John Broome has to say about CBA and the long-term future. Broome is a defender of standard economic analysis in normal contexts.[35] However, about climate change he claims:

> Cost-benefit analysis, when faced with uncertainties as big as these, would simply be self-deception. And in any case, it could not be a successful exercise, because the issue of our responsibility to future generations is too poorly understood, and too little accommodated in the current economic theory.[36]

These are very strong claims. Broome does not say merely that CBA will make mistakes about climate change, or even that it is fundamentally flawed. Instead, he claims that it *could not be successful*, and calls any attempt *simply self-deception*.

Why does Broome claim that CBA for climate change would be "self-deception"? He emphasizes uncertainty, saying that in the further future, "society is bound to be radically transformed in ways which are utterly unpredictable to us now."[37] To illustrate this, he quotes Thomas Schelling's remarks about the view from 1890:

> Electronics was not dreamed of ... Transatlantic travel by zeppelin was a generation in the future ... Russia was czarist ... U.S. life expectancy at birth was 47 ...

34. Spash 2002, 188.

35. "In principle I favour conventional decision theory [i.e., "expected utility theory" (p. 18)]. Nevertheless, when it comes to global warming, I do not think the decision making process can be simply a matter of calculating expected utilities and then going ahead. The problem is too big for that, and the uncertainties—particularly the historical uncertainties—too extreme"(Broome 1992, 19).

36. Broome 1992, 19.

37. Broome 1992, 10.

only a third of the U.S. population lived in places with more than 5,000 inhabitants.[38]

One might add that, in the case of climate change, such changes are not exogenous to the problem at hand. For example, Dale Jamieson points out that the regional effects of climate change are varied and uncertain; predicting human behavior is difficult since climate impacts affect a wide range of social, economic, and political activities; we have limited understanding of the global economy; and there will be complex feedbacks between different economic sectors.[39] Similarly, Stern writes, "what we do now will transform the circumstances and income of future generations."[40] Such worries undermine attempts to extend information drawn from current market prices far into the future.[41]

As well as the general problem of generating realistic cost-benefit information about the further future, there are also serious concerns about the background assumptions of the standard economic approach, especially as these involve claims about human interaction with the natural world. One such concern involves independence. Broome comments on the early work of Nordhaus:

> Nordhaus'[s] estimate appears to be based on the assumption that *everything will be much as it is now, but a bit hotter.* . . . [He] is evidently assuming that *human life is by now fairly independent of the natural world.* . . . I find this assumption too complacent. Nordhaus would presumably have produced a similar estimate for the effect on national income of a similar global cooling. But *a similar cooling would take us most of the way to an ice age,* and I doubt if anyone would expect that to diminish national income by a mere 0.25%. I think we must expect global warming to have a profound effect on history, rather than a negligible effect on national income[42]

Broome accuses Nordhaus of assuming that human systems have become substantially independent of natural systems, and says that this

---

38. Schelling 1983, cited by Broome 1992, 10.

39. Jamieson 1992, 288–89.

40. Stern 2009, 81.

41. Hence, Stern's opposition to the traditional reliance on marginal price information. For worries about Stern's own approach, see Spash 2007.

42. Broome 1992, 25; emphasis added.

assumption is too complacent.[43] The more general problem is that part of what is at issue in climate change is how robust economic and other social institutions are in the face of it. Hence, if a standard approach simply *assumes* this issue away, it seems to miss something essential.

A second concern is related. It is common to all CBA to assume that environmental goods are infinitely substitutable for other goods.[44] In essence, the claim is that in principle improved productivity can always compensate for any other losses. This has a number of implications. First, it suggests that CBA has no inherent objection to the dome world scenario mentioned in chapter 1. Even if humanity were forced into artificial domes, and the rest of life on Earth were extinguished, this might still be preferable in standard economic terms, so long as the survivors were well-off on other ways (e.g., on typical assumptions, by having plenty of consumer goods). But this, of course, is a highly contentious position, and one embodying a major value assumption.

Second, since the idea is that more consumption can always make up for environmental degradation, the claim surreptitiously implies that suitably bigger economies (and domes) are definitely available to us, and can be brought to bear very quickly. But if we are concerned about major climate catastrophe, such claims are question-begging, and so dangerous. As we saw in chapter 7, one question raised by the climate crisis is whether our institutions—including our economic institutions—are up to the task of coping. Simply to assume that they are, no matter what comes, seems to evade a central issue. It also seems to involve judgments that are not themselves narrowly economic, but rather broadly scientific and value laden (including moral and political beliefs about what is worth pursuing and how it should be pursued).

---

43. Thomas Schelling seems in the same territory when he claims: "except for a very low probability of a very bad result . . . [Americans] are probably going to outgrow any vulnerability we have to climate change. And in any case we'll be able to afford to buy food or import it is necessary. You know, very little of the US economy is susceptible to climate. All of agriculture is less than 3% of our gross product. Forestry may be endangered. Fisheries may be endangered. But recreation might actually benefit!" (Clarke 2009). Note that part of the reasoning seems to be that American society is not dependent on agriculture because it is only a small part of the economy. But this seems dubious. As Julie Nelson has complained to me (personal communication): "So what are we supposed to *eat* if US and foreign agricultural systems collapse? Recreation?"

44. Neumayer 2007.

Perhaps in normal settings there is nothing wrong with economists tending to believe that standard economic institutions are remarkably robust, so that in principle "traditional economic growth can be both sustained and answer all our problems."[45] But if this background claim underwrites their policy recommendations, then other, competing perspectives must also be considered.

3. Risk

One sign that conventional CBA is not well-placed to cope with the possibility of truly catastrophic change comes from the work of another mainstream proponent of CBA, Harvard economist Martin Weitzman. Weitzman worries about low-probability, but high-damage scenarios. He claims that "it is quite possible, and even numerically plausible, that the answers to the big policy question of what to do about climate change *stand or fall* to a large extent on the issue of how . . . high-temperature damages . . . are conceptualized and modeled." Yet, he adds, "standard conventional CBAs of climate change *do not even come remotely close* to grappling seriously with this kind of potential for disasters," and this is "an issue that has received minimal treatment thus far in formal models." Hence, he concludes, "by implication, the policy advice coming out of conventional . . . CBAs of climate change must be treated with (possibly severe) skepticism."[46]

Weitzman believes that the relevant low probability, but high damage scenarios are those associated with 11–20 degrees C of climate change over a century or so; hence, he is thinking of risks beyond the IPCC projections. Still, this also reflects a judgment about the robustness of economic institutions in the face of large change. As Broome points out above, a change of 5 degrees C is equivalent to an ice age shift, but in the other direction. This change is within the IPCC projections, and many scientists say that making such a shift in less than a century would be like moving to "another planet." Why then believe that only 10 degrees counts as a "high damage" scenario? Do the economists have a better

---

45. Spash 2007, 706.

46. Weitzman 2009. Weitzman does think that they can be modeled in an unconventional CBA, and so sets out to create one.

grip on what is potentially catastrophic than the scientists? This seems dubious. In any case, it would seem rash to make policy on the *assumption* that they do. If so, there is reason to treat CBAs of (say) 4–5 degrees C with "(possibly severe) skepticism" as well. Indeed, this is one reason why Stern accuses Nordhaus of being "dangerously complacent."[47] Nordhaus's recommendations would "within a few decades, put us in a position where . . . the probability of temperature increases exceeding 4C would be 58% [and] of exceeding 5C, 24%", and Stern asserts that this "is a very dangerous place to be."[48]

III. THE PRESUMPTION AGAINST DISCOUNTING

The problem that arises with discounting is that it discriminates against future generations.

—David Pearce (Pearce 1993, 54)

Estimates of costs and risk both pose very serious challenges to CBA for the further future.[49] However, notice that Broome claimed that *even if this problem could be resolved*, CBA "could not be a successful exercise because the issue of our responsibility to future generations is too poorly understood, and too little accommodated in the current economic theory." There is, then, an even more basic problem for CBA. What does he have in mind? This emerges later in his book, when he says:

> It is people who are now children and people who are not yet born who will reap most of the benefits of any project that mitigates the effects of global warming. Most of the benefits of such a project will therefore be ignored by the consumer-price

47. Stern 2009, 77.

48. Stern 2009, 91–2. Another sign that conventional CBA is not well-suited to cope with catastrophic risk comes from the explicit way that even the more expansive analyses, such as Stern's, deal with risk within the social discount rate. See below.

49. It is true that uncertainty is a challenge for all theories in this context. But presumably the point is that theories that do not demand such specific and fine-grained information are better placed than conventional CBA.

method of project evaluation. It follows that this method is *quite useless* for assessing such long-term projects. This is my main reason for rejecting it [for climate change].[50]

The "main reason," then, that Broome invokes for the failure of conventional economic analysis is that it ignores most of the benefits of climate change mitigation *because* these are deferred to later generations. In essence, the problem is that mitigation constitutes what I earlier (in chapter 5) called a *temporally dispersed good*. As Broome is conceiving it, mitigation is a backloaded good: one with costs for the current generation but whose benefits accrue to later generations.[51] Thus, Broome's point is that since conventional CBA either ignores or undervalues such goods, it must be rejected. To this we might add that the neglect of such goods suggests a manifestation of intergenerational buck-passing.

Why does conventional economic analysis ignore or undervalue temporally dispersed goods? The answer appears to be that it is because it employs a substantial positive "social discount rate" (SDR).[52] Discounting is "a method used by economists to determine the dollar value today of costs and benefits in the future. Future monetary values are weighted by a

50. Broome 1992, 72; emphasis added.

51. I prefer to think of the situation as involving excessive emissions that are front-loaded goods (benefits now, costs later). Assuming excessive emissions and then calling reductions in them "costs" obscures an important aspect of what is happening on ethical views that insist that there is an important moral difference between inflictions of harm and failures to benefit.

52. In his earlier work, Broome rejects positive discount rates for the long-term impacts of climate change, and endorses a rate of zero (Broome 1992, 19, 72, 108). More recently, he has suggested sympathy with Stern, who employs a very low positive rate. In addition, he now frames part of the ethical challenge as one of "determining the correct discount rate", and suggests that "the role of economists is to work out" the relevant theory (Broome 2008, 102). I am skeptical about this framing. First, the discount rate is a technical notion within economics, and it is far from clear that intergenerational ethics can or should be understood in terms of it (see sections IV and VII) . Second, intergenerational ethics is conceptually prior to the discount rate, so that it is far from clear why we should cede the role of working out the relevant theory to economists (see section VIII). Though Broome does at one point make the reasonable claim that "economics can work in the service of ethics" (Broome 2008, 98), he later suggests that the economists are the relevant experts for producing "sophisticated theory" (Broome 2008, 102). In my view, the latter claim is unmotivated.

value <1, or 'discounted' ".[53] The SDR is the rate of discounting: "Typically, any benefit (or cost), B (or C), accruing in T years' time is recorded as having a 'present' value, PV of: $PV(B) = B_T/(1 + r)^T$."[54] In public policy in general, the rates used vary, but are usually in the range of 2–10 percent. In climate change in particular, the traditional economic models employ rates of around 5%: for example, Lomborg says 4–6 percent is "probably reasonable," and Nordhaus uses 5.5%.[55]

Social discount rates reduce the weight of future costs and benefits relative to current costs and benefits. Given the effects of compounding, this has profound effects in the evaluation of very long-term issues, such as climate change. Consider the following table.

TABLE 8.1 Estimated Number of Future Benefits Equal to One Present Benefit Based on Different Discount Rates

| Years in the Future | SDR | | | |
	1%	3%	5%	10%
30	1.3	2.4	4.3	17.4
50	1.6	4.3	11.4	117.3
100	2.7	19.2	131.5	13,780.6
500	144.7	2,621,877.2	39,323,261,827	$4.96 * 10^{20}$

Table reproduced from Cowen and Parfit 1992, 145.

Clearly, the choice of SDR matters. For example, suppose we were trying to decide whether to pursue a project with costs of $10 million this year, and benefits of $100 million in 100 years. With a discount rate of 5%, this project is not justified; with a rate of 1%, it is.[56]

Discounting is the most controversial issue in climate economics. A full treatment of it would probably require another book, and I cannot attempt it here. Nevertheless, in the rest of this chapter I try to give an impression of why discounting is so important, why it is primarily an ethical (not a narrowly economic) issue, and how the dispute about it within economics tends to hide that fact from public view.

53. Toman 2001, 267.
54. Pearce 1993, 54.
55. Lomborg 2001, 314; Nordhaus 2009.
56. At 5%, it has a net present value of $0.76 million, which is easily outweighed by the current cost. At 1%, the net present value is $36.9 million.

There is an initial burden of proof against the use of standard rates for projects involving the long-term future, such as climate change. The burden arises because of four issues. The first is practical. Under positive discount rates, all but the most catastrophic costs disappear after a number of decades, and even these become minimal over very long time periods. As an approach to intergenerational equity, this seems to reduce cost-benefit analysis to absurdity. Consider the following example, from Columbia University economist Graciela Chichilnisky:

> At the standard 5% discount rate, the present value of the earth's aggregate output discounted 200 years from now is a few hundred thousand dollars. A simple computation shows that if one tried to decide how much it is worth investing in preventing the destruction of the earth 200 years from now on the basis of measuring the value of foregone output, the answer would be no more than one is willing to invest in an apartment.[57]

The second issue is theoretical. The SDR lacks a clear, consistent, and general rationale. In a classic article, Tyler Cowen and Derek Parfit point out that in practice the SDR is actually defended in a number of distinct ways. Most commonly, appeals are made to pure time preference, democracy, probability, opportunity costs, excessive sacrifice, special relations, and the idea that our successors will be better off. This is an issue in itself. (Is this an approach in search of a rationale, rather than something independently motivated?) But Cowen and Parfit also point out that the rationales pull in different directions, and that all of them are vulnerable to serious objections in at least some contexts. (More on this below.) Hence, they conclude:

> At most, these arguments might justify using such a rate as a crude rule of thumb. But this rule would often go astray. It may often be morally permissible

---

57. Chichilnisky 1996, 235. She uses the example to illustrate the point that that discounting future utility "can produce outcomes which seem patently unjust to future generations" since "under any positive discount rate, the long-run future is deemed irrelevant." She concludes that it is "generally inconsistent with sustainable development;" and, immediately afterwards, she invokes the issue of climate change, and cites Broome with approval. Alex Dubgaard employs a similar example against Lomborg (Dubgaard 2002, 200–01).

to be less concerned about the more remote effects of our social policies. But this would never be because these effects are more remote. Rather it would be because they are less likely to occur, or would be effects on people who are better off than we are, or because it would be cheaper now to ensure compensation, or it would be for one of the other reasons we have given. All of these different reasons need to be stated and judged separately, on their merits. If we bundle them together in a social discount rate, *we make ourselves morally blind.*[58]

In other words, the worry is that discounting buries the important issues about our relations to the future in a single "all-purpose" rate, and so undermines good ethical analysis.

The third issue is that of indeterminacy. Martin Weitzman tells us that "no consensus now exists, or for that matter has ever existed, about what actual rate of interest to use."[59]

The fourth issue concerns the dominance of the SDR. In general, the results of cost-benefit analysis on long-term projects are "notoriously hypersensitive" to the rate chosen.[60] For example, Nordhaus says of Stern, "the *Review's* radical revision arises because of an extreme assumption about discounting. . . . [It] proposes using a social discount rate that is essentially zero."[61] Similarly critics of Nordhaus often claim that his choice of SDR effectively swamps the contribution of the climate components of his model, rendering them irrelevant.[62]

In conclusion, if the choice of SDR dominates the economics of climate change, but the rate to be chosen is indeterminate, and if the practice of discounting lacks a clear general rationale, but standard rates lead to absurd results, then it seems hard to deny that we have a problem of theoretical inadequacy. At the very least, there seems to be a strong burden of proof on those who insist otherwise.

58. Cowen and Parfit 1992, 158–9; emphasis added.

59. Weitzman 2001, 260–1.

60. Weitzman 2001, 260–1.

61. Nordhaus 2006, 6. The Stern team claim that this is too quick, since damage estimates play a large role (Stern 2006, 669–70; cf. Cline 1992). But note that the two are interlinked. In the long term the effects of compounding mean that the costs of disaster have to be *much* more dramatic to counteract the effects of, say, 5%, than 1%. So, a higher SDR loads the dice substantially in favor of inaction.

62. Schultz and Kasting 1997, cited by Gundermann 2002, 147.

IV. THE BASIC ECONOMICS OF THE DISCOUNT RATE

How might this burden of proof be met? In this section, I consider how economists typically generate their discount rates. In the next, I consider two background arguments.

1. The Productivity Argument

The most obvious defense of a positive SDR is that it accounts for economic growth.[63] Discounting for growth is intuitive under normal circumstances because investment is usually productive. Suppose that I can invest $100 this year in a project that will yield $105 next year. Then, there is a sense in which $105 next year is worth the same as $100 today. This justifies "discounting" the $105 next year to $100 now. If we assume that there is a uniform annual rate of increase on investment, then this becomes the appropriate discount rate (in this case, 5%). This helps to diffuse the worry about absurd results. Emphasizing the flip side of Chichilnisky's remark about the apartment, Nordhaus states:

> In thinking of long-run discounting, it is always useful to remember that the fund used to purchase Manhattan Island for $24 in 1626, when invested at a 4 percent real interest rate, would bring you the entire immense value of land in Manhattan today.[64]

The productivity of investment is the component of the SDR emphasized by Nordhaus. Indeed, he sometimes seems to present it as definitional. For example, he states that "we can think of the discount rate as the rate of return on capital investments," and says that his use of an average discount rate for the twenty-first century of 4% "reflects the observation that capital is productive."[65] In addition, he asserts that the logic of his proposal for modest action on climate change in the near-term is that "in a world where capital is productive and damages [from climate change]

---

63. Nordhaus 2009, 10.
64. Nordhaus 2009, 11.
65. Nordhaus 2009, 10–11.

are far in the future . . . the highest return investments today are primarily in tangible, technological, and human capital."[66]

The idea that we should take economic growth into account in our assessment of the future seems uncontroversial. Still, we should not be too quick to embrace Nordhaus's particular approach to discounting. In fact, matters are more complex than his remarks initially suggest, and ultimately this is not really where the central dispute about discounting lies. Most importantly, the claim that capital is productive is not something at issue between Stern and Nordhaus. Like most mainstream models, Nordhaus and Stern share an assumption about the determinants of the discount rate and their relationship. Following Ramsey, they assert:

$$\rho = \eta g + \delta$$

where ρ is the social discount rate, g is the rate of consumption growth per capita, δ is the pure time or utility discount rate, and η is the elasticity of the social marginal utility of consumption.

Later I shall raise some considerations that cast doubt on the adequacy of the Ramsey equation. But the key point for now is much more limited. In the equation, g is the factor most clearly associated with productivity. But the magnitude of g is not a matter of serious dispute in the climate case. For example, Nordhaus sets it at 2% and Stern at 1.3%. This is a difference, but not a large one. More importantly, it does not account for the major discrepancy between Nordhaus's discount rate (ρ) of 5.5%, and Stern's 1.4%.[67] This rests on their decisions about other the other elements of the Ramsey equation. Specifically, Nordhaus has $\eta = 2$ and $\delta = 1.5$;[68] while Stern has $\eta = 1$ and $\delta = 0.01$. Clearly, the central issue between them is not productivity narrowly construed, but these other factors.[69]

66. Nordhaus 2007, 201.

67. Nordhaus 2009 states that the DICE model has 5.5% for the first half of the century (61) and 4% averaged over the century as a whole (10).

68. Nordhaus 2009, 61.

69. The claim that productivity should be dealt with through a discount rate is also worthy of further investigation. For example, the standard case involves a single individual deciding whether to consume now or defer consumption until later. But when current and future consumption will accrue to different people, there are distributive issues to consider.

2. The Descriptive Argument

In a moment, we'll look at the specific disputes about δ and η. But before doing so, we should observe that Nordhaus's deepest concerns lie elsewhere. Nordhaus has reasons for his ascriptions of η and δ. Nevertheless, he signals that he would comfortable with considering alternatives. His central claim is that whatever is said about δ, η and g is independently constrained by the end result, the discount rate ρ that they produce. In essence, his view is that this must be compatible with observed market rates of return, and so be around 6–9%.[70] As a result, he does not see η and δ as fully independent variables determining the social discount rate (ρ) "from the ground up", but rather as part of the best explanation of a rate set externally, by the market.[71] This discount rate concerns production, but not literal production. Instead, it is the rate of return on capital in the actual marketplace. This is the sense in which it is the "real" rate of return.

This matters because Nordhaus's position contrasts sharply with that of Stern and other like-minded economists. As we shall see below, they do regard discount rate as something to be built "from the ground up," through an independent evaluation of other variables (in this case, those in Ramsey's equation). This difference in methodology roughly coincides with a sharp divide in economic theorizing, between what are sometimes called "descriptive" and "normative" accounts of the SDR.[72] Moreover, this is not a place where alternative perspectives happily coexist. Indeed, advocates on each side tend to be strikingly dismissive of their rivals. For example, Nordhaus ridicules Stern's normative approach for taking "the lofty vantage point of the world social planner," and calls

70. Nordhaus 2009, 170.

71. Nordhaus 2009, 61.

72. Arrow et al. 1996. The dispute also intersects with a wider dispute within economic theory about the appropriate understanding of the enterprise. At one extreme, some interpret economic analysis as akin to other sciences that aim to describe how the world is from some "value neutral" perspective. At the other extreme, some see economics as the embodiment of a particular grand theory of ethics, utilitarianism. Somewhere between these extremes, another traditional view sees economics as treating only one value ("efficiency"), leaving other values (especially "equity") to other venues, usually politics. (For discussion, see Hausman and McPherson 2006.) Given these diverse understandings, it is not surprising that disputes arise when we turn to contentious issues with real world implications.

Stern's ethical SDR "largely irrelevant" to "the actual investments and negotiations about climate change."[73] Moreover, he suggests that Stern's *Review* is biased in its ethics, representing only a narrow and somewhat idiosyncratic set of values, and even complains that it attempts to impose these values on others, "stoking the dying embers of the British Empire."[74] Similarly, Stern claims that engagement with values cannot be avoided, and so that the SDR is inescapably normative in climate policy. Hence, he denies that the "descriptive" approach is really possible. Moreover, he suggests that those who pursue it are making fundamental mistakes in economic theory. In a section of his book entitled "Why some economists got it so badly wrong," Stern asserts that authors such as Nordhaus make assumptions that are "totally implausible" and claims that the fundamental reason for this that many "forgot, overlooked, or never knew the basic necessary underlying theory."[75] In short, there is a deep division between leading economists concerning how to think about the status of the Ramsey equation, and this division partly reflects antagonism about the place of values in the discipline, and which values should be accommodated.

All of this resonates with our thesis that a focus on current economic approaches brings on paralysis. But more needs to be said about what is at stake here, and in particular about why characterizing the dispute as between "descriptive" and "normative" approaches is likely to mislead.

To begin with, there is an obvious sense in which analyses like Nordhaus's play a "normative" role in policy formation. Most obviously, they prescribe solutions to real world problems. For example, they result in policy recommendations, such as for particular carbon taxes (e.g., \$34 in 2010), and defend these prescriptions against the proposals of the rival (more overtly normative) camps. Less obviously, they assume that employing a SDR that is driven by market rates is the *appropriate* method to use in modeling climate economics. Given this, they cannot avoid coming into dialogue with (more openly?) normative discussions which claim that different SDRs are warranted, and as a consequence produce different results.

Because of this, it is misleading for Nordhaus to claim that his approach "does not make a case for the social desirability of the distribution of

73. Nordhaus 2007, 682.
74. Nordhaus 2007, 683.
75. Stern 2009, 95–6.

incomes over space or time of existing conditions, any more than a marine biologist makes a moral judgment on the equity of the eating habits of marine organisms in attempting to understand the effect of acidification on marine life."[76] Nordhaus is aiming to provide "policy relevant" advice. This is more like the biologist who tries to determine what level of ocean acidification can be "tolerated" by marine organisms in order to make a policy recommendation, assuming that not exceeding the limits of tolerability matters, and that she can identify the factors that are relevant to meeting this goal. This involves normative judgments, and does not seem so different from Stern's project.

The more contentious issue is whether and to what extent the "descriptive" account is intrinsically normative, in the sense that it brings with it a set of value assumptions, and how this sense of "normative" might be different from rival accounts. In the current context, it makes sense to consider Nordhaus's own perspective. Here is what he says:

> The *calculations of changes in world welfare from efficient climate-change policies* examine potential improvements within the context of the existing distribution of income and investments across space and time. As this approach relates to discounting, it requires that we look carefully at the returns on alternative investments—at the *real* real interest rate—as the benchmarks for climatic investments.... When *countries weigh their self-interest in international bargains* about emissions reductions and burden sharing, they will look at the actual gains from bargains, and the returns on these relative to other investments, rather than the gains that would come from a theoretical growth model.[77]

He adds:

> The normatively acceptable real interest rates prescribed by philosophers, economists, or the British government are irrelevant to determining the appropriate discount rate to use in the actual financial and capital markets of the United States, China, Brazil, and the rest of the world.[78]

Much could be said about these remarks. But for current purposes, two quick points may suffice.

76. Nordhaus 2007, 692.
77. Nordhaus 2007, 692–3; emphases added.
78. Nordhaus 2007, 692–3

First, there are internal reasons to question the "descriptive" adequacy of Nordhaus's approach. At first glance, Nordhaus seems to be advocating a "real world" approach, based in existing social and economic realities. But this impression is misleading. First, his analysis mentions two aims: "calculations of changes in world welfare from efficient climate-change policies" and "countries weigh[ing] their self-interest in international bargains." But these seem in tension, and it not clear how they are to be reconciled. Most obviously, it seems doubtful both that most national governments are strongly motivated by world welfare or globally efficient policies, and that they see these as unambiguously in their interests. Less obviously, the idea that countries actually pursue something that can univocally be called 'the national interest' is also questionable. For one thing, often they appear to pursue the ends of particular constituencies or elites; for another, even when they seem concerned for the interests of their citizens more generally, in the perfect moral storm we must worry that this is limited to the interests of their current citizens.

Second, the claim that, in bargaining with others, countries "will look at the actual gains from bargains, and the returns on these relative to other investments" of the sort delivered by Nordhaus's analysis is both a large empirical assertion, and one that is at odds with standard views in public economics. In the case of the latter, it is commonplace for governments to apply discount rates to their projects that are lower than market rates (for the sorts of reasons that underlie Stern's objections). More generally, it is simply not true that actual rates of return in the marketplace are determined independently of government decisions on such issues. For example, in the United States, the Federal Reserve has for the last few years set its lending rate at close to zero percent in order to make market rates lower. Moreover, it has done this in the service of the larger social objective of trying to prop up the economy and help it to recover from recession. But no one takes very seriously the argument that it should not do this because it does not accord with historical "real" rates of return.

Still, third, this is not the main worry. Faced with the tensions between world welfare and pursuit of national self-interest, Nordhaus seems to face a dilemma. On the one hand, if he leads with world welfare, then his view seems not only overtly normative, but also (like Stern's) to adopt the perspective of the world social planner (albeit with different assumptions about operationalizing the plan). But, on the other hand, if Nordhaus prioritizes providing policy advice for "countries weigh[ing] their self-interest in international bargains," he must explain how his analysis can confront the climate problem as it actually is. In chapter 4, I argued that two principal ingredients of the problem are the prospect of countries representing only the current generation of their citizens, and the problem of skewed vulnerabilities. If an analysis ignores these issues, or essentially frames its recommendations so as to enable them to go unresolved, it does not seem adequate to the problem. One might say that it fails to be "descriptive" in the relevant sense.[79]

3. Pure Time Preference

The central place where the debate about descriptive adequacy manifests itself is in the dispute over the second component of the Ramsey equation: δ, the rate of pure time preference. Empirically it is said that many people show a preference for getting benefits earlier even when this makes them smaller (and postponing costs even when this makes them bigger), and even when other factors, such as risk, are removed. Hence, δ conventionally reflects impatience, the preference that "earlier is better just because it is earlier."

To some economists, δ is an important variable. For example, David Pearce once called it "the essential rationale" for discounting, because of the "sovereignty" of individual preferences.[80] Nevertheless, its role is a matter of considerable dispute between Nordhaus and Stern. Nordhaus sets δ at 1.5; Stern at 0.1. This is a difference of an order of magnitude. How do we understand it?

Resistance to δ is overtly ethical. Many philosophers and economists have argued that a substantial positive rate of pure time preference is morally inappropriate for intergenerational projects because it fails to treat future people as moral equals. For example, the Stern team suggest that Nordhaus's earlier (2007) δ of 3% per annum is implausible, since it "would imply that someone born in 1960 should 'count' for roughly twice someone born in 1985."[81] We might add that it is one thing to

79. If it takes the normative perspective that these problems should be ignored, this raises other issues.

80. Pearce 1993, 54. Note that this involves a normative claim about individual sovereignty and the link with preferences.

81. Dietz et al. 2009.

prefer larger damages in the future over smaller costs now when these are both costs to oneself, but quite another to prefer larger damages in the future over present costs when this means that the damages will come to someone else. Perhaps impatience is "irrational"[82] even when the losses are self-inflicted, but when the losses are imposed on others there is a real threat of injustice. Furthermore, it would be one thing for individuals to value deferring damages to the future, and quite another for governments to make it a central driver of national policy. Arguably, governments are charged with representing the interests of their citizens in perpetuity. To pass on high costs to the future for the sake of avoiding modest cost now for no further reason than that current people prefer it seems to exhibit bias.

In the context of climate economics, Stern and Nordhaus display very different attitudes to δ. On the one hand, the Stern team is sympathetic to the ethical objections, and so rejects the conventional justification for a positive δ. However, rather than endorsing a rate of zero, as most sympathizers do, they take the radical step of assigning δ a new role. For them, it represents "the probability of existence of future human civilisations", which they claim is 0.1% per annum. As they recognize, both the role and the number are controversial. On the first issue, the idea that extinction threats can or should be captured in this way requires further defense.[83] On second, 0.1% implies a "90% chance of human civilization seeing out this century," which may be thought "alarmingly low."[84]

By contrast, Nordhaus does not defend his choice of δ, and addresses Stern's choice only indirectly.[85] First, as discussed above, he emphasizes that it is the real rate of return on capital (ρ) as measured by the market that matters to him, calling its role "decisive", and complains that Stern implies a higher rate of savings than currently observed.[86] This appeal to

82. Cowen and Parfit 1992, 154–5.

83. Why put it in δ rather than η (e.g., perhaps it goes up with growth)? And why put it in ρ at all? Again, there are worries about ad hoc interventions around fundamental ethical issues.

84. Dietz et al 2009.

85. It is surprising that Nordhaus does not attempt a robust empirical defense of δ. But he does not seem to approach the issue in this way. One sign of this is the dramatic difference between earlier values for δ of 3% (e.g., Nordhaus 1999, 2007) and the more recent 1.5%.

86. Nordhaus 2009, 178. This is disputed by Dietz et al. 2009.

"realism" is echoed by Lomborg. In support of one of Nordhaus's earlier analyses, he says:

> When we weigh up our own situation and that of future generations, we usually choose to give priority to our own desires and let the future fend for itself. This is something we may find morally lamentable, but it ought not to get in the way of a realistic analysis of how the wealth distribution in society functions.[87]

What should we think of this "realism"? On the one hand, it threatens to undermine the interest of the approach. Given the large intergenerational component of climate change, a model that simply assumed that the future should fend for itself would be both morally lamentable, and largely irrelevant to the problem at hand. Moreover, it is hardly a surprise that such assumptions lead to the conclusion that we should do very little.

On the other hand, the claim that this is the "realistic analysis" of how things work does not do justice to what is really going on. Lomborg's claim that we "let the future fend for itself" is misleading, and in a way unfair. In principle, conventional CBA is not utterly unconcerned about the plight of future generations. Rather it commits itself to promoting world welfare, and so theoretically licenses all kinds of departures from real world distributions as motivated on ethical grounds.[88] The problem is rather that, having done so, it then imposes sharp limits (though not an absolute prohibition) on intergenerational concern. Moreover, it assumes that these limits should be inferred from the impatience individuals exhibit in their personal consumption decisions (as if these signaled their views about future generations), and then that these should be seen as sovereign over the goal of promoting world welfare. Though this is a strange (even bizarre) view, it is not narrowly "self-interested" in the usual sense.[89]

Nordhaus's second response to Stern reflects the ethical aspects of his view. He argues that Stern's rate is not ethically compelling, given that future people will be richer. I defer substantive discussion of this

---

87. Lomborg 2001, 314.

88. Stanton In press.

89. Nordhaus says that δ "measures the importance of the welfare of future generations relative to the present . . . a zero . . . rate means that future generations are treated symmetrically with present generations; a positive . . . rate means that the welfare of future generations is reduced . . . compared with nearer generations" (Nordhaus 2009, 60).

complaint until the next section. But first, let us see how it also arises when we turn to the remaining component of the Ramsey equation, the consumption elasticity η

4. The Consumption Elasticity

Nordhaus sets η at 2, and Stern at 1.[90] This is important because η functions as a multiplier in the Ramsey equation. Hence, the effect of Stern's choice is to leave the value of growth as it is, whereas Nordhaus's choice doubles it. The η component is interesting theoretical device. Stern says that η "plays three roles, guiding (a) intratemporal distribution, (b) intertemporal distribution, and (c) attitudes to risks."[91]

The main point to be made here is that this is a startling claim. The idea that three such important issues—distribution across space, time, and risk—could be captured *in a single number* is deeply surprising, even shocking, from a philosophical point of view. The Stern team is surely right to acknowledge that η is "problematic . . . because a great deal of information appears to be of relevance to η and yet it is contradictory."[92] Moreover, since η covers issues that are right at the heart of the ethics of long-term environmental policy, it seems hard to deny that there is a problem of theoretical inadequacy.[93]

This worry does not dissipate when we consider how the single number is generated. On the one hand, for Nordhaus, the value of η is (like δ) an "unobserved normative parameter" of the discount rate, and so to be inferred on the basis of the observed market rate. Hence, he takes the bold steps of suggesting (i) that our beliefs about intergenerational relations and risk, and how they relate to one another, can somehow be divined

90. Other economists have suggested values as high as 4 and lower than 1. See Dasgupta 2006, Atkinson, T. and A. Brandolini 2007.

91. Stern 2008, 15. Nordhaus claims that it "represents the aversion to inequality of different generations," such that "a high value . . . implies that decisions little heed whether the future is richer or poorer than the present" (Nordhaus 2009, 60).

92. Dietz et al 2009.

93. After all, η is the central operation that is performed on the long-term growth rate in order to generate the SDR. To try to capture it in a single number seems worryingly close to the bare intuition that dealing with the future requires doing *something* with long-term growth. Stern's choice of 1 suggests the "something" is to leave it as it is.

from our normal investment and consumption decisions, and (ii) that this provides good information to guide policy. Moreover, as with δ, he changes his value of η significantly over the years, from 1 to 2.[94]

On the other hand, for Stern the assignment of η is based not just in ethical, but distinctly philosophical thinking:

> Thinking about η is, of course, thinking about value judgements—it is a prescriptive and not a descriptive exercise. But that does not mean that h is arbitrary; we can, and should, ask about *"thought experiments"* and observations that might inform a choice of η.[95]

There is something to this methodology, but also something perplexing. Philosophers typically think that such thinking generates elaborate theories of justice and ethics with complex institutional implications. The idea that the same approach could yield a single number to be inserted into a larger economic equation is jarring.[96]

In conclusion, in light of these worries about g, δ and η, we should acknowledge that if this is the state of thinking at the cutting edge of contemporary economic theory, then important though it may be (and I don't dispute that it is important in context), the claim that we are in the grip of a theoretical storm seems reasonable. More generally, it seems clear that the initial burden of proof against discounting explained in the previous section cannot be met merely by elaborating on the basic disputes within climate economics. Given this, in what remains of this chapter I will briefly consider two alternative approaches. The first invokes explicitly ethical claims, and underlies Lomborg's idea that it is better to help the current poor than future generations. The second is the recent attempt within economics to head off some of the above objections by employing schedules of temporally declining discount rates.

---

94. Nordhaus and Boyer 2000, 16; Nordhaus 2009, 61.

95. Stern 2008, 15.

96. I do not mean to denigrate the efforts of the Stern team. They have done much to highlight the fact that "combining value judgements on risk, intertemporal inequality and intratemporal inequality into one parameter may be a non-trivial simplification" and "disentangling these three issues is an important topic for future research." Moreover, they have made contributions that help with the next steps, such as providing a sensitivity analysis on values of η (Stern 2007, 667), and attempting to evaluate it using coarse-grained ethical and political claims (Dietz, Hope, Stern and Zenghelis 2007).

V. DISCOUNTING THE RICH?

Lomborg claims that the climate change problem ultimately reduces to the question of whether to help poor inhabitants of the poor countries now or their richer descendents later.[97] This claim is already problematic, since it assumes that climate poses no serious threats to current or future inhabitants of richer countries, to animals, or to the rest of nature. But suppose that, for the sake of argument, we let the claim stand. If so, Lomborg argues that the right answer is to help the current poor now, since they are poorer than their descendents will be, because they are more easily (i.e., cheaply) helped, and because in helping them, one also helps their descendents.[98] For example, Lomborg once claimed that a mitigation project like Kyoto would "likely cost at least $150 billion a year, and possibly much more," whereas "just $70–80 billion a year could give all Third World inhabitants access to the basics like health, education, water and sanitation."[99]

1. Opportunity Costs

Lomborg's approach incorporates two main ideas. The first is a straightforward appeal to opportunity costs. Lomborg claims that the resources used for climate change mitigation could produce greater net benefits if used in other ways instead; specifically, to attack poverty.[100] Mitigation efforts like Kyoto are, he says, a "bad deal."[101]

We should begin by acknowledging that opportunity costs often matter. As we have seen, resources can be productive. Hence, those not used to protect the future might be reinvested to produce greater net benefits, and this is relevant to the SDR. Specifically, if we can more than fully *compensate* the future for a loss of world GDP in 200 years due to climate change by making alternative investments (e.g., putting aside a nest egg), then this may be a better strategy than trying to prevent the loss. Hence, Lomborg claims:

97. Lomborg 2001, 322.
98. Lomborg 2001, 322. See also Lomborg 2007, 51–2.
99. Lomborg 2001, p. 322. See also Lomborg 2007, 51–2.
100. Lomborg 2001, 314–15.
101. Lomborg 2007, 40.

> It is probably reasonable to have a discount rate of at least 4–6 percent. But [this] does not mean that ∴ . . we are saying to hell with future generations. It actually means that we are making sure we administer our investments sensibly . . . [low interest rate investments] would all in all probably leave our children and grand-children with far fewer resources.[102]

In some contexts, such arguments are compelling. But we should be careful about their import for climate change and other similar problems. Let me identify three worries.

The first is the threat of a false dichotomy. Arguments from opportunity cost crucially rely on the idea that if a given project is chosen, then that choice *forecloses* some other option.[103] But this is not the case in Lomborg's version. Helping the poor and mitigating climate change are not obviously mutually exclusive alternatives. First, dealing with poverty is not strictly-speaking an *opportunity* cost of mitigating climate change. As Lomborg himself admits, "we are actually so rich that we can afford to do both."[104] Hence, acting on climate change does not foreclose poverty alleviation. Second, it is not clear even that the two projects are independent of each other, in the sense that they are fully separable "opportunities," rather than necessarily linked and perhaps mutually supporting policies. After all, severe climate change is likely to have adverse effects in the poor countries—including on health and water (two items Lomborg mentions)—and there are realistic worries that failing to mitigate may undermine other efforts to aid the poor. For example, perhaps digging new wells in Africa won't make much difference if climate change induces a severe drought (perhaps it will even be simply a waste of resources), and perhaps some mitigation projects also help the poor (e.g., by reducing air pollution).[105] Third, it is not clear that the opportunity that Lomborg wants to emphasize is really available. As Peter Singer points out, Lomborg's position seems to show a giant leap of political optimism. The problem of global poverty has been

102. Lomborg 2001, 314–15.

103. One project (X) is an opportunity cost of another project (Y) only if in choosing Y the decision maker removes the option of choosing X. Suppose I have money enough to buy either a Prius or a boat, but not both. Then buying the Prius will have the opportunity cost of foreclosing the option of buying the boat.

104. Lomborg 2001, 324.

105. See also Stern 2009, 89.

around for a long time. Given this, Singer suggests that if their past record is anything to go by, the rich countries are even less likely to contribute large sums of money to help the world's poor directly than they are to do so to combat climate change. In the face of this problem, he adds, it may be that action on climate is the best available strategy for helping the poor, even if it is second-best overall.[106] Fourth, politically, this might give us every reason to be wary of a "bait and switch" strategy. Perhaps it is easy to persuade the affluent that poverty is more important than climate change when they have no intention of doing much about poverty. If so, the "foregone" opportunity of poverty reduction is spurious; indeed, its role seems to be to facilitate moral corruption. Notice here that the ethics of the "opportunity cost" argument against climate action would look different if the alternative actually pursued with the postulated extra income were not poverty reduction but a grand party for the current generation of the world's affluent.

The second worry about the opportunity cost argument concerns the compensation rationale more generally. Although theoretical welfare economics often assumes that it is enough even if compensation could *potentially* be paid,[107] most people have the intuition that potential compensation is no compensation at all. This intuition is apparently widely shared. According to an authoritative collection, "even hard-nosed benefit-cost analysts" agree that the claim that future people could be compensated by an alternative policy loses relevance if we know that the compensation will not actually be paid.[108] This worry is a live one in the case of climate. The main idea behind the economic analysis is not that we will set aside a separate nest egg for future generations. Instead, the claim is that the future will be compensated simply by its inheritance of a larger world economy. But this idea is questionable. On the one hand, as we have already seen, one of the worries about climate change is that it may threaten the global economy. In the face of climate stress, the "alternative bequest" may cease to grow, and if the stress is catastrophic, it may even shrink in drastic ways (e.g., the Stern Review's 20% loss of global product). On the other hand, even a "successful" bequest may not

---

106. Singer 2002, 26–7. The fact that this objection comes from Singer, the most vocal and radical advocate of assistance to the global poor, lends it extra salience.

107. In economics this view has a name: the Kaldor-Hicks criterion.

108. Portney and Weyant 1999, 6–7.

be adequate compensation. An otherwise richer future beset by severe climate change may not be better off, all things considered, than an otherwise poorer one without such problems even if it does have plenty of money to throw at the problem. (Perhaps throwing money at the problem does not help that much.)

The third worry about the opportunity cost argument is that, because it assumes that we can compensate the future for failure to act on climate change with a larger economy, the argument overlooks the possibility that future people may be entitled to both. This is an important omission. If we owe it to our successors both that we refrain from climate disruption and that we try to improve their material conditions, then we cannot simply substitute one for the other and say that we are even. This would be a morally mischievous slight of hand. It would be like arguing that we should not save for our own retirements but invest in our kids' education instead, because then they will be able to look after us in our old age. On a standard view of things, we owe our children freedom from the burdens of supporting us when we are older, and also some help in securing a good education. The satisfaction of one obligation does not simply silence the other.

2. The Affluence of the Future

This brings us to Lomborg's second main idea, that future people will be better off:

> We know that future generations will have more money to spend. Because of growth we are actually the poor generation, and future generations will be richer than us. We expect that in 2035 the average American will be twice as rich as she is now. For this reason it is perhaps not entirely unreasonable that society expects richer, later generations to pay more towards the costs of global warming—in exactly the same way as high income groups in our society pay higher taxes.[109]

This is perhaps the most popular argument for adopting a significant positive discount rate. Many economists argue that we should "tax the future" more, because they will be richer, and that we are justified in using a discount rate to do so, since this reflects economic growth over time.[110]

109. Lomborg 2001, 314.
110. Helm 2008; Barrett 2008.

This position is also open to challenge in the case of climate change. First, the approach ignores all issues of responsibility. If our generation causes the climate problem, and engages in buck-passing in doing so, it is far from clear that the future victims should pay to fix it (or pay disproportionately). This is so even if they happen to have more resources. We do not *always* think that those who have a greater ability to pay should pay (or pay more). For example, sometimes we think that those who caused the problem should pay instead.

Second, future people may not be richer. For one thing, many of the world's poorer people in 2050 or 2100 may be better off than they are today, but still much worse off than current Americans or Europeans. So, there is no reason to make them pay more. For another, if climate change has severe effects on matters such as food, water, disease, and the regional economies, then many people in the future may be worse off than people now. (Indeed, some will simply be killed.) So, again, there is no reason to "bill these people at a higher tax rate."

Lomborg objects to the last point by claiming that "the threat is vastly exaggerated," and that people tend to underestimate the fact that "global warming will have positive impacts."[111] It is perhaps possible that he will turn out to be correct. Still, it is not clear that this is the right point to be emphasizing. As it stands, the scientific community is saying that business-as-usual will result in a temperature rise of between 2.4 and 6.4 degrees Celsius by 2100, with a best estimate of 4.0 degrees.[112] Lomborg's remarks suggest that he is confident either that we will end up at the low end of these projections, and/or that human life can adapt fairly easily to the change. Unfortunately, this obscures the crucial issue.[113] The question for us concerns what we are morally entitled to assume in our deliberations, given the best information we have. And here it is morally reckless simply to hope for low temperature rises and modest impacts and plan accordingly; we are obliged to take the more severe projections offered by the scientific community seriously. Future generations will not think well of us if we only consider the best-case scenario. This is so even if the best turns out to transpire. Previous saving for retirement does not suddenly become irrational when your novel turns into a Hollywood blockbuster.

Finally, the claim that future people should pay more because they are richer (again) ignores the difficult issue of what we owe the future.

111. Lomborg 2007, 38.
112. IPCC 2007a, 11.
113. Brown 2002.

Perhaps we should not inflict climate instability on them even if they are richer. For one thing, their being richer does not license us doing anything we like to them, or inflicting any manner of damages. Nor does it imply that we have no responsibilities of our own. (Maybe richer Americans should do more for the country than the middle class, but that does not mean that the middle class owe nothing.) For another, we often recognize intergenerational responsibilities of this sort. For example, as mentioned above, we help our children through college, even though their lifetime incomes will probably be much higher than ours. We do not demand that they subsidize our retirements instead.

I conclude that a strong prima facie case can be made against these two rationales for adopting standard discount rates for climate change in general, and Lomborg's arguments in particular. No doubt there is more to be said. But the burden of proof is there, and it is significant. Moreover, many of the issues are clearly ethical, not narrowly economic. Since much depends on the SDR, they ought not to be ignored.

VI. DECLINING DISCOUNT RATES

I turn now to an alternative approach to discounting. A few years ago, an overview piece published by the OECD describes a "revolution" in the economic literature. The revolution takes the form of a rejection of uniform positive discount rates in favor of a schedule of positive rates that decline over time. So, for example, Martin Weitzman suggests that, based on his theoretical manipulation of a survey of the opinions of economists, the following schedule of rates should be adopted.[114]

TABLE 8.2 "Approximate Recommended" Sliding-Scale Discount Rates

Time period	Name	Marginal discount rate (Percent)
Within years 1 to 5 hence	*Immediate* Future	4
Within years 6 to 25 hence	*Near* Future	3
Within years 26 to 75 hence	*Medium* Future	2
Within years 76 to 300 hence	*Distant* Future	1
Within years more than 300 hence	*Far-Distant* Future	0

114. Weitzman 2001, 270.

According to the OECD report, such a schedule constitutes a "middle way" on the topic of discounting, since it is consistent with the theoretical underpinnings of CBA, but "does much to overcome the tyranny of discounting so widely noted by philosophers and environmentalists."[115] In short, the revolution is said to substantially diminish the problem of absurdity but in such a way as to be consistent with mainstream economics.

1. Absurdity

The first question to ask is whether a schedule of declining rates really does solve the absurdity problem. Here, there are several reasons for caution. First, it is not true that the employment of temporally declining rates considered merely *as such* will allow us to avoid absurd results. Everything depends on the magnitude of the rates. Examples such as that given above from Weitzman look encouraging, to be sure. But this is primarily because the magnitudes of the rates they employ are relatively low (1–4%), come down quickly, and then reduce to zero; hence, they appear to be a substantial improvement over conventional CBA (uniform 5%, continued indefinitely). This obscures the fact that the considered by itself the formal idea of temporally declining discount rates is consistent with an infinite number of possibilities schedules of magnitude and timing, many of which would actually make the absurdity problem worse. Consider, for example, the following schedule:

- 1–5 years: 27%
- 6–10 years: 24%
- Over 10 years: 22%

This would have the effect of reducing a benefit of 1 million dollars 100 years from now to a net present value of 17 cents, whereas a standard uniform rate of 5% would "only" reduce it to $7604. In short, merely invoking temporally declining discount rates as such does not solve the absurdity problem. We need to know the magnitudes. This

115. Pearce et al. 2006, 189.

makes it very relevant to recall that indeterminacy about the magnitude of the discount rate was the fourth of the standard problems mentioned above.

The second reason for caution is that even declining rates of low magnitudes seem merely to mitigate the absurdity problem rather than actually to solve it. For even very low rates do show considerable compounding effects over very long time periods. First, consider Chichilnisky's example. She points out that at a standard discount rate of 5%, the value of the world's output 200 years in the future reduces to a net present value of a few hundred thousand dollars. But a very low uniform discount rate of 1% would reach the same conclusion in around 980 years.[116] This raises some obvious questions. For example, if the result is absurd in 200 years, why isn't it absurd at 980 years? Is there some time-horizon over which it ceases to be absurd? What is it? Why? Moreover, by choosing smaller, or declining rates, haven't we just deferred the absurdity problem, rather than actually solving it? And what justifies the choice to defer it for 200 rather than 980 years?

Second, Weitzman's proposal avoids the same conclusion by putting a zero rate in place after 300 years. In effect, this means that there is a cap on the maximum amount of discounting that can occur: after 300 years, the net present value of $1 is fixed at 1.8 cents. But, again, there are obvious questions. Does a weighting of 1.8 cents give rise to absurd results? (If not, why not?) And why stop discounting at 300, rather than 400 or 500 years? (If we did that, the cap would be set at around 0.7 cents or 0.25 cents per dollar respectively.)

We can conclude that it is not at all obvious that the idea of temporally declining rates does help to solve the absurdity problem. Clearly, the hope is that by reducing the magnitude of the effects of the SDR in the long-term future, the SDR becomes more intuitively acceptable. Perhaps it does. But this ignores the more fundamental issue. Even if a schedule of temporally declining rates did *seem* to deal with the absurdity problem, it would be vital to know *how* it did so. Merely asserting a schedule of declining rates would not be enough. We would need to know why we were justified in applying such a schedule. Without a rationale, the kind of table produced above threatens to be merely a dangerous distraction from what is really at

---

116. For 200 years, a uniform 5% rate produces a discount factor of 5.8×10^{-5}.; a uniform 1% rate produces the same discount factor in 981 years.

stake. In short, the array of numbers creates an illusion of precision which merely serves to dignify the basic intuition that the impacts of low and declining positive rates on the future somehow "feel" better than those of moderate and constant positive rates. This would hardly be enough to count as a robust theory of intergenerational ethics or economics.

2. Rationales

As it turns out, a number of different rationales have been offered for temporally declining rates. Some claim that such schedules have an empirical basis in people's actual behavior; others that they evolve out of attempts to incorporate various kinds of uncertainty into decision making; and still others that they are necessary in order to prevent the complete dictatorship of one generation's interests over another's.[117] It has even been argued that they reflect the "professionally considered gut feeling" of economists.[118]

The first point to make is that the sheer diversity of defenses on offer is itself a major issue. It resonates with the second standard criticism of discount rates, namely that they lack a clear and consistent rationale, and also with the more specific claim that existing accounts fail to give completely general reasons for discounting, and may come into conflict. This makes Cowen and Parfit's suggestion plausible. Instead of folding everything into a discount rate, we should take each of these arguments on its merits; otherwise we are in danger of making ourselves "morally blind."

The second point is that the various rationales do not seem to be of the *right kind* to address the problems of intergenerational justice that need to solved. Suppose, for example, that one is concerned about the absurdity problem, and in part because one believes that the minimal concern discounting displays for some future generations manifests buck-passing. Then, one finds out that temporally declining discount rates mitigate that problem somewhat. At first, one might be reassured. But suppose then that one learns of the various rationales for declining rates.

The first is based on the preferences of each generation. (The last is based on the preferences of each generation's economists.) But this reintroduces the worry about the intergenerational buck-passing. If each

---

117. Frederick et al., 2002; Weitzman 1998, 1999, and Gollier 2002; Chichilnisky 1996.
118. Weitzman 2001, 271.

generation's preferences are dominantly generation-relative, then we have reason to be concerned about policy based on purely descriptive claims about such preferences, partly because it would not be surprising to find that they undervalue the future to at least some extent. This suggests that if we take a generation's preferences seriously, it will be at least partly because we have *independent reason* to think that these preferences embody or reflect an acceptable theory of intergenerational justice. But this implies that the real justification for declining rates must be elsewhere.

The second rationale is uncertainty. One worry about this rationale is that it seems too contingent. It suggests that if only we knew more about the future we would still be justified in using standard discount rates, even given the absurdity problem. But, again, this claim requires independent defense. Another worry is that even if the rationale is reasonably secure in practice (given, for example, Broome's point about historical uncertainty about the further future), it seems to provide the wrong kind of basis for intergenerational justice. Suppose, for example, that intergenerational buck-passing occurs and we intentionally adopt policies that leave future generations impoverished. Is it plausible to claim that what went wrong is that we failed to take uncertainty into account?

The third rationale comes from social choice theory. The most prominent proposal here comes from Graciela Chichilnisky. She argues that a concern for sustainable development requires allowing neither present nor future generations to completely dictate policy, and that this is compatible with temporally declining rates. On the face of it, this sounds promising. But, again, there are important problems. Though the claim that sustainable development requires nondictatorship of both present and future generations has the ring of truth to it, it is important to understand what "dictatorship" might mean here. There seem to be two possibilities. On the one hand, "nondictatorship" might mean simply that the interest of all such generations must be taken into account in deliberation in some way. Unfortunately, this claim risks triviality. Even standard rates of discount do allow some role for the interests of future generations. The problem is not that such interests are not taken into account at all, but rather that the degree to which they are taken into account is absurdly small. Hence, if this is all that is being proposed, the nondictatorship requirement itself is in danger of being absurdly minimal. On the other hand, the requirement might be understood in a more substantive way, as asserting at least a minimal theory of intergenerational justice. But then everything depends on what that theory is. Clearly we need some moral and political philosophy.[119]

In conclusion, the apparent revolution in economic thinking about discounting does little to address the basic philosophical challenges faced by the practice. Instead, the recent works tends to illustrate the fact that more robust theory is needed.

VII. TWO OBJECTIONS TO NOT DISCOUNTING

Before closing, it is perhaps wise to say something about two prominent objections to criticisms to the social discount rate. The first is that "not

---

119. Chichilnisky's own approach is not compelling. First, she suggests that we "assign weights which decline into the future, and then assign some extra weight to the last generation" (Chichinisky 1996, 243). But, other than wishing to avoid dictatorship, it is not clear what the rationale for this approach is, or what it amounts to in practice. (Much, of course, depends on what the requisite "weights" are; but we also need to understand what it means to say that the last generation is to get "some extra.") Second, Chichilnisky recognizes that her view could do with additional philosophical underpinnings. But her gloss on this issue is hard to fathom, and her solution unnecessarily radical. The key problem, as she sees it, is that we need to understand our concern for the future when "nobody alive today, not even their heirs, has a stake in the welfare of 50 generations into the future" (Chichinisky 1996, 250). Fair enough. But then she understands this as the question: "Whose welfare do sustainable preference represent?" (Chichinisky 1996, 250). This is a strange question. The obvious answer is: the welfare of present and future generations. But this is not how Chichilnisky understands the problem. We can see this from her immediate answer:

> Perhaps an answer for this riddle may be found in a wider understanding of humankind as an organism who seeks its overall welfare over time. . . . If such unity existed, humankind would make up an unusual organism, one whose parts are widely distributed in space and time and who is lacking a nervous system on which the consciousness of its existence can be based. Perhaps the advances in information technology described at the beginning of this article, with their global communications reach, are a glimmer of the emergence of a nervous system from which a global consciousness for humankind could emerge. (Chichilnisky 1996, 250–1)

It is clear from this that Chichilnisky thinks that making sense of intergenerational ethics requires positing an entity with intergenerational preferences that persists through the realization of those preferences. (For Chichilnisky, this means that it must have its own welfare and consciousness.) But her reason for taking such a view is opaque, and many less extreme solutions are available.

discounting" is the same as discounting at 0% rate of discount and this has its own problems."[120] There is much that might be said on this topic; but again I will limit myself to just one general point. On the face of it, this objection is simply mistaken. It is true that many who reject discounting in some contexts—such as Broome in the case of the further future—end up endorsing a zero rate of discount. But this does not mean that rejecting discounting *implies* endorsing a zero rate.

To see this, consider how discounting is defined:

> Discounting refers to the process of assigning a lower weight to a unit of benefit or cost in the future than to that unit now. The further in the future the benefit or cost occurs, the lower the weight attached to it.[121]

According to this definition, discounting involves three main components: first, it assigns weights to future benefits and costs; second, these weights are lower than those assigned to current benefits and costs; and third, the weights are lower the further in the future the benefit or cost is.[122] To these definitional features, we might add that, in the views we have been considering, those who discount assign the same weight to *all* costs or benefits that occur within the same time period, making no distinctions between different kinds of costs and benefits.

The practice of discounting is thus a complex phenomenon. Given this, it seems both that one might reject it by disputing any number of its constituent claims, and that in doing so one need not thereby be endorsing a discount rate of zero. Consider the following examples of ways of rejecting discounting. First, the view that the same weight should be assigned to all kinds of costs and benefits might be rejected by some theories of justice on the grounds that it is necessary to distinguish between luxuries and basic necessities. For example, perhaps there are good reasons not to discount necessities that do not apply to luxuries. Second, the view that weights should decline over time might be rejected because one thinks that some things (e.g., lives, the value of a beautiful view)

120. Pearce et al. 2006, 184.
121. Pearce et al. 2006, 184.
122. I take it that "weights" here refers to discount factors rather than discount rates, since traditionally, most proponents of CBA adopt a uniform SDR which (hence) does not itself decline, but has compound effects which mean that the associated discount factors decline over time.

do not decline in importance over time, or even perhaps get more important as time goes on.[123] Third, one might reject the view that future benefits and costs must receive lower weights than current benefits and costs because one believes that the current generation has a strong obligation to ensure that future people are better off. Finally, and most noticeably, one might even reject the claim that weights *can* be assigned to some future benefits and costs, or at least that such an assignment is anything other than arbitrary, and thereby useless. As we have seen, one reason to think this would be that such costs and benefits cannot be known with the precision necessary to make fine-grained calculations possible.

Now, very few of these rationales for rejecting discounting seem to *imply* the acceptance of a zero rate. First, and most obviously, the claim that weights cannot even be assigned to future costs and benefits directly rules out *any* kind of weighting, including a uniform rate of zero. Second, the goal of making future people better off than current people might justify weighing future benefits *more heavily* than current benefits, and so imply a *negative* rate (e.g., of –2% per year) rather than one of zero. Third, a desire to distinguish between luxuries and necessities might imply a complex schedule of positive, zero, and negative discount factors for different kinds of benefits and costs in different time periods. (In advance of the announcement of a particular theory of intergenerational justice, how would one know?)

These examples show that rejecting discounting in no way commits one to endorsing a uniform rate of zero. Given the prevalence of the contrary claim, this is an interesting result in itself. But in the present context its relevance is this. Even if there are problems with zero rates of discount, these need not undermine the criticisms of normal discount rates considered as such. This point is sufficient to restore the presumption against such rates.

The second objection to not discounting is that to do so would be extremely burdensome to the current generation. Discussing zero rates, Lomborg says that failure to discount leads to a "grim surprise":

> If the welfare of future generations means just as much (or almost as much) to us as our own, then we ought to spend an extremely large share of our income on

123. Cowen and Parfit 1992; Broome 1994.

investment in the future, because the dividend payable on investments will be much greater in the future.[124]

David Pearce adds, "Everything would be transferred to the future . . . pure equality of treatment for generations would . . . imply a policy of total current sacrifice."[125]

The key thought here is that if we do not discount, many more future-oriented projects become feasible, and so, other things being equal, less is available for the present. If we must save more (or work harder) for the future, then we must consume less (or work less hard for) ourselves. By contrast, standard positive discount rates protect the current generation from excessive demands. Because they sharply reduce the impact of future generations on the rests of a cost-benefit analysis, they prevent our concerns being swamped by theirs.

This argument is correct in observing that there would be something morally problematic in requiring current people to endorse "a policy of total sacrifice." But the problem here is with the discounting, not the ethics of rejecting it. Consider two quick points. First, it is not true that low, or even zero, rates cause the problem. In principle, if the future benefits of a policy are extremely high, then even standard rates could lead to the same conclusion. For example, even though one benefit now is worth more than 131 benefits in 100 years at a rate of 5%, a standard CBA that employed such a rate would still come to the conclusion that we should give up everything for the sake of the future if every foregone benefit could produce (say) 135 benefits in 100 years. Hence, if standard rates save us, it is only because there are no such projects.[126]

Second, the first point reveals that the real problem is elsewhere, in the basic idea of cost-benefit analysis: the claim that a project is worth doing if the benefits exceed the costs. This idea counts for nothing how benefits and costs are distributed. Hence, like its distant parent

---

124. Lomborg 2001, 314. Relatedly, Arrow suggests that it may involve the assertion of an "agent-centered prerogative" (Arrow 1999; cf. Scheffler 1990).

125. Pearce 1993, 58.

126. Similarly, if zero rates doom us, it is only because there are long-term projects to displace all current ones at that rate and not higher. In both cases, this is an empirical point that would have to be shown, not just asserted.

utilitarianism, it can be criticized for demanding too much of some, for the sake of others. Clearly, commonsense morality rebels at the suggestion that some should be subjected to "a policy of total sacrifice" just to make others much better off than they are. But this only implies that there are principles of justice that are in conflict with simple CBA.[127]

There is much more that might be said about CBA in general and discount rates in particular. But for present purposes we can draw two important conclusions. First, even some enthusiasts for CBA in normal contexts are deeply suspicious when it comes to cases that involve the long term future such as climate change. Second, they have good reason to be so. The problem of theoretical inadequacy is thus very much with us.

VIII. THE "ANYTHING GOES" ARGUMENT

Before closing, I want briefly to mention one last argument for CBA that seems implicit in the attitudes of many of its proponents, and which contributes to some of the confusion around discounting. This argument suggests that in principle the approach must be able to cope with any problems that seem to beset it, because in the end any difficulty or objection can be accounted for and absorbed in a suitably sophisticated cost-benefit analysis. In other words, *"anything goes"*, and *the devil is in the details*.

This argument is importantly different from the ideological claim that cost-benefit analysis reflects the correct moral theory (e.g., utilitarianism) and that any problems can be dealt with by that theory. Instead, the argument is ostensibly nonideological. It asserts that *whatever the correct ethical theory, ultimately it must be possible to model that theory in cost-benefit terms*. Echoing some of the claims of the last chapter, the thought is that CBA can absorb and neutralize any substantive external criticism, because the materials of such criticism can always be accommodated within the approach. If moral information is left out of a given

---

127. Cowen and Parfit suggest, "No generation can be morally required to make more than certain kinds of sacrifice for the sake of future generations" (Cowen and Parfit 1992, 149).

CBA, then we can put things right simply by adjusting the costs, the benefits, or the ways in which they are integrated.[128]

This idea is worth discussing at some length. But here I have space for just three preliminary remarks. First, the idea may be a heroic one. It is not obvious that it is philosophically defensible. In the context of actual economic CBA, the basic claims seem to be (a) that any moral theory might be modeled in mathematical terms, and (b) that any such modeling could appropriately be labeled "cost-benefit analysis."

These claims are striking: (a) comes close to asserting that 'cost-benefit analysis' is just another name for *ethical analysis*, appropriately formalized, while (b) suggests that this is because the key terms -'cost', 'benefit', and 'analysis' – are infinitely malleable. Moreover, it is far from clear that this bold thesis is correct. In general, (a) raises deep questions about the limits of mathematical modeling, and (b) about the flexibility of the phrase "cost-benefit analysis". Both also bring back worries about vacuousness, opacity and evasiveness in the face of the perfect storm (see chapter 7).

One sign of the challenges for (a) and (b) is that the claims face early pressure from some mainstream approaches to moral philosophy. Suppose, for example, that virtue ethics, particularism, or situationism were true.[129] Are we really so confident that these theories could be mathematically modeled? Is it plausible to claim that the behavior of the virtuous person can be adequately captured in cost-benefit terms? And what of the particularist's reasons, whose existence, strength, and valence depend on the wider context in which they arise? Since most advocates of these views would probably regard such claims as deeply implausible, there is a strong burden of proof against the anything goes argument.

Second, even if granted, the theoretical prospect of mathematical modeling would not guarantee practical relevance. CBA strives to provide a tool for decision making. But perhaps the correct mathematical model of morality is not very useful for that. For example, perhaps only a morally virtuous person would be able to generate or apply such a

128. This is often claimed in economics, but also has some philosophical supporters. For example, Kristen Shrader-Frechette argues that CBA is "a formal calculus amenable to the weights dictated by any ethical system" and "allows one to count virtually any ethical consideration or consequence as a risk, cost or benefit" (Shrader-Frechette 1991, 182-3).

129. Hursthouse 1999; Dancy 1993, 2004; McDowell 1979; Hooker and Little 2000; Doris 2002.

model, because only she could understand the terms;[130] or perhaps the model itself would have to be so complex that it could not be used for making normal policy decisions.

Third, and perhaps most importantly, the claim that "anything goes" seems to concede much of what is at issue. Clearly, if the role of CBA is to model the correct theory, then we need to know what the correct theory is. Ethics needs to come first, or at least be a very explicit component of the development of CBA. On the nonideological reading, the idealized CBA is clearly derivative from our ethical judgments, not prior to, or a replacement for, such judgments. In practice, this is an important point. Obviously, one of the aims of contemporary CBA is to provide some kind of shortcut through at least some forms of ethical decision making. But this aspiration needs to be handled with caution. The basic questions will always be: Is this possible, and is it a good or accurate shortcut? These questions cannot be answered simply by declaring that the devil is in the details. As we have seen in the discussion of the SDR and η, aspiring to a legitimate alternative to deeper theorizing is not the same as having one.

IX. CONCLUSION

This chapter has sketched some of the deep and ongoing disputes within climate economics. These disputes stem from serious differences in fundamental assumptions, and result in strongly divergent policy recommendations. Contrary to initial appearances, these differences do not revolve around narrow technical issues within economic theory, but rather concern deep ethical claims that fill fundamental gaps in that theory. Moreover, recent economic arguments do not fill these gaps, and neither does the (perhaps heroic) claim that some appropriate kind of economic modeling must in principle be possible. This does not mean that good climate economics is not worth pursuing. But it does suggest that we are far from the position where we can confidently rely on such analysis when deciding how to shape the future of the planet.

130. Gardiner 2005.

I conclude that the problem of theoretical inadequacy—the third storm—is very much with us. I should add that I suspect it has wider relevance. In the perfect storm, a focus on climate economics is likely to facilitate moral corruption. For one thing, the apparent intractability of the basic disputes facilitates further procrastination and delay. Hence, a preoccupation with economics threatens to induce a convenient paralysis. For another, it does so by hiding the ethical arguments behind concepts (such as the SDR and η) that on the surface appear narrowly technical. In his review of Stern, Nordhaus says of discounting: "At first blush, this area would appear a technicality that should properly be left to abstruse treatises and graduate courses in economics."[131] This is a dangerous impression, and one we should work hard to counter.

---

131. Nordhaus 2007, 9 (draft version). He notes that divergent ethical perspectives are possible and would lead to dramatically different results; however, he also describes ethical discount rates as "largely irrelevant" (Nordhaus 2007, 693).

PART E

Moral Corruption

CHAPTER 9

Jane Austen vs. Climate Economics

In the tradition of political theory, corruption is a disease of the body politic.
Like a virus invading the physical body, hostile forces spread through the
political body, enfeebling the spirit of the laws and undermining the principles
of the regime.

—Dennis Thompson (Thompson 1995, 28)

We turn now to the last element of our account. In a perfect moral storm, we (the current generation and especially the relatively affluent) are ethically vulnerable. Not only is it the case that we can pass the buck onto the poor, the future, and nature, but we face strong temptations to do so. This makes us ethically vulnerable. One way in which we may succumb is to refuse to acknowledge that there is problem at all.[1] But even if we initially accept that we face a serious moral challenge, our resolve remains vulnerable to corrupt mechanisms of persuasion. One especially serious threat is corruption that targets our ways of talking and thinking, and so prevents us from even seeing the problem in the right way. If we are interested in being ethical, this should be of real concern. Serious moral agents strive to protect themselves against rationalization, self-deception, and moral manipulation.

Moral corruption is often subtle, indirect, and hard to pin down. But we have some experience of it in other settings. This chapter illustrates this problem by drawing on a classic example offered by Jane Austen.

---

1. My main audience in this chapter is those who accept that there is a problem, but are vulnerable to the mechanisms of moral corruption in how (and whether) they address it (i.e., most of us). Not all resistance to the problem manifests corruption, but I suspect that some does. For a few comments, see Appendix 2.

This example occurs in a setting that resembles the perfect storm in important respects. Moreover, the corrupt arguments revealed by Austen have close parallels to those prominent in recent climate policy, with the same result: inaction. These similarities are disturbing, and should make us wonder whether we might be the victims of (or even complicit in) moral corruption in the perfect storm. This gives us reason to work harder at the ethics of climate change in the public sphere, and especially at "defensive ethics" that aims to protect the quality of the discourse.

I. CORRUPTION

The central idea of this chapter is that if we are tempted by buck-passing, but reluctant to face up to moral criticism for succumbing to it (our own, or that of others), we are likely to be attracted to weak or deceptive arguments that appear on the surface to license such behavior, and so to give such arguments less scrutiny than we ought. A particularly deep way of doing this is through the corruption of the very terms of the debate. Hence, we must beware of arguments that work to subvert our understanding of what is at stake. In the perfect moral storm, such vigilance becomes especially important. Not only are the harms and injustice that might occur potentially catastrophic, but many of the victims of our bad behavior (the poor, future generations, and nature) lack the ability not only to resist, but even to make their concerns heard. Given this, it becomes even more necessary than usual to be vigilant about our own reasoning.

Unfortunately, addressing corruption of the understanding is not easy. Not only are the motivational forces that support it powerful, but in its most sophisticated forms it seeks to co-opt important values (such as moral and epistemic values) that otherwise ought to be respected. This is part of the genius of such corruption, and combating it requires serious effort. Fortunately, we are broadly familiar with the phenomenon. This chapter illustrates it by comparing some of the recent climate debate with a classic reconstruction of morally corrupt reasoning put forward by Jane Austen. The aim is to point out the strong resemblances between Austen's story and our own. If we accept that Austen's case is a paradigm case of moral corruption—and it is, after all, designed to be such—then these resemblances should give us pause. Morally serious agents would not want to be portrayed as Austen portrays her subjects.[2]

The chapter proceeds as follows: This section introduces the notions of regular and distinctively moral corruption. Sections II-V discusse the parallels between Austen's story and the contemporary climate debate. Section VI briefly draws some general lessons from this comparison, including how it suggests a need for defensive ethics.

1. Corruption in General

To be corrupt is to be "immoral or dishonest, especially as shown by the exploitation of a position of power or trust for personal gain."[3] Currently, we lack a strong philosophical account of corruption, and some authorities doubt that one is possible.[4] One sign of the difficulties emerges from the definition of "corruption" just mentioned. First, not all immorality is also corrupt. See, for example, a case suggested by Seumas Miller:

> Consider an otherwise gentle husband who in a fit of anger strikes his adulterous wife and accidentally kills her. The husband has committed an act that is morally wrong; he has committed murder, or perhaps culpable homicide, or at least manslaughter. But his action is not necessarily an act of corruption.[5]

Second, matters do not improve if one makes the "especially" clause a necessary condition of corruption, so that all corruption must involve "the exploitation of a position of power or trust for personal gain." For one thing, not all corruption is for personal gain. For example, sometimes corrupt officials and executives act to benefit their friends, their favorite causes, or rival institutions. In addition, not all corruption is most naturally described as involving the exploitation (or taking

---

2. The main argument of the chapter is one from analogy, and the specific criticisms of arguments against action on climate change are intended merely to make the analogy plausible. This is not to say that the criticisms do not have merit, only that more work may need to be done to prosecute them successfully.

3. Encarta® World English Dictionary. The OED has "morally depraved; wicked," or "influenced by or using bribery or fraudulent activity."

4. Miller 2005.

5. Miller 2005.

advantage)[6] of a position of power or trust. Sometimes we say that a group (or institution or individual) is corrupt even if it has no power and no one trusts it. So, for example, we might say of a given political party or social movement that it failed to gain power or influence precisely because it was corrupt.

Despite these drawbacks, the dictionary definition is useful in positing as a core case of corruption the illegitimate taking advantage of a position of superior power for the sake of personal gain.[7] Moreover, a focus on this case is sufficient for present purposes, since it seems central to the perfect moral storm. In the global storm, the main threat is that the rich will take unjust advantage of the poor. In the intergenerational storm, it is that earlier generations will do the same to later generations. In the ecological "storm", the kick the dog scenario suggests the further exploitation of nonhuman nature by humanity. When the various threats are combined, the risk of corruption becomes severe.

The idea that the perfect storm brings on a threat of corruption fits nicely with at least one standard usage in political philosophy. Consider, for example, Dennis Thompson's description (in the epigraph above) of corruption as "a disease of the body politic . . . enfeebling the spirit of the laws and undermining the principles of the regime." Similarly, one might see the threat posed by the perfect moral storm as a "virus" that infects social and political systems, weakening their commitments to explicit and implicit moral norms. In the perfect moral storm, the threat is acute, even potentially fatal, because of the severe nature of some of the asymmetries of power and because those who are damaged by them—the poor, future generations, animals, and the rest of nature—are poorly placed to defend themselves against it.

We can conclude that the claim that the perfect moral storm brings on a threat of corruption seems reasonable. Still, we must be aware that corruption takes many forms. (Like money in politics, corruption has a way

---

6. "Exploitation" is often used as a technical term in political philosophy. But here I assume that the dictionary definition of "corruption" intends only a colloquial sense, meaning something like the illegitimate taking of advantage.

7. Of course, as stressed in chapter 2, this purpose can be broadened to include generation-relative aims more generally. Michael Blake suggests to me that we might understand corruption more generally, as something like "acting in a powerful role without acting on the norms that would legitimate that power." This is a good suggestion, but I cannot pursue it here.

of finding the cracks.) Some of these forms are quite direct. Paradigm cases of corruption arise when individual politicians take bribes for personal gain, engage in outrageous nepotism, or are simply the unabashed agents of some special interest, rather than their constituents and the common good. However, we are also used to manifestations of corruption that take a more circuitous route. Consider, for example, the "revolving door" problem that arises when officials in one political administration grant special favors to some industry or labor group in the full expectation of joining them as lobbyists in the next election cycle and collecting a fat check. Given the possibility of such indirect manifestations, we should not be too naïve about what counts as genuine corruption.

Threats of corruption are pervasive in modern political life, hence they are doubtless also present in climate policy. (Indeed, it would be rash to assume otherwise.) Presumably, some nations, industries, corporations, and unions will try to use climate policy as a tool through which to advance their own (typically short-term economic) agendas at the expense of others, and sometimes they will employ corrupt means for doing so. Moreover, the perfect moral storm can explain how such direct corruption can be extended to include global, intergenerational, and other forms of exploitation. Presumably, some social, political, and economic elites will try to capture the framing of climate policy in various fora at the expense of the less well-funded and well-connected. Similarly, we might see fairly overt intergenerational corruption: the twisting of climate policy to fit the perceived interests of the current generation at the expense of the future.

Confronting such familiar kinds of corruption will require deep and sustained social effort, and I do not wish to diminish that task. (After all, the rest of contemporary politics hardly offers a shining beacon of hope, since we cannot claim to have already solved the familiar problems there.) Still, in this chapter my focus will be on more subtle forms of corruption— those which target our ways of *talking and thinking* about moral problems such as climate change at their basis, at the level of ethics itself. This is what I earlier refer to as distinctively moral corruption, since it strikes at our ability even to understand what is going wrong in moral terms, by subverting moral discourse to other (usually selfish) ends.[8]

8. Another form of corruption of the understanding would be epistemic. (see Appendix 2). Relatedly, see Jon Elser's classic discussion of "sour grapes" (Elster 1983).

2. Moral Corruption

How should we understand moral corruption? I will not attempt to offer a rigorous account here. Instead, I will try to motivate the general idea by gesturing towards Kant.

Kant offers us an initial description of the nature and root causes of moral corruption that is both illuminating and probably sufficient for current purposes.[9] He begins by considering an objection to sophisticated moral reasoning: "Would it not therefore be more advisable in moral matters to leave the judgment of common reason as it is?"[10] In other words, do we really need strong guidance from principles or theory to do the right thing? Can't we just rely on people's normal, common-sense moral judgments? Kant thinks not.

First, he says: "There is something splendid about innocence; but what is bad about it, in turn, is that it cannot protect itself very well and is easily seduced."[11] In other words, everyday moral thinking is vulnerable to external manipulation.

Second, he adds that such manipulation is to be expected:

> Reason issues its precepts unremittingly, without thereby promising anything to the inclinations . . . from this there arises . . . a propensity to rationalize against those strict laws of duty and to cast doubt upon their validity, or at least upon their purity and strictness, and, where possible, to make them better suited to our wishes and inclinations, that is, to corrupt them at their basis and destroy all of their dignity.[12]

In essence, the trouble with morality is that it opposes the regular inclinations, and in an uncompromising way, without promising them anything in return.[13] As a result, the inclinations provoke rationalizations that seek

---

9. Although Kant's account does involve reference to some distinctively Kantian claims about the nature of morality and moral psychology, fans of other traditions could, I believe, easily translate his remarks into their own favored theoretical setting. In addition, since the invocation of Kant is mainly illustrative, nothing much depends on its historical accuracy.

10. Kant 1998, 17.

11. Kant 1998, 17.

12. Kant 1998, 17–8.

13. Kant believes that morality is based in reason, and on the surface his phrasing suggests that the conflict is between reason and inclination considered as such. This initial impression may not even be accurate as an interpretation of Kant; more importantly, we might reject such theoretical claims and yet still accept the basic vision of moral corruption that Kant implies.

to undercut or weaken the moral prescriptions, so as to reconcile them with their own aims. Such corruption, Kant tells us, strikes morality at its foundation, and in doing so destroys its dignity. Though Kant does not explicitly say so, let us postulate that the kind of attack that is central is one that seeks to transform the moral claim itself. The deepest threats to morality seek to pervert our understanding of its status and content.

The thoughts that I take from Kant are, then, that moral corruption is: (a) a tendency to rationalize, which (b) casts doubt on the validity and/or strictness of moral claims, by (c) seeking to pervert their status and substance, and in doing so (d) aims to make those claims better suited to our wishes and inclinations, and (e) destroys the characteristics in virtue of which we respect them (e.g., what Kant calls their "dignity"). According to Kant, the root cause of such corruption is the fact that moral claims are in some sense uncompromising, and in particular do not seek to accommodate other sources of motivation, often and especially the inclinations of the agent on whom the claims are made. Given this, such rival concerns try to undermine the status and content of moral claims, by transforming them into something more amenable to their aims.

Understood in this way, moral corruption poses special difficulties in social life. Unlike the paradigm examples of political corruption mentioned above (such as bribery), many forms of moral corruption are subtle and indirect, and some are systematic. Under such circumstances, it can, from the external perspective, be difficult to find anyone to blame in the usual way. After all, those who offer bad arguments or mistaken values *may* act in good faith, as might many of those who accept their positions. And generally we hold people less morally liable (if liable at all) for such apparently (and "merely") cognitive failures. Moreover, often the problem is not quite that the values or arguments are bad or mistaken considered simply as such; instead, they would be good values and correct arguments in a more limited context, but are misappropriated or badly applied. Given this, it is doubly difficult to find fault with those who are "misled."[14]

Still, we must be careful. Presumably, part of the genius of some methods of moral corruption, and one reason for their enduring effectiveness and popularity, is precisely their ability to obscure abuse. If one

---

14. This is not to deny that such corruption is a serious ethical failing on the part of an agent, which we all have strong reason to avoid.

can twist or pervert otherwise plausible moral claims to a corrupt end, then one can both hoodwink some into thinking that they do right when they do wrong, and also provide moral cover for the more discerning. The first possibility is important. Some people have only to hear a moral term to be carried away by it to action, however confused or inappropriate the application. Hence, the invocation of morality is a useful motivational tool. But the second possibility is equally relevant. In a situation where the moral requirements are otherwise clear, the discerning will be reluctant to go against them without some (at least vaguely) plausible rationale for doing so. Here rival (but specious) moral claims can be very attractive. They allow one to neglect unpleasant moral demands while still apparently seizing the moral high ground; indeed, they may even license the denouncing of the correct demands as actually immoral. In the context of a perfect moral storm, such bogus "morality" can become a powerful weapon.

Since the modes of moral corruption are so rich and varied, and because it is hard to isolate the morally corrupt from the merely mistaken, charges of moral corruption are difficult to prosecute. Still, in the current context, this may not be a major worry. In the perfect moral storm, it is not clear that prosecution is our primary concern. The main reason for this is that to a considerable extent it is us (individually and collectively) who have to make decisions about what to do; hence, we are the ones vulnerable to moral corruption. Given this, our main interest in moral corruption is really with how to fight it, not who to blame for it. This suggests that our focus should be on understanding and resisting the temptation of various forms of buck-passing. Concerns about blame, though also important, are secondary.[15]

How then are we to understand and resist? One suggestion is that we should simply invoke the correct theories of global, intergenerational, and environmental ethics, show that they are correct (and all other approaches are in error), and then proceed directly on the basis of them. But this approach is probably naïve. First, as I claimed in Part C, we lack strong theory. Indeed, this is one central feature of the problem that faces us: it is the theoretical component of the perfect moral storm. Second, the straightforward "invoke and apply" model simply ignores the problem of moral corruption, and so underestimates the seriousness

15. See Gardiner forthcoming.

of the perfect moral storm. Specifically, the perfect storm reveals that our assessment of theories and their consequences is not made in a neutral evaluative setting. Hence, even if the best theories were to hand, it is not obvious that we could rely on ourselves simply to grasp and then correctly apply them. The apparent temptations not to do so and the subtle mechanisms of moral corruption are formidable obstacles. In ignoring them, the "invoke and apply" model fails to take seriously the problem at hand.

The challenge posed by the theoretical storm and the problem of moral corruption is thus severe. Still, we are not completely unarmed. First, we have a general grasp of some of the constraints. Intuitively, there are at least some clear cases, and any correct theory of global, intergenerational, or environmental ethics must either accommodate these cases or else face a severe burden of proof in not doing so. Hence, there are some guidelines. For example, as we have already seen, the idea that all would be fine if humanity simply built self-contained domes to live in on the desolate surface of the earth seems to violate one plausible constraint, and the failure of the global test would violate another (see also chapter 11).

Second, problems of moral corruption are not completely unfamiliar. Indeed, paradigm cases are common fodder in literature, history, and philosophy. So, there is some hope that making ourselves aware of the subtle mechanisms of moral corruption in other settings can help us when we face the perfect moral storm. With this thought in mind, I now turn to one such illustration.

II. THE DUBIOUS DASHWOODS:
INITIAL PARALLELS

A classic example of the subtle processes of moral corruption can be found in the first two chapters of Jane Austen's *Sense and Sensibility*.[16] The novel begins with a description of an old gentleman of property

---

16. Austen 1923, volume I. All quotations are from chapter 2 of this edition unless otherwise noted. The situation is also vividly captured (albeit in an abbreviated form) by the opening scenes of Emma Thomson's Academy Award-winning screenplay for Ang Lee's film.

who is looked after in his declining years by his nephew Henry Dashwood, and Henry's wife and daughters. Henry and his family are sincerely attentive to the old man and provide him with "every degree of solid comfort which his age could receive." They also have an interest in his affairs. Henry stands to inherit the estate. However, he is more concerned for the provision it might offer to his wife and daughters after his own death than for himself. For without some extra inheritance, they will be left with relatively little.

When the old man ultimately dies, he does leave the property to Henry as expected. However, he also entails it on to Henry's independently wealthy son, John, and grandson, Harry, with only a small provision for the ladies in the event of Henry's death. Initially, Henry is severely disappointed, but hopes to overcome the problem, thinking that "he might reasonably hope to live many years, and by living economically, lay by a considerable sum from the produce of an estate already large, and capable of almost immediate improvement." Unfortunately, it is not to be. Within a year, Henry is on his deathbed, faced with the imminent prospect of leaving the women in difficult circumstances. Alarmed by this, Henry sends for his son and begs him to take care of them. John promises to do so. Moreover, after his father's death, John initially intends to fulfill this pledge in a reasonable and substantial way, by giving his vulnerable relatives three thousand pounds.

Unfortunately, as things turns out, John quickly loses his resolve. Under the influence of his wife Fanny's arguments, the sum is initially reduced to fifteen hundred pounds, then to one hundred pounds a year, and then to fifty pounds "now and then." Ultimately, John resolves to give no money at all, and instead to provide only the occasional small gifts that might have been expected of him as a more distant relative or neighbor who had made no promise at all.

At first glance, the concerns of the affluent upper classes in late eighteenth century England may see very far from those of twenty-first century environmental policy. But like much great literature, a central part of Austen's narrative transcends its context. Our interest lies in Austen's vivid account of how easily John Dashwood moves from accepting a serious and apparently unassailable moral commitment to help his stepmother and half-sisters into dismissing that commitment almost entirely. Her tale illustrates just how seductive and familiar the devices of moral corruption are, and how vulnerable we are to them. Moreover, it highlights the influence of moral corruption not merely on the "mean and grasping"[17] (e.g., Fanny Dashwood), but also on those otherwise "steady respectable" types who are merely normally "rather coldhearted and selfish" (e.g., John Dashwood).[18] Interestingly, Austen explicitly suggests that such devices lie dormant, waiting for the chance to be realized. She writes that Fanny "had had no opportunity, till the present, of shewing them with how little attention to the comfort of other people she could act when occasion required it." We might wonder whether the perfect moral storm provides us with a similar opening.

I will now try to make clear the general relevance of Austen's story to our discussion of the perfect moral storm through an examination of specific passages. I hope to show that many of the specific moral considerations mentioned by John and Fanny Dashwood have close parallels in recent discussions of climate change. In essence, my idea is that the phenomenon described so eloquently by Austen more than two hundred years ago casts light on our own problems of political inertia.

Of course, as is usually the case in such comparisons, the analogy is not perfect. Nevertheless, the resemblances should be striking enough to give us pause. In general, both Austen's case and the perfect moral storm centrally involve serious asymmetric vulnerability, where those with a duty to act not only suffer little or no negative consequences from their failure, but also stand to benefit from it. Hence, we should not be too surprised if we and John Dashwood are susceptible to similar arguments. If we acknowledge that the reasoning he ultimately accepts represents a paradigm case of moral corruption, its reflection in the contemporary climate debate should be deeply worrying.

Austen's account develops in a number of steps. The first is the death-bed promise. As we have seen, Henry Dashwood is well-aware of the plight of his wife and daughters, but unable to do much for them while

---

17. Poplawski 1998, 116.

18. Austen says of John Dashwood: "He was not an ill-disposed young man, unless to be rather cold hearted and rather selfish is to be ill- disposed: but he was, in general, well respected; for he conducted himself with propriety in the discharge of his ordinary duties. Had he married a more amiable woman, he might have been made still more respectable than he was:—he might even have been made amiable himself; for he was very young when he married, and very fond of his wife. But Mrs. John Dashwood was a strong caricature of himself;—more narrow-minded and selfish." Austen uses the label "coldhearted selfishness" for Fanny again in chapter 35.

he lives. So, on his deathbed, he entreats his son "with all the strength and urgency which his illness could command" on their behalf. In response, John Dashwood, "affected by a recommendation of such a nature at such a time . . . promised to do every thing in his power to make them comfortable." In short, both men realize what is at stake, and John Dashwood (even lacking "the strong feelings of the rest of the family") makes an explicit commitment to his father in light of this.[19]

There are some broad similarities between this scenario and that present in the perfect moral storm. Consider just three. First, there is a transfer of power across generations, and John is about to possess most of the resources of his generation, somewhat at the expense of his sisters, who are left with very modest means. Hence, there are parallels between John's circumstances and those of the current generation of the world's affluent. Second, Henry's own ability to help his daughters directly is very limited, and so he must rely on his son to carry out his wishes.[20] Hence, his position is similar to that of an earlier generation whose efforts to benefit the further future depend on the cooperation of intermediate generations.[21] Third, Henry pleads with his son to take on that responsibility, and binds him with a promise. The normative authority of this promise plays a role similar to that of norms of global and intergenerational ethics in the perfect moral storm.

The similarities between the two cases are striking. Still, we should also acknowledge two important disanalogies. The first is that John makes an explicit commitment to aid that is conspicuously lacking in the global and intergenerational case. In my view, this disanalogy is not too important, since I doubt that duties of global and intergenerational justice require this kind of consent. Moreover, it seems likely that John makes the promise in large part because of his own understanding

19. This is clear from his early remarks in weak resistance to his wife: "The promise . . . was given, and must be performed," and "one had rather, on such occasions, do too much than too little."

20. Something similar is true of the old gentleman, who does intend to pass the estate onto John and Harry, and does consciously pass over the Dashwood women (though perhaps without anticipating Henry's premature death). However, he has a legal agreement on his side, and no one suggests trying to undermine that agreement. Hence, his wishes are substantially protected.

21. This is so even though, of course, John and his sisters are roughly of the same generation.

of his intergenerational responsibilities to his father and relatives as the new head of the family.

The other disanalogy is more relevant. Climate change might be thought to involve a violation of negative duties not to harm rather than positive duties to aid. As far as we know, John has done nothing to bring about the plight facing his relatives. But the parallel claim does not hold in the perfect moral storm. Instead, in the case of climate change, our actions are likely to play the biggest role in shaping the problems of the future. Of course, other things being equal, this increases rather than decreases our obligation to act. Hence, it only adds to the normative authority of the demands on us.

In the second phase of Austen's story, we turn to matters of content. John is left to determine exactly how he is to discharge his promise. He decides that a gift of three thousand pounds would be appropriate, and notes that he can easily afford it. The latter idea seems entirely reasonable. John is already very well-off through an inheritance from his mother, and the terms of his marriage to Fanny. In addition, he has just inherited an extra four thousand pounds a year and a sizeable lump sum (the other half of his mother's wealth) from his father. Austen adds that John's resolve is initially solid: "He then really thought himself equal to it. . . . He thought of it all day long, and for many days successively, and he did not repent."

Again, there are parallels with the perfect moral storm. On the one hand, in each case the broad outlines of what to do seem clear enough. In Austen's scenario, this is apparent to John. He has no trouble settling on an appropriate amount, and he sticks to it for some time. Moreover, there is no suggestion in the text that this initial plan is unreasonable: Austen does not explicitly criticize him for it.[22] Similarly, in the case of

---

22. There may be an implicit criticism, but the issue is a little unclear. The interest on three thousand would lift their income to six hundred and fifty pounds a year. On the one hand, writers at the time seem to suggest that between seven hundred and a thousand is required for a prosperous family life (Copeland 1997, 136). So, wouldn't a gift of six thousand (lifting the ladies to an income of eight hundred a year) be at least worth considering? If this is right, perhaps Austen thinks it typical of John Dashwood to aim low. On the other hand, the "domestic economists" of the time declare the women's existing five hundred pounds a sufficiency (Copeland 1997, 135); so perhaps John is indeed adding luxury to their lives. In context, however, this looks dubious. Austen ridicules Fanny for saying that five hundred is enough, and she has the unextravagent and practical Elinor declare that a thousand a year would be her "wealth" (Austen 1923, 91).

climate, scientists and politicians seem to have little trouble announcing long-term targets that seem generally appropriate. As we have seen, in the early nineties many developed nations endorsed the target of stabilization of emissions at 1990 levels by 2000. More recently, the Copenhagen Accord endorses the overall objective of limiting temperature rise to 2 degrees C over pre-industrial levels. In addition, there is some convergence in the scientific and policy communities over such specific goals as a 20% cut by 2020, and a 50–80% cut by 2050 for the industrialized countries. In short, in climate politics too, there is a tradition of initially thinking oneself equal to the task.

Still, on the other hand, in both cases a lack of specificity in the content of the obligation coupled with a sharp asymmetry of power creates plenty of wiggle room for moral corruption. In Austen's story, the decision about what is owed to his sisters and stepmother is ultimately simply up to John. Things are similar in the perfect storm. First, given the problem of skewed vulnerabilities, the world's rich have a disproportionate influence over what happens. Second, in the intergenerational storm, particular generations have the power to decide how to discharge their obligations to the future and the past. Third, given the theoretical storm, both the rich and the present make their decisions in a context where the specific content of their obligations is unclear, and the various proposals lack robust theoretical grounding.

III. THE OPENING ASSAULT ON THE STATUS OF THE MORAL CLAIM

The possibility of moral corruption begins to manifest itself in the third step of Austen's discussion. John's resolve soon faces opposition: Fanny is aghast. (Austen says: "Had he married a more amiable woman, he might have been made still more respectable than he was."[23]) Fanny's initial assault is on the status of the moral claim. There are four moves.

First, she greatly exaggerates the negative consequences of the plan for her husband and son. She claims that little Harry will be

---

23. This suggests a parallel with Kant's account of corruption. Some sets of inclinations might be less opposed to morality than others (either by nature or moral training).

"impoverished to a dreadful degree," and John will "ruin himself, and their poor little Harry, by giving away all his money." (Call this move *excessive burdens.*[24])

Second, Fanny implicitly dismisses the idea that they are under any obligation to assist. In particular, her language presupposes that all of the money is legitimately theirs. She speaks of John "giving away all *his* money," and indeed of his *robbing* his only son by honoring the promise. (Call this move *prior entitlement.*)

Third, Fanny invokes the idea of special relationships. She argues that there are important bonds between John and his son that do not exist between him and his half-sisters. On the one hand, she speaks of Henry "begging" John "to give away half [his] fortune from [his] *own child*," as if the request is deeply unreasonable given the nature of the parental relationship.[25] On the other hand, she diminishes the relationship between John and his sisters, declaring that "no affection was ever supposed to exist between the children of any man by different marriages," and adding that she considers "half blood . . . no relationship at all."[26] (Call this *competing special relationships.*)

Finally, Fanny seeks to undermine the source of the claim, John's father, by accusing him of being not in his right mind, and so unreasonable: "He did not know what he was talking of, I dare say; ten to one but he was light-headed at the time."[27] (Call this move *unreasonable aadvocates.*)

---

24. I thank Michael Blake for suggesting some of these labels.

25. She says this despite the fact that Henry is himself John's father and Harry's grandfather, and so might be expected to have a similar and strong bond with each of them.

26. Fanny does not mention here that, even by her lights, Henry had a very legitimate reason to be concerned for the girls, as they are *his* children. However, later in the chapter, she twists this point, declaring: "Your father thought only of *them.* And I must say this: that you owe no particular gratitude to him, nor attention to his wishes; for we very well know that if he could, he would have left almost everything in the world to *them.*" Of course, there is no suggestion of this. (In Emma Thompson's screenplay, Henry says to John of the bequest, "I am happy for you and Fanny.") Moreover, even if Henry would have left everything to his daughters given the chance, this would not necessarily have been unreasonable, given John's ample inheritance from his mother.

27. As we shall see, later she adds that he was biased in favor of his daughters, suggesting moral corruption on his part.

Interestingly, each of these moves has some parallel in the debate about climate policy. (Again, the analogies are hardly perfect, but they are close enough to be disconcerting.) The first move, excessive burdens, is common. The fear that strong action on mitigation in particular would impoverish the rich nations, and perhaps the current generation of the world's people more generally, pervades the political discussion. Not all such concerns are unwarranted. For example, as I said in chapter 1, we (rightly) do not even consider an instant cessation of all anthropogenic emissions, for the reason that the world economy would likely collapse, causing a humanitarian catastrophe for current people. Nevertheless, we must be careful that such worries do not become over-blown. After all, as we have already seen, in the Austen case the claim is preposterous, and John knows it. Their side of the family was already very rich, and has just become much richer; moreover, there is no question of their giving away anything but a small percentage of their wealth. Is something similar true for climate?

Consider the usual estimates of costs offered by those who oppose substantial mitigation. For instance, Bjorn Lomborg cites with approval the claim that Kyoto would have cost between U.S.\$346 and \$75 billion per year, and tends to focus on \$150 billion per year.[28] As we have seen (chapter 8), there are reasons to treat all such estimates as dubious. However, even if correct, emphasizing these costs obscures what is at stake in the same way as Fanny's complaints. Specifically, though the amounts seem large when considered in absolute terms—three thousand pounds, or \$150 billion—they are not so considerable when taken in context.

In Austen's case, three thousand pounds was a substantial sum in the early nineteenth century. Still, to a family like John Dashwood's—already rich, and having just become much richer—it is only of marginal significance. For one thing, the extra amount just would not make much difference to their lives. For another, since they have not yet been relying on these funds, they will not *experience* a loss or decline in their fortunes.

Similarly, in the case of climate change, though \$150 billion a year would be a large amount of money considered in normal contexts, it is not so large when considered against the evolution of the world economy

28. Lomborg 2001, 303, 322.

over time.[29] As we noted in chapter 8, Thomas Schelling claims that "if someone could wave a wand and phase in, over a few years, a climate-mitigation program that depressed our GNP by two percent in perpetuity, *no one would notice the difference*."[30] Seen in that context, the costs of mitigation do not seem unmanageable.[31] Moreover, the need to avoid catastrophe seems to justify them. Just as Fanny's focus on the costs to her immediate (affluent) family seems inappropriate when her (much poorer[32]) relations are those whose interests are most severely affected by the decision, so a focus on the (relatively marginal) costs of abatement for climate change seems to leave out the most salient feature of the situation—the costs of climate catastrophe, especially as they are visited on the most vulnerable.[33]

Fanny's second move, prior entitlement, is also well known in climate circles. For example, it is common to calculate the "costs" of mitigation against the yardstick of "business-as-usual" (i.e., those emissions that would occur in the absence of action on climate change).[34] But this strongly suggests that those who emit at these levels are *entitled to do so*, regardless of the "costs" they impose on others (such as the world's poor, future generations, and nonhuman nature) through this behavior. Similarly, it is standard to frame climate policy in terms of national targets based on each country's emissions in some base year (e.g., the

29. At the rates current in January 2009, it counted as only about 20% of a U.S. economic stimulus package. Few people seem to argue that this is an unreasonable investment in the future (even if a fair number argue that it is the wrong kind of investment in the future, and others claim that it amounts to stealing from future generations).

30. Schelling 1997; emphasis added.

31. To be fair, Lomborg ultimately concedes this, and his central issue really lies elsewhere. See chapter 8.

32. One notable disanalogy between the two cases is that the poorer Dashwoods are only relatively so. They will have fallen dramatically from their former state of considerable wealth. Still, their lives remain privileged: they retain two servants, and do not have to work for their income. Hence, they are wealthy compared to most people of their time, and many of the world's poor today. Still, their relative poverty does seem to threaten them with a catastrophe in terms of social status and exclusion.

33. Battisti and Naylor 2009.

34. The use of this term has become contentious over the years. Initially, the IPCC labeled one of its scenarios "business-as-usual," but now it does not, on the grounds that no one knows how the world's economy will evolve over time. Still, most people continue to think of the new A2 scenario as business-as-usual.

currently popular "20% cut on 1990 or 2000 levels by 2020, and 50% by 2050"). But this is to embed historical patterns of emission. It assumes, in effect, that countries with historically higher emissions begin with some kind of entitlement to that higher level that those with historically lower emissions do not have. For example, a uniform cut by all countries of 50% by 2050 would have the United States reducing from 5.32 metric tons per capita to 2.66 per capita (36722 tons to 18361 tons), and India reducing from 0.35 tons per capita to 0.175 tons per capita (2824 tons to 1412 tons).[35]

Now, in Austen's case it seems clear that the prior entitlement argument obscures the relevant facts. It is, of course, true that John already has a legal right to the property, and so that what to do with it is in one sense up to him. However, the real question here concerns his moral responsibilities. By ignoring this, Fanny's way of putting things implicitly treats the wider claims of John's father, stepmother, and sisters as having little or no status. This seems incorrect. After all, since John has already made the promise, it does not seem right to speak as if all of the money is still "his," at least in the very robust sense, of "his to do with exactly as he pleases." Similarly, it does not seem appropriate to insist that his son has a right (or even a reasonable expectation) of inheritance over everything that is in his father's power. For one thing, as we have just noted, others may also have legitimate claims. For another, if young Harry did have a right over everything in his father's power, then John would have no real property "rights" of his own at all. More generally, the whole property regime is based on the idea that women need not own much, since their male relations should use their property rights to take care of females in their own families. Hence, to assert the property right against such claims seems bizarre.

Assumptions of previous entitlement are also problematic in the climate case. First, even if one wanted benchmarks of this general kind, there are alternatives to business-as-usual and current national emissions. Suppose, for example, that some countries are at very high

---

35. Of course, for reasons stated at the outset of chapter 1, there are problems of transition away from carbon-intensive economic activity. So, one might have good reasons not to expect identical cuts in absolute terms from different countries, at least in the short term. Still, it does not follow from this that best way to proceed is to think in terms of identical relative cuts in the longer term.

levels of per capita emissions and some are not, or that some could cut emissions 30% for the same cost as others cutting 15%. Wouldn't this suggest that equal per capita rates, or the marginal costs of reducing emissions, provide better benchmarks than absolute levels of current emissions?[36]

Second, a different reference point altogether might be more morally defensible. For example, why not make our touchstone the situation where no one is harmed by climate change, or where human rights violations are minimized, or something like that? Or, why not count the baseline scenario as the one where we prevent a temperature rise above two degrees (which the EU and others define as "dangerous"), and see what the costs are of doing more than that?[37]

Third, assuming a benchmark based on current practices encourages the perception that cuts in emissions from that paradigm are appropriately seen as a *sacrifice* made by the current generation, or by particular countries, of something to which they are otherwise entitled. But this is surely not a good way to think about the issue. If current practices impose large costs on the world's poor, future people, animals, and the rest of nature, it seems bizarre to assert that the current generation has an overriding claim to, or even a legitimate expectation of, continuing with them indefinitely into the future. So, why take that situation as the relevant benchmark against which to calculate "costs"?

Fourth, and more generally, it is of course true that the current generation (and especially the affluent and politically influential) have some kind of de facto entitlement to act. Just as John Dashwood is authorized to act by his legal right of inheritance, so they have the power to decide what to do when their generation is in the ascendance. But this is hardly the same as being released from moral considerations all together. Just as the Dashwoods should consider the wider moral context and not pronounce themselves safely cordoned off from it by their legal right to choose, so the current generation (and especially the powerful within it) should take global and intergenerational

36. Note that I am not endorsing either of these alternatives. They are simply illustrations. For commentary, see Gardiner 2010a.

37. Again, I'm not arguing that we should actually do these things. I am merely questioning the existing practice, and showing that it lacks a clear rationale.

ethics into account, even though no one doubts its ability not to, given its asymmetric generational power.[38]

Fanny's third move, competing special relationships, is also present in the climate debate. Some simply want to endorse strong versions of the assumptions underlying the perfect moral storm as real limits to what can be done. We must simply accept (they say) that people will be most interested in their own local concerns (e.g., what happens to them, their families, and their local communities in the short- to medium-term), and that they will have very little interest in the affairs of those with whom they do not regularly interact (e.g., those distant in space or time, such as the poor of other countries, future generations, and nonhuman nature). Moreover, even if it is conceded that we do have some broader concerns (e.g., because we are related to the rest of humanity and the other inhabitants of the planet to at least some extent), this might not be enough. Perhaps concern for the "here and now," and the "near and dear," still swamps everything else (see chapter 5). As Fanny Dashwood puts it, "What brother on earth would do half so much for his sisters, even if *really* his sisters! And as it is—only half blood!"

Such motivational concerns often bring on a parallel to Fanny's fourth move, "unreasonable advocates." Fanny accuses Henry Dashwood of having taken leave of his senses in even asking the promise of John. In the climate debate, some are tempted by the claim that there is something completely unrealistic (even utopian) about raising issues of global and intergenerational ethics in the current context. Much as we might like to think in these terms, the thought goes, we must recognize the way the world really is, and set aside such foolishness.

---

38. Some may suspect that this kind of benchmark is justified on libertarian grounds. In the main text, I have tried to pose the issue in a way that sidesteps this problem, by talking in terms of what the Dashwoods and the current generation have reason to take into account in their decisions. Still, as it happens, I do not think that libertarians should resist stronger claims. Most reasonable libertarians accept constraints on property rights when exercise of them would result in serious harm to others, or when they violate the so-called Lockean proviso of "leaving enough and as good for others." Moreover, some such constraints seem necessary in order to make libertarianism remotely plausible. Hence, it seems likely that libertarians ought to concede that the "right" to emit is itself dependent on wider moral norms, and that these include at least some norms of global and intergenerational ethics.

In short, we must be realistic—hard headed, rather than "light headed"—about international politics and human nature.

These last two moves are deep and serious. They raise skeptical challenges to the very idea of global and intergenerational ethics and community, and these challenges deserve attention. Still, we have reason to worry about their invocation here. In particular, there is a concern about selective skepticism. Some people assert these objections because they are dubious about moral motivation in general. They believe that (narrow) self-interest always holds sway, so that talk of ethics is never anything other than superfluous. Such general skepticism constitutes an intellectually serious position. But it is also a radical one with wide-ranging implications. Because of this, few people actually accept it when pressed. For example, they find it hard to explain many common facts about human life, such as the love of parents for their children, bonds of friendship, charitable donations to strangers, etc. Moreover, most find that skepticism cannot make adequate sense of other central tenets of contemporary political philosophy, such as the importance of individual and human rights, the justification for democracy, and so on. In short, there is a presumption against thoroughgoing skepticism. Given this, there is something problematic about its invocation against long-term climate policy. If moral motivation is impossible, or even unrealistic, then many things we want to say about ethics and the world can no longer be said. Since this normally counts as a reason not to accept such general skepticism, the skeptic needs to say why we are justified in invoking it against climate policy specifically. The worry of course is that it is not justified. Selective skepticism merely serves the purpose as we seek to pass the buck.[39]

IV. THE ASSAULT ON CONTENT

In Austen's story, John is also initially unmoved by Fanny's skeptical assaults. Though he laments having been put under the obligation— "Perhaps it would have been as well if [my father] had left it wholly to myself. He could hardly suppose I should neglect them"—John remains

---

39. See Appendix 2.

firm in his conviction that, as it is, "the promise . . . was given, and must be performed." Given this, his wife begins a second line of attack, this time on the content of the obligation, rather than its status. (This is the fourth step of Austen's account.) Since her husband concedes that a particular sum was not specified, she questions the amount of three thousand pounds: "Well, then, *let* something be done for them; but *that* something need not be three thousand pounds."

Fanny's first argument rests on the idea that the money might be "lost" to the family. She says, "When the money is once parted with, it never can return. Your sisters will marry, and it will be gone for ever."[40] (Call this move *demanding mutual benefit*.) This is, of course, an odd consideration. For one thing, a good part of Henry Dashwood's intent in making the request of his son was presumably to provide dowries for his daughters and so make them more eligible for marriage. (This is explicit in Emma Thompson's screenplay: she has Henry say " . . . nothing for the girls' dowries. You must help them.") Hence, it is bizarre to dismiss the need for the money on the grounds that the girls might marry, especially since they would presumably continue to benefit from the funds as a result. More generally, the objection seems premised on the assumption that the promise is only justified if the transfer continues to benefit those giving it in at least some way (i.e., it needs to be what we might call a "gift that keeps giving back").[41] Yet the demand that any transfer to their poorer relatives must be something that might ultimately benefit the rich Dashwoods seems unreasonable, and immoral.

This argument has close parallels in the political debate about climate change. First, in general, it is commonplace that many national negotiators are more interested in how they might gain economic or geopolitical benefits from a climate regime than in whether it actually reduces emissions. Indeed, some have gone so far as to suggest that the largest polluters, the United States and China, ought to be "compensated" for

40. John chimes in sympathetically: "The time may come when Harry will regret that so large a sum was parted with. If he should have a numerous family, for instance, it would be a very convenient addition." Again, the focus is shifted away from the needs of the poorer relations now to the hypothetical needs of the richer later. Moreover, no consideration is given to the thought that the sisters may have large families.

41. Fanny continues, "If, indeed, it could be restored to our poor little boy—"; and Henry responds ("very gravely"), "Why, to be sure, that would make great difference."

joining any agreement to reduce climate change with side-payments from other nations.[42] (We might label this "the polluters get paid" approach to contrast it to the more usual "polluter pays" principle.)

Second, as we saw in chapter 2, some suggest that the burden is on those in favor of climate action to show that it will bring major benefits to the current generation, and to rich and poor countries alike, as well as aiding future generations and nonhuman nature. So, the implicit assumption is that climate action must be a "win-win" situation for all concerned to be viable. If such action does turn out to benefit all, this would be a welcome truth. Neverthetheless, in my view, our principal, and moral, reasons for acting on climate change would persist even if the scenario is not "win-win" and real costs had to be endured to avoid catastrophe. We should refrain from exploiting the poor, the future, and nature even if doing so does not benefit us. *Demanding* that we profit from the refraining seems just as immoral as the Dashwoods requiring that they profit from John's promise.

At this point in Austen's story, John proposes, somewhat arbitrarily, to cut the amount of the transfer in half, to five hundred pounds for each of the three girls. Fanny extols his generosity, emphasizing that they are mere half-sisters, and John congratulates himself. Though he is implicitly yielding something to his wife's skepticism, he seeks to cover this by sanctimoniously declaring, "one had rather, on such occasions, do too much than too little," and "no one, at least, can think I have not done enough for them: even themselves, they can hardly expect more."

Still, Fanny is not satisfied. She quickly responds: "There is no knowing what *they* may expect . . . but we are not to think of their expectations: the question is, what you can afford to do." (Call this move *budget constraint*.) This discussion is, of course, bizarre. John signaled at the outset that he believed twice the sum to be appropriate, and that he could afford such a sum. Still, Fanny's remark represents a critical move. She sees that John's lingering resolve to act depends crucially on his concerns about what others, and especially his sisters, may think of his actions. Hence, she aims to shift his focus inward, from their concerns to his. Now the moral demand is to be seen as something to be traded off against his other, more personal priorities, rather than something with a distinct status.

42. Posner and Sunstein 2007; Posner and Weisbach 2010.

This move, is, of course, utterly pervasive in climate policy and politics. In practice, discussions of what to do invariably proceed very swiftly away from the moral reasons for action to concerns about what they will mean for the current generation, and especially the affluent ("what can we afford?"). Instead of global targets, such as 2 degrees or 450 parts per million, actual political discussion has (thus far) focused on country-by-country or sector-by-sector goals, usually set by negotiation between the affected parties. Importantly, and unsurprisingly, this almost always has the effect of watering down the ultimate effects of action.

In Austen's story, however, Fanny's attempt is not immediately successful. John readily admits that he can afford the fifteen hundred pounds. Nevertheless, he goes on to add: "As it is, without any addition of mine, they will each have about three thousand pounds on their mother's death—a very comfortable fortune for any young woman." (Call this move *diminish the victims' needs.*) This, of course, is nonsense. John and his father have already agreed that the girls need his assistance. There is no question of their existing inheritance being adequate. Why then make the claim? One possibility is that John is merely trying to defend the sufficiency of his largesse (which, after all, he has just cut in half on dubious grounds). But another is that Fanny's thought has given him pause, so that he is already implicitly shifting his focus to his own finances, by diminishing the claims of his sisters.

Whatever the root of the remark, Fanny pounces on the concession: "To be sure it is; and, indeed, it strikes me that they can want no addition at all. They will have ten thousand pounds divided amongst them. If they marry, they will be sure of doing well, and if they do not, they may all live very comfortably together on the interest of ten thousand pounds." This time, the pressure is successful. John concedes the point, but not the whole issue. Instead, he moves in a new direction: "That is very true, and, therefore, I do not know whether, upon the whole, it would not be more advisable to do something for their mother while she lives, rather than for them—something of the annuity kind I mean.—My sisters would feel the good effects of it as well as herself. A hundred a year would make them all perfectly comfortable."

This new argument is interesting.[43] John's key ideas are that it will be better to help his stepmother, and his sisters through her, than to try to

---

43. Initially, the shift to an annuity seems inexplicable. Why not just transfer the fifteen hundred, or a similar sum, directly to John's stepmother? But Fanny immediately provides a reason: "To be sure, it is better than parting with fifteen hundred pounds at once."

secure the future of his sisters, since this (he has suddenly been persuaded) seems bright in any case. Hence, he tries to find another less demanding (and ultimately more easily resisted) way to meet his obligations. (Call this *shifting the playing field.*) This move has a close parallel in the climate debate. Infamously, Lomborg claims that the climate change problem ultimately reduces to the question of whether to help poor inhabitants of the poor countries now or their richer descendents later.[44] Moreover, he argues that the right answer is to help the current poor now, because they are poorer than their descendants will be, because they are more easily (i.e., cheaply) helped, and because in helping them, one also helps their descendants.[45]

As I explained in chapter 8, in my view, Lomborg's argument is far from compelling. Still, it is worth reviewing a few points to draw parallels with Austen. First, Lomborg appears to assume that helping the poor now and acting on climate change are mutually exclusive alternatives. But this seems simply mistaken; just as John could aid both his stepmother and his sisters, so (as Lomborg himself eventually acknowledges) "we are actually rich enough to afford both."[46]

Second, the argument looks worrying in the current political setting. For one thing, it seems to show a giant leap of political optimism. As Peter Singer puts it, if their past record is anything to go by, the rich countries are even less likely to contribute large sums of money to help the world's poor directly than they are to do so to combat climate change.[47] More importantly, this gives us reason to fear a "bait and switch" strategy. Once the direct obligation to the future is supplanted, will the one to the present (through which it was to be indirectly discharged) then be conveniently forgotten, as it so often was before the issue of climate change arose? After all, this is what happens in Austen's example, with the result that none are helped. Indeed, given this worry, we may have an *extra* reason to act on climate change: even if Lomborg is right that there are better ways to help the current poor, "a comparatively inefficient way of helping [them] may be better than not helping them at all."[48] In short, perhaps climate policy is justified on direct

---

44. The following draws on Gardiner 2004a.
45. Lomborg 2001, 322.
46. Lomborg 2001, 324; Grubb 1995, 473, n. 25.
47. Singer 2002, pp. 26–27.
48. Singer 2002, 26–27.

humanitarian grounds in addition to on environmental grounds (some of which are indirectly humanitarian).

Third, the original claim that the future poor will be better off than their predecessors is dubious in this context, just as the claim that the Dashwood girls are "sure of doing well" in marriage, and otherwise would "live very comfortably together" without assistance is dubious in Austen's example. On the one hand, as we saw in chapter 6, climate change threatens future generations with impacts that are severe and likely to disrupt social and economic systems. Under such circumstances, it seems rash to assume that future people in general (and the future poor in particular) will be better off than their current counterparts. On the other hand, it is worth saying that, even on an optimistic account of future circumstances, many of the future poor will still be considerably worse off than the current rich. Hence, it is not clear that their (potentially) being better off than their currently poor counterparts absolves us of all responsibilities towards them.

V. INDIRECT ATTACKS

Returning to Austen, Fanny now tries three kinds of indirect attack.

1. Problems of Implementation

In the fifth step of the argument, she claims that there are serious problems of implementation. Her first concern is that the annuity may end up costing them more in the long run than the lump sum. Fanny says: "If Mrs. Dashwood should live fifteen years we shall be completely taken in." John bridles a little at this suggestion: "Fifteen years! my dear Fanny; her life cannot be worth half that purchase." In response, Fanny concedes the spirit, but not the substance of the point: "Certainly not; but if you observe, people always live for ever when there is an annuity to be paid them; and she is very stout and healthy, and hardly forty." Of course, Austen means the suggestion that people go on living merely to collect their annuity to be an amusing one. But there is also a deeper thought here. Fanny seems to be arguing that granting the annuity will itself have a causal influence that will result in further burdens. (Call this move *opening the floodgates*.) This has a ready parallel in the case of climate change. There the worry is that if the developed countries get involved in a policy that requires aid to the developing nations, the demands on them will continue indefinitely into the future. In Austen, Fanny says: "An annuity is a very serious business; it comes over and over every year, and there is no getting rid of it. You are not aware of what you are doing." Similarly, though the political talk tends to be of medium-term targets (20% by 2020, and so on), the reality of long-run climate policy is that additional, and tougher, targets will need to be set decade by decade over the next century or so, probably until the global economy is completely de-carbonized. Thus, the developed nations have a realistic concern that any initial agreement to a climate policy involving short-term or "transitional" aid for the developing countries will evolve into an ongoing financial commitment. As I mentioned in chapter 1, there is also a worry that such an agreement puts the developed countries on a path that leads inexorably to wider norms of global justice and community, where these place demands that are both perpetual and potentially much more onerous.

Fanny's second concern is with the additional administrative burdens associated with the annuity. Offering the example of her mother's experience with "three old superannuated servants" she says "twice every year these annuities were to be paid; and then there was the trouble of getting it to them; and then one of them was said to have died, and afterwards it turned out to be no such thing." (Call this *onerous logistics*.) Similarly, many in the developed world worry about the logistics of becoming directly involved in development elsewhere. How is this aid to be given? Who is to administer it? How are we to ensure that it going to the right people and being used correctly? Most importantly, doesn't the presence of these issues imply that the developed countries are liable to still more (costly) obligations of implementation and oversight?

Fanny's third concern about the annuity signals the core worry. In the end, her mother, she reports, "was quite sick of it . . . Her income was not her own, she said, with such perpetual claims on it." John agrees, saying that "to be tied down to the regular payment of such a sum . . . takes away one's independence." (Call this move *undermines autonomy*.) This complaint is connected to the earlier assumption that the income still legitimately belongs to them. As we have seen, in the sense at stake here, this claim is questionable: if they agree to an annuity, the foregone income is no longer theirs to be disposed of as they please. Moreover, the worry about independence is specious: given John's overall wealth, their ability to do as they please with their lives would not be at all compromised by the annuity.

Similar points can be made in the case of climate change. First, suppose that a just climate policy would involve regular claims on some of the resources of the developed countries and the world's richer people. Should it be rejected just for this reason? Presumably not: if justice requires such claims, then these resources have a new status. Second, is it credible to think that the developed nations will lose their "independence" through the transfer? This seems unlikely. For one thing, though climate assistance would improve the position of the developing nations, it is unlikely to undercut the autonomy or even the preeminence of the developed world (at least, not by itself), which has much else going for it. For another, the more serious threat to that autonomy would be the need for serious reductions in emissions itself, which could potentially cripple the global economy in general, but especially in those places which are currently fossil-fuel intensive, such as the United States. But this concern also turns out to be unrealistic. Present proposals, involving reductions phased in over decades (20% by 2020, 50% by 2050 and so on) are popular precisely because it is assumed that gradual change does not impose too big a shock to current economic systems, so that "independence" (and much else) is preserved.[49]

Fanny's fourth complaint is that the recipients of annuities are not grateful: "You have no thanks for it. They think themselves secure, you do no more than what is expected, and it raises no gratitude at all." (Call this move *lack of appreciation*.) The first point to be made here is that the basic claim is questionable. People do often express gratitude to those who give what is owed, especially when they recognize that they might (immorally) withhold it. Indeed, given their characters, it is hard to imagine the other Dashwood women not expressing thanks to John if

---

49. Bigger cuts, which may have more radical impacts on economies, and which many scientists and environmentalists believe are needed, would probably have to be facilitated by other mechanisms to preserve individuals and their communities if they were to be at all sustainable.

he were to act on his promise. Still, even if the basic claim were realistic, any worry about gratitude hardly seems to justify John's failing to help. After all, he promised his father, and he has other moral reasons to assist. Similarly, in the case of climate change, some might complain that the developing nations, or the world's poor more generally, will not be grateful to the developed nations for their assistance, but will simply expect it, as a matter of justice. This may simply be mistaken—the developing nations may well think better of the developed if the latter showed willingness to act justly on climate change—but, in any case, it is unclear why this issue would justify acting differently. Justice is its own warrant.

Fanny's next substantive suggestion seems to build on the previous threat to independence. She says: "If I were you, whatever I did should be done at my own discretion entirely." John agrees, and offers an additional, moral reason for this approach: "Whatever I may give them occasionally will be of far greater assistance than a yearly allowance, because they would only enlarge their style of living if they felt sure of a larger income, and would not be sixpence the richer for it at the end of the year." (Call this move *discretionary aid*.) John's point is familiar from debates about aid to the poor more generally, and is not foreign to climate policy. First, it is often said that aid does not improve the long-term prospects of the poor. The responses are equally familiar: that there are ways to design aid so that it does help in the long term ("teaching a man to fish" as opposed to giving him a fish, as the proverb has it); that short-term help is at least a benefit in the short term (and so better than nothing); and that in many cases it is questionable whether those providing the aid are best placed to make (or even morally should be making) consumption decisions for the recipients. Similar points could be made in the case of the Dashwoods. Second, domestic and international climate policy has often retreated into calls for "voluntary commitments" by interested industries and states. The track record of such efforts is poor, and (according to the perfect moral storm) sadly predictable.

At this point in Austen's narrative, John finds the considerations against the annuity decisive. Agreeing with his wife, he concedes that "A present of fifty pounds, now and then, will prevent their ever being distressed for money, and will, I think, be amply discharging my promise to my father." Fanny agrees ("To be sure it will," she says).

2. Radical Reframing

Nevertheless, Fanny is not yet fully content. In the sixth step of the account (and second round of indirect attacks), she seeks to reframe the context of the obligation. First, she aims to remove all thought of explicitly financial assistance:

> Indeed, to say the truth, *I am convinced within myself that your father had no idea of your giving them any money at all.* The assistance he thought of, I dare say, was only such as might be reasonably expected of you; for instance, such as looking out for a comfortable small house for them, helping them to move their things, and sending them presents of fish and game, and so forth, whenever they are in season. I'll lay my life that he meant nothing farther; indeed, it would be very strange and unreasonable if he did.[50]

The idea here is clearly that John's obligations may be discharged in indirect ways, through substantive logistical assistance, rather than the provision of resources. (Call this *indirect methods.*) This move has a clear parallel in the case of climate policy, where the developed countries show much more enthusiasm for technological transfers and assistance than for monetary ones. (Of course, as with the Dashwoods, whether this enthusiasm ultimately translates into action is a further question. Again, there is a worry about "bait and switch.")

Fanny then resumes the earlier attack on the notion that her in-laws will have any real needs at all, by urging a radical shift in perspective about their situation. (Call this *blessing in disguise.*) She says:

> Altogether, they will have five hundred a-year amongst them, and what on earth can four women want for more than that?—*They will live so cheap!* Their housekeeping will be nothing at all. They will have no carriage, no horses, and hardly any servants; they will keep no company, and can have no expenses of any kind! *Only conceive how comfortable they will be!* Five hundred a-year! I am sure I cannot imagine how they will spend half of it; and as to your giving them more, it is quite absurd to think of it. *They will be much more able to give you something.*

In context, this final claim is clearly outrageous. How can Fanny possibly assert that her in-laws will actually be better placed than John, *precisely*

---

50. Emphasis added.

because they will be much poorer? Moreover, how could John conceivably allow this thought to influence his interpretation of the deathbed promise to his father, made precisely on the assumption that his mother-in-law and sisters would need help? But this, of course, is exactly what he does: "Upon my word, I believe you are perfectly right," he says, "My father certainly could mean nothing more by his request to me than what you say. I clearly understand it now, and I will strictly fulfill my engagement by such acts of assistance and kindness to them as you have described."

Presumably, Austen intends the shocking nature of Fanny's claim to signal that the Dashwoods have finally plunged into complete absurdity. But this should give us pause. For again, similar claims influence the climate debate.[51] After all, there is one way in which Fanny is correct. The expenses of the Dashwood women will certainly be much lower than those of their rich relatives, because they will be forced to retrench. Similarly, it is sometimes suggested that the global poor, and those in the developed countries more generally, do not need the resources of those in the developed world, since their expenses are much lower. Just as Fanny asserts that the Dashwood women will be forced to live their lives on a smaller scale now that they have a smaller income, and this will mean that they will engage in some activities as much lower cost, so the basic cost of living is much higher in the United States, for example, than it is in India. In both cases, it is true that resources go further when one lives on a smaller scale. So, is Fanny's outrageous claim justified after all?

I think not—but it takes a little work to show why. On the one hand, Fanny's remark does hint at important insights about happiness. First, there is certainly truth in the idea that some people in the world live as well, or almost as well, as others but on much less income. Austen clearly agrees with this idea, and indeed appreciates both the moral and practical necessity of retrenchment under some circumstances, and the absurdity of saying that it cannot be done. For example, in *Persuasion*, she considers a family in such a predicament, and mocks the attitude of those members of it who react in horror at the mention of cutting back.[52] Moreover, the characters she mocks (Sir William Eliot and his eldest daughter Elizabeth) are very like

51. Of course, our knowledge of the conditions of the future is much less secure than Fanny's of those of her relatives. So, arguably, we are much more vulnerable to romanticizing their fate.

52. Austen 1923, volume V, chapter 2.

Fanny Dashwood in their selfish and narrow concerns for social prestige. In addition, the compromise that Sir William eventually accepts, that of decamping to Bath, is justified to him on the grounds that this is a place where one "can be important at comparatively little expense." Hence, Austen gives explicit recognition to the possibility of living well with less under different social circumstances. Second, there is much to the related idea that happiness does not require riches, and may even sometimes undermine it. Again, Austen seems to be in agreement. Her characters often express opposition to the values that imply that wealth is necessary for happiness, and to their corrosive influence on people's lives.[53]

Still, on the other hand, one must be careful not to push this point too far, or to use it to justify injustice. First, poverty is obviously a major obstacle to happiness, as (arguably) is pronounced economic inequality, especially when it leads to rigid social hierarchies and social exclusion. Though wealth is not everything, some resources are necessary. (As Elizabeth Bennet puts it in *Pride and Prejudice*, "handsome young men must have something to live on as well as the plain ones.")[54] Hence, the most egregious component of Fanny's argument is the idea that her in-laws will be comfortable *because* they will have no money for entertaining or transportation. On the contrary, this is one of the primary harms that are to befall the Dashwood women, for it is a major cause of their social exclusion.

Second, their lack of resources threatens a value that Fanny herself has already asserted as important: that of independence. Mrs. Dashwood and her daughters can no longer do much on their own, and so must depend on others. Hence, for example, Elinor and Marianne must frequently bear the embarrassing "raillery" of Mrs. Jennings and Sir John Middleton, their good natured but somewhat uncouth benefactors, because they are indebted to them for their new home, and rely on them as their

---

53. For example, in *Sense and Sensibility*, Edward Ferrars rejects his family's emphasis on driving a barouch in favor of a quiet country parish; in *Mansfield Park* Mary Crawford's resistance to marrying a mere clergyman is portrayed in a negative light; and in *Persuasion* Captain Benwick is in anguish about not marrying his betrothed before going to sea because of "fortune."

54. Austen 1923, Volume II, Chapter III.

entry point into local society. As Marianne puts it, "I realize the rent is low, but I do believe we have it on very hard terms."[55]

Third, we should note the hypocrisy of Fanny's claim. The values that drive both Fanny and the older Eliots—"being important"—involve precisely the kind of social resources that Fanny claims that the other Dashwood women will have no need of in their new life. For example, in *Persuasion* the point of the Eliots' relocation is precisely to preserve much of their previous lifestyle, and so allow them to retain their existing social status. Sir William protests that a retrenchment at home "could not be put up with." Specifically, he says: "What! every comfort of life knocked off! Journeys, London, servants, horses, table—contractions and restrictions every where! To live no longer with the decencies even of a private gentleman! No, he would sooner quit Kellynch Hall at once, than remain in it on such disgraceful terms."[56] On the plausible assumption that Fanny Dashwood would share this understanding, her claim that the Dashwoods will be "comfortable" is not one that she would be willing to make on her own behalf. Her argument is *directly opposed to her own values*, and can only succeed if she is prepared to demand that the Dashwoods have different values. (As it happens, they do have somewhat different values, and do cope with the change better than Fanny might have done. But this does not at all imply that they would willingly forego the assistance that John has promised.)

In summary, though there is some truth to the idea that in some settings one can live better on less resources than in others, Fanny's assertion of this claim is self-serving and hypocritical in light of her own values. Something similar seems to be the case for those who claim that the poor of the developing world would or could be "comfortable" with less than the residents of developed countries. As a matter of moral theory, there may be something right about this claim; nevertheless, in the current context, it obscures much of what it at stake, such as what might be *owed* to the developed countries as a matter of justice rather

55. Such concerns afflict even the rich in Austen's novels. In *Sense and Sensibility*, John Willoughby complains of his Aunt's demand that he return to London that she is "exercising the privilege of riches on a poor dependent cousin." Similarly, in *Persuasion*, once the Eliots are in Bath they are at pains to ingratiate themselves with their richer cousins, the Dalrymples, in order to take advantage of the latter's superior social position and resources.

56. Austen 1923, volume V, chapter 2.

than welfare, the reluctance of the rich to give up the more lavish lifestyles that they would so readily deprive the developing nations of, and the importance of "independence."

3. Resentment

We now come to the seventh and last step of the account. John has already reached a self-satisfied conclusion: "I clearly understand it now, and I will strictly fulfill my engagement by such acts of assistance and kindness to them as you have described. When my mother removes into another house my services shall be readily given to accommodate her as far as I can." But he also adds, "Some little present of furniture too may be acceptable then." Fanny is unhappy even with this last small concession. "Certainly," she says, "But, however, *one* thing must be considered. When your father and mother moved to Norland, though the furniture of Stanhill was sold, all the china, plate, and linen was saved, and is now left to your mother. Her house will therefore be almost completely fitted up as soon as she takes it." John agrees: "That is a material consideration undoubtedly. A valuable legacy indeed! And yet some of the plate would have been a very pleasant addition to our own stock here." Encouraged, Fanny goes on: "Yes; and the set of breakfast china is twice as handsome as what belongs to this house. A great deal too handsome, in my opinion, for any place *they* can ever afford to live in."

In short, now the Dashwoods move in the direction of actually coveting the limited possessions of their poor relations.[57] (Call this *covet the victims' goods*.) But it does not stop there. Fanny is quick to blame their dissatisfaction on John's father: "But, however, so it is. Your father thought only of *them*. And I must say this: that you owe no particular gratitude to him, nor attention to his wishes; for we very well know that if he could, he would have left almost everything in the world to *them*." Hence, she tries to undermine any lingering claim John may feel by suggesting that his father was biased against them, and so is owed nothing. (Call this

---

57. I am not sure that there is a direct parallel to this claim in the climate debate. Echoes of it may occur in the claim that future generations of less developed countries stand to be much better off than their ancestors and so should bear the burdens of climate change (even though they will be poorer than many residents of the rich nations are now).

recasting oneself as the victim; see also lack of appreciation, above.) Austen concludes: "This argument was irresistible. It gave to his intentions whatever of decision was wanting before; and he finally resolved, that it would be absolutely unnecessary, if not highly indecorous, to do more for the widow and children of his father, than such kind of neighborly acts as his own wife pointed out."

The parallel in climate policy is presumably this. The claims of justice are simply too demanding, it is said. Those who present them are strongly biased in favor of the poor and the future, and care nothing for us now. Given this, we are more than justified in ignoring their arguments.

One instance of such an argument is the objection frequently made against employing low social discount rates on intergenerational projects. Many economists protest that this would involve excessive sacrifice on behalf of current people. Lomborg puts the point this way:

> It is . . . tempting to suggest that future generations should be given as much consideration as our generation, and that the discount rate should be zero or almost zero. This seems like the nice and ethically just way to go. However, this apparently sound assumption leads to a grim surprise. If the welfare of future generations means just as much (or almost as much) to us as our own, then we ought to spend an extremely large share of our income on investment in the future, because the dividend payable on investments will be much greater in the future.[58]

As I argued in chapter 8, this argument is deeply misleading. The real problem here is not low discount rates as such, but the background idea that our sole social objective should be the maximization of welfare (at least as understood in the way cost-benefit analysis does). Clearly, commonsense morality tells us that distribution matters, and some sacrifices ought to be prohibited. So, what is happening here is that bad theory is being invoked to attack better ethics, and the blame is put on the ethics.

More generally, attempts to claim the mantel of the victim are simply implausible in this context. Consider first Austen's story, where Fanny's reaction is highly dubious and self-serving. Henry has not demanded that John give up his inheritance to his sisters and stepmother, or even that he split its proceeds with them. He merely asks John to promise to assist them. This is so even though it is not clear that stronger demands

---

58. Lomborg 2001, 314.

would be unreasonable. Similarly, in current climate policy, the central issue is not whether the developed world should give over its excess wealth to the developing nations, or even share it evenly with them. The claim is only that the needs and aspirations of the less privileged should be taken into account in any agreement, so that it is not constructed solely for the benefit of the rich. Moreover, this is so even though some would argue that much stronger demands are not unreasonable.

VI. THE MORAL OF THE STORY

The upshot of this long discussion is as follows. Few of Fanny's objections have any real weight when considered in isolation—but the cumulative effect is spectacular. A rich man who has made a deathbed promise to his father to help his impoverished stepmother and sisters is moved from acknowledging a serious commitment to rejecting anything beyond the minimal claims appropriate to a neighbor. Moreover, he justifies this in part by declaring that his father and sisters have failed to acknowledge what is owed *to him*. The comparison with climate policy is worrying. Many of the steps in Austen's narrative have close parallels in the social and political discussion, and are similarly open to objection. Yet, arguably, the cumulative effect of this discussion over twenty years has been more or less them same. Very little of substance has been done. The poor, the future, and nature have been left to fend for themselves. The only serious difference is that in Austen's case the rich Dashwoods refrain from helping, but are not themselves the originators of the wrong. In our case, this is not so.

In addition to being generally unsettling, the analogy between the two cases sheds additional light on both. On the one hand, both Austen's case and the perfect moral storm centrally involve serious asymmetric vulnerability, where those with a moral duty to act not only suffer little or no negative consequences from a failure to act, but also stand to benefit from that failure. The global and intergenerational storms display this feature more vividly than the case of the Dashwoods, but the central problem seems the same. Because of this, in both cases the central agents are ripe for moral corruption; so, we should not be surprised to find similarly corrupting arguments made in each. On the other hand, the Austen case demonstrates how persuasive and subversive morally corrupt arguments can be, and in a context where the moral requirement is almost indisputable. This is helpful when we come to climate change, where the theoretical storm looms large, and can seem to obscue matters. The clarity of the Dashwood's folly helps us to see many of the corrupt arguments in the climate debate for the dangerous temptations they are.

In closing, it is worth mentioning two more general lessons one might draw from this chapter. The first is (as I have already suggested in previous chapters) that moral argument already abounds in the climate debate, but some of this is not very good argument. This should be unsurprising. Moral concerns are just as central to the climate problem as scientific concerns, and moral reasoning is just as open to misuse as scientific reasoning. Moreover, there are circumstances in which outright abuse is likely, and the perfect moral storm is one of them. In such settings, practical ethics can help. For one thing, it can facilitate an understanding of our moral situation, and careful separation and scrutiny of the arguments involved. For another, it can also operate defensively, to preserve initially sound moral intuitions against unscrupulous or misguided attacks. If we don't want to end up like John Dashwood—a victim of moral manipulation and self-deception—we need such philosophy.

The second lesson is that we should beware the cumulative effect of poor arguments. If we look more closely at Austen's example, we can see that the Dashwoods are actually engaged in a sophisticated "all-out assault" on the moral demands they face. If we revisit the central moves, the following picture emerges. Some seek to dispute the application of the moral claim (excessive burden, prior entitlement, competing special relationships, and unreasonable advocates); others claim that compliance will have unintended bad consequences (opening the floodgates and undermining autonomy); a third group aims to reduce the magnitude of the moral demand (budget constraint, demanding mutual benefit, diminishing victims' needs, shifting the playing field, and blessing in disguise); a fourth seeks to undermine the implementation of the duty (onerous logistics, discretionary aid, and indirect methods); and a fifth group aims to breed resentment on the part of the duty-bearer (lack of appreciation, coveting the victims' goods, and recasting oneself as the victim). This is a very robust offensive.

The "all-out assault" strategy has major advantages. Although, as I have argued above, none of the specific arguments looks very compelling at first glance, when advanced together—and in quick succession—they become more difficult to resist. This is part of the genius of Austen's narrative. In addition, it seems highly relevant to the perfect moral storm. In an age dominated by sound bites and intense political partisanship, by limited engagement and short attention spans, by superficial media and spin, are we not also vulnerable to such a barrage? Indeed, is this not at least one part of a compelling explanation for the ongoing political inertia? Again, the perfect storm analysis seems worryingly on target.

CHAPTER 10
Geoengineering in an Atmosphere of Evil

So convenient it is to be a reasonable Creature, since it enables one
to find or make a Reason for everything one has a mind to do.

—Benjamin Franklin (Franklin 1986, chapter 4)

One might have the idea that the unthinkable was itself a moral category . . . in the
sense that [a man] would not entertain the idea of doing [such actions] . . .
Entertaining certain alternatives, regarding them indeed as alternatives,
is itself something that he regards as dishonourable or morally absurd.

—Bernard Williams (Smart and Williams 1973)

Chapter 9 developed the idea that the perfect moral storm threatens our ethical discourse by drawing an analogy between the climate debate and a classic case of moral corruption presented by Jane Austen. This chapter aims to make that idea more vivid by focusing on a specific proposal for future climate action that is now beginning to gain traction. The proposal is that we should pursue the possibility of intentional intervention in the earth's climate system on a global scale ("geoengineering") in order to prepare for a nightmare scenario where such intervention has become "the lesser evil." My main claim will be that, though such a proposal need not manifest moral corruption, in context there is a high risk that it will. This is so even if, ultimately, good arguments can be found for pursuing geoengineering. The perfect moral storm not only makes it highly questionable that the best arguments will move us, but also suggests that the arguments that succeed are likely to trade on deep forms of corruption, and perhaps involve some form of moral schizophrenia.

Given the chapter's overall aim, my discussion will be in some ways unusual. On the one hand, I raise various challenges to "lesser evil" arguments for geoengineering as they are usually presented, and in doing so claim to have shifted the burden of proof back onto the geoengineers. Hence, my method looks familiar from other philosophical settings. However, on the other hand, opposing the pursuit of geoengineering as such is not my purpose. In particular, I am not here concerned with identifying whether geoengineering can, in the end, be justified, and under what conditions. Moreover, I do not take myself to have offered any argument that establishes that it cannot.[1] Though my analysis is relevant to such projects, the goal of this chapter is tangential. It is to illuminate the possibility of moral corruption when geoengineering is pursued, and explore the ethical implications of this. In my view, this is an important concern in the nonneutral evaluative setting of the perfect moral storm, where the threat of shadow solutions looms large. Indeed, for reasons that should become clear, I regard it as in many ways more pressing than the wider issue of (merely) possible justification.

I. AN IDEA THAT IS CHANGING THE WORLD

The term "geoengineering" lacks a precise definition, but is widely held to imply the intentional manipulation of the environment on a global scale.[2] For most of the last thirty years, there has been a strong presumption that such manipulation would be a bad idea. However, in August 2006, Paul Crutzen, the climate scientist and Nobel laureate, published an article which reignited debate about whether we should explore geoengineering "solutions" as a response to escalating climate change.[3] This was soon followed by other contributions and proposals,[4] and now

---

1. Indeed, I shall implicitly suggest some lines of argument for geoengineering that are worthy of further investigation. Nevertheless, I defer that project for another occasion. This is partly because I suspect that an ethical geoengineering policy would be far more demanding than any proposal currently being considered. Hence, as we shall see, its relevance is compromised by the perfect moral storm.

2. Schelling 1996; Keith 2000.

3. Crutzen 2006. Crutzen's piece appeared in *Climatic Change*, accompanied by a set of responses from other distinguished scientists, including Bengtsson 2006; Cicerone 2006; McCracken 2006; Kiehl 2006; Lawrence 2006.

4. Such as Wigley 2006.

interest in geoengineering has become widespread in both academia and the world of policy. As a result, *Time* magazine recently listed geoengineering as one of its "Ten Ideas that are Changing the World."[5]

Geoengineering is a relatively new and underexplored topic. This is true both of the science and the ethics. Just as we are not close to fully understanding exactly how to geoengineer if we were to choose to do so, or what the impacts of any geoengineering scheme would be, so we are also not sure how to understand the normative dimensions of undertaking geoengineering. Indeed, at this point almost no moral and political philosophy has even been attempted.[6] In such a setting, it is useful to get some sense of the moral terrain: of what the major issues might be, how they might be investigated, and in which ways understanding might move forward. To do so, I focus on one prominent argument for geoengineering, raising a number of serious challenges that have wider application.

In my view, these challenges are sufficient to seriously threaten the argument, at least in its most prominent and limited form, and so shift the burden of proof back onto proponents of geoengineering. Still, (again) my purpose is not to determine whether the pursuit of geoengineering can, in the end, be morally justified.[7] Instead, my concern is with the moral implications of such pursuit. This explains my focus on current reasoning in our existing context, rather than hypothetical reasoning in some ideal. Given that (I suspect) the scientific and political momentum is such that serious research is almost certain, and ultimate deployment also probable (at least on moderately pessimistic assumptions about what the future holds), this setting should be taken seriously. In particular, the arguments I consider explicitly concede that geoengineering is some kind of "evil." But if we are to set an evil course, the moral costs should be exposed. This is so even if, as I shall argue, these involve debts that few have any intention of paying.

5. Walsh 2008.

6. In ethics, the main exception is the groundbreaking Jamieson 1996. Other early articles with something to say about ethics include Bodansky 1996, Keith 2000, Schelling 1996, Schneider 1996, and Kellogg and Schneider 1974.

7. After all, I focus on only one argument for geoengineering when many others might be offered, I consider only a fairly limited version of that argument, and I admit in advance that the challenges I raise may not be decisive.

Ethical discussion of geoengineering is made more difficult by the complexity of the terrain. First, a number of interventions are already being proposed for combating climate change, and it is not clear that all of them should be classified together. For example, some suggest deflecting a small percentage of incoming radiation from the sun by placing huge mirrors at the Lagrange point between it and the earth; some advocate fertilizing the oceans with plant life to soak up more carbon dioxide; some suggest a massive program of reforestation; and some propose capturing vast quantities of emissions from power plants and burying them in sedimentary rock deep underground. But do these interventions raise the same issues? Should we count all of them as "geoengineering"?[8]

Second, different arguments can be (and often are) offered in favor of the same specific intervention. For example, some advocate a given geoengineering "solution" because they think it much more cost-effective than mitigation, others say that it will buy time while mitigation measures are implemented, and still others claim that geoengineering should only be implemented as a last resort, to stave off a catastrophe. Such differences in rationale are important because they often make for differences in research and policy implications. For example, they can affect what kinds of geoengineering should be pursued, to what extent, and with what safeguards.

This chapter focuses on one specific intervention, and one rationale currently being offered for it. The intervention is that of injecting sulfate aerosols into the stratosphere in order to block incoming solar radiation by modifying the earth's albedo.[9] The rationale is a certain kind of "lesser

8. For an overview, see Keith 2000.

9. This approach is especially appealing because it has a natural precedent whose implications are generally understood: the cooling effects of a large volcanic eruption. Nevertheless, it should be noted that whereas volcanic eruptions are usually isolated events whose effects on temperature last only a year or two, the geoengineering proposal involves continuous injections of aerosols for a period of at least decades and possibly centuries. Not only is this a different proposition—amounting to continuous sustained eruption rather than an isolated event—but there are worries that it soon becomes effectively irreversible. First, because the sulfate particles only mask the effects of increasing greenhouse gas concentrations in the atmosphere, and because they dissipate quickly, any attempt to halt the experiment would probably commit the earth to a swift rebound effect. Second, if the masking effect is large, then the rebound effect will likely also be so, and this is relevant in the current case. Under the circumstances envisaged by the current proposal, the masking effect is of comparable magnitude (2–6 degrees Celsius) to the kind of catastrophic climate change that

evil" argument. It begins by conceding both that mitigation—direct and substantial reductions in anthropogenic emissions—is by far the best approach to climate policy, and that there is something morally problematic about geoengineering proposals. However, it goes on to claim that so far progress on the preferred policy has been minimal,[10] and that, if this failure to act aggressively continues, then at some point (probably forty years or more into the future) we may end up facing a choice between allowing catastrophic impacts to occur, or engaging in geoengineering. Both, it is conceded, are bad options. But engaging in geoengineering is less bad than allowing catastrophic climate change. Therefore, the argument continues, if we end up facing the choice, we should choose geoengineering. But, it is alleged, this puts us in a bind: if we do not start doing serious research on geoengineering now, then we will not be in a position to choose that option should the nightmare scenario arise. Therefore, it is concluded, we should start doing that research now. Call this the "arm the future argument" (AFA).

I focus on this combination of intervention (sulfate injection) and rationale (the AFA) for three reasons. First, it is currently the most popular proposal under consideration, and the one that most strongly motivates Crutzen.[11] (For this reason, I shall also call it "the core proposal.") Second, the focus on sulfate injection helps us to sidestep the definitional worries about what constitutes geoengineering. Such direct intervention into the chemistry of the stratosphere appears to be a clear case, both scientifically and ethically. Third, appeals to the lesser evil are attractive to a wide audience, including those who are otherwise strongly against technological intervention. Indeed, in the current context such appeals

---

the intervention is trying to prevent. Third, since the speed of the change is itself a factor, this would probably make unmasking worse than allowing the original climate change. Hence, many scientists believe that once we have been doing sulfate injection for a while, we will in effect be committed to continuing indefinitely (e.g., Matthews and Caldeira 2007).

10. We could add to this that there has been a similar lack of progress on the other necessary policy, adaptation.

11. The attribution to Crutzen requires some interpretation, since his claims are not fully explicit. Though I believe that it is reasonable, I am not completely confident. Still, this should not diminish the interest of the present chapter, since the AFA is clearly one major and widespread argument for geoengineering. As Stephen Schneider put it: "In this case, the messenger is the message" (Morton 2007, 133). More recently, similar claims appear in Victor et al. 2009.

are often seen as irresistible, constituting a straightforward and decisive move that no sane person could reject. Hence, such arguments seem among those most likely to justify geoengineering.

Before proceeding, it is worth considering one objection to this "core case" approach. Some would like to jettison the term geoengineering because, they say, it covers too many things that are too dissimilar. Hence, they may sympathize with the attempt to narrow in on the clear instance of sulfate injection, but nevertheless argue that it would be better not to use the term geoengineering to describe it. Indeed, they may complain that regarding sulfate injection as a core case continues to imply similarities with other methods of intentional intervention in the climate system that do not exist. In particular, they may suspect that the problems I later identify with sulfate injection do not generalize to these other methods, with the result that my description of these problems as arising for geoengineering becomes misleading. We can illustrate this worry with an example. Some critics may lament the fact that I have not revised my nomenclature in light of a recent Royal Society report which claimed that we should embrace a sharp distinction between what it called "carbon dioxide removal" methods (such as reforestation and direct capture from the air) and "solar radiation management" methods (such as sulfate injection), and acknowledge that these two raise very different issues.[12] Why don't I just say that sulfate injection is, at best, a clear case of solar radiation management, and leave it at that? Why appear to drag carbon dioxide removal methods in as well?

Though I cannot take up this topic at length here, let me offer two quick responses, focusing on the Royal Society's distinction. First, the core case approach is less bold than the Royal Society's. It does not assert (nor does it reject) the claim that forms of intervention can be classified into two rigidly defined types with common properties. Instead, it allows for more modest assumptions, such as that there might be a continuum of forms of intervention, and so permits the thought that there may be more or less degenerate forms of geoengineering, to which the current analysis will apply only imperfectly, and perhaps at the margin not at all.[13] Second, there are reasons to prefer this methodology. For example, imagine the

12. See Shepherd et al. 2009. Gardiner 2011b provides a commentary on the report's ethics.

13. One consequence of this is that the approach weakens worries about having an arbitrary cutoff point between what counts as geoengineering and what does not.

following scenario. Suppose that someone were to invent a machine capable of sucking carbon dioxide from the air in massive quantities in a very short period of time. Assume also that this machine is capable of reducing the current atmospheric concentration of around 380 ppm to a preindustrial concentration of around 270 ppm in six months. This would be huge and amazingly fast perturbation of the climate system. Serious science would have to be done to consider its potential effects, and many ethical issues (e.g., relating to governance) arise. Given this, the machine scenario seems to have much more in common with the kind of sulfate injection envisioned by the core proposal than with other forms of carbon dioxide removal, such as reforestation, or nongeological carbon capture and storage. This is so even though ambient air capture is paradigmatically a form of carbon dioxide removal on the Royal Society's reckoning. Given this, there are reasons not to prejudge what counts as geoengineering. The core case method facilitates this caution.

Returning to the matter at hand, as I have indicated, the main aim of this chapter is to explore the moral context of the decision to pursue geoengineering. Still, as a secondary matter, I will argue for three more specific conclusions. First, the arm the future argument is far from straightforward or decisive. Instead, it assumes much that is contentious, and—at least in its most prominent political and scientific forms—is overly narrow in its conclusions. Second, the argument obscures much of what is at stake in the ethics of geoengineering, including what it means to call something an "evil," and whether doing evil has further moral implications. Third, in the context of the perfect moral storm, the argument should be viewed with suspicion. Since we—the current generation, and especially those in the affluent countries—are particularly vulnerable to moral corruption, we should be especially cautious about arguments that appear to diminish our moral responsibilities. As Franklin suggests in the opening epigraph, we must beware the "conveniences" of being "reasonable creatures."

The discussion proceeds as follows. Sections II–III set out the context in which the core proposal emerges. Section IV presents some internal challenges to the arm the future argument. Section V considers whether an "arm the present" argument may do better. Sections VII–IX consider some general challenges that face lesser evil arguments considered as such, and discuss why they may arise in the case of geoengineering. The discussion centers on what it means to call something "evil," and what kinds of moral reasons evils provide.

II. POLITICAL INERTIA REVISITED

Before we turn to the core proposal itself, it is worth examining how it emerges. Crutzen's position is largely motivated by what I have called "the problem of political inertia."[14] Crutzen asserts that, despite the fact that mitigation is "by far the preferred way"[15] to address climate change, so far efforts to lower carbon dioxide emissions have been "grossly unsuccessful."[16] Similarly, the Royal Society reports that "early and effective" emissions reductions offer the "safest and most predictable" approach to dealing with climate change, and that increased interest in geoengineering among scientists is motivated by a concern about "the lack of progress of the political processes."[17] The grounds for such skepticism are easy to understand. As we have seen, since the IPCC's first report in 1990, humanity's overall response has been disappointing (chapters 3 and 4). Given such inertia, Crutzen infers that "there is little reason to be optimistic" about future reductions,[18] adding that the hope that the world will now act decisively is "a pious wish."[19] This is his ultimate reason for proposing geoengineering.

If political inertia is the key problem, what causes it? Crutzen does not say. But, of course, I have been arguing that a good part of the explanation is that climate change constitutes a perfect moral storm

14. The centrality of the problem of political inertia can be obscured by the fact that Crutzen initially gives most prominence to a different issue concerning lower-level aerosols. As policy makers tackle normal air pollution problems by reducing sulfur dioxide emissions, Crutzen worries that they will thereby increase global warming, and the increase may be dramatic. However, despite the prominence Crutzen gives this "Catch-22" situation, the problem of inertia appears more fundamental for him. He explicitly claims that the aerosol problem could be solved through mitigation, and indeed that this would be the best solution: "By far the preferred way to resolve the policy makers' dilemma is to lower the emissions of the greenhouse gases" (Crutzen 2006, 211–2; see also 217). Hence, his view is *not* that the aerosol problem as such makes geoengineering necessary (e.g., because it puts us into new territory, where mitigation alone will not be enough, so that geoengineering must be considered as well).

15. Crutzen 2006, 211.

16. Crutzen 2006, 212.

17. Shepherd et al. 2009, ix and 1.

18. Crutzen 2006, 217.

19. Crutzen 2006, 217.

that threatens our ability to behave ethically. If this is correct, the central question to ask about any geoengineering proposal is whether it provides a serious way out of the perfect moral storm, or whether, instead, it amounts only to a shadow solution. In the present case, the issue becomes whether the core proposal (and the growing clamor in its favor) poses a solution, or is itself part of the problem. Since the perfect moral storm makes us vulnerable to moral corruption, we should be on our guard.

III. TWO PRELIMINARY ARGUMENTS

The economics of geoengineering are—there is no better word for it—incredible.

—Scott Barrett (Barrett 2008, 49)

The core proposal acknowledges that geoengineering is a bad thing. But why concede this? Why consider geoengineering an evil at all? To motivate this idea, it is useful to consider briefly two other arguments for geoengineering that lurk in the background.

1. The Cost-Effectiveness Argument

The first argument claims that geoengineering ought to be pursued simply because it is the most cost-effective solution to the climate crisis. Hence, some enthusiasts claim that albedo modification is relatively cheap and administratively simple to deploy. It is said to be relatively cheap because (it is claimed) the basic mechanism for inserting sulfur into the stratosphere, though expensive in absolute terms, is orders of magnitude cheaper than switching whole economies to alternative energy. It is said to be administratively simple because action need not require full international agreement. Indeed, in theory, the actual deployment could be done by one country or corporation acting alone.[20]

---

20. Schelling 1996, Barrett 2008.

The "cost-effectiveness argument" has not (yet) proven persuasive to many people. This is presumably because a number of important considerations seem to count against it. First, since sulfate injection does not remove carbon dioxide emissions from the atmosphere, but rather allows their accumulation to continue accelerating, some important effects—such as ocean acidification, and its implications for marine organisms and systems—remain untouched. Thus, at best this intervention deals with only one part of the problem; and at worst, it implicitly assumes the deployment of further technological fixes, so that sulfate injection becomes only the tip of a geoengineering iceberg.[21]

Second, the claim that albedo modification is cheap appears to focus only on the costs of actually delivering sulphur into the stratosphere, using cannons mounted on ships, or especially modified airliners. But this seems curiously myopic. (One doesn't decide whether to embark on brain surgery by focusing on the price of the scalpel.) In particular, it appears simply to *assume* that this kind of geoengineering will have no expensive side effects. But worries about side effects are, of course, many people's main reason for rejecting all geoengineering proposals.[22]

Third, the claim that geoengineering is administratively simple appears morally and politically naïve.[23] Can we really imagine that major countries will happily stand aside while a single power or corporation modifies the climate without their input and oversight? At the very least—given that the effects of geoengineering are likely to vary across different countries and regions—won't there be debate about which kind of geoengineering should be pursued, and to what extent? Aren't there major issues of liability to be resolved? In short, isn't this the kind of issue on which international agreement will be absolutely necessary if serious social, economic, political, and military conflict is to be avoided?

Finally, the basic cost-effectiveness argument ignores important issues about the human relationship to nature. Given the wider context of

21. Cf. Lovelock 2008, 3887.

22. For example, some are concerned that sulfate injection may lead to further destruction of stratospheric ozone. Crutzen (himself a pioneer of the ozone problem) is optimistic that this problem is small, given the quantity of sulfate to be injected, and also suggests that alternatives to sulfates might be tried. Still, as he acknowledges, this requires more research. (See Crutzen 2006, 215–6.)

23. Bodansky 1996.

escalating species extinction, rampant deforestation, dramatic population increases, and so on, is it not cavalier to assume that the *only* issue that arises with climate change is whether to employ a "quick" and "cheap" technological fix? Indeed, some have even gone so far as to suggest that, even if successful, adopting a geoengineering "solution" might turn out to be worse for humanity in the long run than the problem it is supposed to solve. Perhaps, they say, it would be better all things considered to endure a climate catastrophe than to encourage yet more risky interventions in, and further domination of, nature.[24]

For these and other reasons, most people have concluded not only that the cost-effectiveness argument does not justify sulfate injection, but also, on the contrary, that such intervention is something we have serious reason to avoid: an "evil" in the most modest sense. (I consider less modest senses later on.) This is an important claim, since it imposes a burden of proof on other arguments for this kind of geoengineering. They must show that its merits are, all things considered, serious enough to override the "evils" involved.

2. The Research First Argument

The second lurking argument comes from Ralph Cicerone, president of the National Academy of Sciences. Cicerone believes that we should separate out questions about research on geoengineering from those concerning actual deployment. On the one hand, he supports allowing research and peer-review publication, since this will help us to "weed out bad proposals" and "encourage good proposals," and because knowledge is worthwhile for its own sake, a consideration that (he says) backs the normal presumption in favor of freedom of inquiry. On the other hand, Cicerone concedes that deployment raises special issues. Hence, he proposes that scientists get together and agree on a moratorium on testing or deploying geoengineering. Once some good concrete proposals have emerged from research, he believes that the process should be opened up to public participation.

There is something attractive about Cicerone's proposal, and about the model it implies of science and its role in society. However, there are

---

24. Jamieson 1996.

serious concerns about how good that model really is, and in particular how it holds up in the real social and political world in which we live. To begin with, although almost everyone will like the idea of "weeding out" bad geoengineering proposals, Cicerone's aim of "encouraging" the good ones is contentious. So, much depends on his third rationale: that we should promote the acquisition of knowledge for its own sake. But there are some significant issues here.

The first is that it is not obvious that any particular research project should be supported just because it enhances knowledge. To begin with, in the real world, there are limited resources for research. Since we cannot fully support everything, projects compete with one another for funding and expertise. Given this, the claim that geoengineering research increases knowledge is insufficient to justify our pursuit of it. If we prioritize geoengineering, other knowledge-enhancing projects will be displaced. Some rationale is needed for this displacement.

Second, some kinds of knowledge-enhancement seem trivial. Suppose, for example, that someone proposes a project to count (not estimate) the number of blades of grass in each individual backyard in Washington State. Do we really have a reason to support this research? Similarly, some experts claim that geoengineering research may turn out to be in some sense trivial. For example, they suggest that it is highly unlikely to yield the kind of results needed to justify action on the time-scale envisioned,[25] and that the rate of technological progress is so fast that it may make little sense even to try.[26]

Third, there are such things as morally bad projects. Consider, for example, research whose aim is to find the maximally painful way in which to kill someone, or the cheapest way to commit genocide against a specific minority population. Arguably, if such projects succeed, they increase knowledge. But it is not clear that this alone gives us reason to

25. Bengtsson 2006, 233.

26. Thomas Schelling warns that if we are preparing for intervention that is fifty years or more off, this may be pointless preparation: technological change over such a period may be so profound as to make the preparation worthless. The precise import of this claim is unclear. (Should we prepare less than we otherwise might? Should we do comparatively more basic climate research and less technical research?) But it does cast doubt on the claim that the best we can do for future generations is geoengineering research. See Schelling 1996.

support them. Similarly, if, as we have seen suggested above, geoengineering really is some kind of evil, why encourage the pursuit of "good" ways to do it? Why not promote research with better aims (e.g., green technology)?[27]

The second issue about the knowledge-enhancement argument concerns the conclusion that we should support research. There is a crucial ambiguity here, because "support" is not an all-or-nothing affair. There are major differences between, for example, individual scientists and journals being willing to review and publish papers, major funding agencies encouraging geoengineering proposals, and governments providing massive resources for a geoengineering "Manhattan Project." The kind of support Cicerone emphasizes is that of the participation of reviewers and journals in publishing work on geoengineering. This is a very limited kind of support. But others want something *much* more substantial, amounting to a substantial shift in the existing research effort. Surely, giving this kind of preeminence to the cause of geoengineering research cannot be justified merely by appealing to the value of knowledge for its own sake. Instead, a much more robust argument is needed.

The final issue with Cicerone's argument is that it is unclear whether geoengineering activities can really be limited to scientific research in the way he suggests. First, there is such a thing as institutional momentum. In our culture, big projects that are started tend to get done.[28] This is partly because people like to justify their sunk costs; but it is also because starting usually creates a set of institutions whose mission it is to promote such projects.[29] For such reasons, sometimes the best time to prevent a project

---

27. Some scientists sympathetic to Cicerone's argument are confident that, in the end, there are no good geoengineering proposals to be had. Hence, they support research on the grounds that it will reveal this "fact" more clearly, and so prevent geoengineering strategies from being implemented merely for political reasons. But this is a different rationale. Note that it assumes not only that good proposals will not emerge, but also that further science will be enough to circumvent the political forces in favor of geoengineering (even when existing science has not), and that it is worth "wasting" scarce scientific resources in this effort.

28. Jamieson 1996.

29. Don Maier also suggests to me (i) that often such institutions compete, so that we should expect geoengineering institutions to discourage those that promote mitigation, and (ii) that such institutions create psychological momentum: individuals do not like to abandon projects in which they have invested time, energy, money, and emotion.

proceeding is before the costs are sunk and the institutions created. Second, there are real concerns about the idea of a moratorium. After all, if the results of research are to be published in mainstream journals that are freely available online or in libraries across the world, what is to stop some rogue scientist, engineer, or government deciding to use that research? Third, there are worries about who gets to make such decisions and why, and about how they are enforced. If the future of the planet is at stake, why is it that the rest of humanity should cede the floor to something that might amount only to a "gentleman's agreement" among a specific set of scientists? Fourth, there are issues about conducting geoengineering research in isolation from public input, and in particular divorced from discussions about the ethics of deployment. The background assumption seems to be that such input and discussion has *nothing to tell us* about the goals of geoengineering research or how it should be conducted. But it is not clear why we should accept this assumption.[30] After all, many do not accept it for other important scientific issues, such as research on stem cells, genetic enhancement, and biological warfare.

In summary, stronger arguments are needed for considering substantial investment in geoengineering research, and a more robust account of the conditions under which deployment would be considered is also necessary. This is where lesser evil arguments enter the discussion.

IV. ARMING THE FUTURE[31]

> Life's toughest choices are not between good and bad, but between bad and worse. We call these choices between lesser evils. We know that whatever we choose, something important will be sacrificed. Whatever we do, someone will get hurt. Worst of all, we have to choose. We cannot wait for better information or advice or some new set of circumstances. We have to decide now, and we can be sure that there will be a price to pay. If we do not pay it ourselves, someone else will.
>
> —Michael Ignatieff (Ignatieff 2004, vii)

30. Jamieson argues for just the opposite conclusion: that geoengineering research could only be justified if accompanied by research into the ethics of geoengineering (Jamieson 1996).

31. Some parts of this section draw on Gardiner 2007.

If there is a presumption against geoengineering, how might this be met? One promising approach is based on the general idea that "we may reach the point at which [geoengineering] is the lesser of two evils."[32] This idea has been influential in discussions about geoengineering for climate change since the earliest days, and has appealed to both its enthusiasts and its detractors. For example, Stephen Schneider, himself generally an opponent of geoengineering, reports that, back in 1992, the concerns of a National Academy of Science panel were "effectively countered" by the following argument: "Let us assume . . . [that] the next generation of scientific assessments . . . converged on confidently forecasting that the earth had become committed to climate change . . . serious enough to either require a dramatic retrenchment from our fossil fuel based economy . . . or to endure catastrophic climatic changes. Under such a scenario, *we would simply have to practice geoengineering as the 'least evil.'*"[33]

1. The Basic Argument

The core proposal offers one kind of lesser evil argument, and so appears to fit neatly into this framework.[34] As we have seen, the basic structure of this argument seems to be as follows:

> (AFA1) Reducing global emissions is by far the best way to address climate change.
> (AFA2) In the last fifteen years or so, there has been little progress on reducing emissions.
> (AFA3) There is little reason to think that this will change in the near future.
> (AFA4) If very substantial progress on emissions reduction is not made soon, then at some point (probably forty years or more into the future) we may end up facing a choice between allowing catastrophic impacts to occur, or engaging in geoengineering.
> (AFA5) These are both bad options.
> (AFA6) But geoengineering is less bad.

32. Jamieson 1996, 332–3.
33. Schneider 1996, 295–6; emphasis added. Schneider attributes the argument to Robert Frosh.
34. Crutzen cites the Schneider passage with approval.

(AFA7) Therefore, if we are forced to choose, we should choose geoengineering.

(AFA8) But if we do not start to do serious scientific research on geoengineering options soon, then we will not be in a position to choose it should the above scenario arise.

(AFA9) Therefore, we need to start doing such research now.

The arm the future argument is complex. But, on the surface at least, it does seem to be the right *kind* of argument. For one thing, it acknowledges that geoengineering is problematic, and that there is a burden of proof against it. For another, it offers a weighty moral reason to endorse geoengineering—that of preventing a catastrophe—and it is easy to see why this reason addresses the deficiencies of the cost-effectiveness and research first arguments. The threat of catastrophe appears both to meet the burden of proof against geoengineering, and to justify prioritizing research on it over other kinds of research. Finally, the arm the future argument appears to address a significant aspect of the perfect moral storm. Under the scenario it sketches, geoengineering research emerges as one way of assisting future generations. If the world really isn't going to do very much about reducing emissions, then substantial investment in geoengineering research emerges as an alternative strategy for meeting our intergenerational obligations.

At first glance, then, the arm the future argument appears to make a very strong, even overwhelming, case for geoengineering research, and also (under the stated circumstances) ultimate deployment. However, I will now argue that matters are not as straightforward as they initially seem.

To begin with, we would do well to proceed with caution. In general, arguments from moral emergency are perennially popular in both private and public life, and for an obvious reason. Clearly, part of the point of claiming that one is in morally exceptional circumstances is in order to secure an exemption from the usual norms and constraints of morality. But this fact should give us pause. After all, there will always be those who would prefer that morality not apply to them or their projects, and all of us are vulnerable to such thoughts at some time or other. Morality sometimes seems inconvenient to us (like truth, as Al Gore reminds us)—and in such cases we'd often like to have an exemption. Hence, we should be wary of arguments from emergency; clearly, they are open to manipulation. (This explains why arguments from emergency—and declarations of states of emergency when normal political processes and rights are suspended—are often employed by political despots.) Moreover, in the case of climate change we have a further reason for caution. In a perfect moral storm, the incentives for moral corruption are high. Given all this, the core proposal should be subjected to special scrutiny.

2. Five Challenges

In the remainder of this section, I focus on five challenges that face the arm the future argument specifically, and consider two responses. In subsequent sections, I raise some wider worries that apply to lesser evil arguments considered more generally. Ultimately, I conclude that the AFA faces a serious burden of proof.

(i) Which Nightmare?

The first challenge to the AFA concerns the salience of its nightmare scenario. In general, we should not simply accept *as a stipulation* that some policy that is said to be an evil (like geoengineering) should be endorsed because under some circumstances it would be a lesser evil than some other policy (such as allowing a catastrophic climate change). Instead, we should ask important questions such as: How likely is this emergency situation (where one has actually to decide between these two options) to arise? Is it the most relevant emergency situation? Is it true that the two evils are the only alternatives? Is the lesser evil really lesser, all things considered?

As it happens, the answers to these questions seem very much in doubt in the present case. In the AFA, the "nightmare scenario" is one where a decision must be made between embarking on geoengineering, or allowing catastrophic climate change to occur. But consider two points.

First, for a group of decision makers actually to face this emergency situation, they would need to know at least the following: that the planet was on the verge of very serious climate impacts; that geoengineering was very likely to—and the only thing likely to—prevent them; and that the side effects of deployment (including not just the physical and ecological effects, but also the human and political effects) would be minor in relation to the harm prevented. But this, I submit, would be a pretty unusual scenario. Moreover, given this, it is questionable whether it makes sense to organize policy around it. For one thing, the scenario may be so unusual that it is worth asking whether it is even *worth* preparing for. (After all, it does not seem to make sense to prepare for every possibility.[35]) For another, there may be other emergency situations that are more salient; and if so, it may be better to prepare for these emergencies. For example, the more salient emergency situation might be one where choices have to be made about how to cope with, or reverse, a catastrophic change that has already occurred.[36] In general, the claim that the nightmare scenario described by the arm the future argument is *the* nightmare that we should be concerned to address requires further support.[37]

Second, in one respect the core proposal may not be neutral here. The arm the future argument proceeds as if the decision to do research will have no influence on the likelihood of the nightmare situation's arising. But it is not clear what justifies this assumption. Many people worry that substantial research on geoengineering will itself encourage political inertia on mitigation, and so help to bring on the nightmare scenario and deployment.[38] If this is so, we may have strong reason to limit or resist such research at this stage. We do not want to create a self-fulfilling prophecy.

These points illustrate a weakness in hypothetical lesser evil arguments like the AFA. Even if one accepts in principle that one should make a lesser evil choice in a highly stylized case like the nightmare scenario, this fails to justify a policy of preparing to make that choice.[39] The salience of the scenario to current policy still needs to be demonstrated. By itself, this kind of hypothetical lesser evil argument is not enough.

35. Perhaps it is possible that you will win ten million dollars in the lottery this year. But that doesn't mean that you should *now* hire an investment banker to develop a plan on how to spend it.

36. Perhaps this scenario is simply more likely, or perhaps preparing for it would help us to deal with the nightmare scenario as well, at least to some extent.

37. One response to this argument would be simply to concede and claim merely that the nightmare scenario is at least one among a number of emergencies for which we should prepare. For more on this kind of argument, see below.

38. It may also facilitate inertia on adaptation, and so increase the severity of any given climate catastrophe by undermining people's ability to cope.

39. This basic idea is familiar from another context. Proponents of torture try to force their opponents to admit that in the case of a ticking bomb—where you, the

(ii) Other Options?

The second challenge to the core proposal concerns its account of the current options. The arm the future argument does not involve a straightforward appeal to moral emergency, since it explicitly concedes that the nightmare scenario is not *yet* upon us. According to the argument, we are not *now* in the relevant lesser evil situation, having to choose between the evils of allowing catastrophe and pursuing geoengineering;[40] instead, the decision currently to be made is about whether and how to prepare for such a situation.[41]

This shift is important because it puts questions about how the emergency is supposed to arise back in play. One of the usual effects of actually being in an emergency is to make many of the background conditions much less salient. For example, if I see a small child drowning in a pond, whom I could easily save by reaching down to pick him out, we do not normally think that I should to stop to mull over questions such

---

authorities, know that your prisoner has hidden a nuclear device under the streets of a major city, but don't know where it is—torture is permissible, and then to infer from this that torture is justified. In a classic move against this kind of lesser evil argument, Henry Shue concedes that torture may be permissible in the ticking bomb case, but argues that this does not imply anything about what the policies of those not confronting such a case should be (Shue 1978, 2005). For one thing, the case may be theoretically possible, but in practice so very, very improbable as to make planning for it irrational; for another, actually planning for the case—for example, by creating a bureau for torture and training torturers—may have such profound and predictable negative consequences that this is decisive reason to reject it.

40. Crutzen is explicit about this: the idea is that we must prepare for the possibility of an emergency, not that we are actually in one right now. Hence, his core position is that we should develop geoengineering to serve as a backstop technology, to deploy if the situation eventually deteriorates. The AFA is explicitly a "backstop argument."

41. One could embellish the AFA to claim that we are already in a different lesser evil situation. So, suppose the argument is: (1) current research on geoengineering is an evil, because it really does increase the probability of deployment; but (2) given the possibility of the nightmare scenario, we must take the risk and choose this evil; and (3) we must do so *now*, or else risk being too late. This embellishment probably makes the original argument more promising. Nevertheless, it is also challenged by many of the other considerations raised in the text. For one thing, we (now) have alternatives to geoengineering including mitigation and investment in alternative energy, to name just two; for another, there are serious questions about whether geoengineering research will succeed, and about whether this is even a good time to begin.

as how he came to be there, and who is officially responsible for saving him. The relevant question is what to do here and now. But none of this is the case if one is *anticipating* an emergency. Then it is perfectly appropriate to consider how the emergency might arise.

First, sometimes the best way to plan for an emergency is to *prevent* its arising. In the case of the pond, for example, one might erect a small wall to prevent toddlers falling in. Similarly, suppose—as the arm the future argument suggests—that we are interested in preventing a catastrophic climate change brought on by the failure to reduce emissions directly, through regulation and political leadership. Even given this failure, we still have other options. For example, perhaps we can prevent the emergency by indirect means, such as by investing in a massive Manhattan Project that produces very cheap alternative energy by 2030.[42] The general point here is that if a good option is available that will prevent the emergency situation arising, the fact that we would choose a (lesser) evil if it did arise may be irrelevant to what to do now. Again, the nightmare scenario loses its salience.

Second, considering how the emergency might arise can also help us to put other options on the table for dealing with it even if it does ultimately come about. In the present case, the AFA implicitly suggests that the *very best* we can do now to help future people faced with the threat of an imminent climate catastrophe is to research geoengineering. But this claim is unsupported and open to challenge. Most conspicuously, there are other ways in which we might aid future people on the brink of such a calamity. For example, perhaps we could prepare them for a massive emergency deployment of existing alternative energy technology (e.g., we could establish a Strategic Solar Panel Reserve), or perhaps we could establish a robust international climate assistance and refugee program; or perhaps we could do both of these things, together with any number of other alternatives. Given that some of these policies

42. Some have argued that such an approach is not only more feasible than geoengineering, but also secures a better outcome: "I do consider it more feasible to succeed in solving the world's energy problem, which is the main cause to the present concern about climate change, than to successfully manage a geo-engineering experiment on this scale and magnitude, which even if it works is unable to solve all problems with the very high concentration of greenhouse gases in the atmosphere" (Bengtsson 2006, 233; responding to Crutzen).

may not be "evil" in any respect, we might even have strong prima facie reasons to prefer them over research on geoengineering. In any case, their relative merits should be discussed.

(iii) Additional Liabilities?

The third challenge facing the core proposal concerns additional liabilities. The arm the future argument concedes that it is probably not *us*—our generation—who will actually make the decision to deploy the lesser evil. The assumption is that the nightmare scenario will not unfold until the second half of this century at the earliest, if at all.[43] There are probably two basic reasons for this. First, mainstream scientists suspect that the kind of threshold effects most likely to produce the nightmare scenario are some way off, if they are plausible at all.[44] Second, many believe that the basic research needed on the possible methods and impacts of geoengineering will take a similar time period to emerge. Discussion of the problem is very much in its infancy, much of the relevant work is at a highly speculative stage, and good scientific guidance will take a long time to materialize. Hence, in a recent review Stephen Schneider emphasizes that "strong caveats, which suggest that it is premature to contemplate implementing any geoengineering schemes in the near future, are stated by all responsible people who have addressed the geoengineering question."[45]

43. Schelling, an economist, explicitly assumed that the decision was at least fifty years off in the mid-1990s (Schelling 1996). Moreover, Crutzen assumes that geoengineering will only be necessary if mitigation efforts fail. But such efforts will have almost no impact on temperature rise in the next thirty years, and a limited impact in the next forty to fifty years.

44. See, for example, Lenton et al. 2008. Victor et al 2009 explicitly invoke such "tipping points." However, Alan Robock has suggested to me that the future generation assumption may not be widely shared by scientists, since there will be substantial climate impacts during the next fifty years. The latter claim is highly plausible if one is referring to gradual effects rather than abrupt changes. Still, I suspect that such concerns push towards an "arm the present" argument, and perhaps one that does not focus on catastrophe and suggests fairly quick deployment. My impression is that such arguments are not yet mainstream. In any case, they require independent treatment. For a few remarks, see Section V.

45. Schneider 2008, 3856. In the current context, though the idea of sulfate injection has been around for a while, little work has been done on the impacts of a sustained

Given these things, it seems highly likely that, if the nightmare scenario arises, it will confront future generations, not the current generation. The arm the future argument tends to obscure this point by referring to what "we" will be forced to choose, where this refers to some temporally extended sense of "we," such as humanity as such, or the United States considered across time. But once the point is made clear, the role of the argument becomes to imply that the responsibility of the current generation is (merely) to aid future generations in choosing the best kind of geoengineering possible. Unfortunately, this conclusion tends to obscure a vital moral feature of the situation: the potential crisis is to be brought about by *our* (the current generation's) *failure* to pursue better climate policies.[46] Acknowledging this matters because there is usually an important moral difference between (on the one hand) preparing for an emergency, and (on the other hand) preparing for an emergency that is *to be brought about by one's own moral failure*.

Many things might be said about this. But here let me make just two remarks. First, if someone puts others in a very bad situation through a moral failure, we usually do not think it enough for her to respond merely by offering the victims an evil way out. Instead, we believe that the perpetrator has substantial obligations to help the victims find better alternatives, and also, if the alternatives are costly or harmful, to compensate them for making this necessary. If this is right, then even if the arm the future argument were correct in other respects, we should not conclude from it that current people owe future generations *only* research on geoengineering; much more seems required. For example, we might owe them a very substantial compensation fund, or we might be obliged to run graver risks ourselves on their behalf. These are potentially very serious implications. For example, if we force a risky geoengineering project onto future people, we might have to compensate them with a massive climate assistance and refugee

---

intervention of this kind, the extent to which it is irreversible, and its regional and ecological impacts. Bengtsson 2006 lists some of the general worries, and several articles released since Crutzen's paper call into question some of its main claims (e.g., Matthews and Caldeira 2007, Rasch et al., 2008, Robock 2008).

46. This is something that Crutzen himself is very clear about: he argues that we ought to pursue mitigation, but we probably won't; therefore, he concludes, we should research geoengineering.

program, potentially amounting to a global safety net.[47] Similarly, if the threat of catastrophe is extreme, we may be required to forestall it by attempting risky geoengineering on ourselves.[48]

Second, concerns about additional liabilities are heightened in circumstances where we fail to do what we ought to prevent a catastrophic evil *partly because* we know in advance that a lesser evil solution will still be available to others. For example, suppose that we knowingly allow a crisis to unfold, which we could prevent by taking a nonevil option open to us. Suppose also that we do this partly because we know that others will eventually be forced to step in to prevent the coming catastrophe, even though they will have to accept significant evils in order to do so. Finally, add to this that we act in this way simply because we want to secure some modest benefits for ourselves.[49] Surely, such *calculated moral failure* would make us liable for even greater burdens, both compensatory and perhaps punitive.

(iv) Fatal Silence?

The fourth challenge to the core proposal aims to broaden the remit of geoengineering policy still further. The key idea is that the political issues raised by any decision to geoengineering would be profound, so that the proposal's silence on this topic is fatal to its moral acceptability. To motivate this idea, I offer the following simple argument. (Call this, the stalking horse argument (SHA)).[50]

---

47. Kellogg and Schneider 1974 make a similar point about unilateral geoengineering.

48. Cf. Wigley 2006. This possibility reveals that not all geoengineering proposals need manifest intergenerational moral corruption. For example, the attempt to "buy time" by geoengineering may pose more threats to current than future people. If so, they hardly manifest intergenerational buck-passing. Of course, there may be other reasons to resist them (e.g., they are very risky, or pose disproportionate threats to the world's poor).

49. Suppose, for example, that it is my child in the pond, that I let her climb in, that I then just watch the drowning (knowing that you will jump in), and that I do all this even though you are old, much further away, and risk a heart attack from the exertion while I am young and merely concerned about getting my shoes muddy.

50. The name is appropriate because the argument is intended as a placeholder, to stand in for a set of more sophisticated accounts. Such accounts might emerge from with a wide variety of views in global political philosophy (including, for example, cosmopolitanism, Rawlsian nationalism, communitarianism, and libertarianism). The SHA merely offers a general framework within which they might operate.

The first part of the argument concerns political legitimacy:

> (SHA1) The climate system is a basic background condition of human life and social organization on this planet.
> (SHA2) To engage in geoengineering would alter the human relationship to this basic background condition, and the relationship between humans subject to that condition.
> (SHA3) Hence, geoengineering raises new and profound issues of global governance.
> (SHA4) Institutions of global governance must be politically legitimate.
> (SHA5) Hence, any argument for the permissibility of geoengineering has to explain the political legitimacy of those institutions charged with making the decision to geoengineer.

At first glance, the arm the future argument appears to run afoul of this concern for political legitimacy. Because it is silent on the topic, it fails to establish that geoengineering would be permissible.[51]

This bring us to the second part of the argument, which concerns norms:

> (SHA6) A basic principle of modern political thought is that institutions of governance are legitimate only if they can be justified to those who are subject to them.
> (SHA7) Hence, geoengineering institutions must be justified to those who are subject to them.
> (SHA8) If a set of institutions is to be justified to those subject to them, it must explicitly or implicitly invoke appropriate norms of justice and community. (For example, it must not be seriously unfair or parochial in its concerns.)[52]
> (SHA9) Therefore, any successful argument for the permissibility of geoengineering must invoke appropriate norms of justice and community.

51. While the AFA ultimately concludes only that research on geoengineering is justified, in doing so it relies on the claim that geoengineering should be chosen in the nightmare situation (AFA7), and no argument about political legitimacy is made there. This suggests that the idea is that *any* decision to geoengineer would be morally appropriate in the nightmare scenario. On this claim, see below.

52. Notice that the SHA makes no assumption about how robust those norms must be. This is because it is designed to allow for a wide spectrum of views in global political philosophy.

Again, the AFA is silent on these matters. But it also faces a more specific threat:

> (SHA10) A good part of the political inertia on climate change is caused by resistance to such norms.
>
> (SHA11) Hence, there is good reason to suspect that the attempt to establish legitimate geoengineering institutions will face similar resistance.
>
> (SHA12) Hence, unless the roots of political inertia can be addressed, any decision to geoengineer is likely to be illegitimate, because it violates norms of justice and community.

The import of this last part of the argument is as follows. Since the arm the future argument not only fails to address the problem of political inertia, but also tries to operate within its constraints, it is likely to license illegitimate geoengineering, and so violations of norms of justice and community.[53] This is reason to reject that argument.[54]

(v) Lingering Inertia?

The fifth and final challenge to the core proposal concerns moral corruption and political inertia. The arm the future argument suggests that geoengineering research is a kind of insurance policy. But presumably there are *many* such policies—that is, many ways in which we might try to aid the future if we think that serious reductions in emissions will not occur. Now, as we have already seen, one issue is that only some of these policies involve geoengineering: there are other options (e.g., the Manhattan Project for alternative energy, the climate refugee project). But it is also true that there are many policies that might

---

53. Victor et al. 2009 raises the issue of legitimacy, and claims that work on establishing norms needs to be done. Still, it seems concerned only with the narrow issue of implementation, assuming that existing political arrangements remain more or less as they are. Moreover, in another recent work Victor envisions the norms arising "through a intensive process . . . best organized by the academies of sciences in the few countries with the potential to geoengineer" (Victor 2008). For obvious reasons, such a process raises concerns if the intent is to generate appropriate norms of justice and community.

54. An obvious retort would be: "But in the nightmare scenario, any decision to geoengineer would be legitimate." On this, see the core component interpretation below.

include geoengineering research as a component. These run the gamut from various "geoengineering research only" proposals (ranging from merely tolerating very limited research to launching a truly massive geoengineering "Manhattan Project") to more general approaches, where geoengineering research is included within a much more robust package (ranging from including substantial compensation to future people and the world's poor to proposing the creation of a new global order for a geoengineered world). Given this plethora of geoengineering policies, there is a real question about which one to choose.

This generates a serious worry. As stated, the arm the future argument advocates only for geoengineering research. It does not even mention wider considerations. Moreover, in context, most advocates of geoengineering seem to envisage only a moderate redirection of scientific resources.[55] In short, the core proposal tends to suggest that the relevant policy is "modest geoengineering research only." But why think that this is the salient backstop policy? The worry is this: "modest geoengineering research only" gains prominence only because it is the approach most compatible with continued intergenerational buck-passing. In essence, we'd be happy to spend a few million dollars on research our generation will probably not have to bear the risks of implementing, and we'd be even happier to think that in doing so we were making a morally serious choice in favor of protecting future generations. But thinking so hardly makes it the case. What makes us confident that our preference for "modest geoengineering research only" is not just another manifestation of moral corruption? Specifically, doesn't it seem likely that the same forces that oppose substantial mitigation measures will also oppose any other policies that involve serious costs or commitments for the current generation of the world's richer countries, including (but not limited to) substantial compensation proposals, the running of extra risks by the current generation on behalf of the future, the setting of punitive damages, and (even) huge

55. American Meteorological Society 2009. By contrast, Victor and company advocate the establishment of a "dedicated international entity overseen by the leading [scientific] academies, provided with a *large* budget." Moreover, they do see a role for social scientists and lawyers in the research that needs to be done. Still, overall, the proposal is at the modest end of what one might expect given the two previous arguments. See Victor et al. 2009.

investment in geoengineering research and deployment, if that were required?[56] More generally, doesn't the focus of the arm the future argument on scientific research conveniently obscure this problem?

3. Refining the AFA?

The last three challenges all rely on the idea that the conclusion of the arm the future argument is too narrow. But perhaps this charge is uncharitable. Specifically, although it is true that the AFA does not explicitly mention things that need to be done other than geoengineering research, as a matter of logic it does not exclude them either. So, perhaps all that is being asserted in the AFA is that we owe the future *at least* geoengineering research.

(i) The Neutrality Interpretation

Are the narrow interpretations uncharitable? It is difficult to say; the answer depends partly on how far one is willing to press the principle of charity. To begin with, while it is true that the AFA does not explicitly exclude more robust geoengineering policies, it also does not mandate them. At best, the overall lesson of the argument is underdetermined. This is worrying in itself. Given the threat of moral corruption, we should be wary of allowing such room for maneuver. More importantly, there are some indications that narrow interpretations are not uncharitable. Consider first the most natural reading of the objection, which we might call the "neutrality interpretation." According to this reading, the AFA establishes only that we owe the future research on geoengineering, and it *simply takes no position* on whether we owe them anything else as well. Is this interpretation plausible?

Two considerations suggest not. First, the context matters. In the public and political discussion of geoengineering there is virtually no mention of compensation, global justice, and the like. *Time* magazine,

---

56. This point does not require the success of the previous arguments. Perhaps we owe the future some of these things because limited geoengineering research will do no good, or because of other past injustices, or because minimal humanitarian duties require it.

for example, does not list either "geoengineering with compensation" or "reforming the global order to facilitate geoengineering" as one of its ten ideas that are changing the world. Instead, the implicit proposal is geoengineering alone, on the assumption that nothing much else changes. Moreover, to the extent that wider considerations are mentioned in the public debate, they are usually seen as obstacles only to mitigation, not to a robust geoengineering policy. For example, the *Time* article concludes: "Unless the geopolitics of global warming change soon, the Hail Mary pass of geoengineering might become our best shot;"[57] there is no thought that the geopolitics might have to change before geoengineering should be seriously considered.

Second, the arm the future argument is under internal pressure. It already requires that political inertia precludes some better options, including at least substantial mitigation, but also probably any radical alternative energy revolution. So, severe political obstacles must be assumed if geoengineering is to seem like a serious option at all. But then there is a real worry that these obstacles will be so severe that "modest research only" really is the only (politically) viable geoengineering policy. If this is not their view, proponents of the AFA need to explain why it is not.

(ii) Core Component Interpretation

Perhaps, then, friends of the arm the future argument should embrace this dark view, accepting that more robust geoengineering policy is unlikely, but still maintaining that the evil of climate catastrophe is so severe that research should be done on geoengineering regardless. The guiding idea would be that, even if more robust geoengineering policies would be better than the modest approach, the urgency of the nightmare scenario means that geoengineering research itself has absolute priority. In essence, the claim is that the moral imperative in favor of at least modest research is quite central and decisive: any such research under any conditions is better than no research at all because in the nightmare scenario we should deploy geoengineering whatever else we do, whatever the wider circumstances, even acknowledging the other moral costs. (Call this the "core component interpretation.")

57. Walsh 2008.

There is some evidence for the core component interpretation in the leading scientific work. The key advocates of research recognize that geoengineering raises broader concerns. Crutzen, for example, acknowledges that "ethical, and societal issues, regarding the climate modification scheme are many;"[58] similarly, Cicerone states: "While a strong scientific basis is necessary for geoengineering, it is far from sufficient. Many ethical and legal issues must be confronted and questions arise as to governance and monitoring."[59] Still, since these are practically the only remarks that these authors address to ethical constraints, both seem to operate under the assumption that whatever the broader concerns are, they are either insufficient to blunt the case for geoengineering research, or can be dealt with later, once research is underway.[60]

How plausible are such views? Can we really isolate the ethical and political considerations in this way? Are they really some kind of afterthought that can be safely deferred? I am not so sure. Let me begin with three preliminary thoughts. First, it would be misleading to suggest that the arm the future argument defers *all* ethical considerations: on the contrary, the lesser evil claim is itself a moral one, and it is central to the argument. So, the real question is not whether ethics can be left until later, but whether, given the central ethical argument, some related moral considerations can be safely ignored or deferred.

Second, the suggestion that the problem of political inertia is so bad that we should organize our policy around geoengineering research alone (deferring or ignoring other ethical considerations) embodies a profound skepticism that should not be conceded without argument. After all, the thought is that neither mitigation, nor adaptation, nor alternative energy, nor compensation, nor geopolitical reform, nor even more extensive geoengineering research has a realistic chance of political success. But why accept this? And if things are really so bad, why think that "moderate geoengineering research only" has better prospects?

Third, not only is such profound skepticism questionable, but its truth would have further important moral implications. If a large

---

58. Crutzen 2006, 217.

59. Cicerone 2006, 224.

60. Cicerone, of course, is explicit about this: he thinks that we should do the research first, and bring in the broader issues at a later stage.

number of alternative policies would be preferable, but none are available because of *our own* political inertia, the scale of our moral failure in choosing modest research at this point would be immense. But this suggests that the sense in which we are now *morally required* to pursue such a policy is sharply attenuated.[61] How are we to understand the force of the obligation to facilitate the lesser evil when we are so conspicuously refusing all prior (and many nonevil) moral demands? Is there not a worrying moral schizophrenia underlying this proposal?[62]

More substantively, we should be careful about the further presuppositions of the core component interpretation. First, the claim that scientific research should be the *sole* central component of any geoengineering policy requires further support. It is not clear that the ethical and geopolitical concerns with geoengineering are any less central than the scientific ones, nor that there are good pragmatic reasons to defer them. For example, arguably we have at least as strong a reason to make sure that any given geoengineering policy does not set off a major geopolitical conflict as to start preparing such a policy in the first place. Severe climate change is not the only catastrophe to be avoided, after all. Global nuclear war would also count; so, presumably, would a genocidal geoengineering intervention designed to systematically destroy the less developed countries in order to spare the developed.

Second, it may be that the moral and political concerns turn out to be *more central* than the scientific ones. On the one hand, there are reasons not to prioritize geoengineering science now. As we have seen, some claim that we simply cannot do the research necessary in the time envisioned, and others believe that the rate of technological progress is so fast that it makes little sense to try.[63] Such worries may be more pronounced if we plan to do only modest research. Moreover, it may be that the best science to be doing now involves continuing to work on the details of how the climate system works. If future generations do need to consider geoengineering, this research may be more useful to them than anything else we can deliver.

---

61. See also the wilderness survival example offered above.

62. The idea that approaches to important moral questions may exhibit some kind of schizophrenia is pioneered by Michael Stocker (1976). I cannot pursue it here.

63. Schelling 1996; Bengtsson 2006.

On the other hand, it may be that failure to deal with the moral and political considerations is more likely to thwart the effort to aid the future than failure to do the science. For example, countries will (rightly) be concerned that geoengineering science and technology might be misused. In particular, they will worry about the possibility of *predatory geoengineering*: intervention to further political goals beyond those of stabilizing the climate, and particularly those contrary to the interests of the some of the nations affected.[64] Hence, if we supply the future only with improved possibilities for geoengineering, and no account of how to implement them in an ethical way, then such concerns may paralyze deployment. This may be so even if the world's people are otherwise persuaded of the importance of geoengineering to climate stability. In short, geoengineering research may only facilitate a different "lesser evil" scenario, one where decision makers must choose between climate catastrophe and geopolitical catastrophe. This is a nastier "nightmare scenario" than that envisioned by the arm the future argument, but it is not clear that it is any less likely, or relevant to policy.

In conclusion, this section identified five specific challenges facing the core proposal: first, it is not clear that the nightmare scenario it envisages is salient; second, there are other ways in which we could prepare; third, if the scenario did arise we would owe the future more than geoengineering; fourth, the argument ignores concerns about political legitimacy and norms of global justice and community; and fifth, its narrow focus is suggestive of moral corruption. In addition, I considered the objection that some of these challenges uncharitably assume that the arm the future argument is too narrow. Specifically, on one interpretation, the argument is simply silent on wider considerations, and on another, it holds that scientific research has absolute priority. Against the former interpretation, I argued that it is implausible in context, and fails to appreciate the internal pressure placed on the AFA by its own claims about political inertia. Against the second interpretation, I claimed that it assumes a profound skepticism that ought not to go unchallenged, that it threatens a serious form of moral schizophrenia, that it falsely prioritizes scientific research over other forms of preparation for climate emergency, and that it fails to appreciate the salience of other nightmare scenarios such as those where the choice is between

---

64. How would the United States feel about geoengineering if it thought that China, Russia, or Iran were going to do it?

climate and geopolitical catastrophe. For such reasons, I conclude that as it stands the AFA is seriously underdetermined, and that efforts to rectify this face substantial obstacles. Because of this, the case it makes for both research on, and ultimate deployment of, geoengineering is far from being straightforward or irresistible.

V. ARM THE PRESENT?

There is a further, more pessimistic, lesser evil argument for geoengineering that I cannot treat fully here, but which is worth a few comments. This argument asserts that there is a significant and scientifically plausible chance that the earth is *already committed* to catastrophic climate change that even our best efforts at mitigation will not stop. On this view, it is no longer true that mitigation is by far our best policy, since it cannot forestall such a catastrophe. Instead, geoengineering needs to be considered as well. More formally, the argument runs:

> (APA1) There is a significant and scientifically plausible chance that the earth is *already committed* to catastrophic climate change that even our best efforts at mitigation will not stop.
> (APA2) Given this, then at some point (perhaps only a decade or two into the future) we may end up facing a choice between allowing catastrophic impacts to occur, or engaging in geoengineering.
> (APA3) These are both bad options.
> (APA4) But geoengineering is less bad.
> (APA5) Therefore, if we are forced to choose, we should choose geoengineering.
> (APA6) But if we do not start to do serious scientific research on geoengineering soon, then we will not be in a position to choose it should the above scenario arise.
> (APA7) Therefore, we need to start doing such research now.

Call this the "arm the present" argument (APA).

The APA departs from the AFA in several important ways. Most prominently, it drops three central assumptions: that mitigation is our best policy; that the risk of the nightmare scenario can be avoided; and that the need to geoengineer is probably at least forty years off. These departures make a significant difference.

To begin with, they imply that the APA moderates some of the worries that beset the AFA. First, if mitigation alone cannot succeed, then pursuit of geoengineering need not in itself constitute a moral failure. Hence, further compensation for the future may not be necessary.[65] Second, since the nightmare could plausibly come soon (e.g., in the next few decades), it may well be us, the current generation, who have to bear the burdens. Hence, preparing to geoengineer need not constitute intergenerational buck-passing. Most prominently, we might be more prepared to believe that the current generation is taking the potential risks of geoengineering seriously if it thinks that these are risks that it may have to take on itself. (More on this below.) Third, if the nightmare is coming soon, there is much less chance that the advance of technology over time will render current research efforts futile. Given the narrow window, perhaps we will have to do what we can with what we have.

Despite these advantages, we should remain cautious about the APA. One reason is that they come at a price. The APA (explicitly) claims that we are already committed, or may be committed, to catastrophic change, and (implicitly) suggests that no other solutions exist. In this way, it aims to overcome the "other options" challenge to the AFA. But such claims might be contested. In particular, it should be emphasized that the APA requires a much higher level of pessimism about our current predicament than the AFA, and one that probably requires going beyond the consensus scientific projections of the IPCC and other bodies. Perhaps this can be justified. Still, the justification cannot simply be assumed; it must be provided. Importantly, these more controversial projections need to be made explicit and defended as scientifically plausible. In addition, the details have implications for policy. For one thing, preparing to geoengineer in five or ten years would be a very different proposition from preparing to geoengineer in thirty, forty, or more. For another, having to geoengineer very soon, before much at all is known about the likely impacts and long-term effects, may reasonably be thought to be more risky than allowing climate change to proceed, and so undermine the "lesser evil" claim.[66]

---

65. Of course, some may still be needed if the current generation bears some responsibility for making the catastrophe inevitable through previous buck-passing.

66. For example, suppose that the potential side effects were severe and that the intervention could not be withdrawn once started without unleashing a very rapid climate change.

A second reason for caution is that the APA leaves some concerns about the AFA untouched. Nothing has been said to show that this is the right nightmare to prepare for, and that other (e.g., geopolitical or post-catastrophe) nightmares are not more salient. In addition, the argument remains silent on the vital issues of global legitimacy and norms. If anything, these latter issues become more urgent if the nightmare scenario is coming sooner, rather than later. Hence, the omission is even more surprising.

A third reason for caution is that the APA appears to make some worries about the AFA worse. Consider lingering political inertia. On the one hand, if we really might be on the threshold of a climate catastrophe that cannot be avoided through conventional means, then a broad array of preparatory measures would seem appropriate not just on the political front, but also including concrete policies on issues such as global public health, climate refugees, and humanitarian assistance. As before, a narrow focus on modest and technical geoengineering research seems unduly complacent in the face of the problem at hand, and the additional urgency of the APA makes that complacency harder to fathom.

On the other hand, we must be wary of shadow solutions (as in chapter 4). Climate change occurs in a dynamic context. Given this, we should be wary that the APA may become a self-fulfilling prophecy. Perhaps the strategy of refusing to mitigate long enough to make the nightmare scenario plausibly in the cards would suit a generation of the affluent who have predominantly self-interested or generation-relative aims. This is important in at least two ways. As we have seen, such calculated moral failure brings with it additional liabilities—for example, for compensatory and perhaps punitive damages. But it might also make one cautious about the kind of geoengineering that a calculating generation might pursue. This is a critical point. Other things being equal, we might expect such a generation to prefer geoengineering strategies that are themselves temporally dispersed, frontloaded goods. Let's find an intervention, the thought would go, where the benefits come quickly and the serious risks are substantially deferred, preferably to after we are dead. If we are going to geoengineer, but we know there are risks, buck-passing geoengineering is best.

Initially, this worry may seem farfetched. But perhaps it is not. For example, consider two claims that are often made about the advisability of sulfate injection: that such intervention is reversible, and that we have sufficient "proof of concept" from volcanic eruptions such as Mt. Pinatubo in the Philippines in 1991. Each of these claims is readily contestable. First, as noted earlier, sulfate injection might not be reversible once it is masking a significant temperature effect, since withdrawing the intervention may then result in a rapid bounce-back at least as dangerous as the climate change it is aimed at preventing. Second, sulfates injected into the stratosphere by volcanoes typically wash out of the atmosphere in a year or two, whereas effective geoengineering would need to be in place for many decades and perhaps centuries. Notice that in both cases, these objections are salient if we care about long-term impacts and long-term reversibility. If we don't, then the standard claims look more relevant.

VI. EVOLVING SHADOWS

These last points suggest that we should be more sophisticated in thinking about shadow strategies. Instead of involving only resistance to action, they can be complex and evolve over time, in response to the increasing severity of problem and the ageing of the generation in question. To illustrate this, consider the following extremely simple (and simplistic) model. (*This section can be safely skipped.*)

Suppose we have four generations of the rich and powerful whose future is encompassed by five time periods. Across these periods the generations all have the following expectations. When thinking in terms of gradual change, in Period 1 (say, 1990–2009) they anticipate no significant climate impacts; in Period 2 (2010–2029) they predict mild climate impacts; in Period 3 (2030–2049) they expect moderate impacts; in Period 4 (2050–2069) they believe that serious impacts are likely; and in Period 5 (2070–2089) they suspect severe impacts. When thinking of abrupt change, they believe that serious negative impacts are unlikely in the first three periods, but possible in Period 4, and a moderate risk in Period 5. Each generation also believes that mitigation policies in a given period only begin to have serious effects two periods later, and have the most effect on the periods after that. Suppose then that each generation only has the ability to substantially affect policy when its members are in either the 41–60 or 61–80 age group. Moreover, assume that each has only self-interested or generation-relative concerns. These are equal for most time periods, except for the last period for that group, when its members will be 81–100. The generation retains some interest in that period, but less than in others.

Suppose that the first generation is 61–80 years old in Period 1, and 81–100 years old in Period 2. (After that, its members assume that they will be dead.) Given this, the previous assumptions imply that the first generation cares only about Periods 1 and 2, and less about 2 than 1, and that it can affect policy only during Period 1. This suggests that it will be against any direct action on climate change. It has nothing to gain. It has no concerns beyond Period 2, and these impacts are already in the cards. It may, however, try to make sure that its goods are secure against mild climate change in Period 2, for example by trying to maximize its wealth and investing in military forces.

The second generation is 41–60 years old in Period 1, 61–80 in Period 2, and 81–100 in Period 3. Thus, it cares mainly about Periods 1 and 2, and less about 3, and can affect policy in Periods 1 and 2. In Period 1, it supports limited (win-win type) mitigation policies, because it believes that it can influence Period 3 conditions. These are projected to be moderate, but can be reduced to some extent. It also supports economic growth and military investment. In Period 2, it no longer supports mitigation, since this has impacts only in Period 4 and thereafter, when it is gone. Hence, in Period 2, it supports national adaptation for Period 3, and perhaps modest geoengineering research in case the moderate impacts of that period can be deferred. It also supports additional economic and military investment to secure goods in the next period.

The third generation is 20–41 years old in Period 1, 41–60 in Period 2, 61–80 in Period 3, and 81–100 in Period 4. It cares about Periods 1–4, but mainly about 2–3. It can affect policy directly only in Periods 2 and 3. In Period 2, it supports modest mitigation, beyond win-win, because the impacts in Period 4 are strong (but its support is not deep, because it cares less about Period 4 than Period 3). Concerns about Period 3 drive it to support greater geoengineering research, since the impacts there are already in the cards. It may also support national adaptation measures, as well as substantially increased military spending. In Period 3 it no longer supports mitigation, but does favor significant adaptation and military spending, as well as geoengineering research in case there are nasty surprises in Period 4.

The fourth generation is 1–20 years old in Period 1, 21–40 in Period 2, 41–60 in Period 3, 61–80 in Period 4, and 81–100 in Period 5. It cares about Periods 1–5, but mainly about 3–4. It can only affect policy directly in Periods 3 and 4. In Period 2, however, it agitates from outside of the system for substantial mitigation, since this is the period where mitigation to affect Periods 4 and 5 is most effective. In Period 3, when it has direct influence, it still supports significant mitigation, since Period 5 impacts are projected to be strong, but since Period 4 is already in the cards, and since the fourth generation will be old in Period 5, its support is less than in Period 2. However, this generation does support substantial adaptation efforts and geoengineering research in Periods 3 and 4, since it is worried about climate and geopolitical catastrophes, especially in Period 4. It also supports a very strong military.

What is the upshot of this simple dynamic model? Let us focus on mitigation and geoengineering. In Period 1 (1990–2009), the decision makers are the first and second generation. One resists action, the other favors win-win mitigation. Given this, one might expect very weak action in the period. In Period 2 (2010–2029), the second and third generations hold sway. One resists mitigation, the other supports it beyond win-win, but modestly so. Both are in favor of modest geoengineering research. Given this, the expectation is for improved, but still modest, all-around action. In Period 3 (2030–2049), the third and fourth generations decide. One resists mitigation, and the other supports a substantial effort, though less than it did before it came to power. Both support substantial adaptation efforts, military spending, and geoengineering research. Given this, mitigation efforts should improve, but the real push will be elsewhere. By Period 4 (2050–2069), much depends on what the impacts are. If they are manageable, then a stronger version of Period 3 may be expected. But if they are very severe, one might anticipate the onset of global conflict, and perhaps also an intergenerational arms race.

In summary:

PROJECTED EVOLVING SHADOW SOLUTION

TABLE 10.1

	Period 1 [1990–2009?]	Period 2 [2010–2029?]	Period 3 [2030–2049?]	Period 4 [2050–2069?]	Period 5 [2070–2089]
Generation 1	61–80 years old IN POWER Support: • Increase Security & Wealth	81–100	Dead	Dead	Dead
Generation 2		41–60 IN POWER Support: • Limited "win–win" mitigation	61–80 IN POWER Reject: • Mitigation Support: • National adaptation • Modest geoengineering research • Military investment	81–100	Dead

	1–20	21–40	41–60	61–80	81–100
Generation 3			IN POWER Support: • Modest mitigation • Greater geoengineering research • National adaptation • Military investment	IN POWER Reject: • Mitigation Support: • Stronger national adaptation • Geoengineering research • Military investment	*Dead*
Generation 4		Agitate from outside the system	IN POWER Support: Significant • Mitigation • Adaptation • Geoengineering • Military Investment	IN POWER Reject: • Mitigation Support: Significant • Adaptation • Geoengineering • Military investment	
RESULTING SHADOW POLICY	*Very weak action*	*Modest all-round action*	*Improved mitigation, substantial adaptation, geoengineering research and military spending*	*Either ramped up from period 3, global conflict, or intergenerational arms race*	*Either ramped up from period 3 & 4, global conflict, or intergenerational arms race*

The point of the model is this. In general, the expected (self-interested or generation-relative) shadow strategy evolves over time. It becomes more friendly towards mitigation as time goes on, and the threats increase, but also supports a heavier emphasis on geoengineering, adaptation, and military preparations. In doing so, it is suggestive of increasing intergenerational concern, without actually incorporating such concern. While obviously not doing enough, it appears at least to do better, even when its action is presumably biased in the wrong directions. The shadow strategy is thus subversive of more serious action on climate policy, and in a way that supports moral corruption. People can continue to say: "To be sure we've done badly in the past; but we are getting better, that's something isn't it?" And so it goes on. Specifically, the APA seems to play a crucial role here. Once the projected impacts reach a certain severity, and once they can be anticipated by a politically influential generation, there is substantial motivation towards geoengineering. But none of this is incompatible with intergenerational buck-passing, or the perfect moral storm more generally. On the contrary, it is just what one might expect.

So far, this chapter has considered a prominent rationale for pursuing geoengineering—the arm the future argument—found it less straightforward and decisive than it is usually taken to be, and suggested that the relevant issues (such as liability, compensation, political legitimacy, and lingering inertia) raise the ethical stakes in geoengineering policy. In addition, it has maintained that an initial attempt to improve on the rationale—the arm the present argument— though more promising in some respects, retains many of the basic concerns, and even exacerbates some. Finally, it has argued that there is a background worry that increased interest in geoengineering, and especially geoengineering that involves short-term benefits and long-term risks, is to be expected within the perfect moral storm as part of an evolving shadow strategy.

The burden of proof on proponents of the push to geoengineer is therefore high. Nevertheless, there remains more to be said about the lesser evil arguments for geoengineering. We have not yet considered what might be at stake in calling something an "evil." It is to this issue that I now turn.

VII. UNDERESTIMATING EVIL

In some way I know I should feel no badness over something I done like that. I see that it was—oh, you know—beyond my control, but it is still so terrible to wake up these many mornings with a memory of that, having to live with it. When you add it to all the other bad things I done, it makes everything unbearable. Just unbearable.

—Sophie (in *Sophie's Choice*) (Styron 1979, 538)

The general idea that geoengineering might be a "lesser evil," and that this justifies both research on it and ultimately deployment, is common in the fledgling literature on the topic.[67] No doubt part of its allure is that it is often seen, by both enthusiasts and detractors of geoengineering, as presenting a simple, decisive, and irresistible consideration. In the previous sections, I argued that in the context of the two most popular arguments, this is not the case. Still, one might wonder about the general idea: "Surely some lesser evil argument must work! After all, geoengineering can't be the very worst thing that could happen."

Sections VII–IX explore this intuition by directly confronting the very idea of the lesser evil. I argue that the notion is less simple, and less decisive, than first meets the eye. One reason is that the term "evil" itself bears closer scrutiny, and can mean very different things to different people, or even to the same people under different circumstances. Another is that claiming that an evil should be chosen because it is lesser need not be the end of the moral story. On some ethical views, those who choose some kinds of evil bear special moral burdens. This adds an extra dimension to the decision to geoengineer, and indeed climate decisions more generally, which the simple appeal to the lesser evil leaves out.

What does it mean to choose the lesser evil? What is at stake? We can begin by acknowledging that there is something morally appealing about the notion of choosing the lesser evil in a situation of grave crisis.

67. It manifests itself in a number of distinct arguments, including the AFA, the APA, and the "buying time" argument (see Gardiner 2011b).

Such a choice can seem heroic, and even to display a deep moral serious-ness. One reason for this is that many people believe that there are cir-cumstances in which normal rules must be overridden because the negative consequences are so severe. Another is that a strong rigorism about moral rules often seems morally unattractive, perhaps even an irrational fetish.

To illustrate the attractiveness of these thoughts, consider a standard varient of the case of the enquiring murderer famously discussed by Kant. In this varient, you are confronted with a Nazi stormtrooper asking whether you are hiding Jews in your house. As it happens, you are. Since lying is normally immoral, are you morally bound to tell the stormtrooper the truth? Many people think not. Sticking to the normal rules in such cases, they believe, would be deeply bizarre: a morally serious person could not do such a thing. Similarly, the lesser evil argument can seem overwhelmingly appealing in the case of geoengineering. Faced with a possible catastrophe, why wouldn't one try geoengineering? Wouldn't failure to do so constitute an irrational fetish?

Clearly, such concerns are important. But matters are not as simple here as they initially seem. To see this, consider three obstacles that a lesser evil argument must seek to overcome.

1. Opacity

The first is the problem of opacity. In the abstract form in which they are usually presented, lesser evil arguments are often inscrutable.[68] For one thing, we are asked simply to compare two bad options and rank one as lesser; but we are not usually asked for the reasons for our rankings. For another, the options themselves are frequently underdescribed. Such opacity creates concerns. Perhaps people's conceptions of the options differ. They implicitly fill in the details of the lesser and greater evils in ways that pick out what features would be most salient to them, and these are

---

68. This worry is especially relevant in the case of geoengineering, where the lesser evil claim is typically not so much argued for as simply asserted as decisive in a sentence or two before the discussion moves on. Of course, lesser evil arguments need not be opaque; but—for the reasons mentioned below—we should pay special attention to opacity when the threat of moral corruption is high.

not the same. Moreover, perhaps their underlying concerns are at odds. Even where they agree on the salient features, they take them to be salient for very different reasons, and where this has different implications.

Such things matter for two reasons. First, any apparent consensus in favor of a lesser evil argument may turn out to be dangerously shallow. Though there is outward agreement that some generic form of action (such as geoengineering) would be permissible under some circumstances, there is deep, but implicit, disagreement about what those circumstances would be. Suppose, for example, that some scientists believe that geoengineering would be permissible in order to prevent the greater evil of a mass extinction, but some economists believe that it would be permissible to prevent the greater evil of a short-term drop in economic growth. In that case, their apparent consensus on the need to pursue geoengineering research may turn out to be shallow. Assent to the lesser evil argument would mask deep disagreements about the appropriate goals of geoengineering policy.[69]

The second reason that opacity matters is that it is likely to obscure the real moral arguments. The true justificatory work is done by the underlying reasons together with whatever features of the underdescribed options the person is regarding as salient. It is these that underlie that person's assent to the basic form of words "lesser evil." Hence, appealing to the lesser evil functions not as an independent argument in favor of some policy, but rather as a convenient umbrella term that covers a number of different considerations. But if this is the case, then such an appeal might fail to do real normative work; indeed, it might hinder that work by drawing attention away from the real justifications for policy.[70]

69. Even among scientists, there are variations in the description of the catastrophic evil to be averted. Is it runaway temperature change, caused by a convergence of positive feedbacks that make mitigation no longer possible? Is it a major abrupt change, such as a shutdown of the thermohaline circulation, or a sudden collapse of the Greenland ice sheet? Is it accelerating extinctions caused by linear climate change? These are distinct scenarios, and may call for quite different emergency measures.

70. Of course, the lesser evil argument might play an appropriate role in summarizing something like an overlapping consensus on a given policy. But this argument would need to be made independently, and would face a substantial burden of proof. The worry is that the lesser evil argument as usually stated is an attempt to avoid meeting that burden.

2. Denial

The second obstacle facing lesser evil arguments is the problem of denial. Some may simply refuse to accept that the lesser evil should be chosen under any circumstances: a lesser evil is still an evil, they will say, and therefore not to be chosen. This, of course, is Kant's attitude to the enquiring murderer case. One ought not to lie *simpliciter* is his position, and let the chips fall where they may.

Now, most people do not find Kant's position compelling in this case. But we should be wary of simply rejecting it out of hand. For one thing, even in the case of the inquiring murderer, it is difficult to *show* how or why an uncompromising attitude is irrational, or otherwise in error. More importantly, even if most of us do not agree with Kant in that case, there are situations in which the same kind of attitude seems more plausible. For example, suppose some great evil could be prevented if you would just kill your own grandmother in cold blood. (If necessary, embellish the case. For example, imagine that your grandmother is morally innocent and that the killing would be against her wishes.) Is it so obvious that you should do this? Surely one can understand why a person might resist, and for reasons that seem at least possibly morally appropriate.

The possibility of resistance has important implications. First, it suggests that lesser evil arguments might turn out to be logically invalid: one cannot infer from the fact that an evil is "lesser" in some sense that it ought to be chosen. Second, it implies that rival attitudes to the relevant evil will be at the heart of many disputes about lesser evil cases. Those who resist lesser evil arguments are likely to protest that such arguments typically assume an *impoverished* account of evil—such as the earlier "something one has serious reason to avoid"—and that it is only because of this that they begin to look plausible at all.[71] In short, lesser evil arguments underestimate what it is to call something an evil.

---

71. This concern resonates with familiar complaints about the way economists tend to reduce moral wrongs to mere "costs," as, for example, when they insist on seeing fines as mere fees. See Goodin 1994.

3. The Unthinkable

At first glance, it may seem that these points stand or fall with the assertion of the strong and uncompromising view that evil ought never to be done. But in fact one need not go this far. In particular, finer-grained distinctions are possible.

Consider, for example, what Bernard Williams says about the category he calls the "unthinkable": "Entertaining certain alternatives, regarding them indeed as alternatives, is itself something that [someone] regards as dishonourable or morally absurd."[72] Perhaps not all "evils" are also unthinkable, and those that are not might sometimes be chosen. Still, if some evils are unthinkable, then one cannot be confident that lesser evil arguments will always go through. Perhaps some evils are "lesser" than others in some respects, but still nonetheless unthinkable.[73] In that case, merely showing that an evil is lesser will not be enough to justify action.

In this case, Williams' focus is not on what should be done, but rather on what options should be entertained. His central claim is that it is dishonorable to regard certain options as legitimate alternatives.[74] Importantly, this thought seems pertinent in the current case. One can certainly see someone arguing that *advance planning* for a nightmare scenario is itself morally inappropriate when that nightmare is to be brought on by *one's own future moral failure*. Hence, some will say that it is morally inappropriate to start planning for geoengineering when mitigation and adaptation are still on the table; instead, all our energies and efforts should go into preventing the nightmare scenario—where geoengineering starts to look acceptable—from arising.

To illustrate the appeal of this attitude, consider a related lesser evil argument. Call this the *climate survival clan*:[75]

---

72. See the second epigraph to this chapter, and Smart and Williams 1973.

73. For example, suppose that coldblooded murder is a lesser evil than genocide, but still unthinkable.

74. Note that even if one thinks that this claim is too uncompromising, it might be weakened if to say that *under some circumstances* it is morally shameful to regard an evil option as a legitimate alternative, *even if perhaps in other situations it is not*. The basic point would remain.

75. This is my example rather than Williams'.

If very substantial progress on emissions reduction is not made soon, then the world may plunge into chaos because of catastrophic climate change. If this happens, my family may face a choice between starvation and fighting for its own survival. Both starvation and fighting for survival are bad options. But fighting for survival is less bad. Therefore, if we are forced to choose, we should choose fighting for survival. But if we do not begin serious preparations for fighting for survival now, then we will not be in a position to choose that option should the circumstance arise. Therefore, my family needs to commence serious preparations for fighting for survival now.

This argument is structurally similar to the AFA. So, should we arm ourselves, build fortified camps in the boonies, withdraw our children from school and train them instead in wilderness survival and combat, and so on? Wouldn't this be a lesser evil than entering the world of climate chaos unprepared? Perhaps. Still, devoting ourselves to such a strategy at this point in time seems not merely unwarranted, but also an unacceptable evasion of moral responsibility. The survival argument, with its focus on the lesser evil, ignores this, and so is to be criticized. This suggests a general flaw in hypothetical lesser evil arguments, and one that the arm the future argument may share.

Finally, Williams goes on to suggest a further worry about the limits of moral reasoning. Perhaps there are some situations so extreme that it would be insane to plan for them, because morality somehow gives out:

[Someone might] find it unacceptable to consider what to do in certain conceivable situations. Logically, or indeed empirically conceivable they may be, but they are not to him morally conceivable, meaning by that that their occurrence as situations presenting him with a choice would represent not a special problem in his moral world, but something that lay beyond its limits. For him, there are certain situations so monstrous that the idea that the processes of moral rationality could yield an answer in them is insane: they are situations which so transcend in enormity the human business of moral deliberation that from a moral point of view it cannot matter any more what happens. Equally, for him to spend time thinking what one would decide if one were in such a situation is also insane, if not merely frivolous.[76]

76. Smart and Willliams 1973.

Now, it seems at least possible that some lesser evil situations are of this sort. (Consider, for example, the one where you must choose to kill your own grandmother in cold blood.) Still, whether the decision to geoengineer is one of these is a more difficult question. Presumably, the answer depends in part on how risky one thinks that a particular method of geoengineering is likely to be, and what kinds of obligations to the future and to other species one thinks we have. In my own view, the nightmare scenario envisioned by the core proposal is not nearly so extreme that "from a moral point of view it cannot matter any more what happens." Still, something related to Williams' concern is relevant. What are we to say about "monstrous" situations that strain normal moral deliberation?

4. Marring Evils

This thought leads to the third obstacle facing lesser evil arguments. As it happens, many people, Williams included, believe that even actions that are normally "unthinkable" must sometimes be done.[77] Yet, even when there is agreement that certain evils are of this sort, people have different attitudes to the relevant moral emergencies. One might be aptly described in terms of the well-known bumper sticker slogan, "shit happens." On this view, the occurrence of a lesser evil situation is an unfortunate fact about the world, more serious than, but otherwise akin to, other shifts in empirical circumstances. But another attitude is quite different. To see this, consider the following classic case. In his novel *Sophie's Choice*, William Styron tells the tragic tale of Sophie, a mother who is put in a situation where she must choose between saving one of her children or submitting both to be killed by the Nazis. Sophie chooses to save her son, but relinquish her daughter. The novel explores her subsequent life as she deals with the fact of her choice and its consequences. Ultimately, Sophie kills herself, unable to come to terms with the decision she made.

77. Consider, for example, Williams's famous example of Jim and the Indians. Jim faces the option of shooting one Indian or doing nothing, with the result that Pedro will shoot twenty. Williams famously concludes that Jim should shoot the Indian. But he chastises utilitarianism for reaching the same conclusion too easily, without realizing what is at stake for Jim in such a decision.

Sophie's Choice is a modern literary classic. But it is also of philosophical interest. Most people agree that Sophie's suicide is tragic. For many, this is because they believe that she wrongly blames herself for the death of her daughter. The situation in which she found herself was, it is said, monstrously difficult. Nevertheless, she did the right thing in choosing, and ought not to be wracked by guilt. Others are to blame, not Sophie. She should recognize that and feel better about herself. Perhaps she should even praise herself for being able to make the decision to save at least one person's life (her son's) under such emotionally difficult circumstances. (After all, "shit happens.") For others, however, Sophie's suicide is tragic in a more traditional sense. Sophie does not make a moral mistake. Even though she makes a defensible (perhaps even the best[78]) decision in that terrible situation, and even though she bears no responsibility for being in it, still she is right to think that her choice carries negative moral baggage. Though she is not to be blamed for the decision in the usual way, it is nevertheless true that her life is irredeemably *marred* by it.[79] Though we might admire Sophie in certain respects, no one would say that she lives the kind of life that it is desirable for a human being to live. No one would want to be Sophie.[80] Interestingly, this second attitude seems to be Sophie's own, and the one that ultimately leads her to suicide. She says: "In some way I know I should feel no badness over something I done like that. I see that it was—oh, you know—beyond my control, but it is still so terrible to wake up these many mornings with a memory of that, having to live with it. When you add it to all the other bad things I done, it makes everything unbearable. Just unbearable."[81]

---

78. In my own view, Sophie's choice is probably not the best; still, I do not think that we should blame her for it, nor do I believe that it is the existence of some alternative that produces the marring effect.

79. Hursthouse 1999, 73–5.

80. This is so even if we agree that Sophie did the right thing, and perhaps even if we think that there is a sense that she made a heroic choice. Even if we think that our everyday behavior falls morally far short of Sophie's choice, there is still a clear sense in which we don't want to be Sophie. We'd rather fall short under normal circumstances than make a heroic choice in this one. It is not clear whether this attitude is best characterized as a moral one, or one which seeks to restrict the relevance of morality. But it is clearly an evaluative one.

81. Styron 1979, 538.

The idea that a life can be marred from a moral point of view, and possibly irredeemably, is a controversial one in moral theory. So, let me make three quick points about how I'm understanding the claim. First, I propose using the phrase *marring evil* in a special, technical sense, to refer to a negative moral evaluation of an agent's action (or actions), that is licensed when the agent (justifiably) chooses the lesser evil in a morally tragic situation, and which results in a serious negative moral assessment of that agent's life considered as a whole.[82]

Second, I propose this because I assume that the evil that torments Sophie is a special instance of a more general category of ills. People's lives are subject to serious negative evaluation even when their choices are not "forced" by circumstance in the way that a lesser evil decision is said to be. For one thing, normally evil actions—such as those of premeditated murder or genocide—stain or tarnish lives too. For another, some believe that a person's life can be compromised by circumstances beyond their control even if they themselves make no evil choices.[83] In short, "marring" is just one way in which a life may be morally compromised, or "tarnished."[84] Third, we need not assume that all tarnishings (or marrings) are irredeemable. Perhaps some can be outweighed or expunged (e.g., by other good actions), with the result that a positive (or neutral) overall evaluation of the agent's life is restored. Still, some tarnishings may be irredeemable. I will call these "blighting evils."

With these points in mind, let us return to Sophie. The dispute over how to understand her choice is sometimes described as turning on the question of whether or not there are genuine moral dilemmas: situations in which an agent cannot help but act in a way that is morally reprehensible in at least some sense. Those in the first camp say that there are no genuine moral dilemmas—and so no marring evils in my sense—those in the second say that there are.

82. I assume that this definition requires refinement. But this is not the place for such work.

83. Aristotle, for example, claims that even though Priam of Troy was virtuous, his life was not a flourishing one. The tragedy that befell his family and city in the Trojan War was sufficient to undermine that claim. (See Aristotle 2009, Book I.9–10).

84. The distinctions to be made between ways in which lives may be tarnished raises interesting questions in ethical theory, but these cannot be pursued here. For present purposes, the mere signaling of the category, and the fact that it does not automatically disappear in a "nightmare scenario," is all that is needed.

Now, I suspect that many of you are already thinking that a discussion of *Sophie's Choice* seems oddly (perhaps even shockingly) out of place in a paper on climate change and geoengineering. I admit that Sophie's choice is an extreme case. Nevertheless, I mention it because attention to the dispute about genuine moral dilemmas helps us to see some important issues within the ethics of geoengineering.

First, the dispute helps to make sense of some of the angst present within the debate. Consider the contrast between those who see geoengineering as merely one among a set of possible policy options—to be chosen simply on the basis of a set of normal policy criteria, such as technical feasibility, likely side effects and cost-effectiveness—and those who are reluctant to consider geoengineering even as a last resort, and even then are unhappy about having to do so. My suggestion is that there may be a connection between, on the one hand, the first group and those who deny the existence of genuine moral dilemmas, and, on the other hand, the second group and those who accept that such dilemmas exist. This connection might explain why, when the first group goes on about technical feasibility and the like, these arguments do not really seem to address the core concerns of the second. Even when it is said that geoengineering is a necessary evil, the second group are not happy; they don't seem to process the term "necessary evil" in the same way.[85]

Second, introducing the categories of tarnishing, marring, and blighting evils enriches the debate. These senses of "evil" are distinct from, and much more morally loaded than, the modest sense of "evil" as "something one has serious reason to avoid." But they are also less uncompromising than that implied by the claims that evils ought never to be done, that they should never even be considered, or that they exceed the bounds of moral deliberation. Tarnishing, marring, and blighting evils

85. For whatever it is worth, I have found that when I present this paper in public, the audience is divided on whether there are such things as marring evils and whether geoengineering might constitute one. Typically, one third will have no truck with marring evils at all. Of the rest (who believe that marring is possible), somewhere between two-thirds and one third think that geoengineering may be a marring evil. This wide range may reflect moderate disciplinary biases. On average, mainstream economists and political scientists seem less friendly to marring arguments for geoengineering, whereas scientists, environmentalists, and the public at large are more so. Within moral philosophy, consequentialists are traditionally opposed to marring arguments, while virtue ethicists and some deontologists are more sympathetic.

can often be thought about, and perhaps sometimes ought to be chosen. Still, they come with considerable moral baggage, which a morally serious person cannot ignore. If we suppose for a moment that there are, or might be, such evils, then precisely how to categorize the "evils" at the center of a lesser evil argument becomes an important issue.

Third, if such evils exist, this raises a question about whether putting someone in a marring situation—one where they might be required (or have strong reason) to incur such an evil—constitutes a special kind of moral wrong, or at least one which greatly increases the moral gravity of the action. Surely, the thought goes, there is a significant moral difference between putting others in a situation where they must choose between (normally) bad options, and putting them in a situation where their choice will tarnish or even blight their lives. Other things being equal, we have much stronger reason to avoid the latter situation, and so are liable to greater censure if we fail to do so. Indeed, this reason may be so strong that ignoring it—and so unnecessarily inflicting a marring choice on others—itself counts as an evil that blights *our* lives.

This third issue may turn out to be especially serious in the case of climate change. Consider just two kinds of cases. First, perhaps the inaction of some countries (e.g., the high-emitting developed countries) will inflict marring choices on the people of other countries (e.g., the lower emitting developing countries). For example, if current and past emissions cause Bangladesh to flood and force its people to migrate, it is not beyond the realm of possibility that some parents (or the Bangladeshi government, or other agencies) may be placed in situations similar to the one confronting Sophie. Second, the current generation, by exploiting its temporal position, may put some future generation in a position where it must make a marring choice. For example, perhaps our actions will cause that future generation to confront an abrupt climate change so severe that they must choose to burn a large amount of fossil fuel in order to prevent an immediate humanitarian disaster, even knowing that this will then impose further catastrophes on some later generation.[86] In this case, we are responsible for putting the first future generation in a position where it must inflict a great harm on the second, and so mar itself. This seems a serious moral wrong. It may also be a blighting evil.

86. See chapter 6.

VIII. AN ATMOSPHERE OF EVIL

The arrogance of human beings is just astounding.

—Oceanographer Sallie Chisholm (quoted in Monastersky 1995)

Of course, none of the above explains why geoengineering specifically might bring on a marring evil. Presumably, successfully answering this question would require a much larger project. Moreover, since here we are only trying to survey the moral terrain, an answer is not strictly necessary. Still, since the very idea of marring is controversial in itself, and perhaps especially so when applied to geoengineering, it may be worth at least gesturing at the shape the relevant reasons may take.

Some possibilities emerge from considering how many climate scientists (some specifically responding to the core proposal) argue against geoengineering. First, it is common to imply that pursuing geoengineering manifests arrogance and recklessness. For example, Jeff Kiehl writes: "On the issue of ethics, I feel we would be taking on the *ultimate state of hubris* to believe we can control Earth. We (the industrially developed world) would essentially be telling the (rest of the) world *not to worry* about our insatiable use of energy."[87] Similarly, Stephen Schneider argues: "Rather than pin our hopes on the *gamble* that geoengineering will prove to be inexpensive, benign and administratively sustainable over centuries—*none of which can remotely be assured now*—in my value system I would prefer to start to lower the human impact on the earth through more conventional means."[88]

Second, climate scientists frequently claim that pursuing geoengineering represents a kind of blindness, a failure on the part of humanity to address the underlying problem. For example, Kiehl says, "In essence we are treating the symptom, not the cause. Our species needs to begin to address the cause(s) behind the problem."[89] Moreover, it is often suggested that this reluctance to address the underlying problem is somehow short-sighted, obstinate, or even bizarre. For example, Schneider likens the

87. Kiehl 2006, 228; emphasis added.
88. Schneider 1996, 300; emphasis added.
89. Kiehl 2006, 228.

climate change problem to heroin addiction, and compares the decision to pursue geoengineering to choosing "a massive substitution of [planetary] methadone" over "slowly and surely" weaning the addict.[90] Similarly, Gavin Schmidt offers the analogy of a small boat being deliberately and dangerously rocked by one of its passengers. Another traveler offers to use his knowledge of chaotic dynamics to try to counterbalance the first, but admits that he needs huge informational resources to do so, cannot guarantee success, and may make things worse. Schmidt concludes: "So is the answer to a known and increasing human influence on climate an ever more elaborate system to control the climate? *Or should the person rocking the boat just sit down?*"[91]

Two features of these criticisms of geoengineering strike me as especially intriguing. The first is the hint that at least one core wrong associated with geoengineering is best captured by gesturing at certain character traits such as hubris, recklessness, and an obstinate resistance to look at the central problem. The second feature is the tendency to see the moral issue as one which faces us as members of collectives: e.g., whole societies, the industrialized world, or even humanity considered as such. In short, one worry that these scientists have about the decision to pursue geoengineering concerns what it might show about us: our lives, our communities, our generation, our countries, and ultimately our species. What kind of people would make the choice to geoengineer? Would they be reckless, hubristic, and obstinate people? Would this be a generation or country consumed by its own (perhaps shallow) conception of its own interests, and utterly indifferent to the suffering and risks imposed on others? Would it be a species that was failing to respond to a basic evolutionary challenge?

Such concerns are relevant to political inertia over climate change in general. On one natural way of looking at things, groups with which many of us identify are predominantly responsible for creating the problem, are currently largely ignoring the problem, and are also refusing to address the problem in the best way possible because of a strong attachment to lesser values. These are serious moral concerns, and give rise to substantial moral criticism. Who would want to be associated

---

90. Schneider 1996, 299–300.
91. Schmidt 2006, responding to Crutzen. Emphasis added.

with such groups and implicated in such behavior? Are we not saddened, even ashamed? Is this not a tarnishing evil?

Perhaps. But what about geoengineering specifically? Why might choosing it tarnish a life? Again, let me emphasize that this is not the place for a full account, and that such an account is not necessary for current purposes. Still, we can gesture at three worries that give us some sense of what such an account might look like.

Consider first those who cause the nightmare scenario to arise. One way in which our lives might be tarnished would be if the commitment to geoengineering becomes a vehicle through which we (e.g., our nation and/or our generation) try to disguise our exploitation of other nations, generations, and species. Specifically, our willingness to facilitate (or engage in) geoengineering might show that we have failed to take on the challenge facing us, and instead have succumbed to moral corruption. Indeed, the decision to geoengineer might reveal *just how far we are prepared to go* to avoid confronting climate change directly, and this may constitute a tarnishing, even blighting, evil. Think about what people mean when, in tragic circumstances, they say: *"Has it really come to this?"*[92]

Consider now those who choose geoengineering as the lesser evil in some nightmare scenario. Why might this be marring? One reason is that through their choice they inflict grave harms on innocents that may otherwise not have occurred. Suppose, for example, that geoengineering really does cause less harm than climate catastrophe, but that this harm accrues to different individuals.[93] Or suppose that geoengineering saves humanity, but only through the destruction of many other species and ecosystems. Suppose, for example, that it involved the extreme of creating the dome world scenario (see chapter 1), and that this required either leaving the earth's other living creatures to burn, or else actively bringing about their destruction (e.g., through a radical form of terraforming). In these cases, when we choose geoengineering innocents are harmed through our agency, and this may be a marring evil, even if it is in some sense a "lesser" evil overall. One can certainly imagine it being

92. Another root of tarnishing would be if geoengineering led to the infliction of marring choices on others. See above.

93. Robock 2008.

something that people find, as the expression goes, *hard to live with*. Indeed, this is a prominent feature of other marring cases.[94]

Finally, and more controversially, consider the position of humanity more generally. Pursuing geoengineering may be taken as a sign that we have failed to meet a basic challenge, and should be saddened or ashamed for that reason. The thought is this. Humanity is, in geological and evolutionary terms, a recent arrival on the planet, and is currently undergoing an amazingly rapid expansion in terms of sheer population numbers, technological capabilities, and environmental impact. A basic question that faces us as humans, then, is whether, amidst all this, we can meet the challenge of adapting to the planet on which we live. In this context, the decision to geoengineer might be taken to show that we have, to a significant extent, failed; and such a failure may be blighting.[95]

More specifically, suppose the basic idea is that, as a species, we already had a perfectly serviceable planet to live on, but now we are undermining that. We have, in elementary terms, "fouled the nest." We could clean it up—that would be the most direct approach, the one most likely to work—but so intent are we on continuing our messy habits, that we will pursue any means to avoid that, even those that impose huge risks on others and involve further alienation from nature.[96] In this case, so the

94. Perhaps what is at stake in Williams' Jim and the Indians case is a marring evil. Note that even though the Indian that Jim shoots would have died anyway, Jim's complicity in the death makes a moral difference, even if only to Jim.

95. Of course, the charge of failure is controversial. In this context, "adaptation" is a complex and value-laden term. First, the basic survival of the species might be one necessary component. Surely (pace Lenman 2002) it would be grounds for shame if our inaction led to extinction. Fortunately, most scientists do not think that this is likely, even under extreme scenarios. Still, the more credible extremes are not very comforting. For example, James Lovelock (2006) believes that the worst-case scenario is a few hundred thousand humans hunkered down at the poles. Who would want to be implicated in bringing that about? Second, alternatively, some might say that it would count as adaptation if a few million humans survived, living in huge artificial domes atop a desolate planet. But this also seems to miss something. Many believe that part of the human challenge is to develop an appropriate relationship to nature, including to other species inhabiting the earth. Surviving in domes does not satisfy that demand. If this is the best that humanity can manage, it might still be a source of sadness and shame. Though the core proposal is far from a commitment to domes, it begins to enter similar territory.

96. Indeed, perhaps we are pushed in this direction by the very factors (e.g., ways of life, institutions, values) that caused the mess in the first place.

thought goes, the decision to geoengineer constitutes the crossing of a new threshold on the spectrum of environmental recklessness, and so embodies a recognition of our continued and deepening failure. On this view, it is natural to think that it will be a sad and shameful day in the life of humanity when such a decision is made, that (if the choice is "forced" as a lesser evil) such a decision mars the lives of those who make it, that it blights those who bring about the nightmare situation, and perhaps even that it tarnishes humanity as such.

In summary, I have gestured at three reasons for thinking that the decision to engage in geoengineering might involve tarnishing. Some of these are, of course, highly controversial, and embody distinctive perspectives on global environmental issues.[97] Still (I emphasize again), the purpose of this discussion is not to defend such views, but merely to survey the moral terrain. The general point is only that simple lesser evil arguments fail *even to consider the possibility* that there might be such things as tarnishing evils. Thus, such arguments are too quick, and obscure important ethical issues. More specifically, if we focus on the core proposal in its most abstract and simplistic form, we might miss much of what is at stake in the decision to geoengineer.

IX. "BUT . . . SHOULD WE DO IT?"

In conclusion, the purpose of this chapter has been to survey some of the moral landscape relevant to geoengineering. This has been done through an exploration of the ubiquitous idea that geoengineering is some kind of "lesser evil," and that this offers a straightforward and decisive reason for pursuing it.

In the first half of the chapter, I considered two popular arguments of this kind, the arm the future argument and (to a lesser extent) the arm the present argument. I argued that contrary to initial appearances, these arguments are neither simple, nor irresistible. First, they assume

97. We should not be too quick to conclude this. For example, it may be tempting for consequentialists to claim that recognizing marring evils and "fouling the nest" would be irrational on their view. But we should respect Jamieson's dictum. Perhaps recognizing these things brings about the best consequences in the long run, and so is justified on consequentialist grounds.

much that is contentious, including that geoengineering is our only (or most central) option, that it is less risky than other options, and that the time to pursue geoengineering is now. Second, they are overly narrow in their focus. For example, they do not even consider the serious issues of compensation, political legitimacy, and the role of political inertia in framing geoengineering policy.

In the second half of the chapter, I addressed the more general idea that sometimes lesser evils must be done, and claimed that there is more to this idea than first meets the eye. For one thing, the idea obscures deeper moral considerations, such as what is at stake in calling something evil, whether evils ought sometimes to be chosen, whether there are marring choices, and whether putting others in situations where they are forced to choose a marring evil is an extra, and special kind of, moral wrong. For another, the idea is seriously underdetermined. When presented (as it often is) simply as a generic idea, with the presumption that this is enough to justify moving forward on geoengineering, the claim that lesser evils must sometimes be done surreptitiously assumes that any consensus on the need to geoengineer will not be shallow, but deep enough to guide policy. But such an assumption is dubious in the context of the perfect moral storm, and dangerous given that moral corruption is likely. In such a setting, a generic appeal to the lesser evil runs the risk of being glib, cavalier, and even perhaps morally irresponsible.

What lessons should we draw from this discussion? One we cannot draw is that no lesser evil argument for research on, or deployment of, geoengineering can ever succeed. Our survey of the terrain raises serious difficulties for such arguments, but does not show that these cannot be overcome. Still, progress has been made. First, the survey dispels the illusion of irresistibility, and hence shifts the burden of proof back onto proponents of geoengineering. Second, it strongly implies that, if we pursue geoengineering at all, then a broad range of obligations—far beyond mere scientific research—must be considered. These flow from our responsibility for the climate problem, our failure to choose nonevil solutions, our creation of nightmare scenarios that are potentially marring for others, and our infliction on the future of the special liabilities and political realities associated with geoengineering. Third, the discussion suggests that these extended obligations are likely to be demanding, involving not just technological assistance, but also substantial compensation, and wider commitments to norms of global justice and community.

Some will want to craft such points into a new case for geoengineering, suggesting that the survey reveals some shapes that such a defense might take. One obvious thought is that perhaps geoengineering can be justified as part of some broad climate policy portfolio that includes many of the alternative policies I mention, suitably embedded in wider ethical and political concerns. For example, perhaps what should be pursued is geoengineering that embraces claims of compensation and norms of global justice.

This approach is tempting and may be correct; still, we must be cautious. First, the urge to find *some* kind of argument for geoengineering should give us pause. Is this a policy in search of a rationale? Are we simply looking for an argument that will justify geoengineering, rather than seeing where the arguments lead? In the perfect moral storm, this is a worrying thought.

Second, and more importantly, the idea that such a "fully moralized" lesser evil argument might justify the pursuit of geoengineering may be more interesting in theory than in practice. Politically, such an approach seems likely to curb the current enthusiasm for geoengineering in many quarters, restoring many of the same motivational obstacles that face conventional climate policies, and introducing further moral and political objections. Indeed, for many the mere mention of wider and more demanding obligations will be enough to undermine geoengineering's status as any kind of "lesser" evil, all things considered. Given this, we must take seriously the possibility that robustly moralized lesser evil solutions will be even less available politically than the nonevil options.

Third, this, of course, tends to shift the focus back to modest geoengineering research only. Nevertheless, it suggests a crucial point. Now it has been revealed that such an approach counts as the lesser evil only in a severely attenuated sense. Modest geoengineering research only is likely to be *far down the list even of evil options*. Talk of the lesser evil covers this up. In a perfect moral storm, this is an important conclusion. As Franklin might put it, "how convenient."

This concludes my attempt to motivate the problem of moral corruption. Hence, the account of the perfect moral storm is complete. In Part F, I consider how modest ethical theorizing might help us to navigate the way forward, especially through defensive moral and political philosophy, and then turn to summing up.

PART F

What Now?

CHAPTER 11

Some Initial Ethics for the Transition

The bulk of this book focuses on describing the general ethical challenge posed by climate change, rather than responding to it. It also claims that a full response requires deep work in moral and political philosophy, since one basic component of the challenge is our lack of robust theory in many of the key areas, such as intergenerational ethics, international justice, environmental philosophy and scientific uncertainty. Despite this, it does not follow that ethics has nothing substantive to say about our current predicament, and the shape of the direction forward. This chapter illustrates the potential for such work through a brief commentary on five central aspects of climate policy: scientific skepticism, responsibility for past emissions, the setting of mitigation and adaptation targets, and the relationship between individual and collective responsibility. In doing so, it urges a modest redirection of the public debate.

Before beginning, let us frame the discussion with a distinction. Roughly-speaking, projects in *ideal* ethical theorizing aim to work out the best way in which to deal with some domain or issue in an otherwise neutral (or even moderately encouraging) practical setting.[1] As a result, such projects often assume that many current and contingent constraints on change - such as the existence of background injustice, maladapted institutions, or deeply hostile agents - can, from the point of view of theory, be set aside. For example, in ideal theory we are free to envision the target at which people of reasonably goodwill would like to aim, without thought as to how or even if this aim might be feasible under current real world conditions.

---

1. Rawls says ideal theory "assumes strict compliance and works out the principles that characterize a well-ordered society under favorable circumstances" (Rawls 1999, 216). Presumably, strict compliance and well-orderedness might be subsumed under "favorable circumstances". However, I am not concerned with pursuing a precise definition here.

By contrast, projects in the *ethics of the transition* articulate how we might proceed ethically starting from existing, and sometimes deeply constrained or ethically compromised, social realities in the direction of better solutions and general circumstances.[2] Sometimes such projects operate in the service of a robust ideal theory, but more often the challenge is how to muddle through even in the absence of a guiding "grand theory." Either way, the ethics of the transition aims to identify how policies should be targeted and assessed given our actual constrained starting position. This is typically done through the use of intermediate normative criteria, parameters, benchmarks, and so on.

In the case of the global environmental crisis, this project seems especially important. For one thing, we lack robust theory in many of the relevant areas (e.g., intergenerational ethics, global justice) even when these are considered in isolation. For another, these areas require integration, both with each other and with other domains where we are more confident. Sensing that modern life has significant vices, but also major virtues, many hope to transform serious environmental concern into social change. But they also want this transformation to be responsive to, reflective of, and integrated with wider values. Given this, there is a need for an ethics of the transition that tries to synthesize such concerns in new and creative ways. In the absence of a grand integrative theory, in the interim we must pursue more indirect strategies. These include searching for ethical constraints by identifying intuitively clear cases of failure[3], trying to articulate those constraints more fully, searching for levels of overlapping consensus across existing theories, and defending such benchmarks against the forces of moral corruption.

In my view, ideal theory has an important role to play in addressing the global environmental crisis. But this chapter will focus on how we might make some modest progress with the ethics of the transition, focusing specifically on climate change. Section I points out how the foundational international agreement already takes a first step in that

---

2. For example, some contemporary work in cosmopolitan political theory imagines what a world would (and should) look like that transcended state institutions and boundaries. This is work in ideal theory. By contrast, other cosmopolitan writing considers how existing institutions might be reformed to function in ways either more in keeping with cosmopolitan ideals, or more likely to lead eventually to better cosmopolitan structures (and hopefully both).

3. Rawls 1999, 253.

direction, and how this creates a strong prima facie duty to act. Sections II-V confront some key arguments obstructing effective action. Section II addresses objections based on scientific uncertainty and the alleged irrationality of precaution. Section III confronts objections to considering past emissions. Section IV considers what to do about future emissions, and current and future damages. Section V addresses the problem of reconciling individual and collective responsibility. In closing, Section VI briefly considers the feasibility of postponing ideal theory. Inevitably, since these are large topics, the treatment will be preliminary and overly simplistic. Nevertheless, it should help to push the debate forward, by providing a starting-point for further discussion.

The main claims of the chapter can be summarized in eight propositions:

1. Ethical Concerns are Already at the Basis of International Climate Policy

The United Nations' Framework Convention on Climate Change (UNFCCC) relies on ethical concerns in framing its motivation, main objective, and guiding principles. Since the convention has been ratified by all major nations, the main actors have already acknowledged that they have ethical responsibilities, and so that there is a burden of proof against inaction. Moreover, since the convention was negotiated nearly two decades ago, and since very little of substance has been achieved in the interim, those responsible are subject to ethical criticism.

2. Scientific Uncertainty Does Not Justify Inaction

Arguments for inaction based on appeals to scientific uncertainty face an additional burden of proof. First, there is reason to think that climate science is not uncertain in the technical sense. Second, even if it were technically uncertain, this does not justify inaction. Uncertainty is a fact of life, and we often face situations where we must act in the face of it. Moreover, this is a case where we have a serious body of empirical and theoretical information on which we can rely. We are far from under-standing nothing about the climate threat, and what we do understand seems more than sufficient to justify significant action.

3. Precaution is Theoretically Respectable

Arguments for inaction are often articulated as objections to the notion of precaution. In particular, the precautionary principle is sometimes said to be vacuous, extreme, or myopic. There is something to these charges if the principle is conceived of in a completely open-ended way. But there are more restricted ways to understand it, and under these kinds of conditions the principle signals a reasonable concern. In addition, the case for precaution is stronger when the decision-makers are not those vulnerable to unacceptable outcomes, but impose the threat of them on innocent others. Given that the main actors have already accepted the need for precaution as part of the UNFCCC, the burden of proof on inaction is even greater.

4. Past Emissions Matter

There are large differences between the past emissions of developed and developing countries, and these are roughly correlated with economic prosperity. Some argue that they should be ignored on the grounds of ignorance, the idea of "first-come, first-served," the fact that many past emitters are now dead, or political infeasibility. But these arguments are too quick, and ought not be accepted without further discussion. The burden of proof remains on those who would reject all historical accountability.

5. The Intragenerational Burdens Should Fall Predominantly on the Developed Countries

There is a strong ethical consensus surrounding the general direction of future policy. In the short- to medium-term, significant emissions reductions are needed, and most of the burdens of this shift away from fossil fuels must be borne largely by the developed nations, and especially the wealthy within those nations. The consensus is grounded by the convergence of concerns about historical responsibility, equal treatment, and the moral priority of subsistence emissions. The ethical consensus carries over to the question of how to deal with unavoided impacts. This involves issues of adaptation, compensation, recognition, and reconciliation.

6. Specific Intergenerational Trajectories Require Ethical Defense

The issue of how quickly global emissions should come down is also the subject of a rough consensus among scientists, policymakers, and activists. Although the general shape of action seems ethically justified, more specific benchmarks must be defended from the ethical point of view, and there are significant differences between them.

7. The Right to Self-Defense Is an Important, but Sharply Limited Rationale

An appeal to self-defense can explain why the current generation of the world's affluent are not required to completely ruin their own lives in order to comply with climate justice. However, this right is sharply limited. For example, it can be invoked only when there are no intermediate policies, and implies a need for compensation when this is not the case. Current climate policies are far from satisfying such constraints.

8. Individuals Bear Some Responsibility for Humanity's Failure

According to a traditional view in political thought, social and political institutions are legitimate because, and to the extent that, citizens delegate their own responsibilities and powers to them. On this account, if the attempt to delegate effectively has failed, then the responsibility falls back on the citizens again, either to solve the problems themselves, or else, if this is not possible, to create new institutions to do the job. If they fail to do so, then they are subject to moral criticism for having failed to discharge their original responsibilities.

This chapter aims to give an initial sense of why these propositions seem plausible. In doing so, it draws on the main strategies of an ethics of transition, including the identification of moral constraints, arguments for overlapping consensus, and especially the practice of defensive moral and political philosophy.

I. AN ETHICAL FRAMING

The claim that climate change is an ethical issue may initially seem surprising. However, it should not be. After all, ethical concepts play a central role in the foundational legal document, the UNFCCC, which has been ratified by all major nations, including the United States. This treaty states as its motivation the "protection of current and future generations of mankind," declares as its major objective the prevention of "dangerous anthropogenic interference" with the climate system, and announces that this objective must be achieved while also protecting ecological, subsistence, and economic values.[4] In addition, the text goes on to list a number of principles to guide the fulfillment of these objectives, and these make heavy use of value-laden concepts. For example, appeals are made to "equity," "common but differentiated responsibilities" (Article 3.1), the "special needs" of developing countries (Article 3.2), the "right" to development (Article 3.4), and the aim of promoting a supportive, open, sustainable, and nondiscriminatory international economic system (Article 3.5) (See chapter 1.1 for a more direct argument for the relevance of ethics.)

Substantive ethical concerns are therefore central to how international climate policy is framed, and this framing adopts a strategy familiar in the ethics of the transition. The UNFCCC seeks to guide future policy by announcing a set of intuitive criteria that require further articulation and integration, but nevertheless are useful in pointing towards clear and egregious violations. This is relevant in the current political context. Since the main actors have acknowledged that they have ethical responsibilities, there is a serious burden of proof against both inaction and action that does not take the relevant values seriously. Since the convention has been in place for nearly two decades, the lack of major progress since then suggests that those responsible are subject to strong ethical criticism.[5]

---

4. For example, Article 2 states: "Such a level should be achieved within a time-frame sufficient to allow ecosystems to adapt naturally to climate change, to ensure that food production is not threatened, and to enable economic development to proceed in a sustainable manner."

5. Chapters 3–4; Brown 2002.

Given that the project of confronting climate change, seen in ethical terms, already has considerable standing in the real world, establishing its relevance is, arguably, not the most pressing task of the ethics of the transition. Instead, the main issues seem to be: (1) how to interpret, reconcile, and implement the relevant values; (2) whether the convention's account of them should be challenged or extended; and (3) most importantly, how to address the fact that those who have openly committed themselves to these values have apparently failed to be guided by them.

This is not the place to attempt the large projects of synthesizing or assessing the values of the framework convention. Instead, the remainder of this chapter will focus on the third question, and in particular how substantive ethical analysis can help in confronting many of the arguments currently used to stall effective action.

II. THE ETHICS OF SKEPTICISM

On the face of it, the claim that climate change poses a substantial threat demanding action is supported by a broad scientific consensus.[6] Still, in the public realm it has been subject to two prominent challenges.[7]

1. Scientific Uncertainty

The first asserts that the science remains uncertain, so that current action is unjustified. This claim raises important epistemic and normative questions about what constitutes relevant uncertainty, and what amounts to appropriate action under it. We can make some progress on the first question if we begin with a distinction. In economics, situations involving uncertainty are distinguished from those involving risk. Suppose one can identify a possible negative outcome of some action. That outcome is a risk if one can also identify, or reliably estimate, the probability of its occurrence; it is uncertain if one cannot.[8]

---

6. IPCC 2007; Oreskes 2004; UNFCCC 1992.

7. A third challenge is the claim of many mainstream economists that only modest steps should be taken since (they say) the costs of substantial action outweigh the benefits. I address this argument in chapter 8.

8. Knight 1921.

An initial objection to the first challenge is that, on this standard account of uncertainty, it is unclear whether mainstream climate science is uncertain in the technical sense. As it turns out, the IPCC assigns probabilities to many of its projections, making the situation overtly one of risk. Moreover, many of these assignments are both high, and associated with substantial negative damages; hence, they seem more than sufficient to justify significant action.[9]

The initial objection is powerful. However, there may be a way to rehabilitate the challenge. Most of the IPCC's probability assignments are based on expert judgment, rather than, say, on direct appeals to causal mechanisms. Hence, these are "subjective," rather than objective probabilities. Appeal to subjective probabilities is common in many approaches to risk. (Indeed, some claim that all probabilities are ultimately subjective.[10]) But if one is suspicious of subjective probabilities in general, or has particular reasons to be skeptical in this case, one might reject the IPCC assignments and continue to regard climate change as genuinely uncertain in the technical sense.

Still, granting this concession is not enough by itself to make the skeptic's case. Even if we were to assume for a moment that we lack robust probability information, there remains something troubling about the claim that one should refuse to act just because of this. Arguably, some kind of uncertainty "is an inherent part of the problem."[11] For instance, if we knew precisely what was likely to happen, to whom, and whose emissions would cause it, the problem might be more easily addressed; at the very least, it would have a different shape. [12] Hence, to refuse to act because of uncertainty may be either to refuse to accept the climate problem as it is, insisting that it be turned into a more respectable kind of problem first, or else to endorse the principle that "do nothing" is the appropriate response to uncertainty. But neither looks appealing. The former suggests a head-in-the-sand approach that seems clearly unacceptable, and the latter is also dubious. After all, in real life,

9. IPCC 2007c.

10. Friedman 1976.

11. Broome 1992, 18.

12. For example, using ozone depletion and deforestation as his case studies, Rado Dimitrov argues that the crucial variable in resolving global environmental problems is knowledge of their cross-border consequences, rather than of their extent and causes, since this "facilitates utility calculations and the formation of interests" (Dimitrov 2003, p. 123).

we neither can pick and choose the problems we face, nor simply ignore the one's we don't like the look of.

More generally, perhaps the most crucial point to make about the problem of uncertainty is that it is important not to overplay it. On the one hand, many decisions we have to make in life, including many important decisions, are also subject to considerable uncertainties.[13] But this does not imply that I should do nothing, or that I cannot make a decision. On the other hand, not all uncertainties are created equal. For instance, in some cases I may know almost nothing about the situation[14], but in others I may know a great deal.[15] Moreover, uncertainty in some kinds of case seems clearly worse than in others.[16]

These points are relevant because it seems reasonably clear that we have to make some kind of decision about climate change, that it is not an unfamiliar kind of decision, and that we do have a considerable amount of information. As Donald Brown argues: "A lot of climate change science

13. For example, suppose I am weighing a job offer in a distant city, and that one major consideration is what kind of life my eighteen-month-old son will have. The information I have about this is riddled with uncertainty. I know that my current location offers many advantages as a place for children to grow up (e.g., the schools are good, the society values children, there are lots of wholesome activities available) but some considerable disadvantages (e.g., great distances from other family members, a high youth suicide rate). But I have no idea how these various factors might affect my son, particularly since I can only guess at this stage what his personality might turn out to be. So, I am in a situation of uncertainty.

14. For example, suppose that the position is on the other side of the world in New Zealand, but I have never been there, nor know anyone who has. Then, I might be completely bereft of information on which to make a decision. (These days, of course, I have the Internet, the local library, and Amazon.com. But pity the situation of the early settlers.)

15. For example, suppose I'm now thinking about my fifteen-year-old daughter. In this case, I do have considerable information about her personality, preferences, goals, and aspirations. But this does not mean there is not considerable uncertainty about how good the move would be for her. Suppose, for example, that I know that the most important thing from her point of view is having a group of very close personal friends. I also know that she is good at making friends; but I don't know whether a suitable group will present itself. Uncertainty, then, can come with more or less information attached, and information of very different kinds.

16. E.g., The "never been to New Zealand" case seems clearly worse than "fifteen-year-old daughter".

has never been in question . . . many of the elements of global warming are not seriously challenged even by the scientific skeptics, and . . . the issues of scientific certainty most discussed by climate skeptics usually deal with the magnitude and timing of climate change, not with whether global warming is a real threat."[17] But if this is right, then the inference from uncertainty to inaction does not seem compelling.

To see this point more clearly, let us briefly examine a number of sources of uncertainty about global warming. The first concerns the direct empirical evidence for anthropogenic warming itself. This has two main aspects. First, systematic global temperature records, based on measurements of air temperature on land and surface-water temperature measurements at sea, exist only from 1860; satellite-based measurements are available only from 1979. For earlier measurements, we have to rely on more patchy observations and indirect (proxy) data. This makes long-term comparisons more difficult. Second, there is no well-defined baseline from which to measure change.[18] While it is true that the last couple of decades have been the warmest in human history, it is also true that the long-term climate record displays significant short-term variability, and that, even accounting for this, climate seems to have been remarkably stable since the end of the last Ice Age 10,000 years ago, as compared with the preceding 100,000 years.[19] Hence, global temperatures have fluctuated considerably over the long-term record, and it is clear that these fluctuations have been naturally caused.

The skeptics are right, then, when they assert that the observational temperature record is a relatively weak data set, and that the long-term history of the climate is such that even if the data were more robust, we might be mistaken in concluding solely on this basis that humans are

17. Brown 2002, 102. Thus our situation seems more like the fifteen-year-old daughter case than "never been to New Zealand."

18. There is, of course, an important presumption here. Dale Jamieson points out that the very idea of climate change presupposes a paradigm of stability versus change, and this brings with it a need to distinguish signal from noise (Jamieson 1991, 319–21).

19. According to data largely from Arctic ice cores, in the last 10,000 years the variation in average global temperatures is less than one degree Celsius; in the preceding 100,000 years, variations were sometimes experienced of up to five or six degrees Celsius in less than 100 years (Houghton 1997, chapter 4).

causing the recently observed rises.[20] Still, we should not infer too much from this. For it would be equally rash to dismiss the possibility of warming on such grounds. Even though it is possible that the empirical evidence might be consistent with there being no anthropogenic warming, it is also true that it provides just the kind of record we would expect from such warming.

This paradox is caused by the fact that our epistemological position with respect to climate change is intrinsically very difficult. Indeed, it may simply be impossible to confirm climate change empirically from our current position, at least to a very high standard of scientific proof (see Appendix 2). This is because our basic situation may be a bit like that of a coach who is asked whether the existing performance of a fourteen-year-old athlete shows that they will reach the highest level of their sport. Suppose the coach has the best evidence that she can have. It will still only be evidence for a fourteen-year-old. It will be at most consistent with reaching the highest level. It cannot be taken as a certain prediction. But that does not mean it is no prediction at all, or worthless. It is simply the best prediction she is currently in a position to make. Presumably, a major league scout would regard the prediction as worthwhile information, even if not conclusive. This is particularly so if the scout knows that waiting to be sure–until the prospect is twenty-one, say–will substantially increase the cost to the club of acquiring him.[21]

20. Interestingly, this does not imply that we should not have a global warming policy to limit emissions. It could be that the observed warming trend is natural but if it were to continue, this might be just as potentially disastrous for current patterns of human life on the planet as artificially induced warming would be. It might then turn out that some abatement of projected anthropogenic emissions would be justified as a counteracting measure.

21. The analogy with the climate case is as follows. What really concerns us about climate change is the prospect of a dramatic climate shift over the next century or two, of the sort suggested by a substantial rise in average global temperature, such as 1.1–6.4 C. (This is like being concerned with the eventual mature athlete.) However, we are currently still fairly early in the evolution of climate change impacts. (The athlete is still young.) The leading scientific authority is telling us that thus far observed "warming of the climate system is unequivocal" and "very likely" (meaning a probability of 90% or more in their judgment) due to human activity.[21] At this point, the IPCC is referring to an observed global temperature rise of around 0.8 C, and is essentially saying that global warming provides a good explanation for this, and nonanthropogenic explanations are not forthcoming. (The coach who is monitoring the young athlete thinks that he is a very good prospect.) But there is still some chance that this judgment may turn out to be mistaken. (The coach might admit that the probability is only 90% in her judgment,

Fortunately, in the case of climate change the empirical temperature record is far from our only evidence. Instead, we also have strong theoretical grounds for concern. First, the basic physical and chemical mechanisms that give rise to a potential global warming effect are well understood. In particular, there is no scientific controversy over the claims (a) that in itself a higher concentration of greenhouse gas molecules in the upper atmosphere would cause more heat to be retained by the earth and less radiated out into the solar system, so that other things being equal, such an increase would cause global temperatures to rise; and (b) that human activities since the industrial revolution have significantly increased the atmospheric concentration of greenhouse gases. Hence, everyone agrees that the basic circumstances are such that a greenhouse effect is to be expected.[22]

Second, the remaining scientific dispute, insofar as there is one, concerns the high level of complexity of the global climate system, given which there are the other mechanisms that might be in play to moderate such an effect. The issue here is whether there might be negative feedbacks that either sharply reduce or negate the effects of higher levels of greenhouse gases, or even reduce the amount of them present in the atmosphere. Current climate models suggest that most related factors will likely exhibit positive feedbacks (water vapor, snow, and ice), while others have both positive and negative feedbacks whose net effect is unclear (e.g., clouds, ocean currents). Hence, there is genuine scientific uncertainty.

However, again, we must be cautious about inferring too much from this. On the one hand, uncertainty about feedbacks is already represented in mainstream projections of climate change. For example, it is

---

so that there is a 10% chance that the prospect won't mature into a top-class athlete; and also, that she might be mistaken about the 90% judgment.) Nevertheless, it does provide information relevant to decision making, especially given that delaying action will make action much more expensive, or even impossible. (The mature athlete will be very expensive, maybe too expensive for the club to buy.) This is especially so if there are some things that can be done initially that are relatively easy and not too costly. (Perhaps the club could offer a contract with opt-out clauses, and performance incentives.)

22. As pointed out in chapter 3, the potential gains from carbon emissions are far from exhausted, given the low per capita rates in most parts of the world. Hence, even if global warming were not yet occurring, we would, other things being equal, expect it at some time in the future, as global emissions rise.

one major reason why the IPCC offers a range of projected temperature rises over the current century (e.g. of 1.1°–2.9°C for a low emission scenario, with a best estimate of 1.8°C, and of 2.4°C–6.4°C for a high emission scenario, with a best estimate of 4.0°C).[23] It is not therefore a compelling reason for dismissing such projections.[24] On the other hand, we should not assume that any residual uncertainty cuts in favor of less action. There may be no more reason to believe that we will be saved by unexpectedly large negative feedbacks, than that the warming effect will be much worse than we would otherwise anticipate due to unexpectedly large positive feedbacks.[25]

In conclusion, while there are uncertainties surrounding both the direct empirical evidence for warming and our theoretical understanding of the overall climate system, these cut both ways. In particular, while it is conceivable (though currently unlikely) that the climate change problem will turn out to be chimerical, it is also possible that global warming will turn out to be much worse than anyone has yet anticipated. More importantly, the really vital issue does not concern the presence of scientific uncertainties, but rather how we decide what to do under such circumstances, and the ways in which this is open to ethical assessment. To these issues we now turn.

2. Precaution

The UNFCCC makes the claim that "where there are threats of serious or irreversible damage, lack of full scientific certainty should not be used as a reason for postponing [precautionary] measures [to anticipate, prevent, or minimize the causes of climate change and mitigate its adverse effects]" (Article 3.3). Hence, the treaty explicitly rules out some kinds of appeal to uncertainty as justifications for inaction, and it does so precisely in an attempt to block the kinds of skepticism mentioned above.

23. IPCC 2007a.

24. One may try to argue that the IPCC ranges are inadequate, but this is a separate argument, to be assessed on its merits.

25. In particular, there is no reason to assume that our planet's atmosphere is robustly stable in the face of different inputs. The atmosphere of Venus, for example, has undergone a runaway greenhouse effect. (It is easy to forget that what we are dealing with fundamentally is a band of gases around the earth that is just a few miles wide.)

Since the convention has been ratified, there is a strong ethical reason for the main actors to abide by this provision.

Stated as it is in the convention, this appeal to precaution is extremely minimal and underdeveloped. However, some have tried to generate a more general precautionary principle.[26] According to one standard statement, this asserts "when an activity raises threats of harm to human health or the environment, precautionary measures should be taken even if some cause and effect relationships are not fully established scientifically."[27] However, such claims have frequently been dismissed as extreme, myopic, and ultimately vacuous. Couldn't a precautionary principle be invoked to stop *any* activity, however beneficial, on the basis of any kind of worry, however fanciful? If so, the critics charge, surely it is irrational, and ought to be rejected. This is the second challenge to action on climate change.

Let us consider two basic replies to this challenge. The first addresses the rationality and general coherence of the precautionary principle. Understood in a completely open-ended way, the principle may be vulnerable to some of the objections listed above. However, it is plausible to restrict its application by introducing criteria to guide when the principle should be applied. Elsewhere, I illustrate this using John Rawls's criteria for the application of a maximin principle: that the situation is uncertain, in the sense that the parties lack reliable probability information; that they care little for potential gains above the minimum they can secure by acting in a precautionary manner; and that they face outcomes that are unacceptable.[28] This approach not only diffuses the original objections, but suggests that many disputes about precaution ultimately do not rest on a rejection of the principle, but rather on disagreement about whether the relevant criteria are met.[29] This significantly reframes

26. Others have proposed addressing uncertainty with various default rules and institutional mechanisms that are sometimes discussed under the heading of precaution but sometimes not. See, for example, Cranor 1994, 2004, 2006; Michaels 2008; Shrader-Frechette 1993.

27. Wingspread 1998.

28. I add a fourth condition to Rawls's list: that "the range of outcomes considered are in some appropriate sense 'realistic,' so that, for example, only credible threats are considered" (Gardiner 2006, 51–2). See also Cranor 2003, 2004.

29. For example, the criticism that the resources spent on precautionary policies would produce major benefits if used elsewhere suggests an attack on the "care little for gains" condition.

the theoretical debate. Rather than foundational disagreements about whether the notion of precaution makes any sense, we are instead engaged in more substantive disputes about (for example) whether the relevant outcomes are really unacceptable, whether we do care more about potential gains of nonprecautionary behavior, and whether we have trustworthy probabilities.

At a more practical level, a reasonable case can be made that the Rawlsian precautionary principle applies to climate change. First, it seems clear that some of the projected impacts, being severe or catastrophic, are morally unacceptable. Second, we have already seen that there may be uncertainty in the technical sense.[30] The third condition—that we care little for the gains that can be made beyond those secured by precautionary action—is more contentious. For example, Cass Sunstein has argued that this condition threatens to confine the Rawlsian version of the principle to trivial cases, and in particular undermines the application to global warming because the costs of mitigation amount to hundreds of millions of dollars.[31] However, I remain unconvinced. Though Sunstein is surely right that more work needs to be done in fleshing out the precautionary principle, it is not clear that the problem with the third condition is that it is "trivial." Remember that Rawls is speaking of gains that can be made *above some minimum we can guarantee* through eliminating the worst-case scenario. Hence, much depends on how one understands the alternative options. To see this, consider an example. Suppose we could avoid the possibility of catastrophic climate change and guarantee a decent quality of life for everyone, all at the cost of slowing down our rate of accumulation of purely *luxury* goods by only two years.[32] This might satisfy the "care little for gains" condition even if the cost of those luxury goods in dollar terms were very large. For instance, perhaps the importance of averting catastrophic climate change might simply make such a loss seem relatively unimportant. (Suppose, for example, that the hit were taken by the global budgets for cosmetic research, Hollywood movies, or professional sports teams.[33])

30. If there is not, then the probabilities of severe impacts seem large enough to justify action on other grounds.

31. Sunstein 2005, 112. Because of this, he tries to "build on" the Rawlsian version to develop an alternative "catastrophic harm precautionary principle" (Sunstein 2006, 168).

32. Shue 1993; Gardiner 2006a.

33. Recall that Rawls says only that we must care "little" for the gains of an alternative strategy, not that we need not care at all.

Given this point, the real issue seems to revolve around the interpretation and elaboration of the "care little for gains" condition, rather than whether it is "too stringent."[34] Resolving this issue is likely to involve a substantive project in normative ethics.

The second basic reply to the challenge to precaution is a moral one. If precaution is often reasonable in cases involving actors who impose threats of unacceptable outcomes on themselves, it seems even more reasonable when they impose such threats on innocent others. Intuitively, there are risks that I can choose to run for myself that I ought not to make you run on my behalf. Moreover, the moral problem in such cases is heightened when the benefits to me are minor in comparison to the disaster I may inflict on you, and when you are completely vulnerable. Naturally, more remains to be said here. But the basic point is enough to disrupt the initial case against precaution.

In conclusion, neither of the two challenges to climate action seems decisive when pressed. When we understand the state of the science and the intellectual respectability of precaution, much contemporary skepticism about action on climate change becomes unwarranted. At best, skeptical concerns would justify some caution about the way in which we frame and implement climate policies moving forward. But they do not seem to license either inaction, or the current trajectory of global emissions. Indeed, what we do understand about climate change suggests that a robust skepticism about action is likely to be profoundly reckless and unethical. Faced with this kind of situation and this kind of evidence to continue to accelerate hard into the problem, exposing the global poor, future generations and the rest of nature to a profound threat, seems very difficult to justify. At the very least, the burden of proof seems very squarely on those who would claim otherwise. Given that the main actors have already accepted the need for precaution as part of the UNFCCC, this burden is even greater.

III. PAST EMISSIONS

If action is warranted, who should take it, and what should be done? The UNFCCC asserts that countries should act "on the basis of equity and in

34. Contra. Sunstein 2006, 156.

accordance with their common but differentiated responsibilities and respective capabilities [such that] . . . the developed country Parties should take the lead in combating climate change and the adverse effects thereof" (Article 3.1). Hence, there is a strong presumption that the developed countries should move first, and take the largest initial burden. As we shall see, this claim also seems to be a matter of strong ethical consensus, although precisely how to interpret it in policy poses more difficult questions.

One proposal for action is that responsibility should be assigned in light of past emissions. Two kinds of argument are prominent. The first invokes historical principles of responsibility, along the lines of the commonsense ideals of "you broke it, you fix it" and "clean up your own mess."[35] Such principles are already familiar in environmental law and regulation, appearing, for example, in various versions of the "polluter pays" principle. They imply that those who cause a problem have an obligation to rectify it, and also assume additional liabilities, such as for compensation, if the problem imposes costs or harms on others. The second kind of argument appeals to fair access. The thought is that the atmosphere's capacity to absorb greenhouse gases without adverse effects is a limited resource that is, or ought to be, held in common. If some have used up the resource, and in doing so denied others access to it, then compensation may be owed. The latecomers have been deprived of their fair share.

Such rationales for considering past emissions seem straightforward and readily applicable to climate change. Moreover, it is easy to see their general tendency. For example, the United States is responsible for 29% of global emissions since the onset of the industrial revolution (from 1850–2003), and the nations of the EU 26%; by contrast, China and India are responsible for 8% and 2% respectively. In light of this, it is natural to conclude that their duties to act are different.

Despite this, appeals to past emissions have been subject to four prominent objections.

1. Ignorance

The first asserts that past polluters were ignorant of the adverse effects of their emissions, and so ought not to be blamed. They neither intended nor foresaw the effects of their behavior, and so should not be held

---

35. Shue 1999; Singer 2002.

responsible. This objection occurs in academic writings,[36] but also has political prominence. As the top U.S. negotiator, Todd Stern, put it at the Copenhagen meeting: "I actually completely reject the notion of a debt or reparations or anything of the like. For most of the 200 years since the Industrial Revolution, people were blissfully ignorant of the fact that emissions caused a greenhouse effect. It's a relatively recent phenomenon."[37]

The ignorance objection initially seems compelling, but turns out to be more complicated when pressed. First, it is worth distinguishing blame as such from responsibility. Though it is true that we do not usually blame those ignorant of what they do, still we often hold them responsible. Hence, showing that blame is inappropriate is insufficient to dismiss past emissions.[38] Second, there are reasons for holding the ignorant responsible in this case. On the one hand, consider the "you broke it, you fix it" rationale. If I accidentally break something of yours, we usually think that I have some obligation to fix it, even if I was ignorant that my behavior was dangerous, and perhaps even if I could not have known. It remains true that I broke it, and in many contexts that is sufficient. After all, if I am not to fix it, who will? Even if it is not completely fair that I bear the burden, isn't it at least less unfair than leaving you to bear it alone?[39] On the other hand, consider the fair access rationale. Suppose that I unwittingly deprive you of your share of something and benefit from doing so. Isn't it natural to think that I should step in to help when the problem is discovered? For example, suppose that everyone in the office chips in to order pizza for lunch. You have to dash out for a meeting, and so leave your slices in the refrigerator. I (having already eaten my slices) discover and eat yours because I assume that they must be going spare. You return to find that you now don't have any lunch. Is this simply your problem? We don't usually think so. Even though I didn't realize at the time that I was taking your pizza, this does not mean that I have no special obligations. The fact that I ate your lunch remains morally relevant.

36. Caney 2005 (but see Caney 2011); Posner and Sunstein 2007; Posner and Weibach 2010.
37. Revkin and Zeller 2009.
38. Shue 1999.
39. Shue 1999, 2009.

2. First-come, First-served

The second objection emerges from the claim that there is a disanalogy between the pizza case and that of past emissions. In the pizza case, you have a clear right to the eaten slices, because you have already paid for them. But in the case of emissions, where the shares of the latecomers are used up by those who come earlier, it might be maintained that the latecomers have no such claim. Perhaps it is simply "first-come, first-served," and hard luck to the tardy.

In my view, this response is too quick. We must ask what justifies a policy like first-come, first-served in the first place. To see why, consider one natural explanation. If a resource initially appears to be unlimited, then those who want to consume it might simply assume at the outset that no issues of allocation arise. Everyone can take whatever they want, with no adverse consequences for others. In this case, the principle is not really first-come, first-served (which implies that the resource is limited, so that some may lose out), but rather "free for all" (which does not). Since it is assumed that there is more than enough for everyone, no principle of allocation is needed.

But what if the assumption that the resource is unlimited turns out to be mistaken, so that free for all becomes untenable? Do those who have already consumed large shares have no special responsibility to those who have not, and now cannot? Does the original argument for free for all justify ignoring the past? Arguably not. After all, if the parties had considered at the outset the possibility that the resource might turn out to be limited, which allocation principle would have seemed more reasonable and fair: "free for all, with no special responsibility for the early users if the resource turns out to be limited," or "free for all, but with early users liable to extra responsibilities if the assumption of unlimitedness turns out to be mistaken"? Offhand, it is difficult to see why a ignoring the past would be favored. Indeed, there seem to be clear reasons to reject it: it makes later users vulnerable in an unnecessary way, and provides a potentially costly incentive to consume early if possible. Given this, first-come, first-served looks unmotivated. Why adopt an allocation rule that so thoroughly exempts early users from responsibility?[40]

40. Of course, the case is even stronger if one takes into account negative side effects. "Free for all, with no special responsibility for the early users if their use turns out to harm others" looks highly implausible in most settings.

3. Dead Emitters

The third objection to considering past emissions emphasizes that, since significant anthropogenic emissions have been occurring since 1750, many past polluters are now dead. Given this, it is said, "polluter pays" principles no longer really apply to a substantial proportion of past emissions; instead, what is really being proposed under the banner of polluter pays is that the descendents of the original polluters should pay for those emissions, because they have benefited from the past pollution (because of industrialization in their countries). However, the argument continues, this "beneficiary pays principle" is unjust because it holds current individuals responsible for emissions that they did not cause (and could not have prevented), and in ways which diminish their own opportunities.[41]

Much could be said about this objection,[42] but here let me make just two comments. First, the claim that polluter pays does not apply is more complex than it first seems. For example, it does apply if it refers not to individuals as such but to some entity to which they are connected, such as a country, people, or corporation. Moreover, this is the case in climate change, where polluter pays is usually invoked to suggest that countries should be held responsible for their past emissions, and these typically have persisted over the time period envisioned.

Many proponents of the objection recognize this complication. To meet it, they typically reject the moral relevance of states, and instead invoke a strong individualism that claims that only individuals should matter ultimately from the moral point of view. Still, [second] note that this move makes the argument more controversial that it initially appears. On the one hand, even many individualists would argue that states often play the role of representing individuals and discharging many of their moral responsibilities. Given this, more needs to be said about why the fact of membership is irrelevant for assigning responsibility. On the other hand, the argument ignores the issue that a very strong individualism would also call into question many other practices surrounding inherited rights and responsibility. Put most baldly, if we are not responsible for at least some of the debts incurred by our ancestors, why are we entitled to

---

41. Caney 2005; Posner and Sunstein 2008.
42. See also Gosseries 2003; Meyer and Roser 2006.

inherit all of the benefits of their activities? In particular, if we disavow their emissions, must we also relinquish the territory and infrastructure they left to us? The worry here is that, if successful, the attempt to undermine polluter (or beneficiary) pays is liable to prove too much, or at least to presuppose a radical rethinking of global politics.

4. Practicality

The fourth objection to taking past emissions seriously claims that doing so would be impractical. Instead, it is said, if agreement is to be politically feasible, we must ignore the past and be forward-looking in our approach. The most prominent response to this objection is that it makes a rash claim about political reality. On the contrary, it will be said, since a genuinely global agreement is needed to tackle climate change, and since many nations of the world would not accept an agreement that did not explicitly or implicitly recognize past disparities, any attempt to exclude the past from consideration is itself seriously unrealistic.[43]

In conclusion, prominent attempts to exclude past emissions from consideration on ethical grounds do not appear to succeed. Still, how to include such emissions in climate policy remains an important and nontrivial question. One reason for this is that it is difficult to disentangle the role of past and future emissions. On the one hand, the future emissions that make climate change pose such a large threat do so principally against the backdrop of past emissions. Not only do these remain in the atmosphere for a long time, but they also make any given level of future emissions more dangerous than it might have been.[44] Hence, the past constrains the future, and past emitters might be held liable for that. On the other hand, a similar point applies in reverse. The "liability" of the past is in part determined by future behavior. Past emissions become more dangerous if there are greater future emissions. Hence, though it might initially be tempting to assign responsibility for adaptation efforts solely on the basis of past emissions, this obscures the fact

43. Athanasiou and Baer 2002.

44. For example, if we had not already seen an increase in atmospheric concentration of carbon dioxide from 270 to 380 ppm, then we would have another 110 ppm to play with. (I thank Henry Shue for discussion on this point).

that how much adaptation is ultimately necessary (or feasible) will depend on future emissions as well. Given these points, the issue of past emissions casts a notable shadow over other allocation questions.

IV. FUTURE EMISSIONS

If something must be done to limit future emissions, then imposing such a limit will have the effect of transforming an open access resource into one that must be distributed.[45] This raises profound ethical questions, and especially ones of procedural and distributive justice.

1. Procedural Justice

Procedurally, the main issue is how to get an agreement that pays due respect to all of the parties involved. In practice, international discussion has treated emissions reductions as a matter for political horse-trading. Individual nations offer cuts in terms of their own emissions in exchange for cuts from the others, and other nonclimate-related benefits. However, in an international system characterized by historical injustice and large imbalances of power, the prospect that such bargaining will be fair to all parties seems dim. Moreover, as Henry Shue argues, there is a threat of compound injustice.[46] Those treated unfairly in the past are likely to be more vulnerable to current injustices because of their past treatment. Finally, there are worries that the interests of those most affected by future climate change—future generations, the very poor, animals, and nature—are not adequately represented. Why expect an agreement driven by representatives of the current generation of the world's most affluent people to produce justice in this context?

The question of how to arrange a climate regime that is procedurally fair is an important one. But some of the concerns might be met if we had a good idea of what a fair distributive outcome might look like. At the theoretical level, this issue is complex. But one natural way to frame it is in terms of three questions.

45. Shue 1995.
46. Shue 1992.

2. The Allocation Question

The question that has received most attention so far asks how those emissions allowable at a particular time should be allocated. A large number of proposals have been made, but nevertheless there seems to be a strong ethical consensus supporting the basic idea of "common, but differentiated responsibilities", that the richer, developed nations should take the lead in acting on climate change, and bear the greatest burdens. To see why, let us briefly review just three basic proposals, to get a sense of the terrain and suggest some further complications.[47]

a. Equal Per Capita

The first proposal is that of equal per capita entitlements.[48] The intuitive idea is that, other things being equal, permissible carbon emissions should be distributed equally across the world population, because no individual has a presumptive right to more than an equal share.[49] A shift to per capita entitlements would generally support the ethical consensus, since national emissions levels are strongly linked with economic prosperity as conventionally understood. However, it faces two initial challenges.

First, it has radically different implications for particular nations. In 2005, global per capita emissions were at 1.23 metric tons of carbon. But national averages show wide discrepancies. In the United States, for example, the average in 2005 was 5.32; in the United Kingdom it was 2.47; in China 1.16; in India 0.35; and in Bangladesh 0.08.[50]

Suppose, for example, that we were to call for roughly a 20% cut in global emissions in the next decade, and distribute the remaining emissions

47. More complex proposals exist (cf. Bear et al. 2007; Chakravarty et al. 2009). But these remarks should provide an entry point into thinking about those too.

48. Agarwal and Narain 1991; Meyer 2000; Jamieson 2001; Athanasiou and Baer 2002; Singer 2002.

49. Sometimes this rationale may be based in a basic egalitarian intuition. But it is also supported because per capita allocation serves wider ethical goals (Singer 2002), or (perhaps most often) because it is viewed as a pragmatic principle that at least moves in the right direction (away from grandfathering huge international inequality in emissions levels, for example), and has the advantage of comparative simplicity.

50. Boden et al. 2009.

on a per capita basis, at roughly 1 metric ton each. This would imply that citizens of the United States would have to cut their emissions by more than 80%, those of the United Kingdom by nearly 60%, and those of China by around 14%, while the Indians could increase their emissions by around 65% and the Bangladeshis by 92%. In short, on the face of it, the burden of the shift to equal per capita entitlements seems very different for different countries. As a result, it is often said that it would be more dislocating, and therefore unfair, for those who emit the most to make such drastic cuts since much of their infrastructure depends on much higher rates of emission.

The second initial challenge is that people in different parts of the world have different energy needs. For example, those in northern Canada require fuel for heating that those in more temperate zones do not. Hence, there is a question about whether equal resource entitlements really do treat people as equals. This resonates with a deep issue in political philosophy about what the appropriate aim of equality should be: equality of resources, welfare, capabilities, or something else.[51]

In practice, most proponents of the equal per capita approach suggest that these two challenges can be largely dealt with by making the right to pollute tradable once allocated. On this version of the proposal, those for whom the costs of reduction are high can buy unused allocations from others whose costs are low. In addition, it is usually thought that allocations will actually be made to states on the basis of their populations, rather than directly to individuals.[52] In practice, then, the thought is that the effect of the per capita proposal is that developed nations will end up buying large amounts of currently unused capacity from the developing world in order to make their own cuts more manageable.

This more complex proposal raises many new issues. On the one hand, there are concerns about feasibility. For one thing, on the face of it, trading seems to involve a massive transfer of wealth from the rich to the poor nations. For another, the proposal of giving the allowances to states may lead far away from the initial intuition towards equality.

---

51. Sen 1980; Dworkin 2000; Page 2007.

52. This reflects the fact that the per capita proposal was originally conceived within the context of national allocations (as an alternative to grandfathering and similar schemes) and the appeal of administrative simplicity.

In many countries, the thought goes, such allowances are likely to become just another resource for the elite to plunder, perhaps in collusion with, and on behalf of, outside forces. What then of individuals in poor countries to whom the right is nominally given? Does the appeal to individualism turn out merely to be a convenient illusion? On the other hand, concerns about fairness remain. Do tradable allowances simply allow the rich countries to continue their polluting habits by "buying off" the poor? Perhaps they are morally akin to environmental indulgences, simply a fancy way for the rich to spend their way out of the implications of their bad behavior;[53] and perhaps they also undermine a sense of collective moral endeavor.[54]

More generally, it may be that in practice the main appeal of the "equal per capita plus trading" proposal lies not in equal division as such, but elsewhere: in the way it appears to reconcile concern for the future with recognition of the past, and with global justice more generally. After all, because current prosperity is highly correlated with past emissions, the trading mechanism provides a way for the rich nations to provide some compensation to the developing world (and without overtly appearing to do so). If the numbers had worked out differently (if, that is, the poor countries turned out to be the big current polluters per capita), then it may be that the per capita approach would have little support.

Perhaps then "equal per capita" is best seen as a hybrid proposal, aimed at reconciling a number of different desiderata. In addition to accommodating some notion of equality and responsibility for the past, it also seems to facilitate resource transfers to the least well-off, to allow the rich to protect themselves against too painful a transition, and to provide incentives for technical innovation.

b. Subsistence Emissions

The second proposal for allocating future emissions initially appears to overcome some of the worries about the modified per capita approach by putting concern for the poor and for individuals right at the heart of its approach. Henry Shue maintains that individuals have an inalienable

53. Goodin 1994.
54. Sandel 2005; Sagoff 1999.

right to the emissions necessary for their survival or some minimum level of quality of life. He proposes that such emissions should be open neither to trading, nor appropriation by governments, and that they ought to be sharply distinguished from other emissions, especially those associated with luxury goods[55]. At first glance, this proposal has a different logic than that of tradable per capita rights. On the one hand, subsistence emissions rights are inalienable, suggesting not only that they cannot be exchanged, but also that they should be guaranteed even if this would predictably lead to serious harm to others, such as future generations. On the other hand, subsistence emissions are subject to a strict threshold, implying that emissions above that threshold might be distributed according some principle other than equality.

Of course, the subsistence emissions proposal also raises new difficulties. Most obviously, what counts as a "subsistence emission"? After all, former U.S. president George H. Bush infamously stated at the Rio Earth Summit in 1992 that "the American way of life is not up for negotiation." Does that mean that we should regard an emissions rate of 5.32 metric tons per capita as the subsistence level for Americans? Surely not. Yet even subsistence at a minimal level of quality of life presumably does include some social and cultural factors,[56] and these may involve different levels of absolute emissions. So, how do we decide what is necessary and what is not? Again, some moral and political philosophy seems needed.

Less obviously, in practice it is not clear that the proposal has real advantages over the equal per capita approach. On the one hand, the two may not be easily separable. Given the fungibility of the notion of "subsistence," it seems likely that the task of determining an adequate minimum may turn out to be very close to that of deciding on an appropriate long-term trajectory (see below) and then assigning equal per capita rights. On the other hand, if the two approaches do diverge, it is not clear that the subsistence approach does a better job of protecting vulnerable individuals. Consider some examples. If culturally sensitive subsistence emissions overshoot the equal per capita allocation, then they justify an increase in the burdens on future generations. Alternatively, if they undershoot that allocation, then the "excess" emissions need to be distributed in some other way. If this is equal per capita, then

55. Shue 1993, 13.
56. Traxler 2002.

(again) the two approaches may amount to much the same thing. But if it is not—and in particular if they are to be distributed by market forces—then the subsistence approach may end up being less favorable to the poor than equal per capita.

c. Equal Burdens

The third allocation proposal is that nations should share the costs of mitigation fairly amongst themselves by trying to equalize their marginal costs in reducing emissions. This is presumably part of the appeal of nations declaring percentage reduction targets. The thought is that if each reduces their own emissions by, say, 20% in a given period, then all take on equal burdens. Martino Traxler suggests that an equal burdens approach has major political advantages. No nation has any stronger reason to defect than any other, and each experiences the maximum moral pressure to participate.[57]

I am not so sure. First, the proposal is entirely future-oriented. Not only does it ignore past emissions; it also has the effect of embedding recent emissions levels. For example, a cut of 20% would reduce per capital levels in the United States to 4.26, and in India to 0.28. Is this fair, given that the United States is so much richer? Even more starkly, if ultimately the global cut needs to be 80%, is it fair that the equal percentage cut approach reduces the U.S. level to 1.64 per capita, when this is still significantly higher than current Chinese and Indian levels, and when Bangladesh is pushed down to a miniscule 0.1 per capita?

Second, as the first point already suggests, the correct measure of "equal burdens" is morally contentious. Consider three proposals. The first aims to equalize the marginal economic cost of reduction in each country. However, assume for a moment that this turns out to be $50 per metric ton. Does it matter that this amounts to the cost of nice evening out for the average American, but more than a month's income for the average Bangladeshi? Presumably, it does. Given this, a second proposal might aim at equalizing marginal welfare instead. But what if the worst off are in so wretched a condition that taking more from them

57. Traxler 2002. However, Traxler is thinking in terms of luxury emissions, and so would presumably not support a uniform 20% cut. (See below.) For a more recent appeal to the metaphor of teamwork, see Miller 2010.

will make little difference to their misery, but the very well off are so accustomed to luxury that even small losses hit their subjective states very hard? Does this justify taking more from the poor? Again, presumably not. Finally, as a third proposal, suppose that we adopt a more substantive account of goods, distinguishing (for example) between luxuries and subsistence goods, and differentiating their importance to welfare. Then we could protect the poor from additional deprivation by insisting that the rich should give up all their luxuries before the poor give up anything.[59] However, even if this is morally correct, it seems highly politically controversial, and so undermines many of the (alleged) practical advantages of the equal burdens approach.

In short, "equal burdens" is a contentious phrase, compatible with many different accounts of equality and burdens. Thus, the real issue is which account of these is correct. But here the usual metric of equal percentage cuts looks untenable, and other versions seem either unacceptable, or else to push back in the direction of the ethical consensus.

In conclusion, this section illustrates why ethical discussion of the allocation problem seems to support the general consensus that the richer, developed nations should take the lead in acting on climate change.[58] However, it also suggests some complications with particular proposals. In addition, it should be said that specific allocation proposals will probably have significantly different concrete implications for particular nations, especially as the climate issue evolves. Hence, though the general direction of ethical action is clear, much more work will need to be done on these questions as we move forward.

3. Unavoided Impacts

The second theoretical question about distribution concerns unavoided impacts. In practice, this has received even less political attention and

58. Approaches that prioritize the interests of the least well-off also endorse the consensus because the developing countries are much poorer than the developed countries. In 2007, average income in 2007 in the U.S. and U.K. was above $45,000 per year; in China it was $2604, in India $976, and in Bangladesh $428 (UN 2009a). Moreover, these averages do not highlight some of the worst problems. In 2005, more than 10% of the world's population lived in absolute poverty, on less than $1 per day, unable to meet their basic needs.

59. Shue 1992; Traxler 2002.

action than mitigation. Although the developed nations have promised substantial funds for many years, these have not yet materialized, much to the chagrin of poor nations. Not only has little been placed in the relevant UN fund, but even those developed countries (such as the EU) who have been publicly supportive seem interested mainly in reallocating existing foreign aid, rather than providing new funds.[60]

As a matter of theory, much of the ethical consensus on allocation seems to carry over to unavoided impacts, since many of the same facts (e.g., concerning historical responsibility and current emissions levels) seem relevant. Nevertheless, there are complications, especially about how to understand the scope of the problem. Consider just two examples.

First, in climate policy, unavoided impacts are usually discussed in terms of assistance for "adaptation," understood as "adjustment in natural or human systems . . . which moderates harm or exploits beneficial opportunities."[61] But this focus is liable to mislead, since it must be acknowledged that adaptation efforts "will not prevent all damages."[62]

On the one hand, some unavoided impacts will simply have to be endured. This raises distinct issues of justice which should not be ignored. Most obviously, there is a case for compensation, and perhaps in forms such as financial resources and immigration rights, rather than technical assistance, the usual focus of "adaptation" measures. Less obviously, since some losses cannot be compensated, and since compensation is not the whole of justice in any case, other modes of restitution, such as recognition and reconciliation, may also become prominent over time. On reflection, this should not be surprising. For example, the loss of indigenous homelands facing small island states (such as the Maldives) appears to have similarities with other, more historical, grievances of indigenous populations, where matters of recognition and reconciliation loom large.

On the other hand, there is the possibility of catastrophic changes than can neither be adapted to, nor endured. For example, if the earth really experiences a warming comparable in magnitude to an ice age shift (e.g., 5 degrees C), but over the course of only a century or so, or if climate change triggers dramatic threshold events, then the impacts on

60. Vidal and Adam 2009.
61. IPCC 2001, 365.
62. IPCC 2001, 226.

humanity might transcend historical experience. In such scenarios, the whole idea that we should address unavoided impacts through "adaptation" may end up seeming "quaint at best."[63]

Second, much depends on what we are willing to call a climate impact. Not only will no one's death certificate ever read "climate change," but many actual deaths will result from the interplay of climate with institutional failures caused by other moral and political problems.[64] As an illustration of this general problem, we might note that while it is often said that we can avoid "dangerous climate change" if the global temperature rise can be limited to 2 C, it is also frequently claimed that climate change is already responsible for around 300,000 deaths per year.[65]

4. The Trajectory Question

The third theoretical question about distribution asks what the appropriate trajectory of global carbon emissions should be over the coming decades and centuries. Conventional climate policy implicitly involves envisioning a long-term aim, and then deciding how quickly to achieve that aim. On the first issue, it seems clear that a business-as-usual path that exposes the future to the scientifically-plausible risk of an ice-age like shift in temperature in less than a hundred years is ethically unacceptable. From this it follows, given scientific projections, that any ethical policy would demand that global emissions peak sometime in the next few decades and then decline significantly for the foreseeable future. Not to make this demand seems to expose the future to extreme risk. A strong rationale would be needed to make this ethically acceptable, and none seems forthcoming.[66] In other words, this is a place where climate policy runs into a serious ethical constraint, one to which any theoretical approach would have to respond in order to be at all plausible.

Despite this promising beginning, work needs to be done to specify a more fine-grained target. In mainstream policy discussion, a number of different proposals have been made. Some claim that we should prevent a temperature rise of above 2 degrees C, some that we should aim at

63. Jamieson 2008.
64. Jamieson 2005.
65. Global Humanitarian Forum 2009.
66. For responses to some objections, see chapter 8.

a specific atmospheric concentration of carbon dioxide (or the equivalent), such as 350, 450, or 550 ppm, and others that we should not exceed a given total of human emissions, such as one trillion tons of carbon.[67] But the differences between these targets are not much discussed. The first reason for this is presumably that, since all the targets actually offered are far from business-as-usual projections, advocates assume that a move towards any would be one substantially in the right direction, and so are disinclined to highlight disagreements on the specifics. A second reason is that there appears to be substantial agreement on the speed at which we should try to reach these long-term goals. Currently, many scientists and activists have converged on the claim that global emissions reductions of 20–40% by 2020, and 50–80% by 2050, are roughly appropriate.

This political consensus is encouraging, and does aid the attempt to find benchmarks for the ethics of the transition. Nevertheless, we should be careful. Such quantitative pronouncements tend to obscure the underlying ethical issues. Most prominently, the question of how quickly to reduce global emissions implicitly requires making a decision on how to balance the interests of the present and the future, and ultimately requires a moral judgment. More specifically, though much talk of specific percentage reductions is carried out in the language of "feasibility," and so seems technical, this is a mistake. Presumably, it would be perfectly *technically* feasible for us all to reduce our emissions by 50–80% tomorrow, or even to eliminate them completely. We could, after all, just turn off our electricity for a large portion of the day, refuse to drive, and so on. The problem here is not that this cannot be done; it is rather that, given our current infrastructure, we assume that a very rapid reduction would cause social and economic chaos, and a humanitarian disaster for the current generation (see chapter 1). If this assumption is correct, we are justified in not considering such drastic measures. But the justification is moral: a policy that demanded them of us would be profoundly unjust.

This move away from the "feasibility" rationale makes an important difference. Even if emissions cuts are disruptive at some levels, presumably at some point the risks imposed on future generations are severe enough to outweigh them. Perhaps the current proposals—such as 20%

---

67. E.g., Copenhagen Accord 2009, McKibben, Allen at al. 2009.

by 2020—capture the appropriate tradeoff point. Nevertheless, it would be nice to see some argument for this claim, especially since an issue of intergenerational justice is at stake, and since we are likely—given the perfect storm—to be biased in our own favor. To see why this is important, consider two issues.

First, the trajectory concern is already arising for some of those most vulnerable to climate impacts. For example, some world leaders criticized the Copenhagen Accord's endorsement of a two degree limit as too high. For example, Mohamed Nasheed, the president of the Maldives, asserted:

> Anything above 1.5 degrees, the Maldives and many small islands and low-lying islands would vanish. It is for this reason that we tried very hard during the course of the last two days to have 1.5 degrees in the document. I am so sorry that this was blatantly obstructed by big-emitting countries.[68]

And Lumumba Stanislaus Di-aping, the Head of the G-77 group of developing countries went so far as to declare:

> [The draft text] asks Africa to sign a suicide pact, an incineration pact in order to maintain the economic dominance of a few countries. It is a solution based on values, the very same values in our opinion that funnelled six million people in Europe into furnaces.[69]

Whatever one thinks of the rhetoric of these claims, the basic ethical worry is clear. Any decision on the trajectory of emissions limits implicitly makes choices about what kinds of impacts are acceptable and unacceptable, and the values driving those choices are currently being hidden in technical language.[70]

Second, if the essential rationale for the current generation's continuing with relatively high levels of emissions in the near term were one of self-defense,[71] this would have further implications. Rights of self-defense usually come with sharp limits, especially when directed

---

68. BBC 2009.

69. BBC 2009.

70. Some claim that it is better to help the current generation of the world's poor at the expense of climate action. For a response, see chapter 8.

71. Traxler 2002.

towards the morally innocent.[72] For example, one is normally required to use other (nonharmful) means of escaping the threat if possible; and if it is not possible, one is permitted only to use the minimum force necessary. In addition, one is usually required to provide some form of restitution (e.g., financial compensation) if the victim is innocent. Interestingly, such stringent restrictions seem to play very little role in current discussions of the trajectory question. Instead, the focus is on how the current generation may preserve its own expectations into the future by implementing a policy that allows as much as possible to go on exactly as before. It is far from clear that this is a morally defensible policy. Unfortunately, the perfect storm analysis easily explains it.

In conclusion, the ethical consensus surrounding strong action led by the developing nations looks compelling. Nevertheless, we should be aware of a range of deeper issues moving forward. For example, on the allocation question, differences in rationale are likely to have significant implications for specific allocations, which may make a large difference to particular actors; on the impacts question, the issue of what to count as an unavoided climate impact will have profound distributive implications; and on the trajectory question, the current consensus on medium-term objectives obscures some important ethical assumptions about what is owed to the future. Such issues put pressure on existing theoretical approaches, especially as mediated through the ethics of the transition. So, in a moment I turn to some brief remarks about more ideal forms of theorizing. Before doing so, let us turn briefly to the issue of responsibility.

V. RESPONSIBILITY

If action is needed, and the rough shape of the burdens clear, who is responsible for making it happen?[73] At first glance, this question may seem almost impossible to answer. There are two main reasons. First, it seems plausible to claim that our existing institutions were simply not

72. Some maintain that such rights do not apply when the rights-holder is responsible for bringing about the situation, or when the victim is innocent. There is a vast philosophical literature on such matters. For an entry-point, see McMahan 2002, 2005.

73. This section draws on Gardiner 2011c.

designed for, and did not evolve in response to, global environmental problems that play out over many generations. Hence, it is unclear who has the responsibility and authority to act. Second, it might also be claimed that our ethical frameworks are also not up to the task. For example, Dale Jamieson has suggested that our current values evolved relatively recently in "low-population-density and low-technology societies, with seemingly unlimited access to land and other resources," and so are ill-suited to a globalized world.[74] More specifically, he asserts that these values include as a central component an account of responsibility which "presupposes that harms and their causes are individual, that they can be readily identified, and that they are local in time and space."[75] But, he claims, problems such as climate change fit none of these criteria, so that a new value system is needed.[76]

Both of these worries raise serious issues in global ethics, and I cannot offer a full response here. Nevertheless, some preliminary remarks may help to diffuse the initial challenge. According to a long tradition in political theory, political institutions and their leaders are said to be legitimate because, and to the extent that, citizens delegate their own responsibilities and powers to them. The basic idea is that political authorities act in the name of the citizens in order to solve problems that either cannot be addressed, or else would be poorly handled, at the individual level, and that this is what, most fundamentally, justifies both their existence and their specific form. This simple model suggests an equally simple account of failures of ethical responsibility.

First, it seems to follow straightforwardly that the most direct responsibility for the current failure of climate policy falls on recent leaders and current institutions. If authority is delegated to them to deal with global environmental problems, then they are failing to discharge the relevant responsibilities and are subject to moral criticism for this failure.

Against this, it might be reasserted that such institutions were not designed to deal with large global and intergenerational problems; hence, the assignment of responsibility is unfair. There is some truth to this. Nevertheless, we should not concede too much too quickly. After all, existing leaders and institutions have not been slow to take up the issues and assume the mantel of responsibility—making many fine

74. Jamieson 1992, 148; Jamieson 2010.
75. Jamieson 1992, 148.
76. Jamieson 1992, 147.

speeches, organizing frequent meetings, promising progress, making the topic a campaign issue, and so on. In addition, we have the explicit commitment to act, and act ethically, registered in the UNFCCC and its ratification. Hence, even if this role was not originally envisioned, many political actors have acted as if it did belong to them, and that they were capable of discharging it. They did not, for example, simply declare to their constituencies that the topic was outside of their purview or competence, nor did they advocate for fundamentally new or different institutions (e.g., by declaring the need for a new global council on the topic, or even a global constitutional convention). Given this, it is far from clear that they cannot be held at least partly responsible for assuming the role, and for their subsequent failure to deliver. They can hardly claim to be ignorant of, or to have refused, the responsibility.

Nevertheless, second, the more important issue is the following. Suppose that it is true that humanity currently lacks the appropriate institutions to deal with global environmental change. What follows? If political institutions normally operate under delegated authority from the citizens, the answer seems clear. This is a case where the delegation has either not happened, or else has failed to be successful. How do we think about this? Again, there is a natural answer. If the attempt to delegate effectively has failed, then the responsibility falls back on the citizens again—either to solve the problems themselves, or else, if this is not possible, to create new institutions to do the job. If they fail to do so, then they are subject to moral criticism, for having failed to discharge their original responsibilities.

At first glance, this move may seem startling. If the world's leaders and institutions are failing to deal with climate change, the average person might ask, how does that suddenly become *my* problem? Moreover, isn't that deeply unfair?

In response, let me make two comments. First, although the move is startling, it is a traditional one in political theory, and often made in mainstream arguments about rights of civil disobedience, revolution, and the like.[77] In short, this is not a foreign, or even unusual, model of political responsibility. Indeed, arguably, it is built into the foundations

---

77. E.g., Rawls 1999. I am not advocating these measures. How to respond to political failure is a complex and difficult question. Moreover, one must be sure not to overlook either the successes of conventional institutions, nor the potential for certain kinds of intervention to make matters (much) worse.

of democratic thinking and institutions more generally, as a natural consequence of their basic rationale. Hence, if there is a problem, it is not new, and not specific to climate change. The whole idea that citizens might be politically responsible for the behavior of their institutions is in some respects a radical and demanding one.

Second, the fact that the move seems startling to many contemporary readers may itself be the consequence of a certain vision of modern political justification. Some democratic thinkers believe that the role of social and political institutions is to discharge as many ethical responsibilities as possible for the citizenry, so that under an ideal system individuals would not have to worry at all about such responsibilities, but would instead be maximally free to engage in their own pursuits (subject to the external constraints set out by the system). But here it is noticeable that success breeds the elimination of responsibility at the individual level. The better the rest of the system is at discharging responsibilities on behalf of individuals, the fewer direct demands such responsibilities make on the individual. Hence, it is likely that the demands themselves become unfamiliar, and indeed perhaps invisible to the individual herself. If this is right, it seems plausible to think that the more effective a social system is (or is perceived to be) in discharging responsibilities in general, the more demanding any significant unmet responsibilities will seem. Or, to put the point in another way, for those used to very wide freedom to pursue their own ends without worrying about wider responsibilities, the emergence of a serious failure to discharge is likely to be deeply jarring. The issues will seem very unfamiliar and the nature of the responsibilities extreme. But this may say more about the past successes of the delegated responsibility paradigm than its likelihood of current or future failure.

Whatever the cause of the jarring problem, it seems clear that we need better ways of understanding our collective responsibilities and how to discharge them. This can be a part of the ethics of the transition, but also raises questions in ideal theory. To this, I now turn.

VI. IDEAL THEORY

The ethics of the transition aims to influence policy through existing institutional constraints and gradual attempts to modify those constraints. But it is reasonable to ask whether this is a feasible project. Early signs are not encouraging. Recent history implies that existing institutions have both allowed the threat to arise, but are (at best) reluctant to address it. Hence, the ethics of the transition is haunted by two more radical thoughts. The first is that current institutions might be seriously—and perhaps fatally—flawed and so should be rejected.[78] The second is that "you can't get there from here." Perhaps existing institutions and theories must be radically reconceptualized to reflect new global and ecological realities, and perhaps the necessary moves overwhelm the logic of a climate-focused account.[79]

In the face of such worries, some concessions seem inevitable. In general, most political philosophers working today believe that the current world order is seriously unjust. More specifically, it seems wise to acknowledge that climate change involves issues which current political institutions and theories do not seem designed for, nor obviously well-equipped to handle. Hence, whatever one thinks about the ethics of the transition, it seems clear that ideal theory matters. Most prominently, climate change is one of a number of contemporary global problems that casts doubt on the traditional philosophical strategy of constructing basic justice on the model of a single self-sufficient nation-state. If we have truly entered a new epoch on the earth, a geological era dominated by humanity—the "anthropocene"[80]—then such a model seems at least seriously incomplete, and perhaps hopelessly outdated. Theorists should ask whether this requires revising their grand visions of ethics and justice. Given these things, the project of ideal theory seems pressing.[81]

78. Dryzek 1987. See also chapter 7.

79. Perhaps it is even the case that a conventionally unfair climate deal leads to less injustice overall.

80. Crutzen and Stoermer 2000.

81. The basic moral logic of the situation may also drive us away from the status quo. For example, considering the allocation problem, no one cares much about carbon emissions for their own sake, but only about the role they play in human lives. Hence, some have advocated moving away from the focus on national emissions targets towards metrics such as development rights (Baer et al 2007), human rights against environmental harm (Caney 2005; Vanderheiden 2008), or basic capabilities (Holland 2008; Schlosberg 2009). Such a shift may be morally justified; but it does suggest a substantial departure from current political norms and institutional structures. Consider, for example, that if there is a "Germany in China," there must be something like a Pakistan or Bangladesh too (in order to generate China's low average per capita emissions). China could address this by pursuing greater internal equality if it wished. But if we insist that international policy must be adjusted instead—to ensure that different classes of Chinese emitters are treated differently—we seem to be saying that the international community should exert significant authority over China's internal affairs.

Nevertheless, we should not be too quick to dismiss the ethics of the transition. Even if existing institutions and theories are hopelessly inadequate, we can hardly expect a transformation to better overnight; so, there remains a place for intermediate theorizing. In addition, we should recognize that such theorizing might play a number of different roles. At the extremes, some will conceive of climate ethics as operating completely in isolation of other, nonclimate concerns (the isolation model), while others will see climate change as opening the door to a dramatically new world order (the vanguard model). But there are more moderate conceptions. For example, perhaps transitional climate policy should merely aim for modest improvement in other areas, insofar as it intersects with them (the mild rectification model); or perhaps it should remain content with not making wider injustice worse (the neutrality model). Importantly, discussions of the merits of these rival models seem part of the ethics of the transition rather than an obstacle to it.

More generally, it is important to note that what is at stake here is likely to depend as much on background beliefs about political reality as anything else, and so raise serious questions about the boundaries of the ideal. Practical "political reality" is, of course, a treacherous notion, as geopolitical events of the last fifty years (e.g., the fall of the Berlin Wall, the end of apartheid in South Africa) have shown. But such worries infect ideal theory as well. Rawls, for example, claims to found his own political philosophy on a notion of "realistic utopia" that aims to reconcile the real constraints of human nature and the world with the (equally treacherous) concept of "utopia." But how are we to decide what the "real constraints" on ideal theory are? Given this problem, perhaps the differences between ideal and nonideal cases are more a matter of degree than of kind. This issue is itself a matter for serious theoretical discussion.

VII. CONCLUSION

The aim of this chapter was to illustrate how substantive ethical theorizing is relevant to current debates about climate policy, and thereby suggest a modest redirection of the public debate. The main claims were:

1. Ethical considerations are already at the basis of international climate policy.

2. Scientific uncertainty does not justify inaction.
3. Precaution is theoretically respectable.
4. Past emissions matter.
5. The intragenerational burdens should fall predominantly on the developed countries.
6. Specific intergenerational trajectories require ethical defense.
7. The right to self-defense is an important, but sharply limited rationale.
8. Individuals bear some responsibility for humanity's failure.

Obviously, more needs to be done to fully develop and defend these propositions. But I hope that they help to give shape to the emerging ethics of the transition. At this point in time, getting started is the most important thing.

In closing, I want to make one final point about how to think about the roles of both ideal theory and the ethics of the transition. Some may be pessimistic about the ability of current institutions and their likely successors ever to deal with climate in anything like an ethical way—and perhaps this initial discussion only heightens such fears. I would resist this pessimism. Nevertheless, even if it turns out to be well founded, I would still insist that there is some point to work on climate ethics. While it is true that a central purpose of ethics is to guide change, it can also have other roles. In my view, prominent among these is the task of *bearing witness* to serious wrongs even when there is little hope of change. Ideal theory is central to this task. However, the ethics of transition can also play a part. Though we may not yet know either what a fully ethical approach to climate would look like, or how to get there in the long term, visions of what might count in the near term are still of some value in holding us accountable. This is so even if all they do is remind us that what we do now falls far short of any morally defensible goal.

CHAPTER 12

The Immediate Future

*It is a difficult thing, . . . and one that merits much praise, to live your whole life
justly when you've found yourself having ample freedom to do what's unjust.
Few are those who prove to be like that.*

—Socrates (Gorgias 526a)

Reality is made up of six billion voices. It is about us, and it is about ethics.

—Mary Robinson (Robinson 2009)

We face a looming global environmental tragedy. Given that we see it
coming, why has our response been so limited? This book addresses this
question through the metaphor of the perfect moral storm. This storm
has three dimensions; global, intergenerational, and theoretical. At its
core is the asymmetric power of the rich, the current generation, and
humanity as such over the future of the planet, and the corresponding
vulnerability of the poor, future generations, and the rest of nature.
These asymmetries make it tempting for the powerful to externalize the
costs (including the serious harms) of their activities over space, time,
and species. The possibility of such buck-passing threatens to undermine
ethical action, and even moral discourse itself.

Sadly, it appears that our current major institutions (such as the
market and short-term democratic institutions), though useful in other
respects, facilitate and encourage taking advantage of others in these
ways. Worse, we seem to lack structures that effectively facilitate their
natural rivals, such as direct concern for future generations, the environment, and the global poor. In addition, our main theories seem inadequate to the task. Most notably, conventional economics—the dominant
approach to public policy of our age—lacks the resources with which to

deal with large-scale problems involving the long-term future. More generally, our best political and ethical theories remain largely silent. Worryingly, there are signs of complacency, opacity, and evasiveness, and this is itself a ground for criticism. Conventional approaches may not only fail the global test, but also be accused of a basic abdication of moral responsibility. Finally, the task of moving forward is made more complicated by the fact that the perfect moral storm leaves us vulnerable to moral corruption, the subversion of our moral discourse by rival motivations. As Kant might have put it, in our (theoretical) innocence we are easily seduced. If we cannot wake ourselves from our dogmatic slumbers (and it is convenient for us not to awaken), then other things being equal, and unless we get lucky,[1] humanity is heading for global tragedy.

The focus of this book has been on global climate change. Unfortunately, the history of climate policy in the last twenty years offers strong evidence that the perfect moral storm is manifest there, and that current institutions and theories are failing the global test. Clearly, we should, and must, do better. What then of the future?

In January 2009, as I wrote the first draft of this conclusion, much hope filled the air. In the United States, a new administration was talking seriously about action on climate change, and the world was less than a year from a meeting in Copenhagen whose goal was to set a new path for reducing emissions. Clearly, the time was ripe (indeed overripe) for serious progress. Let me recount what I said then before turning to a more recent reflection:

> With luck, we are on the threshold of a new era, and one in which the climate storm will be successfully addressed. Still, we ought not simply assume that this is the case, and would be wise to show caution. First, we have been here before. Major geopolitical meetings to address climate change took place in 1993 (the Rio Earth Summit), 1997 (the Kyoto Protocol), and to a lesser extent 2001 (Bonn-Marrakesh). Moreover, initially, and on the surface, the results of those meetings appeared to be positive. After all, commitments were made to avoid dangerous climate change, to stabilize national emissions in the developed world, to cut emissions by 5% by 2012, and so on. Still, as we have seen, fine speeches and promissory notes are not enough. The facts speak for themselves. Emissions are

---

1. Many problems are solved by luck. Still, relying on luck to save the day is often morally impermissible, and a sign of deep corruption.

up substantially almost everywhere, and have been growing even more rapidly recently. Clearly, we might see "positive" agreements again, with a similar result. Moreover, even a move towards some genuine action would not show that we have successfully addressed the perfect moral storm. Shadow solutions still abound. Perhaps the asymmetrically powerful will decide that some limited action suits their narrow purposes. That will not show that we have overcome the perfect storm. Most importantly, on the face of it, we need global commitments and sustained cooperation over the long-term. This will not happen in one meeting, and is unlikely without widespread institutional, political, and ethical support. We should beware the temptation of another round of long-range targets that foist the political heavy lifting on others, passing the buck to the future. Sadly, the perfect moral storm can explain much.

Second, though leadership can help, we should not assume that the perfect moral storm can be solved by leadership alone. Beware the view that one man or administration makes all the difference (e.g., that Bush was responsible and Obama will solve it). This account of how the world works is surely too simplistic. In general, there are reasons why certain people and views come to the fore, why particular results come about, and why even "good" leaders are constrained. (Recall that Al Gore, who has done more than any politician to put climate change on the agenda, was U.S. vice president from 1993–2000.) More specifically, the perfect moral storm analysis suggests some of the strong background pressure on attempts to solve climate change. In light of it, we must beware how convenient it would be for the rest of us merely to set up a "great man" as the solution and then decry his failures. This is a very tempting form of moral corruption.

Third, we should resist the suggestion that the perfect storm can be solved *merely* by global good will and cooperation, as appeals to the "next big meeting" tend to suggest. Even the more optimistic battle of the sexes and tragedy of the commons models imply that good regulatory structures are needed in order to facilitate the desired outcome, and not just goodwill. And the perfect moral storm is worse. On the surface, it seems to require mutual *self-regulation* rather than "mutual coercion mutually agreed upon." In other words, to solve it the rich, the current generation, and humanity as such must impose limits *on themselves* that prevent the exploitation of the poor, future generations and nature. This is a more difficult task. In meetings of the powerful, the problem of shadow solutions looms large.

As things turned out, Copenhagen was not the turning point many had hoped for (see chapters 3–4). At the current time of writing (February 2010), the mood is more pessimistic. Although some point to the Copenhagen Accord's endorsement of the goal of stabilizing global temperature below 2 degrees Celsius as an important step forward, and hope that the next big meetings (set for Cancún (in late 2010) and Durban (in late 2011)) might deliver the substantial agreement necessary to make this possible, many fear that momentum has been lost, and that new impetus will be needed that is not yet forthcoming, or even perhaps conceivable, in the near term.

What then should we say? How might future climate policy succeed where the past has failed? If I am right to suggest (above) that mutual self-regulation is needed, then it is unlikely that the conventional grab bag of public motivations will deliver. Self-interested consumption and interest group politics as conventionally understood do not seem up to the task. Instead, our best chance of addressing the storm seems to rest with ethical motivation, and especially concern for future generations. If this is correct, knowing how to channel such motivation into appropriate institutions, capture it in good moral theories, and support its development in people's characters and lives becomes a major task. Many can contribute here, at all levels of society. In the academy itself, psychology, law, economics, political science, sociology, and many other disciplines all have a role to play. But we should not lose track of philosophy, especially moral and political philosophy. Clearly, the perfect moral storm in general, and the pure intergenerational problem and global test in particular, pose substantial challenges to business-as-usual.

In closing, I would like to make one last point. Since at least the time of Socrates, philosophers have been fond of "throwing down the gauntlet," and playing the gadfly. Indeed, articulating and addressing fundamental challenges to orthodoxy has always been a central part of the philosophical tradition, and a major cause of its continued vigor. Some philosophers relish this task, enjoying the discomfort that it causes those who are challenged. But this is no part of my attitude here. In my view, the global environmental tragedy raises profound questions for most of those likely to read this book, myself included.[2] The ethical challenge is unusually difficult, the stakes extremely high, and it will not be easy for us to emerge morally unscathed.[3] Moreover, the intellectual task is daunting, and it is not yet clear that we are up to it. The time to think seriously about the future of humanity is upon us. Neutralizing the perfect storm would be a good place to start.

2. See chapter 9.
3. See chapter 10.

APPENDIX I

The Population Tragedy

In discussions of global environmental problems, the issue of world population is often raised as an objection to demands being made on the world's more affluent countries. Climate change is no exception. Population growth is the core problem, some say, and this is occurring primarily in the poorer countries. Hence, they continue, the emphasis should be on population policy in the developing world rather than consumption elsewhere.

This appendix confronts an influential argument for this view. In his classic article "The Tragedy of the Commons", Garrett Hardin argues that world population is the central global environmental tragedy, that it has the structure of a tragedy of the commons, and that this implies that the only tenable solutions involve either coercion or immense human suffering.[1] I argue that Hardin's arguments are deeply flawed.[2] The population problem as he conceives it does not have the structure of a tragedy of the commons; and even if it did, this would not necessitate the extreme responses he canvasses. In addition, I contend that the basic facts about carbon emissions imply that the reproduction of the world's poorer people is not at the heart of the climate

1. I am grateful to Nick Sturgeon for introducing me to Hardin's views on population and framing much of my subsequent thinking about them.

2. Hardin's work been criticized before, but I have not found the criticism I will make in the literature. First, most of the criticism is empirical—especially that offered by proponents of a benign demographic transition hypothesis, who maintain that population will be curbed by development. Unfortunately, valuable though it is, this work does not directly address Hardin's main argument, which is not empirical but theoretical. Second, much of the theoretical criticism of Hardin revolves around his metaphors in his "Living in a Lifeboat" article, not those in "The Tragedy of the Commons." For a good discussion of the major views and their weaknesses, see Ryberg 1997.

challenge. Though I do not deny that population is an issue, my remarks cast it in a very different light.

I. HARDIN'S ANALYSIS

Human population is increasing rapidly. In 1804, after a wait of approximately 2 million years, it reached 1 billion. One hundred twenty-three years later in 1927, it topped 2 billion; 33 years later, in 1960, three billion. By 1974, 14 years later, there were four billion people; 13 years on, in 1987, five billion; and 12 years after that, in 1999, six billion.[3] By early 2010, the number had reached 6.8 billion and was on pace to reach seven billion by late 2011. This is an amazing rate of progression. Bill McKibben reports that if the world's population had increased by the same number each year throughout its history as it did in 1994, then thinking backwards from its current total, the proverbial Adam and Eve would have to have started out in 1932.[4]

There are some positive signs. For example, the rate of increase in the number of humans appears to be slowing down.[5] Nevertheless, since this rate is being applied to an expanding base of people, the absolute number of births will only come down to what it is today by the second quarter of this century. Furthermore, because people are living longer, the total population will still be rising at the mid-century mark, to around nine billion on mid-range projections; that is, by around 2050, global population will be fifty-per cent larger than it was in 2000. Hence, the problem of population growth is very much with us.[6]

Population is a problem mainly because both the increased absolute number of people and the rate of increase itself are likely to have a severe

3. UN 1998.

4. McKibben 1997.

5. The U.S. Bureau of Census estimates the peak to have been in 1962–1963 at 2.19% per year. (http://www.census.gov/ipc/www/worldpop.html)

6. The low and high projections capture a range between 8–10.5 billion by 2050. These would be increases of roughly 33–75% over 2000. See UN 2009b.

impact on the planet. Extra people place extra demands on food, water, and energy supply, and their activities cause environmental damage. Given this, it is important to understand what or who[7] is causing the problem, and perhaps thereby determine what if anything can be done about it.

Hardin offers some dramatic answers to these questions. First, he claims that the population problem is a tragedy of the commons. Left to their own devices, people will have large families, causing misery to themselves and their communities and untold damage to the environment. The structure of their preferences *"remorselessly generates tragedy."*[8] Second, Hardin sees the problem as one primarily caused by, and affecting, those in the developing nations of the third world. Third, he argues that the only available solutions are severe. In one article, he argues that we should abandon the UN's declaration that the freedom to reproduce is a fundamental human right.[9] Instead, Hardin thinks, we should use coercive instruments to prevent people from reproducing, or reproducing more than is wanted. In another article, Hardin argues that the affluent nations should refuse to assist their poorer neighbors in times of humanitarian crisis. Instead, he endorses Tertullian's claim that we would be wise to think of "pestilence, famine, wars, and earthquakes" as "prun[ing] away [their] luxuriant growth."[10]

Hardin's idea is that the earth provides a corrective to the problem of population through natural catastrophe. But, he thinks, human interference has disrupted the natural mechanism. Misguided altruism, in the form of the welfare state and food aid to overpopulated countries, has meant that the costs of overpopulation no longer fall on those who have the children. These institutions have created a tragedy of the commons that spells ruin for all.

---

7. This is not to say that the issue is one of whom to blame, in the moral sense. For example, on Hardin's view, "the concepts of blame and punishment are irrelevant" (1974, 563): "each human being, like every other animal, is genetically programmed to seek its own good," so that "the tragedy is brought on not by individual sin ('greed'), but by the system itself" (1993, 218.).

8. Hardin 1968, 1244; emphasis added.

9. Hardin 1968, 1246; 1999, 145.

10. Hardin 1974, 564.

Hardin's recommendations are difficult to accept.[11] Indeed, there is a strong moral presumption against them. They imply that the rich countries should deliberately allow hundreds of millions of people to die, when they could help them at relatively small cost to themselves. This conflicts with even a very weak principle of beneficence,[12] and may also be resisted on other moral grounds.[13]

Given the presumptions against Hardin's solutions, surely we should think on moral grounds that if almost anything else will work, then that is what we should do. This makes it relevant to consider alternative ways in which a tragedy of the commons might be resolved, ways which do not involve coercion. At least three are pertinent here. The first is to change people's motives, and so alter the preference structure that generates the problem. Hence, one might try to make people value some aspect of the situation in a new way[14], or one might try to make people value cooperation itself.

The second solution is to appeal to broad considerations of self-interest. For example, it is well known that the dynamics of a commons tragedy can be changed if the parties will meet again in other bargaining situations in the future. If we know that we must make a bargain again, we are much more likely to give up some gains from noncooperation now in exchange for the expectation of gains to be made from an overall strategy of cooperation.

The third solution is to appeal to a sense of fair play, and in particular to the notion of reciprocity. This is present in almost all societies, and supports a social attitude of rebuke to those who do not cooperate: they

11. Ryberg argues that even if Hardin is right about the severity of the problem, it may not necessitate his solutions, because aid to the "overpopulated" countries coupled with regulation of population via famine and environmental disaster may still be best on Hardin's consequentialist grounds (Ryberg 1997, 212–15).

12. A principle of beneficence may be conceived of as either a principle of moral goodness (or virtue), or as a moral requirement. I directly intend the former, as beneficence is less controversial as a moral ideal (say, of charity), than as a moral requirement. But the weak principle is also plausible as a requirement.

13. See, for example, Onora O'Neill 1985, 1993.

14. For example, in the fairly recent past, many people have come to disparage disposable Styrofoam cups to such an extent that they are willing to carry a reusable cup around with them.

are socially shunned. This too can work to solve some problems without the need for coercive state interference.[15]

These points imply a problem for Hardin. Even if the population problem were a tragedy of the commons, it seems plausible to think that any one of these solutions (or some combination) might help to resolve it. The appeal to broad self-interest looks especially promising. The economic costs of having children are huge, and the noneconomic costs are also frequently high. Though, arguably, the noneconomic benefits of parenthood are similarly large, it seems more than possible to persuade people either to forgo these altogether (e.g., by having no children of their own, and making do with being biological or nonbiological aunts or uncles), or to have less of these benefits (by having less children), in exchange for the savings incurred by not having children.[16] Indeed, arguably, this is at least part of what has already happened in the developed countries, and has reduced the number of children there.

However, Hardin seems to treat the possibility of such solutions with outright disdain. In particular, he seems to think that an appeal to broad self-interest will not work because self-interest[17] is far too deeply tied to the production of children for any change in reproductive behavior to occur. And he regards an appeal to fairness as not only ineffective, but also self-eliminating. These attitudes suggest that Hardin regards the population problem not just as a tragedy of the commons, but as one which

15. In the original standard "tit for tat" solutions to the prisoner's dilemma, the second and third strategies fit together. Robert Axelrod reports that "the two requisites for cooperation to thrive are that the cooperation be based on reciprocity, and that the shadow of the future is important enough to make this reciprocity stable" (Axelrod 1984). For egoists, these conditions hold when there is prolonged interaction over time and where this interaction holds the promise of great benefits to both sides.

16. For an overview, see Hacker 2000.

17. Hardin says, "Ruin is the destination towards which all men rush, each *pursuing his own best interest* in a society that believes in the freedom of the commons" (1968, 1244, emphasis added); about the population problem in particular he says, "the individual *benefits as an individual* from his ability to deny the truth [about the population tragedy] even though society as a whole, of which he is a part, suffers" (1968, 1244; emphasis added).

depends on circumstances of a particularly deep and intractable kind. Hence, in order to understand Hardin's attitudes, we must look at his arguments for the claim that population is a tragedy of the commons.

II. POPULATION AS A TRAGEDY OF THE COMMONS

If population is a tragedy of the commons, then it should have at least the following features:

> (Population TC1) It is *collectively rational* to have smaller families: each agent prefers the outcome produced by everyone having smaller families over the outcome produced by everyone having large families.
>
> (Population TC2) It is *individually rational* to have a large family: when each individual has the power to decide whether or not she will have a large or small family, each person (rationally) prefers to have a large family, no matter what everyone else does.[18]

The first problem for Hardin, which is widely noted, is that, on the assumption that most actual people are individually rational to this extent, Population TC2 seems empirically false. This is true both of its content and its form.

With regard to content, the raw data is remarkably consistent.[19] First, as is often pointed out, there has been a significant transition in Western Europe over the past 100 years or so. All agree that Western Europe is *below* replacement level, and that this is almost true now in North America.[20] There was a spurt of population growth with industrialization,

---

18. Hardin tends to speak in terms of "overbreeding," and seem to intend by this "having as many healthy, surviving children as possible." But his general argument requires only the more modest "have a size of family above replacement level," and this is what I intend here. (I have avoided the term "breeding." An anonymous reviewer pointed out to me that this term may seem offensive, and in any case encourages the animalistic connotations Hardin tries to give human behavior, connotations I resist below.)

19. UN 2009b.

20. The North American population figures are complicated by large immigration to both the United States and Canada. Without immigration, North America is likely to be slightly below replacement.

but now this is over. Furthermore, this has happened without coercion. So, Population TC2 is not true of the behavior of people in these nations.[21] Second, the UN reports that *global* fertility rates have fallen significantly in the recent past (to 2.56 in 2005–2010, from 5 in the early 1950s); and, furthermore, this reflects a decline in fertility in *all* regions of the world (in the last 40 years, 6.69 to 4.61 in Africa, 4.76 to 2.35 in Asia, 5.01 to 2.26 in Latin America and the Caribbean).[22] So, Population TC2 seems unlikely to be true of the behavior of the world as a whole either. All seem to be following the downward trend towards smaller family size.

As well as being in stark conflict with the raw data, Population TC2 also takes an overly simplistic form. It reduces the question of reproduction to the issue of family size. But even in the developing nations, matters are much more complex than this. For example, the Indian census has suggested that ultrasound technology is enabling Indians to follow the Chinese in aborting female fetuses at abnormally high rates. In India, then, it seems clear that sex plays a significant role in reproductive choice, and one that affects family size. This fact is clearly relevant for population policy.[23]

The second problem for Hardin is that Population TC2 seems independently implausible. What makes it in my interest to have a

---

21. It is not true even in those nations officially in favor of more rather than less children. For example: Italy is officially Catholic, but nineteenth-century Italy had a fertility rate of 5 children per woman; now it is down to significantly below that necessary for replacement. Indeed, the UN predicts very substantial immigration will be necessary to maintain its current population.

22. This data is used by optimists about population in support of their view that there will be a benign demographic transition to lower total population. The pessimists may argue that these declines are coming too late (and they may be right). But this does not help Hardin's argument. This is an empirical question, to be answered by the data; but Hardin doesn't provide any data. He provides a conceptual argument to show that the population problem is a prisoner's dilemma, and that coercion is required.

23. A major cause of the problem seems to be that these societies have no universal social security systems, and that women are effectively relieved of all responsibilities for their own family when they marry. This tends to make the rationality of having a child depend on its sex, and perhaps the rationality of having an additional child depend on the sex of the preceding children. See Dugger 2001; Sen 1992, 1999.

large family *whatever anyone else does*? For a prisoner's dilemma, we
need this incentive structure:

TABLE A.1

	Couple B merely replaces	*Couple B has a large family*
Couple A merely replaces	2nd, 2nd Maintain current population	4th, 1st
Couple A has a large family	1st, 4th	3rd, 3rd Population explosion

But why would we think that couples have these preferences, so that the
preferred outcome for all is to have a large family, and what is feared
most of all is for others to have large families while we do not? Under
moderately favorable conditions, it seems more plausible that some
people will prefer replacement, or close, no matter what everyone else
does, that very few people will prefer having lots of children just for the
sake of it, and that some will prefer no children (or one). Indeed, the
empirical evidence from the developed countries suggests that overall,
taking everyone's preferences into account, uncoerced decisions produce a level of reproduction that is *below* the replacement level for a
whole society.

To resist this argument, Hardin has to claim that it is always to the
advantage of the individual to have a large family.[24] But why should we
believe this? It is not clear. But Hardin seems tempted by the view that
it is because it is *biologically advantageous* to have a large family. For
example, he says:

> *If* each human family were dependent only on its own resources; *if* the children of
> improvident parents starved to death; *if*, thus, overbreeding brought its own "pun-
> ishment" to the germ line—*then* there would be no public interest in controlling
> the breeding of families. But our society is deeply committed to the welfare state,
> and hence is confronted with another aspect of the tragedy of the commons.

24. Hardin seems to realize this. He says that the independent herdsman "dare not
refrain" from overloading the commons, because if he did so he would "suffer more"
than a "selfish" one who does (1974, 562), and would be (correctly) condemned as a
"simpleton" (1968, 1246).

In a welfare state, how shall we deal with the family, the religion, the race, or the class (or indeed any distinguishable and cohesive group) that adopts overbreeding as a policy to secure its own aggrandizement? To couple the concept of freedom to breed with the belief that everyone born has an equal right to the commons is to lock the world into a tragic course of action.[25]

This argument faces two problems. First, it is concerned with groups and germ lines. It says nothing about the interests of the *individuals* involved. Therefore, it does nothing to justify the claim that it is always to the advantage of the individual to have a large family. Second, this claim would be plausible only if one posited a strong correlation between the biological interests of a germ line and the self-interest of individuals carrying that germ line. But, on any plausible theory of the interests or well-being of an individual, an individual's self-interest does not consist in, nor is it dominated by, even his or her own biological interests, let alone the biological interests of the group.[26]

But perhaps Hardin has a second argument that does not depend on people's interests. When arguing against the idea that an appeal to conscience might solve the population problem (my "fair play" suggestion), he says:

People vary. Confronted with appeals to limited breeding, some people will undoubtedly respond to the plea more than others. Those who have more children will produce a larger fraction of the next generation than those with more susceptible consciences. The difference will be accentuated, generation by generation. . . . The argument assumes that conscience or the desire to have children (no matter which)

---

25. Hardin 1968, 1246; emphasis in original. As is often noted, this seems to be an inaccurate description of the motivation of those in above replacement countries. People in some societies have reason to have many children because there is no one else to look after them when they become old and there is high infant mortality. This makes it risky not to have lots of children, from the point of view of self-interest. This is actually worse than a prisoner's dilemma situation. Here the parents are likely not prefer the constrained outcome (Population TC1), because they fear abandonment in old age more than general population problems.

26. There is also a question about whether one can make sense of biological interests in evolutionary terms (and also, perhaps, whether one can make sense of the notion of biological interests). Such an approach is tried by Varner 1998. But note that even Varner believes that individuals have psychological interests in addition to their biological interests, and that the psychological interests trump the biological ones.

is hereditary—but hereditary only in the most general formal sense. The result will be the same whether the attitude is transmitted through germ cells, or exosomatically ... The argument has been stated in the context of the population problem, but it applies equally well to any instance in which society appeals to an individual exploiting a commons to restrain himself for the general good—by means of his conscience. To make such an appeal is to set up a selective system that works towards the elimination of conscience from the race.[27]

Hence, Hardin argues that reproductive restraint will be eliminated by natural selection: those who practice restraint will have less descendants than those who do not, and since the attitude of restraint is transmitted between generations, this attitude will become progressively less common.

This argument faces serious practical, empirical, and theoretical problems. The practical problem is that natural selection works over very long time scales. Hence, it is unlikely to work fast enough to prevent the appeal to conscience working for a while. And perhaps a while is all we need worry about, if the benign demographic thesis is correct. The empirical problem is that if Hardin were right, we would expect people already to have the desire for as many children as possible, since we would expect the selection procedure to have been at work for generations.[28] But the empirical evidence suggests the opposite: global fertility rates are falling. The theoretical problem is the assumption that the attitude of restraint is transmitted between generations. There is simply no reason to believe that people's consciences will be the same as their parents, nor in particular that they will have the same attitude towards reproduction. Indeed, the empirical evidence stands squarely against it.

27. Hardin 1968, 1246.

28. I.e., we would expect people already to have the desire for as many children as would maximize the chance of the genes being passed on. Against this, Hardin would presumably argue that the historical natural pruning had an effect on reproductive motivation, but one which is being undermined by the more recent welfare state and foreign aid programs. But here it is worth pointing out (a) that those countries without the welfare state are the ones which have sustained the high birth rates rather than held them back, and (b) the decline in birth rates has occured in rich countries even given the introduction of welfare. (Against (b), Hardin might argue that it is too early to tell what will happen in these countries, given that welfare is fairly recent; but still the empirical evidence does not look promising for him.)

I conclude that Hardin's analysis of the population problem as a tragedy of the commons is untenable. It relies on flawed assumptions about human motivation which rest on extremely dubious appeals to evolutionary biology.

III. TOTAL ENVIRONMENTAL IMPACT

How then should we think about the population problem? This is not the place for a full account. But it may be worth observing that the important issue about population is not really how many people there are. In itself, this tells us nothing and threatens little. The issue is the environmental impact that people have, in particular on the so-called carrying capacity of the earth.[29] Thus, the population element of global environmental problems concerns how the number of people in the world interacts with the environmental impact per person to produce the total environmental impact of humanity.[30]

On this issue, however, there is reason to believe that for some problems the most important variable is the environmental impact per person, not the total human population.[31] Consider our case of climate change. Here there is a presumption that per capita emissions are the more important variable, at least in the short- to medium-term.

First, there is a large discrepancy between many developed and developing nations. Total global carbon emissions in 1990, the usual benchmark year, were 6.164 billion metric tons of carbon.[32] This would correspond to a global per capita emission rate of 1.16 tons. But in 2005, the U.S. population emitted at a rate of 5.32 tons per capita. This is roughly equal to the average emissions of nearly five Chinese people,

---

29. Determining the carrying capacity is a difficult, and extremely value-laden business, which raises philosophical issues of its own. For a helpful discussion, see Cohen 1995: chapter 12 and appendices 3–4.

30. For a similar view, see Ehrlich and Holdren 1971.

31. See Griffin 1988, 223–4; Ehrlich and Ehrlich 1989.

32. The following figures are drawn from Marland 2008. Emissions are sometimes reported as tons of carbon dioxide, rather than carbon. This gives higher numeric values (as CO_2 is heavier), but the same qualitative results.

fifteen Indians, and sixty-six Bangladeshis. Clearly, the impact of one average American is much higher than that of many extra Indians and Bangladeshis. Indeed, if the rest of the world (currently 6.7 billion people) were to follow suit, this would produce a global total of more than 35 billion tons. If we factor in an increase in world population to 9 billion—that expected by mid-century—the number rises to nearly 48 billion tons. Clearly, such increases would be dramatically unsustainable. Given this, to focus on population growth in India and Bangladesh seems seriously misleading. The key considerations seem to be that the emissions of people in developed countries are very high, whereas those in developing countries are generally very low. Of course, it does not help that many Indians and Bangladeshis (for example) aspire to live like Americans (at least in terms of energy consumption), and that American emissions are increasing, in good part because it is growing its own population (primarily through immigration rather than reproductive choices). Nevertheless, population growth per se in places like India and Bangladesh is a much lesser component of the problem.

Second, it is stunning fact that the current activities of many developing countries are in one sense sustainable. Scientists typically advocate a reduction of between 50–80% in global emissions over the coming decades. If world population were kept constant, a 50% cut would yield a per capita rate of 0.58 tons; if it were to increase to 9 billion, the rate would be 0.39 tons. This would require reductions in per capita emissions in the United States of 89–96%, and in the United Kingdom of 77–85%. By contrast, in 2005, many large developing countries were already below 0.58 tons per capita, and some were even below 0.39 tons. Consider, for example, India (0.37 tons), Indonesia (0.41), and Brazil (0.51 tons). Bangladesh and large portions of Africa were even below the 80% reduction benchmark of 0.23 tons per capita (constant population) and 0.15 (population of 9 billion). In short, the raw numbers suggest that the climate problem would not be much affected by many more Indians, Bangladeshis and Africans living as they currently do. The heart of the matter is elsewhere.

If this is right, the benign demographic thesis turns out not to be so encouraging after all. That thesis suggests that the price of a decrease in the absolute number of people is development, but development as we presently understand it requires additional energy consumption, and this in turn tends to involve an increase in the environmental impact per person. This is because the major sources of energy currently supporting the developed countries—especially oil and coal—come with significant environmental impacts. Indeed, the development necessary for the less developed nations to reach a stable or even declining population would, on present technologies, involve a catastrophic increase in energy consumption, and so in the environmental impact per person.

This is bad news. However, as we have seen in chapters 1 and 5, there is worse to come. The problem of an escalating environmental impact per person seems to have a structure similar to the one that worries Hardin, but also in some respects worse. This is the problem of intergenerational buck-passing.

IV. CONCLUSION

Hardin claims that we face global environmental tragedy, that strong regulatory regimes may be needed in order to stop overpollution, and that the benign demographic transition hypothesis should be treated with suspicion. I agree, but for very different reasons.[33]

First, Hardin's regulatory regime mistakes the core problem and the primary culprits. While it is true that for the poor countries to adopt the more energy- and pollution-intensive lifestyles of the West would be disastrous, and so that there is reason to prevent this, even without their contribution existing patterns of behavior in the developed countries would have serious consequences, and must be addressed. It is affluent people in general, and especially in the rich countries, who currently contribute most to our main global environmental problem, so it is essential that they take the lead in action, and quickly. This should be the political priority, especially since it is probably also a politically necessary prerequisite for preventing the developing countries from following a Western path.

---

33. Of course, I do not endorse the kinds of rights-violating regimes he has in mind. I would also emphasize that the problem of overpollution would remain even in the absence of population growth, since energy consumption *per capita* is on an upward spiral.

Second, Hardin is skeptical about the benign demographic transition hypothesis because he doubts the scientific evidence, and is inclined towards a strong evolutionary account of human reproductive behavior. But I am skeptical because, though the empirical evidence for a decline in population seems compelling, I doubt that the expected transition will be benign since it comes at the price of increased development, and on current technologies this means increased energy consumption and pollution. This locates the problem not in the deep nature of human beings and their germ lines, but in ways of life to which some of us are deeply attached, but could, and if it comes to it, should, live without.

Third, Hardin's analysis mistakes the shape of the problem and so underestimates its depth. Instead of a tragedy of the commons where equally vulnerable herdsmen must convince each other to accept "mutual coercion mutually agreed upon", we face a perfect moral storm dominated by degenerate forms of the pure intergenerational problem, where the asymmetrically powerful current generation must overcome the temptations of intergenerational buck-passing, and do so largely through self-regulation.

APPENDIX 2

Epistemic Corruption and Scientific Uncertainty in Michael Crichton's *State of Fear*

Our understanding can be corrupted in a variety of ways. Chapter 9 considers moral corruption; but epistemic corruption is also a major threat in the perfect moral storm. This appendix illustrates this point using an example drawn from the climate debate. A few years ago, Michael Crichton, the celebrated author of novels such as *Jurassic Park*, wrote a work of fiction entitled *State of Fear*. In that book, he suggested that climate change is a green conspiracy, an attempt by environmentalists to hoodwink the public and major institutions into action on environmental issues with a false scare.

Crichton rehearses a number of common objections to mainstream climate science in the novel that I will not address here. Instead, I focus on some general epistemic claims he makes in the author's message at the end of the book, where he tells us his own conclusions.[1] These claims are:

- Nobody knows how much of the present warming trend might be a natural phenomenon.
- Nobody knows how much of the present warming trend might be man-made.
- Nobody knows how much warming will occur in the next century.[2]
  ... But if I had to guess—the only thing anyone is doing, really—I

---

1. Crichton 2005, 625.

2. Crichton adds, "The computer models vary by 400 per cent, de facto proof that nobody knows." This claim is misleading. The nonpartisan Pew Center puts the point this way: "What Crichton is really saying is that the high estimate from IPCC's projected range for 2100 (5.8C) is 400% greater than its lowest estimate (1.4C). This isn't a valid expression of model variation or uncertainty. The variation around the average warming projected by the IPCC of 3.6C is about 60%. Perhaps more importantly, the reason for wide range is not due to the models themselves, but the use of a range of emissions scenarios" (Pew Center 2005).

would guess the increase will be 0.812436 degrees C. There is no evidence that my guess about the state of the world one hundred years from now is any better or worse than anyone else's. (We can't "assess" the future, nor can we "predict" it. These are euphemisms. We can only guess. An informed guess is just a guess.)

At first glance, Crichton's claims can seem rhetorically effective. After all, even the best and most concerned climate scientists will say that there are significant uncertainties associated with climate science. Isn't Crichton just reporting the epistemic facts and drawing logical conclusions from them? I think not.

I. WHAT THE SCIENTISTS KNOW

Let us begin with the assertions themselves. Consider first the claims that "nobody knows" how much of the present warming is natural, and how much is man-made. On the face of it, these seem false. For example, in 2001, the IPCC stated that "there is new and stronger evidence that *most* of the warming observed over the last 50 years is attributable to human activities," and included graphs showing that the combination of natural and human-induced warming provided a good explanation of temperature rise since 1850.[3] So, it looks as though the IPCC at least does know the answers to these questions.

Second, similarly, Crichton claims that "there is no evidence that my guess about the state of the world one hundred years from now is any better or worse than anyone else's." But this claim is hard to understand except as hyperbole. For example, the basic greenhouse effect is not in dispute, nor is the accumulation of carbon dioxide in the atmosphere, nor the increase in human emissions since the Industrial Revolution. Moreover, scientific projections of future temperature rise have remained consistent across the IPCC reports, and indeed for nearly a century since Svante Arrenhius's original calculations. Even if one thought that this

---

3. IPCC 2001c, 5–7. IPCC 2007a stated that the warming trend was now unequivocal, and "very likely" (meaning a probability of 90% or more) due to human activity. However, Crichton's book was written before that report came out; so, here and below, I focus on the information available to Crichton.

evidence was insufficient in some way, it is surely *some* evidence. Some "guesses" are better than others.

Third, a little later Crichton suggests a different argument by proposing a condition for sufficiency that has not yet been met: "Before making expensive policy decisions on the basis of climate models, I think it is reasonable to require that those models predict future temperatures accurately for a period of ten years. Twenty years would be better."[4] However, in context this demand is also problematic. First, the "expensive" claim is contested (see chapter 8). Second, as Donald Brown argues, the bar here is probably set too high. On the one hand:

> Future predictions of human-caused climate events suffer both from scientific uncertainty about how the global physical system will react to increases in greenhouse gas emissions and from ignorance about what levels of these gases will be emitted by human activities in the years ahead. Therefore, if we make high levels of scientific certainty about what will actually happen in the future a test for the rationality of public policy on global warming, we will probably *never* meet the test.[5]

On the other hand, setting the bar so high probably means that even if science meets the test, by the time this evidence is there it will be too late to act. Hence, there is an ethical question about what kind of evidence we should demand before acting.[6] Demanding too much may constitute a fancy method of intergenerational buck-passing. Third, some standards of evidence are being met. A lead author of the 2001 report states that models do "stand up well" against current climate, and are in "qualitative agreement" with past climate.[7]

Why, then, is Crichton so dismissive of the information coming from climate science? One answer, of course, is that he believes that the IPCC are part of a serious scientific conspiracy. This claim looks less credible given the high level endorsements of the basic conclusions of their reports by other scientific bodies, and the degree to which there seems to be a consensus in the scientific community.[8] But perhaps Crichton would respond that this just shows the extent of the conspiracy. However,

4. Crichton 2005, 626.
5. Brown 2002, 113.
6. Brown 2002, 114.
7. Houghton 2005, 100–1.
8. Oreskes 2004.

now we are in difficult epistemic territory. For one thing, conspiracy theories are by their nature very difficult to rebut, partly because they tend to reinterpret any evidence against them as proof that the conspiracy is deeper and more pervasive than people have acknowledged. Hence, it is difficult to know what (if any) evidence would convince a radical conspiracy theorist. For another, there are conspiracy theories on both sides of the climate question. Some believe that the skeptics are part of a "brown" conspiracy funded by the fossil fuel industry and nefarious right wing fanatics. Hence, appeals to conspiracy are a double-edged sword in this context. If we are attracted to them, it is difficult to know which way to be pulled.

II. CERTAINTY, GUESSWORK, AND THE MISSING MIDDLE

Conspiracy theories raise interesting epistemic questions. But I will not pursue them here. Instead, I want to discuss another explanation for Crichton's pessimism about climate science. When he claims that there is "no evidence" in favor of mainstream climate projections, he immediately adds: "We can't 'assess' the future, nor can we 'predict' it. These are euphemisms. We can only guess." This is puzzling. To guess might be said to mean "to form an opinion about something either (a) without enough evidence to make a definitive judgment, or (b) without knowing for sure." But notice that this picture appears to leave something out. Surely there is something between certain knowledge and mere "guessing." Moreover, this missing middle seems to characterize our normal epistemic situation much more readily than either of the extremes. To see this, let us first review a little basic history of philosophy, and then briefly offer a different picture of the epistemic issues.

One way of ignoring the claims of mainstream climate science would be to be very demanding in what one is willing to count as knowledge. It is evident from the rest of the novel that Crichton distrusts the data and methods of the scientists whose work is summarized by the IPCC. (As noted earlier, the IPCC does no science itself, but produces a report of the peer-reviewed science that has been done.) So, perhaps the idea is that the IPCC results are not certain. They could be mistaken; therefore Crichton claims that the IPCC do not "know."

This move is an interesting one. It resonates with two more general epistemic skepticisms familiar from the history of philosophy. The first comes from Rene Descartes. Descartes also had the thought that one should not claim to know something about which one could be mistaken. From this he concluded that knowledge must be based on certainty, and so set out to work out what he "really" knew based on his "method of doubt." He refused to believe anything that he could conceive to be possibly false.

Descartes's project has intrigued epistemologists for centuries. But there is something suspicious about its invocation here. On the one hand, the method of doubt seems successful against climate science. But, on the other hand, if this is so, this is only because it seems more generally successful. On a standard philosophical view of things, it is conceivable that all our scientific beliefs—and indeed most of our beliefs more generally—are mistaken, because, for example, we can imagine that we might be being manipulated by an evil demon, or brains in a vat, or really plugged into *The Matrix*. Given this, a common attitude to the method of doubt is that, if it proves anything, it proves too much. Descartes himself thought that, pushed to its logical conclusion, it would show that the only thing one knows (in the sense of "knows for certain") is that one is thinking when one is thinking. (This is the famous "I think, therefore I am.") Many subsequent philosophers have agreed that it does have this implication, and have become troubled as a result.[9] The problem is that the idea that in order to know something I must "know it for certain" flies strongly in the face of the fact that we usually claim to know all sorts of things, including many scientific facts and theories. (This is why philosophers are still interested in Descartes.)

If the method of doubt does lead in this direction, we seem to have an awkward choice. Either we invoke a different conception of knowledge (and so save our claims to know), or else we admit that knowledge is problematic, and instead decide to re-label much of our normal ways of talking (speaking, for example, of what one is "warranted" in believing). This is important from the theoretical point of view; but, arguably, neither move makes much difference to how we normally talk and think. (Indeed, much of the point of the theoretical discussion is usually to try

---

9. Descartes tried to show that one could reclaim ordinary knowledge based on an argument for the existence of God. Subsequent philosophers find his argument lacking.

to preserve normal practice.) Still, in the current context, this brings us to an important point. It is that the apparent problems with the notion of knowledge as certainty do nothing to imply that climate science considered as such should be seen as a suspect field. If there is epistemic trouble here, it is not in any way peculiar to climate science. The theory of gravity, molecular biology, organic chemistry, and so on, would all be subject to the same worry. But we are not put off relying on these when we make policy decisions.

This implies that there might be an ethical as well as an epistemic problem with Crichton's claim that "nobody knows" the various scientific claims. If it is based on the claims that knowledge requires certainty, and climate science is uncertain, then this may be true in one sense, but nevertheless deeply misleading. To invoke such skepticism selectively against climate science ignores the fact that all science, and almost everything else that we claim to know, is vulnerable to the same charge. And selective skepticism may be a sign of moral and epistemic corruption.

The second general epistemic skepticism that Crichton's claims bring to mind is Hume's problem of induction. Hume argues that scientific knowledge, and indeed empirical knowledge more generally, rests on the hidden assumption that the future will resemble the past. But, Hume argues, this claim cannot be justified. In particular, if one tries to justify it by claiming that inductive methods have always worked in the past, one must rely on the hidden assumption again, in order to justify the relevance of this claim to future projections. Hume concludes from this argument that all of empirical knowledge relies on a much less robust foundation than we pre-theoretically believe. This resonates with Crichton's assertion that "We can't 'assess' the future, nor can we 'predict' it. These are euphemisms. We can only guess."

The first point to make is that, again, there is no reason to single out climate science. If climate projections are "guesses" in this sense, then so is the claim that the law of gravity will continue to hold tomorrow, or in 2100. But we do normally claim to "know" these things, and we are more than willing to make policy decisions based on them. Given this, the claim that "an informed guess is just a guess" is deeply misleading. Crichton can, of course, define terms in whatever way he sees fit. But we should emphasize that his terminology is far from usual practice. We do not normally think of the extrapolation of the theory of gravity or basic organic chemistry into the future as merely "informed guesses."

The second point is that even though there may be something new going on in climate science, so that there might be something to the claim that induction is not justified there, this tends to justify action rather than inaction. What I have in mind is this. It is true that climate projections are made on the basis of the agreements between models and past climate data. Hence, one might worry that as climate change increases, the past performance of the earth's climate system becomes a less reliable guide to future change. Indeed, this is part of what scientists have in mind when they speak of climate change leading us to a "new planet." Nevertheless, this concern does not seem to justify doing nothing. On the contrary, pushing the inductive envelope in this way seems to be something we have good reason to avoid. We have grounds for believing that rapid, unprecedented, and unpredictable shifts in climate would be dangerous, even potentially catastrophic, to human and natural systems. Indeed, this is a primary reason that climate scientists are concerned about anthropogenic climate change in the first place.

III. CONCLUSION

I conclude that Crichton's strong rhetoric about knowledge and climate science is misleading. Construed in normal terms, it is simply not true that our epistemic poverty is so great. Construed in more philosophical terms, it may be true, but this does not have the implications that Crichton suggests. Profound skepticism is an interesting theoretical exercise in epistemology, but ought not to be applied selectively against climate science. Moreover, to do so suggests a worrying kind of epistemic and moral corruption.

References

Ackerman, Frank. 2008. "Hot It's Not: Reflections on Cool It by Bjorn Lomborg". *Climatic Change* 89: 435–446.

Ackerman, Frank and Elizabeth Stanton. 2010. "The Social Cost of Carbon". *Economics for the Environment and Equity Network.*

Adam, David. 2007. "Scientists Warn It May Be Too Late To Save the Ice Caps." *The Guardian*, 19 February.

———.2007b. "Climate Talks Progressing Despite U.S. Opposition to Targets, Benn Says." *The Guardian*, 12 December.

———.2008a. "Analysis: Has the Kyoto Protocol Worked?" *The Guardian*, 8 December.

———.2008b. "World Emissions on Track to Meet Kyoto Targets Says UN Chief." *The Guardian*, 18 November.

Adam, David, Peter Walker, and Alison Benjamin. 2007. "Grim Outlook for Poor Countries in Climate Report." *The Guardian*, 18 September.

Agarwal, Anil, and Sunita Narain. 1991. *Global Warming in an Unequal World: A Case of Environmental Colonialism* (New Dehli: Centre for Science and Environment).

Aldred, Jonathan. 2009. "Ethics and Climate Change Cost-Benefit Analysis: Stern and After." *New Political Economy* 14(4): 469–88.

Allen, Myles R., David J. Frame, Chris Huntingford, et al. 2009. "Warming Caused by Cumulative Carbon Emissions Towards the Trillionth Tonne." *Nature* 458 (Apr.): 1163–6.

Alley, Richard. 2004. "Abrupt Climate Change." *Scientific American* 291: 62–9.

American Meteorological Society, 2009. "Policy Statement on Geoengineering the Climate System." Available at: http://www.ametsoc.org/policy/draftstatements/

Andreou, Chrisoula. 2006. "Environmental Damage and the Puzzle of the Self-Torturer." *Philosophy & Public Affairs* 34(1): 95–108.

———.2007. "Environmental Preservation and Second-Order Procrastination." *Philosophy & Public Affairs* 35(3): 233–48.

———.2010. "A Shallow Route to Environmentally Friendly Happiness: Why Evidence That We Are Shallow Materialists Need Not Be Bad News for the Environment(alist)." *Ethics, Place & Environment* 13(1): 1–10.

Archer, David. 2005. "How Long Will Global Warming Last?" *Real Climate*, 15 March 2005. Available at: http://www.realclimate.org/index.php/archives/2005/03/how-long-will-global-warming-last/#more-134.

————.2006. "Fate of Fossil Fuel CO2 in Geologic Time." *Journal of Geophysical Research* 110: 1–6.

————.2009. *The Long Thaw* (Princeton, NJ: Princeton University Press).

Archer, David, and Bruce Buffett. 2005. "Time-dependent Response of the Global Ocean Clathrate Reservoir to Climatic and Anthropogenic Forcing." *Geochemistry. Geophysics. Geosystems* 6, Q03002, doi:10.1029/2004GC000854.

Archer, David, Michael Eby, Victor Brovkin, Andy Ridgwell, Long Cao, Uwe Mikolajewicz, Ken Caldeira, Katsumi Matsumoto, Guy Munhoven, Alvaro Montenegro, and Kathy Tokos. 2009. "Atmospheric Lifetime of Fossil Fuel Carbon Dioxide." *Annual Review of Earth and Planetary Sciences 37: 117–34.* 10.1146/annurev.earth.031208.100206

Aristotle, 2009. *Nicomachean Ethics.* Ed. David Ross and Lesley Brown (Oxford: Oxford University Press).

Arrow, K. 1999. "Discounting, Morality, and Gaming." In P.R. Portney and J.P. Weyant, eds., *Discounting and Intergenerational Equity* (Washington, D.C.: Resources for the Future): 13–21.

Arrow, K., Cline, C., Maler, K.-G., Munasinghe, M. and Stiglitz, J. 1996. "Intertemporal Equity, Discounting, and Economic Efficiency." In J. Bruce, H. Lee, and E. Haites, eds., *Climate Change 1995: Economic and Social Dimensions of Climate Change* (Cambridge: Cambridge University Press): 125–44.

Athanasiou, Tom, and Paul Baer. 2002. *Dead Heat* (New York: Seven Stories).

Atkinson, T., and A. Brandolini. 2007. *On Analysing the World Distribution of Income* (Oxford: Oxford University Press).

Austen, Jane. 1923. *The Oxford Illustrated Jane Austen.* Edited by R. W. Chapman. (Oxford: Oxford University Press).

Axelrod, Robert. 1984. *The Evolution of Cooperation* (New York: Basic Books).

Babiker, Mustapha H., Henry D. Jacoby, John M. Reilly, and David M. Reiner. 2002. "The Evolution of a Climate Regime: Kyoto to Marrakesh and Beyond." *Environmental Science & Policy* 5: 195–206.

Baer, Paul, Athanasiou, Tom, and Kartha, Sivan. 2007. *The Right to Development in a Climate Constrained World: the Greenhouse Development Rights Framework* (London: Christian Aid.)

Barrett, Scott. 1990. "The Problem of Global Environmental Protection." *Oxford Review of Economic Policy* 6: 68–79.

————.1998. "Political Economy of the Kyoto Protocol." *Oxford Review of Economic Policy* 14: 20–39.

————.2005. *Environment and Statecraft: The Strategy of Environmental Treaty-Making* (Oxford: Oxford University Press).

————.2007. *Why Cooperate? The Incentive to Supply Global Public Goods* (Oxford: Oxford University Press).

————.2008. "The Incredible Economics of Geoengineering." *Environmental and Resource Economics* 39: 45–54.

Barry, Brian. 2005. *Why Social Justice Matters* (Cambridge: Polity).

————.1978. "The Circumstances of Justice and Future Generations." In R. Sikora and B. Barry, eds., *Obligations to Future Generations* (Philadelphia: Temple University Press).

Battisti, David, and Rosamund Naylor. 2009. "Historical Warnings of Future Food Insecurity with Unprecedented Seasonal Heat." *Science*, 9 January 323. no. 5911: 240–4.

BBC 2009. "Copenhagen reaction in quotes". December 19.

Bengtsson, Lenart. 2006. "Geoengineering to Confine Climate Change: Is it at all Feasible?" *Climatic Change* 77: 229–34.

Berner, Robert. 2002. "Examination of Hypotheses for the Permo-Triassic Boundary Extinction by Carbon Cycle Modeling." *Proceedings of the American Academy of Sciences* 99.7: 4172–7.

Bertram, Christopher. 2009. "Exploitation and Intergenerational Justice." In Axel Gosseries and Lukas Meyer, eds., *Intergenerational Justice* (Oxford: Oxford University Press): 147–66.

Binmore, Ken. 2007. *Game Theory: A Very Short Introduction* (Oxford: Oxford University Press).

Black, Ian. 2002. "EU votes for Kyoto and increases pressure on Bush." *The Guardian*, 5 March.

Black, Richard. 2005. "UK Could 'Miss Kyoto Gas Target.'" *BBC News*, 1 April.

———. 2010. "UN Climate Deadline is 'Flexible.'" *BBC News*, 21 January.

Blackburn, Simon. 1998. *Ruling Passions* (Oxford: Clarendon Press).

Blair, Tony. "Climate Change Speech (2004)." URL: http://www.guardian.co.uk/politics/2004/sep/15/greenpolitics.uk

Bodansky, Daniel. 1996. "May We Engineer the Climate?" *Climatic Change* 33: 309–21.

Bohringer, Christoph. 2001. "Climate Politics from Kyoto to Bonn: From Little to Nothing?" *Energy Journal* 23, no. 2.

Booker, Christopher. 2009. "The Real Climate Catastrophe." *Daily Telegraph*, 25 October.

Borger, Julian. 2001. "Bush Kills Global Warming Treaty." *The Guardian*, 29 March.

Bostrom, Nick. 2003. "Astronomical Waste: The Opportunity Cost of Delayed Technological Development." *Utilitas* 15.3: 308–14.

Broome, John. 1992. *Counting the Cost of Global Warming* (Isle of Harris, UK: White Horse Press).

———. 1994. "Discounting for Time". *Philosophy and Public Affairs* 23(2): 128–156.

———. 2005. "Should We Value Population?", *Journal of Political Philosophy* 13(4): 399–413.

———. 2008. "The Ethics of Climate Change". *Scientific American* 298(6): 97–102

Brown, Donald. 2002. *American Heat: Ethical Problems with the United States' Response to Global Warming* (Lanham, Md.: Rowman & Littlefield).

Brown, Gordon. 2009. "Copenhagen Must be a Turning Point." *The Guardian*, 6 December.

Brown, Paul. 2001. "World Deal on Climate Isolates US." *The Guardian*, 24 July.

———. 2003. "Russia Urged to Rescue Kyoto Pact." *The Guardian*, 26 February.

Buchanan, Allen. 2006. "Institutionalizing the Just War." *Philosophy & Public Affairs* 34(1): 2–38.

Burger, Joanna, and Michael Gochfeld. 1998. "The Tragedy of the Commons 30 Years Later." *Environment* 41: 4–27.

Bryden, Harry L., Hannah R. Longworth, and Stuart A. Cunningham. 2005. "Slowing of the Atlantic Meridional Overturning Circulation at 25 Degrees North." *Nature* 438: 655–7.

California Assembly Bill 32 (2006), section 38599.

Caney, Simon. 2005. "Cosmopolitan Justice, Responsibility and Global Climate Change." *Leiden Journal of International Law* 2005: 747–75

———.2008. "Human Rights, Climate Change, and Discounting." *Environmental Politics*,17:4, 536—555.

———.2009. "Climate Change and the Future: Discounting for Time, Wealth, and Risk." *Journal of Social Philosophy*. 40(2): 163–86.

———2010. "Climate Change, Human Rights and Moral Thresholds." In Stephen Humphreys, ed., *Human Rights and Climate Change* (Cambridge: Cambridge University Press).

———.2011. "Climate Change and the Duties of the Advantaged". *Critical Review of International Political Philosophy* (in press).

Carlin, Alan. 2007. "Global Climate Change Control: Is There a Better Strategy than Reducing Greenhouse Gas Emissions?" *University of Pennsylvania Law Review* 155(6): 1401–97.

Carrington, Damian. 2010a. "Cancún Deal Leaves Hard Climate Tasks to Durban Summit in 2011." Guardian Weekly, 14 December.

Carrington, Damian. 2010b. "Cancún Climate Talks 'Anarchic' Says Chris Huhne", Guardian Environment Blog, 15 December.

Chakravarty, Shoibal, Chikkatur, Ananth, de Coninck, Heleen, Pacala, Stephen, Socolow, Robert and Massimo Tavoni. 2009. "Sharing Global CO2 Emission Reductions Among One Billion High Emitters." *Proceedings of the National Academy of Sciences.* doi_10.1073_pnas.0905232106

Chichilnisky, Graciela. 1996. "An Axiomatic Approach to Sustainable Development." *Social Choice and Welfare* 13: 231–57.

Cicerone, Ralph. 2006. "Geoengineering: Encouraging Research and Overseeing Implementation." *Climatic Change* 77: 221–6.

Clarke, Conor. 2009. "An Interview with Thomas Schelling, Part Two." *Atlantic*, July 14.

Cline, William. 1992. *The Economics of Global Warming* (Institute for International Economics).

———.2007. Global Warming and Agriculture: Impact Estimates By Country. (Washington: Center for Global Development and Peterson Institute for International Economics)

Cohen, Joel. 1995. *How Many People Can the Earth Support?* (New York: Norton).

Copeland, Edward. 1997. "Money." In Edward Copeland and Juliet MacMaster, eds., *The Cambridge Companion to Jane Austen* (Cambridge: Cambridge University Press): 131–48.

Costanza, Robert. 1996. Review of *Managing the Commons: The Economics of Climate Change*, by William D. Nordhaus. *Environment and Development Economics* 1:381–84.

Cowen, Tyler, and Derek Parfit. 1992. "Against the Social Discount Rate." In Peter Laslett and James Fishkin, eds., *Justice Between Age Groups and Generations*. (New Haven, CT: Yale University Press: 144–61).

Cranor, Carl. 1993. *Regulating Toxic Substances*. (Oxford: Oxford University Press).

———.2003. "Learning from Law to Address Uncertainty in the Precautionary Principle". *Science and Engineering Ethics* 7: 313–326.

———. 2004. "Towards Understanding Aspects of the Precautionary Principle". *Journal of Medicine and Philosophy* 29(3): 259–279.

———. 2006. *Toxic Torts*. (Cambridge: Cambridge University Press).

Crichton, Michael. 2005. *State of Fear* (New York: Harper Collins).

Crutzen, Paul and E. F. Stoermer. 2000. "The Anthropocene." *Global Change Newsletter* 41: 17–18.

Crutzen, Paul. 2006. "Albedo Enhancement by Stratospheric Sulphur Injections: A Contribution to Resolve a Policy Dilemma?" *Climatic Change* 77: 211–9.

Dancy, Jonathan. 1993. *Moral Reasons* (Oxford: Blackwell).

———. 2004. *Ethics Without Principles* (Oxford: Oxford University Press).

Danielson, Peter. 1993. "Personal Responsibility." In Howard Coward and Thomas Hurka, eds., *Ethics and Climate Change: The Greenhouse Effect*. (Waterloo: Wilfred Laurier Press: 81–98).

Danish Ecological Council. 2002. *Skeptical Questions and Sustainable Answers* (Copenhagen: Danish Ecological Council).

Dasgupta, Partha. 2007. "The Stern Review's Economics of Climate Change." *National Economic Review* 199.

Dean, Cornelia. 2007. "Even Before Its Release, World Climate Report is Criticized as Too Optimistic." *New York Times*, 2 February.

De Leo, Giulio, Rizzi, L., Caizzi, A., and Gatto, M. 2001. "The Economic Benefits of the Kyoto Protocol." *Nature* 413:478–79.

De-Shalit, Avner. 1995. *Why Posterity Matters: Environmental Policies and Future Generations* (London: Routledge).

Des Jardins, Joseph. 1998. *Environmental Ethics: An Introduction to Environmental Philosophy* (Belmont, CA: Wadsworth).

Desombre, Elizabeth. 2004. "Global Warming: More Common Than Tragic." *Ethics and International Affairs* 18: 41–6.

Diamond, Jared. 2004. *Collapse: How Societies Choose to Fail or Succeed* (New York: Viking).

Dietz, Thomas, Elinor Ostrom, and Paul Stern. 2003. "The Struggle to Govern the Commons." *Science* 302: 1907.

Dietz, Simon, Cameron Hepburn, and Nicholas Stern. 2009. Economics, Ethics and Climate Change. In Kaushik Basu and Ravi Kanbur, eds. Arguments for a Better World: Essays in Honour of Amartya Sen. (Oxford: Oxford University Press).

Dietz, S., C. Hope, N. Stern, and D. Zenghelis. 2007. "Reflections on the Stern Review (1): a Robust Case for Strong Action to Reduce the Risks of Climate Change," *World Economics* 8(1): 121–68.

Dimitrov, R. 2003. "Knowledge, Power and Interests in Environmental Regime Formation." *International Studies Quarterly* 47: 123–50.

Doris, John M. 2002. *Lack of Character: Personality and Moral Behavior* (Cambridge: Cambridge University Press).

Driver, Julia. 2001. *Uneasy Virtue* (Cambridge: Cambridge University Press).

Dryzek, John. 1987. *Rational Ecology* (Oxford: Blackwell).

Dugger, Celia W. 2001. "Modern Asia's Anomaly: The Girls Who Don't Get Born." *The New York Times, Week in Review*, 6 May.

Dubgaard, Alex. 2002. "Sustainability, Discounting, and the Precautionary Principle." In *Skeptical Questions and Sustainable Answers*. (Copenhagen: Danish Ecological Council): 196–202.

Dworkin, Ronald. 2000. *Sovereign Virtue* (Cambridge, MA: Harvard University Press).

Ebi, Kristi. 2008. "Adaptation Costs for Climate Change-Related Cases of Diarrhoeal Disease, Malnutrition, and Malaria in 2030." *Globalization and Health* 4:9

Economist. 2007. "Playing Games with the Planet." 29 September.

Edwards, P., and C. Miller, eds. 2001. *Changing the Atmosphere: Expert Knowledge and Global Environmental Governance* (Cambridge, MA: MIT Press).

Eggen, Dan. 2008. "Reflecting on His Tenure, Bush Shows New Candor." *Washington Post*, 2 December.

Elster, Jon. 1983. *Sour Grapes* (Cambridge: Cambridge University Press).

Eilperin, Juliet. 2008a. "Carbon Is Building Up in Atmosphere Faster Than Predicted." *Washington Post*, 26 September.

———. 2008b. "Interim Climate Pact Approved." *Washington Post,* 12 December.

Eilperin, Juliet, and Anthony Faiola. 2009. "Climate Deal Falls Short of Key Goals." *Washington Post*, 19 December.

Ereaut, Gill, and Nat. Segnit. 2006. *Warm Words: How Are We Telling the Climate Story and How Can We Tell it Better?* (London: Institute for Public Policy Research).

European Environment Agency. 2005. *The European Environment: State and Outlooks 2005* (Copenhagen: European Environment Agency).

———. 2008. "EU-15 on Target for Kyoto Despite Mixed Performance." *Press Release,* 16 October.

Frank, Robert. 2005. Microeconomics and Behavior. 6th edition. (Boston: McGraw-Hill).

Frank, Robert, Thomas Gilovich, and Dennis Regan. 1993. "Does Studying Economics Inhibit Cooperation?" *Journal of Economic Perspectives* 7.2: 159–71.

Franklin, Benjamin, J.A. Leo Lemay, and Paul M. Zall. 1986. *Benjamin Franklin's Autobiography: An Authoritative Text, Backgrounds, Criticism* (New York: Norton).

Frederick, S., G. Loewenstein, and T. O'Donoghue. 2002. "Time Discounting and Time Preference: A Critical Review." *Journal of Economic Literature* 40: 351–401.

Friedman, Milton. 1976. *Price Theory* (Chicago, IL: Aldine).

Gagosian, Robert. 2003. "Abrupt Climate Change: Should We Be Worried?" *Woods Hole Oceanographic Institute* 12.

Gardiner, Stephen. 2001a. "The Real Tragedy of the Commons." *Philosophy and Public Affairs* 30: 387–416.

———. 2001b. "Aristotle, Egoism and the Virtuous Person's Point of View." In D. Baltzly, D. Blyth, and H. Tarrant, eds., *Power and Pleasure, Virtues and Vices: Essays in Ancient Moral Philosophy* :239–62.

———. 2003. "The Pure Intergenerational Problem." *Monist* 86: 481–500.

———. 2004a. "The Global Warming Tragedy and the Dangerous Illusion of the Kyoto Protocol." *Ethics and International Affairs* 18: 23–39.

———. 2004b. "Ethics and Global Climate Change." *Ethics* 114: 555–600.

———. 2005. "Seneca's Virtuous Moral Rules." In Stephen Gardiner, ed. *Virtue Ethics: Old and New* (Ithaca, NY: Cornell University Press): 30–59.

———. 2006a. "A Core Precautionary Principle." *Journal of Political Philosophy* 14: 33–60.

————.2006b. "A Perfect Moral Storm: Climate Change, Intergenerational Ethics and the Problem of Moral Corruption." *Environmental Values* 15: 397–413.

————.2006c. "Protecting Future Generations." In Jörg Tremmel, ed., *Handbook of Intergenerational Justice* (Cheltenham: Edgar Elgar Publishing): 148–69.

————.2007. "Is Geoengineering the Lesser Evil?" *Environmental Research Web*. April 18.

————.2009a. "A Contract on Future Generations?" In Axel Gosseries and Lukas Meyer, eds., *Intergenerational Justice* (Oxford: Oxford University Press): 77–119.

————.2009b. "Saved By Disaster? Abrupt Climate Change, Political Inertia and the Possibility of an Intergenerational Arms Race." *Journal of Social Philosophy* 20(4):140–62. Special Issue on Global Environmental Issues, edited by Tim Hayward.

————.2010a. "Ethics and Climate Change: An Introduction." In Michael Hulme, ed., *Wiley Interdisciplinary Reviews: Climate Change* 1(1): 54–66.

————.2010b. "Is 'Arming the Future' with Geoengineering Really the Lesser Evil? Some Doubts About the Ethics of Intentionally Manipulating the Climate System." In Gardiner, Caney, Jamieson and Shue, eds., *Climate Ethics: Essential Readings* (Oxford: Oxford University Press).

————.2010c. "Climate Change as a Global Test for Contemporary Political Institutions and Theories." In Karen O'Brien, Asuncion Lera St. Clair, and Berit Kristoffersen, eds., *Climate Change, Ethics and Human Security* (Cambridge: Cambridge University Press).

————.2011a. "Rawls and Climate Change: Does Rawlsian Political Philosophy Pass the Global Test?" *Critical Review of International Social and Political Philosophy*. Special Issue on Climate Change and Liberal Priorities, edited by Catriona McKinnon and Gideon Calder. (Also to appear as a book with Taylor and Francis.) (In press).

————.2011b. "Some Early Ethics of Geoengineering: A Commentary on the Values of the Royal Society Report." *Environmental Values*. (In press).

————.2011c. "Is No One Responsible for Global Environmental Tragedy? Climate Change as a Challenge to Our Ethical Concepts." In Denis Arnold, ed., *The Ethics of Climate Change* (Cambridge: Cambridge University Press). (In press).

————.2011d. "Climate Justice." In John Dryzek, David Schlosberg, and Richard Norgaard, eds., *Oxford Handbook of Climate Change and Society* (Oxford: Oxford University Press). (In press).

————. Forthcoming. "Are We the Scum of the Earth?" In Allen Thompson and Jeremy Bendik-Kymer, eds., *The Virtues of the Future* (Cambridge, MA: MIT Press).

Gardiner, Stephen M., Simon Caney, Dale Jamieson, and Henry Shue, eds., 2010. *Climate Ethics: Essential Readings* (Oxford: Oxford University Press).

Garvey, James. 2008. *Ethics and Climate Change* (London: Continuum).

Gillis, Justin. 2010. "A Scientist, His Work and a Climate Reckoning", *New York Times*, December 21.

Gilpin, Alan. 2000. *Environmental Economics: A Critical Overview* (Chichester, UK: Wiley).

Glantz, Michael. 1999. "Sustainable Development and Creeping Environmental Problems in the Aral Sea Region." In Michael Glantz, *Creeping Environmental Problems and Sustainable Development in the Aral Sea Basin* (Cambridge: Cambridge University Press).

Global Humanitarian Forum 2009. *Human Impacts Report*. (Geneva: Global Humanities Forum).

Gollier, C. 2002. "Discounting an Uncertain Future." *Journal of Public Economics* 85: 149–66.

Goodin, Robert. 1994. "Selling Environmental Indulgences." *Kyklos* 47: 573–96. Reprinted in Gardiner et al. 2010.

———. 1999. "The Sustainability Ethic: Political, Not Just Moral." *Journal of Applied Philosophy* 16(3): 247–54.

Goodman, Amy. 2009. "US-Led Copenhagen Accord Decried as Flawed, Undemocratic." *Democracy Now*, 21 December. Available at:http://www.democracynow.org/2009/12/21/us_led_copenhagen_accord_decried_as

Gosseries, Axel. 2003. "Historical Emissions and Free Riding." In Lukas Meyer, ed., *Justice in Time: Responding to Historical Injustice* (Baden-Baden, Germany: Nomos): 355–82.

———. 2009. "Three Models of Intergenerational Reciprocity." In Gosseries and Meyer, eds., *Theories of Intergenerational Justice* (Oxford: Oxford University Press): 119–146.

Gosseries, Axel, and Lukas Meyer, eds. 2009. *Theories of Intergenerational Justice* (Oxford: Oxford University Press).

Gray, Louise. 2010. "Climate Change Targets 'Disappointing.'" *Daily Telegraph*, (1) February.

Griffin, Nick. 1988. "Lifeboat USA, Part 1." *International Journal of Moral and Social Studies* 3: 230–31.

Griffin, James. 1989. *Well-Being* (Oxford: Oxford University Press).

Grubb, Michael. 1995. "Seeking Fair Weather: Ethics and the International Debate on Climate Change." *International Affairs* 71: 463–96.

Grubb, Michael, Christian Vrolijk, and Duncan Brack. 1999. *The Kyoto Protocol: A Guide and Assessment* (London: Royal Institute of International Affairs).

Guardian. 2009. "Beyond Copenhagen: Dialogue, Not Diktat." Editorial, 21 December 2009.

Gundermann, Jesper. 2002. "Discourse in the Greenhouse." In *Sceptical Questions and Sustainable Answers* (Copehagen, Denmark: Danish Ecological Council): 139–16.

Hacker Andrew. 2000. "The Case Against Kids." *New York Review of Books*, 30 November: 12–8.

Hansen, James. 2004. "Defusing the Global Warming Time Bomb." *Scientific American* 290: 68–77.

———. 2005. "A Slippery Slope: How Much Global Warming Constitutes 'Dangerous Anthropogenic Interference?'" *Climatic Change* 68: 269–79.

———. 2006. "Can We Still Avoid Dangerous Human-made Climate Change?" Talk presented at The New School University.

Hansen, James, and Makiko Sato. 2004. "Greenhouse Gas Growth Rates." *Proceedings of the National Academy of Sciences* 101: 16109–14.

Hardin, Garrett. 1968. "The Tragedy of the Commons." *Science* 162: 1243–8.

———. 1974. "Living in a Lifeboat." *Bioscience* 24 (1974): 561–68.

———. 1986. "Cultural Carrying Capacity: a Biological Approach to Human Problems." *Bioscience* 36: 599–606.

———. 1993. *Living Within Limits* (Cambridge: Cambridge University Press).

———. 1999. *The Ostrich Factor: Our Population Myopia* (Oxford: Oxford University Press).

Harrabin, Roger. 2008. "UK Seeking CO2 Trading Increase." *BBC News*, September 18.

Harris, Paul. 2010. *World Ethics and Climate Change: From International to Global Justice*. Edinburgh: Edinburgh University Press.

Harvey, Danny, and Zhen Huang. 1995. "Evaluation of the Potential Impact of Methane Clathrate Destabilization on Future Global Warming." *Journal of Geophysical Research* 100: 2905–26.

Harrabin, Roger. 2008. "UK Seeking CO2 Trading Increase." *BBC News*, September 18.

Hausman, Daniel and Michael McPherson. 2006. *Economic Analysis, Moral Philosophy and Public Policy, 2nd ed.* (Cambridge: Cambridge University Press).

Helm, Dieter. 2008. "Climate-change Policy: Why Has So Little Been Achieved?" *Oxford Review of Economic Policy* 24(2): 211–38.

Heyd, David. 2010. "A Value or an Obligation? Rawls on Justice to Future Generations." In Axel Gosseries and Lukas Meyer, eds. *Intergenerational Justice* (Oxford: Oxford University Press).

Holland, Breena. 2008. "Justice and the environment in Nussbaum's 'capabilities approach': Why sustainable ecological capacity is a meta-capability." *Political Research Quarterly* 61, No. 2: 319–332.

Hooker, Brad. 2000. *Ideal Code, Real World* (Oxford: Clarendon Press).

Hooker, Brad, and Margaret Little. 2000. *Ethical Particularism* (Oxford: Oxford University Press).

Houghton, John. 2004. *Climate Change: The Complete Briefing*, 3rd ed. (Cambridge: Cambridge University Press).

Hursthouse, Rosalind. 1996. "Normative Virtue Ethics." In Roger Crisp, ed. *How Should One Live?* (Oxford: Oxford University Press): 19–36.

———. 1999. *On Virtue Ethics* (Oxford: Oxford University Press).

Ignatieff, Michael. 2004. *The Lesser Evil: Political Ethics in an age of Terror* (Princeton, NJ: Princeton University Press).

Intergovernmental Panel on Climate Change (IPCC). 1990. *Climate Change 1990: The Scientific Basis* (Cambridge: Cambridge University Press).

———. 1996. *Climate Change 1995: Economic and Social Dimensions of Climate Change* (Cambridge: Cambridge University Press).

———. 2001a. *Climate Change 2001: The Scientific Basis* (Cambridge: Cambridge University Press).

———. 2001c. *Climate Change 2001: Synthesis Report* (Cambridge: Cambridge University Press).

———. 2007a. *Climate Change 2007: The Scientific Basis* (Cambridge: Cambridge University Press).

———. 2007b. *Climate Change 2007: Impacts, Adaptation and Vulnerability* (Cambridge: Cambridge University Press).

———. 2007c. *Climate Change 2007: Synthesis Report* (Cambridge: Cambridge University Press).

Jamieson, Dale. 1992. "Ethics, Public Policy and Global Warming." *Science, Technology and Human Values* 17: 139–53.

———. 1996. "Intentional Climate Change." *Climatic Change* 33: 323–36.

———. 2001. "Climate Change and Global Environmental Justice." In Paul Edwards and Clark Miller, eds., *Changing the Atmosphere: Expert Knowledge and Global Environmental Governance* (Cambridge, MA: MIT Press).

———. 2003. *Morality's Progress: Essays on Humans, Other Animals, and the Rest of Nature* (Oxford: Oxford University Press).

———. 2006. "An American Paradox." *Climatic Change* 77: 97–102.

———. 2007. "When Utilitarians Should be Virtue Theorists." *Utilitas* 19(2): 160–83.

———.2010. "Climate Change, Responsibility and Justice." *Science, Engineering and Technology Ethics* 16:431–445.

Jordan, Andrew, and Timothy O'Riordan. 1999. "The Precautionary Principle in Contemporary Environmental Policy and Politics." In Carolyn Raffensberger and Joel Tickner, eds., *Protecting Public Health and the Environment: Implementing the Precautionary Principle* (Washington, D.C.: Island Press): 15–35.

Junger, Sebastian. 1999. *A Perfect Storm: A True Story of Men Against the Sea* (New York, NY: Harper).

Kant, Immanuel. 1998. *Groundwork for the Metaphysics of Morals*. Translated by Mary Gregor. (Cambridge: Cambridge University Press).

Kartha, Sivan, Tom Athanasiou, Paul Baer, and Deborah Cornland. 2005. "Cutting the Knot: Climate Protection, Political Realism and Equity as Requirements of a Post-Kyoto Regime." 4. URL: http://ecoequity.org.

Keith, David. 2000. "Geoengineering: History and Prospect." *Annual Review of Energy and the Environment* 25: 245–84.

Kellogg, W. W., and Schneider, S. H. 1974. "Climate Stabilization: For Better or Worse?" *Science* 186: 1163–72.

Kiehl, J. 2006. "Geoengineering Climate Change: Treating the Symptom Over the Cause?" *Climatic Change* 77: 227–8.

Knight, Frank. 1921. *Risk, Uncertainty, and Profit* (Boston and New York: Houghton Mifflin).

Kraut, Richard. 2007. *What is Good and Why: The Ethics of Well-Being* (Cambridge: Cambridge University Press).

Kristof, Nicholas. 2006. "The Big Burp Theory of the Apocalypse." *New York Times*, 16 April.

Kuhn, Stephen. 2001. "The Prisoner's Dilemma." *Stanford Encyclopedia of Philosophy.* URL: http://setis.library.usyd.edu.au/stanford/entries/prisoner-dilemma/#Bib.

Kumar, Rahul. 2003. "Who Can Be Wronged?" *Philosophy & Public Affairs* 31. 2: *99–118.*

———.2009. "Wronging Future People: A Contractualist Approach." In Axel Gosseries and Lukas Meyer, eds., *Intergenerational Justice* (Oxford: Oxford University Press): 251–73.

Lawrence, Mark. 2006. "The Geoengineering Dilemma: To Speak or Not to Speak?" *Climatic Change* 77: 245–8.

Layard, Richard. 2005. *Happiness* (New York: Penguin).

Lean, Geoffrey. 2009. "Copenhagen Climate Conference: More a Planting than a Burial." *Daily Telegraph,* 18 November.

Lee, Jennifer. 2003. "GOP Changes Environmental Message." *Seattle Times*, 2 March.

Leiserowitz, Anthony. 2004. "Before and After the Day After Tomorrow." *Environment* 46: 23–37.

———.2005. "American Risk Perceptions: Is Climate Change Dangerous?" *Risk Analysis* 25: 1433–42.

Lenman, James. 2002. "On Becoming Extinct." *Pacific Philosophical Quarterly* 83: 253–69.

Lenton, Timothy, Hermann Held, Elmar Kriegler, Jim Hall, Wolfgang Lucht, Stefan Rahmsdorf, and Hans Joachim Schnellnhuber. 2008. "Tipping Points in the Earth's Climate System." *Proceedings of the National Academies of Sciences* 105: 1786–93.

Liebrech, Michael. 2007. "How to Save the Planet: Be Nice, Retaliatory, Forgiving & Clear." White Paper, *New Energy Finance*. Cited by Economist 2007. On file with author.

Locke, John. 1988. *Two Treatises on Government*. Ed. Peter Laslett (Cambridge: Cambridge University Press).

Lomborg, Bjørn. 2001. *The Sceptical Environmentalist* (Cambridge: Cambridge University Press).

———. 2007. *Cool It* (New York, NY: Knopf).

Lovelock, James. 2006. *The Revenge of Gaia: Why the Earth is Fighting Back—and How We Can Still Save Humanity* (New York, NY: Basic Books).

———. 2008. "A Geophysicist's Thoughts on Geoengineering." *Philosophical Transactions of the Royal Society A: Mathematical, Physical and Engineering Sciences* 366: 3883–90.

Luce, R. Duncan, and Howard Raiffa. 1957. *Games and Decisions: Introduction and Critical Survey* (New York: Wiley).

Lumer, Christoph. 2002. *The Greenhouse* (Lanham, MD: University Press of America).

Mabey, Nick, Stephen Hall, Claire Smith, and Sujata Gupta. 1997. *Argument in the Greenhouse: The International Economics of Controlling Global Warming* (London: Routledge).

Marland, G., Boden, T. and Andreas, R.J. 2008. "Global CO2 Emissions from Fossil-Fuel Burning, Cement Manufacture, and Gas Flaring: 1751–2005." URL: http://cdiac.ornl.gov/trends/emis/em_cont.html

Marrakesh Accords (advance unedited version). Accord L, Sec. XV, 5; available at unfccc.int/cop7/documents/accords_draft.pdf.

Matthews, Damon, and Kenneth Caldeira. 2007. "Transient Climate–Carbon Simulations of Planetary Geoengineering." *Proceedings of the National Academy of Sciences* 104: 9949–54.

Meyer, Lukas and Roser, Dominic. 2006. "Distributive Justice and Climate Change: The Allocation of Emission Rights." *Analyse & Kritik* 28: 223–49.

MacCracken, Michael. 2006. "Geoengineering: Worthy of Cautious Evaluation?" *Climatic Change* 77: 235–43.

McDowell, John. 1979. "Virtue and Reason." *Monist* 62, 331–50.

McIlroy, Anne. 2002. "Gas-guzzling Canada Divided Over Rush to Kyoto." *Guardian Weekly*, 7 November.

———. 2006. "Emission Failure." *The Guardian*, 15 May.

McKibben, Bill. 1989. *The End of Nature* (New York: Anchor).

———. 1997. "Reaching the Limit." *New York Review of Books*, 29 May.

———. 2001. "Some Like it Hot: Bush in the Greenhouse." *New York Review of Books*, 5 July.

———. 2009. "With Climate Agreement, Obama Guts Progressive Values." *Grist*, 18 December.

McMahan, Jefferson. 2002. *The Ethics of Killing.* (Oxford: Oxford University Press).

———. 2005. "The Basis of Moral Liability for Defensive Killing". *Philosophical Issues* 15: 386–405.

Mendelsohn, Robert O., ed. 2001. *Global Warming and the American Economy* (London: Edward Elgar).

Mendelsohn, Robert, Ariel Dinar, and Larry Williams. 2006. "The Distributional Impact of Climate Change on Rich and Poor Countries." *Environment and Development Economics* 11:1–20.

Michaels, David. 2008. *Doubt is Their Product*. (Oxford: Oxford University Press).

Miller, David. 2007. *National Responsibility and Global Justice*. (Oxford: Oxford University Press).

———.2009. "Global Justice and Climate Change: How Should Responsibilities be Allocated?" *Tanner Lectures on Human Values* 28: 117–156.

Miller, Richard. 2010. *Globalizing Justice*. Oxford: Oxford University Press.

Miller, Seumas. 2005. "Corruption." *Stanford Encyclopedia of Philosophy*.

Monastersky, Richard. 1995. "Iron Versus the Greenhouse: Oceanographers Cautiously Explore a Global Warming Therapy." *Science News* 148, 30 September.

Monbiot, George. 2009. "If You Want to Know Who's to Blame for Copenhagen, Look to the U.S. Senate." *The Guardian,* 21 December.

Montenegro, A., V. Brovkin, M. Eby, D. Archer, and A.J. Weaver. 2007. "Long-term Atmospheric Lifetime of Fossil Fuel CO2." *Geophysical Research Letters* 34: L19707, doi:10.1029/2007GL030905.

Moore, Frances. 2008. "Carbon Dioxide Emissions Accelerating Rapidly." April 9. URL: http://www.earth-policy.org/Indicators/CO2/2008.htm.

Morton, Oliver. 2007. "Is This What it Takes to Save the World?" *Nature* 447: 132–6.

Mulgan, Tim. 2001. "A Minimal Test for Political Theories." *Philosophia* 28: 283–96.

National Assessment Synthesis Team. 2000. *Climate Change Impacts on the United States: The Potential Consequences of Climate Variability and Change* (Cambridge: Cambridge University Press).

Neumeyer, Eric. 2007. "A Missed Opportunity: The Stern Review on Climate Change Fails to Tackle the Issue of Non-Substitutable Loss of Natural Capital." *Global Environmental Change* 17 297–301.

New Scientist. 2008. "World Ahead of Kyoto Emissions Targets." Issue 2683: 18 November.

Nitze, W.A. 1994. "A Failure of Presidential Leadership." In Irving Mintzer and J. Amber Leonard, eds., *Negotiating Climate Change: The Inside Story of the Rio Convention* (Cambridge: Cambridge University Press): 189–90).

Nolt, John. 2011. "Greenhouse Gas Emission and the Domination of Posterity." In Denis Arnold, ed., *Ethics and Climate Change* (Cambridge: Cambridge University Press).

Nordhaus, William. 1999. "Discounting and Public Policies Affecting the Further Future." In Portney, Paul R. and John P. Weylant (eds.) 1999. *Discounting and Intergenerational Equity* (Washington, D.C.: Resources for the Future): 145–162.

———.2007. "A Review of the *Stern Review on the Economics of Climate Change*." *Journal of Economic Literature Vol. XLV*: 686–702.

———.2009. *A Question of Balance* (New Haven, CT: Yale University Press).

Nordhaus, Ted and Michael Shellenberger. 2004. "Death of Environmentalism: Global Warming Politics in a Post-Environmental World." *The Breakthrough Institute*.

———.2007. *Breakthrough: From the Death of Environmentalism to the Politics of Possibility* (New York: Houghton Mifflin).

Nordhaus, William D., and Joseph G. Boyer. 2000. *Warming the World: Economic Models of Global Warming* (Cambridge, MA: MIT Press).

Norton, Bryan. 1995. "Future Obligations, Obligations to." *Encyclopaedia of Bioethics*, 2nd ed. (New York: Macmillan Reference).

———. 1998. "Ecology and Opportunity: Intergenerational Equity and Sustainable Options." In Andrew Dobson, ed., *Fairness and Futurity* (Oxford: Oxford University Press): 118–50.

Nozick, Robert. 1974. *Anarchy, State and Utopia* (New York, NY: Basic Books).

O'Neill, Brian C. and Michael Oppenheimer. 2002. "Dangerous Climate Impacts and the Kyoto Protocol." *Science* 296: 1971–2.

O'Neill, John. 1993. "Future Generations: Present Harms." *Philosophy* 68: 35–51.

O'Neill, Onora. 1985. *Faces of Hunger: An Essay on Poverty, Justice, and Development* (London: Allen & Unwin).

———. 1993. "Ending World Hunger." In Tom Regan, ed. *Matters of Life and Death,* 3rd ed. (Belmont, CA: Wadsworth).

Oleson, Kirsten, Lauren Hartzell and Michael Mastrandrea. 2009. "The Baker's Dozen: Key Nations Can and Should Act to Prevent Further Dangerous Climate Change." *Intergenerational Justice Review* 9, 106–12.

Oppenheimer, Michael, ed. 2006. *Climatic Change 77: Special Issue on Climate Change and the Psychology of Long-Term Risk.*

Oppenheimer, Michael and Annie Petsonk. 2004. "Article 2 of the UNFCCC: Historical Origins, Recent Interpretations." *Climatic Change* 73: 195–226.

Oppenheimer, Michael and Richard Alley. 2004. "The West Antarctic Ice Sheet and Long-Term Climate Policy." *Climatic Change* 64: 1–10.

Oreskes, Naomi. 2005. "The Scientific Consensus on Climate Change," *Science 306,* December 3: 1686.

Ostrom, Elinor. 1990. *Governing the Commons: The Evolution of Institutions for Collective Action* (Cambridge: Cambridge University Press).

———. 2009. "A Polycentric Approach for Coping with Climate Change. Background Paper to the 2010 World Development Report." Policy Research Working Paper 5095.

Ostrom, Vincent. 1999. "Polycentricity—Part 1." In Michael McGinnis, ed., *Polycentricity and Local Public Economies* (Ann Arbor: University of Michigan Press): 52–74.

Pacala, S. and Socolow, R. 2004. "Stabilization Wedges: Solving the Climate Problem for the Next 50 Years with Current Technologies". *Science* 305: 968–972.

Page, E.A., 2006. *Climate change, Justice and Future Generations* (Cheltenham: Edward Elgar).

Palmer, Clare. Forthcoming. "Does Nature Matter? The Place of the Nonhuman in the Ethics of Climate Change". In Denis Arnold, ed., *The Ethics of Climate Change* (Cambridge: Cambridge University Press).

Parfit, Derek. 1986. "The Non-Identity Problem." In his *Reasons and Persons* (Oxford: Oxford University Press).

Patterson, Matthew. 2001. "Principles of Justice and Global Climate Change." In Urs Luterbacher and Detlef F. Sprinz, eds., *International Relations and Global Climate Change* (Cambridge: MIT Press): 119–26.

Pearce, David. 1993. *Economic Values and the Natural World* (London: Earthscan).

Pearce, David, Giles Atkinson, and Susan Mourato. 2006. *Cost-Benefit Analysis and the Environment: Recent Developments* (Paris, France: OECD).

Pew Center. 2005. "Answers to Key Questions Raised by M. Crichton in State of Fear." Available at www.pew.org

Pogge, Thomas. 2002. *World Hunger and Human Rights* (Cambridge: Polity).

Poplawski, Paul. 1998. *A Jane Austen Encyclopedia* (Santa Barbara, CA: Greenwood).

Pravda 2004. "Russia Forced to Ratify Kyoto Protocol to Become WTO Member." 26 October. Available at http://english.pravda.ru/russia/politics/7274-kyoto-0

President's Science Advisory Committee 1965. *Restoring the Quality of Our Environment* (Washington, D.C.: Government Printing Office.)

Prins, Gwyn and Steve Rayner. 2007. "Time to Ditch Kyoto." *Nature* 449, 25 October: 793–5.

Portney, Paul R. and John P. Weylant (eds.) 1999. *Discounting and Intergenerational Equity* (Washington, D.C.: Resources for the Future).

Posner, Eric and Cass Sunstein. 2007. "Pay China to Cut Greenhouse Emissions." *Financial Times*, 6 August.

———.2008. "Climate Change Justice." *Georgetown Law Journal* 96: 1565–612.

Posner, Eric and Daniel Weisbach. 2010. *Climate Change Justice.* (Princeton, NJ: Princeton University Press).

Raffensberger, Carolyn, and Tickner, Joel, eds. 1999. *Protecting Public Health and the Environment: Implementing the Precautionary Principle* (Washington, D.C.: Island Press).

Rawls, John. 1999. *A Theory of Justice.* Revised Edition (Oxford: Oxford University Press).

Reiman, Jeffrey. 2007. "Being Fair to Future People: The Non-Identity Problem in the Original Position." *Philosophy and Public Affairs* 35(1): 69–92.

Revkin, Andrew. 2001a. "Despite Opposition in Party, Bush to Seek Emissions Cuts." *New York Times*, 10 March.

———.2001b. "Bush, in Reversal, Won't Seek Cuts in Emissions of Carbon Dioxide." *New York Times*, 13 March.

———.2001c. "178 Nations Reach Climate Accord; US Only Looks On." *New York Times*, 24 July.

———.2001d. "Deals Break Impasse on Global Warming Treaty." *New York Times*, 11 November.

———.2002. "U.S. Planning Gradual Curb on Emissions, Taking Years." *New York Times*, 6 February.

———.2004. "Bush vs. the Laureates: How Science Became a Partisan Issue." *New York Times*, 19 October.

———.2008, "Issuing a Bold Challenge to the US Over Climate." *New York Times*, 22 January.

Robinson, Mary. 2009. "Closing Remarks." *Three Degrees Conference.* University of Washington, Seattle.

Robock, A. 2008. "20 Reasons Why Geoengineering May Be a Bad Idea." *Bulletin of Atomic Scientists* 64: 14–59.

Rosenthal, Elizabeth. 2007. "UN Chief Seeks More Climate Change Leadership". *New York Times*, November 18.

Rousseau, Jean Jacques. 1997. *The Social Contract.* Ed. Victor Gourevich (Cambridge: Cambridge University Press).

Ryberg, Jesper. 1997. "Population and Third World Assistance." *Journal of Applied Philosophy*, Vol. 14, No. 3: 207–19.

Sagoff, Mark. 1988. *The Economy of the Earth* (Cambridge: Cambridge University Press).

———. 1999. "Controlling Global Climate: The Debate over Pollution Trading." *Report from the Institute for Philosophy and Public Policy* 19.1: 1–6.

Samuelson, Robert J. 2005. "Lots of Gain And No Pain!" *Newsweek*, 21 February: 41.

Sandel, Michael. 2005. "Should We Buy the Right to Pollute?" In his *Public Philosophy: Essays on Morality in Politics* (Cambridge, MA: Harvard University Press).

Sandler, Todd. 2004. *Global Collective Action* (Cambridge: Cambridge University Press).

Scheffler, Samuel. 1990. *The Rejection of Consequentialism.* (Oxford: Oxford University Press).

Schelling, Thomas, ed. 1983. *Incentives for Environmental Protection* (Cambridge, MA: MIT Press).

———. 1996. "The Economic Diplomacy of Geoengineering." *Climatic Change* 33: 303–307.

———. 1997. "The Cost of Combating Global Warming: Facing the Tradeoffs." *Foreign Affairs* 76:8–14.

Schellnhuber, John. 2007. "Kyoto: No Time to Rearrange Deckchairs on the *Titanic.*" *Nature* 450(346): 15 November.

Schiermeier, Quirin. 2006. "A Sea Change." *Nature* 439: 256–60.

Schlosberg, David. 2007. *Environmental Justice* (Oxford: Oxford University Press).

———. 2009. "Rethinking climate justice: Capabilities and the flourishing of human and nonhuman communities." Paper presented at APSA.

Schmidt, Gavin. 2006. "Geoengineering in Vogue." *Real Climate*, June 28.

Schmidtz, David. 2001. "A Place for Cost-Benefit Analysis." *Nous-Supplement* 11: 148–71.

Schneider, Stephen. 1996. "Geoengineering: Could—or Should—We Do It?" *Climatic Change* 31: 291–302.

———. 2008. "Geoengineering: Could We or Should We Make It Work?" *Philosophical Transactions of the Royal Society* A 366, 3843–62.

Schultz, Peter and James Kasting. 1997. "Optimal Reductions in CO2 Emissions." *Energy Policy* 25: 491–500.

Schwartz, Peter and Doug Randall. 2003. "An Abrupt Climate Change Scenario and Its Implications for United States National Security." 2003. URL: www.grist.org/pdf/AbruptClimateChange2003

Sen, Amartya. 1980. "Equality of What?" In S. McMurrin, ed., *Tanner Lectures on Human Values* (Cambridge: Cambridge University Press).

———. 1992. "Missing Women." *British Medical Journal* 304 (March 7: 587.

———. 1999. *Development as Freedom* (New York, NY: Anchor).

Shepherd, John et al. 2009. *Geoengineering the Climate: Science, Governance and Uncertainty.* (London: Royal Society).

Shepski, Lee. 2006. "Prisoner's Dilemma: The Hard Problem." Paper presented at the Pacific Division of the American Philosophical Association, March 2006.

Shrader-Frechette, Kristen. 1991. *Risk and Rationality.* Berkeley: University of California Press.

———. 1993. *Burying Uncertainty.* (Berkeley: University of California).

———. 2002. *Environmental Justice: Creating Equality, Reclaiming Democracy* (Oxford: Oxford University Press).

———. 2011. *Nuclear Power and Climate Change.* (Oxford: Oxford University Press).

Shue, Henry. 1978. "Torture." *Philosophy and Public Affairs* 7: 124–43.

————.1980. *Basic Rights* (Princeton, NJ: Princeton University Press).

————.1990. "The Unavoidability of Justice" In Andrew Hurrell and Benedict Kingsbury, eds. *The International Politics of the Environment* (Oxford: Oxford University Press): 373–97.

————.1993. "Subsistence Emissions and Luxury Emissions." *Law and Policy* 15(1): 39–59.

————.1995. "Equity in an International Agreement on Climate Change". In R. S. Odingo, A. L. Alusa, F. Mugo, J. K. Njihia, and A. Heidenreich, eds. *Equity and Social Considerations Related to Climate Change* (Nairobi: ICIPE Science Press): 385–92.

————.1996. "Environmental Change and the Varieties of Justice." In Fen Osler Hampson and Judith Reppy, eds., *Earthly Goods: Environmental Change and Social Justice* (Ithaca, NY: Cornell University Press): 9–29.

————.1999. "Global Environment and International Inequality." *International Affairs* 75: 531–45.

————.2005. "Torture in Dreamland: Disposing of the Ticking Bomb." *Case Western Reserve Journal of International Law* 37: 231–9.

————.2006. "Responsibility of Future Generations and the Technological Transition." In Walter Sinnott-Armstrong and Richard Howarth, eds., *Perspectives on Climate Change: Science, Economics, Politics, Ethics* (Amsterdam: Elsevier): 265–84.

————.2009. "Historical Responsibility". Technical Briefing for Ad Hoc Working Group on Long-term Cooperative Action under the Convention [AWG-LCA], SBSTA, UNFCC, Bonn, 4 June. Available at: http://unfccc.int/files/meetings/ad hoc working groups/ lca/application/pdf/1 shue rev.pdf.

Singer, Peter. 2002. *One World: The Ethics of Globalization* (New Haven, CT: Yale University Press).

Sinnott-Armstrong, Walter. 2005. "It's Not *My* Fault." In Walter Sinnott-Armstrong and Richard Howarth, eds. *Perspectives on Climate Change* (New York: Elsevier, 2005): 221–253.

Smart, J.J.C. and Bernard Williams. 1973. *Utilitarianism: For and Against* (Cambridge: Cambridge University Press).

Sooros, Marvin S. 1997. *The Endangered Atmosphere: Preserving a Global Commons* (Columbia, SC: University of South Carolina Press).

Spash, Clive L. 2002. *Greenhouse Economics: Value and Ethics* (London: Routledge).

Staff and Agencies. 2003. " 'No Chance' of UK Meeting Greenhouse Targets." *The Guardian*, 3 April.

Stanton, Elizabeth. In press. "Negishi Welfare Weights: The Mathematics of Global Inequality". *Climatic Change*.

Steiner, Hillel and Peter Vallentyne. 2009. "Libertarian Theoreis of Intergenerational Justice." In Axel Gosseries and Lukas Meyer, eds., *Intergenerational Justice* (Oxford: Oxford University Press): 50–76.

Stern, Nicholas. 2007. *The Economics of Climate Change* (Cambridge: Cambridge University Press).

————.2008. "The Economics of Climate Change." *American Economic Review* 98(2), 1–37.

————.2009. *A Global Deal: Climate Change and the Creation of a New Era of Progress and Prosperity*. (New York, NY: Public Affairs).

Stocker, Michael. 1976. "The Schizophrenia of Modern Ethical Theories." *Journal of Philosophy* 14, 453–66.

Stouffer, R.J. et al. 2006. "Investigating the Causes of the Response of the Thermohaline Circulation to Past and Future Climate Changes." *Journal of Climate* 19: 1365–87.

Styron, William. 1979. *Sophie's Choice* (New York, NY: Random House).

Sunstein, Cass. 2006. "Irreversible and Catastrophic." *Cornell Law Review* 91 841.

———. 2005. *The Laws of Fear* (Cambridge: Cambridge University Press).

Tol, R.S.J., T.E. Downing, O.J. Kuik and J. B. Smith. 2004. "Distributional Aspects of Climate Change Impacts". *Global Environmental Change.* 14(3): 259–272.'

Tonn, Bruce. 2003. "An equity first, risk-based framework for managing global climate change." *Global Environmental Change* 13: 295–306.

Toman, Michael. 2001. *Climate Change Economics and Policy* (Washington, D.C.: Resources for the Future).

———. 2006. "Values in the Economics of Climate Change." *Environmental Values* 15: 365–79.

Traxler, Martino. 2002. "Fair Chore Division for Climate Change." *Social Theory and Practice* 28: 101–34.

Turner, R. Kerry. 2007. "Limits to CBA in UK and European environmental policy: retrospects and future prospects." Environment and Resource Economnics 37:253–69.

US Department of Energy 2008. *International Energy Outlook.* URL: http://www.eia.doe.gov/oiaf/ieo/emissions.html.

United Nations 2009a. Social Indicators. Available at: http://unstats.un.org/unsd/demographic/products/socind/inc-eco.htm

United Nations 2009b. World Population Prospects: The 2008 Revision. Department of Economic and Social Affairs, Population Division. New York.

United Nations Environment Program (UNEP). 2007. "Global Environment Outlook 4, Valletta, Malta." URL: http://www.unep.org/geo/

———. 2010. "How Close Are We to the Two Degree Limit?" UNEP Governing Council Meeting & Global Ministerial Environment Forum, 24–26 February.

UNFCCC. 2008. Sixth Compilation and Synthesis of Initial National Communications from Parties Not Included in Annex I to the Convention. Available at <ipcc.ch>

US National Research Council, Committee on Abrupt Climate Change. 2002. *Abrupt Climate Change: Inevitable Surprises* (Washington, D.C.: National Academies Press).

Van der Gaast, Wytze. 2008. "The Challenging Task of Negotiating a Climate Protocol." Presentation delivered at Energy Delta Convention.

Vanderheiden, Steve. 2008a. *Atmospheric Justice* (Oxford: Oxford University Press).

———. Ed. 2008b. *Political Theory and Global Climate Change* (Cambridge, MA: MIT Press).

Varner, Gary. 1998. *In Nature's Interests?: Interests, Animal Rights, and Environmental Ethics* (Oxford: Oxford University Press).

Veblen, Thorstein. 2008. *A Theory of the Leisure Class.* Ed. Martha Banta. (Oxford: Oxford University Press).

Vellinga, Michael, and Richard A. Wood. 2002. "Global Impacts of A Collapse of the Atlantic Thermohaline Circulation." *Climatic Change* 51: 251–67.

Victor, David. 2001. *The Collapse of the Kyoto Protocol and the Struggle to Slow Global Warming* (Princeton, NJ: Princeton University Press).

———. 2008. "On the Regulation of Geoengineering." *Oxford Review of Economic Policy* 24.2: 322–36.

Victor, David, M. Granger Morgan, Jay Apt, John Steinbruner, and Katherine Ricke. 2009. "The Geoengineering Option: A Last Resort Against Global Warming?" *Foreign Affairs*, March/April.

Waldron, Jeremy. 1990. "Who is to Stop Polluting? Different Kinds of Free-Rider Problem." In *Ethical Guidelines for Global Bargains*, Program on Ethics and Public Life, Cornell University. Ithaca, NY.

Walsh, Bryan. 2008. "Geoengineering." *Time*. March 12. URL: http://www.time.com/time/specials/2007/article/0,28804,1720049_1720050_1721653,00.html.

Ward, Hugh. 1996. "Game Theory and the Politics of Global Warming: The State of Play and Beyond." *Political Studies* 44: 850–71.

Weart, Spencer. 2003. *The Discovery of Global Warming* (Cambridge, MA: Harvard University Press.)

Weber, Elke. 2006. "Experienced-based and Description-Based Perceptions of Long-Term Risk: Why Global Warming Does Not Scare Us (Yet)." *Climatic Change* 77: 103–20.

Weitzman, Martin. 1998. "Why the Far Distant Future Should Be Discounted at its Lowest Possible Rate." *Journal of Environmental Economics and Management* 36: 201–208.

———. 1999. "Just Keep Discounting, But. . ." In Paul Portney and John Weyant, eds., *Discounting and Intergenerational Equity* (Washington, D.C.: Resources for the Future): 23–30.

———. 2001. "Gamma Discounting." *Academic Economic Review* 91: 260–71.

———. 2009. "On Modeling and Interpreting the Economics of Catastrophic Climate Change." *Review of Economics and Statistics*, 91(1): 1–19.

Wetherald, Richard T., Ronald J. Stouffer, and Keith W. Dixon. 2001. "Committed Warming and Its Implications for Climate Change." *Geophysical Research Letters* 28: 1535–8.

Wiener, Jonathan B. 2007. "Think Globally, Act Globally: The Limits of Local Climate Policies." *University of Pennsylvania Law Review* 155:1961–79.

Wigley, T.M.L. 2006. "A Combined Mitigation/Geoengineering Approach to Climate Stabilization." *Science* 314: 452–4.

Willetts, David. 2010. *The Pinch: How the Baby Boomers Took Their Children's Future and Why They Should Give It Back* (London: Atlantic Books).

Willot, Elizabeth. 2001. "Population Trends." In David Schmidtz and Elizabeth Willot, eds., *Environmental Ethics: What Really Matters. What Really Works* (Oxford: Oxford University Press).

Wingspread Statement. 1998. Available at http://www.gdrc.org/u-gov/precaution-3.html[OUP_CE23]

Woodward, Richard, and Bishop, Richard. 1997. "How to Decide When Experts Disagree: Uncertainty-Based Choice Rules in Environmental Policy." *Land Economics* 73:492–507

Woodward, James. 1986. "The Non-Identity Problem." *Ethics* 96.4: 804–31.

World Resources Institute (WRI). Climate Analysis Indicators Tool. Available at http://cait.wri.org/.

Zarembo, Alan. 2007. "Kyoto's Failures Haunt New UN Talks." *Los Angeles Times*, 3 December.

Index